A HANDBOOK ON
Old High German Literature

A HANDBOOK ON
Old High German Literature

BY

J. KNIGHT BOSTOCK

Late Reader in German in the
University of Oxford

Second Edition

REVISED BY

K. C. KING

Late Professor of German
King's College
University of London

AND

D. R. McLINTOCK

Reader in German
Royal Holloway College
University of London

OXFORD
AT THE CLARENDON PRESS
1976

Oxford University Press, Walton Street, Oxford OX2 6DP

OXFORD LONDON GLASGOW NEW YORK
TORONTO MELBOURNE WELLINGTON CAPE TOWN
IBADAN NAIROBI DAR ES SALAAM LUSAKA ADDIS ABABA
KUALA LUMPUR SINGAPORE JAKARTA HONG KONG TOKYO
DELHI BOMBAY CALCUTTA MADRAS KARACHI

ISBN 0 19 815392 9

Printed in Great Britain
at the University Press, Oxford
by Vivian Ridler
Printer to the University

Preface to the Second Edition

Dr. Bostock died on 27 June 1963. Expecting that a second edition of his Handbook would be required, though probably not during his lifetime, he had entrusted its revision to his former pupil, Professor K. C. King, whom he rightly took to be the person most competent to perform the task. Professor King died on 3 November 1970, having completed the revision of several chapters and begun work on others. The Clarendon Press then commissioned me, as one who had known the author well and had also discussed the revision with Professor King, to complete the work.

Dr. Bostock's book was the product of a lifetime's study and teaching. It is still the only work of its kind in English and has proved invaluable to students, not only in this country, but in America and even Germany. It was never the author's practice in teaching to present the student with a simplified and single-minded account of a literary problem; he preferred to report fairly all the views which he considered tenable in the present state of knowledge and to encourage the student, by following them up, to arrive at an independent judgement. In his Handbook he attempted to do the same, guiding the student through the Old High German period, acquainting him with the problems it presented and giving full references to the controversial literature. Consequently readers could divine the author's views only from the occasional parenthetical remark or from observing which arguments he chose to elaborate.

Since 1955, when the Handbook first appeared, the study of Old High German literature has seen a number of advances and changes of emphasis, and it soon became clear to Professor King, and later to me, that a thorough revision was necessary. In this the author would assuredly have concurred, for he always encouraged his pupils to recognize superannuated controversies for what they were and to ignore what he called 'the dead wood of scholarship'. We saw no reason, however, to depart from the author's plan, and any changes we have introduced in it are merely minor modifications. The historical thread running through the work has been slightly strengthened, especially in Chapters II, V, X, XI, XIII, and XIV. The minor religious poems have been collected into Chapter XII, and the *Ludwigslied* consequently now has a chapter to itself. The last chapter now includes a brief treatment of the Bamberg Creed and Confession and its companion piece *Himmel und Hölle*, the only works which seem to betray the continuing influence of Notker. The discussion of metre has been lifted from Chapters X and XI and placed in an appendix. Finally, an index has been added.

Dr. Bostock wished to acknowledge the helpful criticism he had received from colleagues, especially the late Professor A. C. Campbell. I should like to record the unfailing consideration shown to me by Mrs. Bostock and Mrs. King, who have put at my disposition all their husbands' papers relevant to the work. I am grateful for the valuable advice I have had from the staff of the Clarendon Press during the preparation of this volume. I should like to express my appreciation of the help given by colleagues whom I have consulted; to single out any by name would be invidious, and I hope they will be glad to recognize as their own contributions some of the new features of the book which may earn their approval. My thanks go also to my daughter Julia for her help in compiling the index. Finally, I should like to pay tribute to the memory of the author, who initiated me into the subject, and of Professor King, to whose scholarship this new edition owes so much.

D. R. M.

London
1 June 1976

Preface to the First Edition

It is a pleasant duty to acknowledge the readiness with which the Clarendon Press undertook the publication of the book and also the valuable advice on technical details given by its officials.

I have pleasure also in recording the interest shown by Dr. E. L. Stahl, Student of Christ Church and University Reader in German Literature.

My obligation to the many scholars from whose work I have profited is indicated, as far as is possible, in the bibliographical references, and here let me add my tribute to the Taylor Institution in which the book was nurtured.

J. K. B.

Oxford
1 January 1954

Preface to the First Edition

Contents

Genealogical Tables

Maps

List of Abbreviations

AfdA	*Anzeiger für deutsches Altertum und deutsche Literatur* (Leipzig/Berlin, 1876–, Wiesbaden 1948–). Published together with *ZfdA* (see below).
AfnF	*Arkiv for nordisk filologi* (Oslo and Lund, 1883–).
Ahd. Gr.	W. Braune, *Althochdeutsche Grammatik*, revd. by W. Mitzka.
Ahd. Lb.	W. Braune, *Althochdeutsches Lesebuch.*
Archiv	*Archiv für das Studium der neueren Sprachen und Literaturen* (Elberfeld and Iserlohn, 1841–; Brunswick etc., 1850–).
ArL	*Archivum Linguisticum* (Glasgow, 1949–; N.S. Menston, 1970–).
DU	*Der Deutschunterricht* (Stuttgart, 1948–).
DPA	*Deutsche Philologie im Aufriß.*
DVjs	*Deutsche Vierteljahrsschrift für Literaturwissenschaft und Geistesgeschichte* (Halle/Stuttgart, 1923–).
Ehrismann	*Geschichte der deutschen Literatur bis zum Ausgang des Mittelalters.* Erster Teil: Die althochdeutsche Literatur (2nd edn.).
Enneccerus	*Die ältesten deutschen Sprachdenkmäler.* In Lichtdrucken herausgegeben von Magda Enneccerus.
Euph.	*Euphorion*, Bamberg; Stuttgart 1894–. Vols. 35–44 (1934–44) were named *Dichtung und Volkstum*. Vols. 45– (1950–) have been published in Marburg.
GGA	*Göttinger Gelehrte Anzeigen* (until 1801 inclusive called *Göttingische Anzeigen von gelehrten Sachen*) (Göttingen, 1753–).
GLL	*German Life and Letters* (Oxford, 1936–; N.S. 1947–).
Gmc.	Germanic
GR	*The Germanic Review* (New York, 1926–).
GRM	*Germanisch-romanische Monatsschrift* (Heidelberg, 1909–43; Neue Folge 1950–).
Grundriß	*Grundriß der germanischen Philologie.*
JEGPh	*Journal of English and Germanic Philology* (Urbana, Illinois, 1897–).
Kz. Grundriß	*Kurzer Grundriß der germanischen Philologie bis 1500*, ed. by L. E. Schmitt.

Kl. ahd. Spdmr.	*Die kleineren althochdeutschen Sprachdenkmäler*, ed. by E. von Steinmeyer.
Med. Æv.	*Medium Ævum* (Oxford, 1932–).
MGH	*Monumenta Germaniae Historica.*
MHG	Middle High German.
MLN	*Modern Language Notes* (Baltimore, 1886–).
MLR	*The Modern Language Review* (London, 1905–).
MSD	*Denkmäler deutscher Poesie und Prosa aus dem VIII–XII. Jahrhundert*, ed. by K. Müllenhoff and W. Scherer. 2 vols. (References are to vol. I unless otherwise stated.)
NddJb	*Jahrbuch des Vereins für niederdeutsche Sprachforschung* (Bremen, 1875–). Vol. 31 and subsequent volumes are called *Niederdeutsches Jahrbuch.*
Neophil.	*Neophilologus* (Groningen, 1916–).
Neuphil. Mitt.	*Neuphilologische Mitteilungen* (Helsinki, 1899–).
NHG	New High German.
OE	Old English (Anglo-Saxon).
OGS	*Oxford German Studies* (Oxford/London, 1966–).
OHG	Old High German.
OLF	Old Low Franconian.
OLG	Old Low German.
ON	Old Norse.
OS	Old Saxon.
PBB	*Beiträge zur Geschichte der deutschen Sprache und Literatur*, begründet von H. Paul und W. Braune (Halle, 1878–1954). From 1955 onwards two independent issues have appeared, one in Halle and one in Tübingen.
Petzet–Glauning	E. Petzet and O. Glauning (eds.), *Deutsche Schrifttafeln des IX. bis XVI. Jahrhunderts aus Handschriften der K. Hof- und Staatsbibliothek in München* (Munich, 1910) (Vol. 1).
P.L.	J. P. Migne (ed.), *Patrologiae Cursus Completus siue bibliotheca universalis . . . omnium S.S. Patrum, Doctorum Scriptorumque ecclesiasticorum qui ab œvo apostolico ad usque Innocentii iii tempora floruerunt. Series (Latina) prima.* (Paris, 1844–).
PMLA	*Publications of the Modern Language Association of America* (New York, 1884–).
Pr. Gmc.	Primitive Germanic (Proto-Germanic).
QuF	*Quellen und Forschungen zur Sprach- und Culturgeschichte der germanischen Völker.*

RhVB	*Rheinische Vierteljahrsblätter* (Bonn 1931–).
Schrifttafeln	H. Fischer (ed.), *Schrifttafeln zum althochdeutschen Lesebuch* (Tübingen, 1966).
TPS	*Transactions of the Philological Society* (London, 1854–).
WGmc.	West Germanic.
WW	*Wirkendes Wort* (Düsseldorf, 1950–).
ZfdA	*Zeitschrift für deutsches Altertum* (Leipzig, 1841–53, Berlin 1856–1944, Wiesbaden 1948–). Vol. 19 and later volumes have the title *Zeitschrift für deutsches Altertum und deutsche Literatur* and appear together with *AfdA* (see above).
ZfdPh	*Zeitschrift für deutsche Philologie* (Halle, 1869–1908, Stuttgart 1909–53, Berlin 1954–).
ZfMaf	*Zeitschrift für Mundartforschung.* (Vols. 1–10 were called *Teuthonista. Zeitschrift für deutsche Dialektforschung und Sprachgeschichte* (Bonn and Leipzig, 1924–34). From 1935 to 1944 (Vols. 11–) it was published under the new title in Halle. Publication was resumed in 1952 in Wiesbaden. In 1969 it was again renamed *Zeitschrift für Dialektologie und Linguistik*.

I

Introduction: the Scope of the Subject

'HIGH GERMAN' is a linguistic term. It denotes those German dialects that have in some measure participated in the consonantal changes known collectively as the Second Sound Shift, and also the standard language that has evolved from them. It is distinguished from 'Low German'. This term denotes the northern dialects of Germany that did not undergo the Shift; at the earliest period they are represented by Old Saxon and in modern times by 'Plattdeutsch'. A separate term, 'Low Franconian', is used for those Franconian (or 'Frankish') dialects that were likewise unaffected by the Shift and whose modern descendants are Dutch and Flemish. The High German dialects are divided into two groups—Upper German, comprising Bavarian and Alemannic, and Middle German, comprising Middle, Rhenish, and East Franconian, together with the, in early times, sparsely attested Thuringian. It has now become customary to associate Lombardic (or 'Langobardic') with High German because it underwent a similar consonant shift. It is also presumed that a form of Frankish, referred to as 'West Frankish', was spoken in northern France for some time after the Frankish conquest, but no certain traces of it have been found in German texts.

The term 'Old' is similarly in the first place linguistic, denoting the early phase of the German dialects, when a variety of vowels existed in unaccented syllables; the subsequent period, in which this variety is no longer found, is called 'Middle High German'. The merging of the various unaccented vowels was far advanced in most dialects by the middle of the eleventh century, though the Old High German type persists in the dialect of the Swiss canton Valais to this day. It is therefore customary to place the transition from the 'old' to the 'middle' period of the language about the year 1050.

This date happens to coincide with the advent of a new type of religious literature, supposed to have been composed under the influence of the Cluny party in the Church. Moreover, the last great figure in German letters before that date, Notker of St. Gall (who died in 1022), seems to have had no successors. It is convenient, therefore, to regard the date 'about 1050' as marking the end of a period of literature too. We can thus speak of 'Old High German literature' as extending from the middle of the eighth century, when the first vernacular documents appear, until the middle of the eleventh. It is customary to include also within the scope of Old High German literature the two biblical epics composed in Old Saxon, the *Heliand* and the *Genesis* (of the latter only three fragments survive). This is convenient, because they would otherwise be isolated, and to some extent justifiable, because they are thought by some scholars to have resulted from literary impulses emanating from the High German south. One might, however, regret the linguistic illogicality and wish for an English term corresponding to the German 'Altdeutsch'.

One can justify the inclusion of these Old Saxon works within a book on Old High German literature on the further ground that they are, after all, composed in the vernacular, the language of the people (*theotisce*), and that the linguistic distinction between High and Low German is anachronistic, being based on the observations of modern philologists. It is not so easy to vindicate the inclusion of Latin works in a book of this sort, and on the whole we shall refer to the rich Latin literature produced in Germany during the period only when it seems to have a bearing upon vernacular texts. An exception is made in favour of two Latin epics, the *Waltharius* and the *Ruodlieb*—of the former because, although Virgilian in style, it treats a native theme which recurs in later German literature, and of the latter because it may credibly be regarded as an indirect precursor of the later chivalric romance.

It should be borne in mind that throughout the Middle Ages Latin was a living language in writing and, to a large extent, in speech also. It may be accepted as a general principle that the written word is always more probably founded in Latin than in a popular oral tradition. This applies with special force to the Old High German period, for at this time German writing in the vernacular was an offshoot of Latin writing.

It may be assumed that the small quantity of vernacular literature

that has come down to us from the Old High German period reflects in some measure—despite probable losses—a relatively small
output. Writing was the province of a small educated class, consisting almost entirely of clerics, whose natural medium of literary
expression was Latin. It is difficult to account for the comparative
richness of Old English literature, except by supposing that the
attitude of the Church to the cultivation of native literature was
less favourable in Germany than it was in England. Nevertheless,
both the quantity and the variety of what has come down to us is
by no means inconsiderable. Although strongly individual personalities may be discerned behind the larger works—the *Heliand*,
the *Evangelienbuch*, and the works of Notker III—there is hardly
any of the original thought or flights of emotion and imagination
that are expected of the modern writer who aspires to even
moderate distinction. There is no lyric, drama, satire, prose fiction,
or history. There is no collection of native lays like the Norse
Edda, and no native epic like the English *Beowulf*. Only a few
faint traces remain of the religion and the ethical code of the pre-
Christian era and of the connection between literature and the
worldly life of the people. The substance of the surviving Old High
German literature is in the main the Christian religion, and the
thought derives almost entirely from the teaching of the Church.
There is, therefore, little scope for aesthetic criticism in the way
that it is applied to modern literature, but there is all the more
room—and all the more need—for interpretation and explanation.

At this period the word 'literature' must be taken in its strict
sense, namely 'that which is written' (in much the same way as
we use the term nowadays to refer to everything from the works
of the poets to official leaflets and advertising brochures). Since
only a handful of works can claim to be 'literature' in the narrow
sense which would exclude everything that was not 'creative
writing', it is customary to talk of the surviving texts as 'monuments', and it is true that many of them have only historical interest. One collection of the shorter texts, that made by Elias von
Steinmeyer, even calls them 'linguistic monuments', as though
they were chiefly interesting for their language. The texts include
every available document in German, even though it be theological, legal, administrative, or medical. Even odd words scribbled
in the margins of manuscripts must be collected and studied.

There is evidence of an 'unwritten literature' or 'oral poetry' in the form of heroic lays, songs, and charms current throughout the period and reaching back far beyond anything which has been preserved in writing. This evidence, however, exists principally outside Old High German 'literature' as it has been defined above, and a discussion of this oral poetry requires a knowledge not only of the Middle High German period, but also of Old English and Old Norse literature, and of the disciplines of Comparative Philology, Prehistory, Archaeology, and Folk-lore. The heroic legends which must have existed in the form of heroic lays will be touched upon in this book only in so far as they are relevant to the *Hildebrandslied* and the *Waltharius*. It will be necessary to draw upon extraneous matter also in the discussion of the ancient German charms. The form of the lost oral poetry will be found relevant too to the biblical epic and the short alliterative poems, and some scholars would have it that it is germane to a discussion of the *Ludwigslied* too.

The Old High German period embraces, therefore, two literatures—the learned Latin literature cultivated in the monasteries, and the native oral literature handed down by professional reciters. With the former we shall be only peripherally concerned, and of the latter we know virtually nothing at first hand. We shall be dealing largely with the remainders which belong to neither. The glossaries and translations, even the masterly translations of Notker, are adjuncts to clerical learning. The baptismal vows were practical instruments of conversion. Even the *Heliand*, for all its formal independence and its employment of the native poetic idiom, was probably intended solely to provide the unlearned with access to the Scriptures, while the *Muspilli* was probably composed as a piece of improving literature directed at the administrators of justice. Even Otfrid, who conceived the grand design of providing his countrymen with a literature worthy of their national qualities, was inspired by Latin models and justified his endeavour by claiming that it would promote the understanding of the Scriptures. The *Merseburg Charms* may appeal to us by their form and rhythm, but their manifest purpose was utilitarian. Only the *Hildebrandslied* can be claimed as a representative of native secular literature. In the normal course of events it would never have been recorded, and we must be grateful for the fact that the two clerics who jotted it down happened, for whatever reason, to have had nothing better to do. It is just possible that in the *Ludwigslied* we have an echo of the ancient songs in praise of native leaders, but it too is imbued with the ecclesiastical spirit. In this period we are dealing with the infancy of a struggling national culture consciously founded on an alien basis.

It can be argued that all the Old High German literature we possess had a mnemonic function. Everything that was written down—the earliest glosses on Latin words, the charms, the extracts from laws and edicts, even the large works of the ninth century— were in some sense aids to the memory. The scholar had to remember his Latin vocabulary, the healer his cures, the administrator his laws, the subject his duties, the retainer the merits of his king, and the Christian the teachings of his Church. Even the *Hildebrandslied* may be considered 'mnemonic writing'. It belongs to an ancient genre which fulfilled the role of history, recording for posterity the deeds of great men *dea erhina warun*; while we admire it for its imaginative power, the contemporary public no doubt valued it too for the 'true' information it contained. The two scribes, who were probably cut off by their calling from frequent access to celebrations of the heroes, may have had imperfect memories and have been impelled to write it down lest they forgot it.

Although we may date and localize the Old High German texts with reasonable accuracy, it is virtually impossible to trace a line of literary development throughout the period. Whereas the study of modern literature is often vitiated by the temptation to see influences at work where there may have been none, and by the difficulty of viewing an individual work as the product of a single creative effort, the student of Old High German literature is frustrated by the virtual isolation of every work he studies. As has been stated already, the most plausible influences are those that spring from the learned, mainly theological, books that the author had read, but even these influences are often impossible to establish. Influences of one native work on another can almost never be presumed, and we must confine ourselves to such tentative statements as that 'Otfrid may have known an early version of the *Muspilli* or another poem from which the *Muspilli* borrowed'. Much has been made, for instance, of the importance of Fulda both as the supposed home of the Tatian translation and as the possible source of the impulse that led to the composition of the *Heliand*, yet neither work can be definitely associated with the house, and much of what has been conjectured may be totally irrelevant. The only poet of the period about whom we know anything is Otfrid, and yet we are exceeding the evidence if we make any unqualified statement about the form of his work, even though, by contemporary standards, he is remarkably informative on the subject. Of all the writers of the period, we know most about Notker, and about his motives and methods, but he had no successors, and his work remains as a colossal monument to the pedagogical zeal of one outstanding scholar. For these reasons it is impossible to write a 'history' of Old High German literature, and all the indications are that Old High German literature, unlike the native poetry or the Latin literature of the Old High German period, in fact had no history. We must therefore be content to call the present volume simply a 'handbook'.[1]

---

[1] See M. Wehrli, 'Deutsche Literaturgeschichte des Mittelalters?', *GLL* (N.S.) 23 (1969) 6–18. For an account of the development of OHG studies up to 1962 see H. Rupp, 'Forschung zur althochdeutschen Literatur 1945–62', *DVjs* 38 (1964), *Sonderheft*, pp. 1–67.

II

The Origin of the German People

TOWARDS the end of the second millennium before Christ there lived in Jutland, on the Danish islands, the eastern shores of the Kattegat, the southern shores of the Baltic, and in the valleys of the Ems and the lower Elbe an agrarian population who buried their illustrious dead in communal graves built of large blocks of stone. The builders of these megalith graves (*Riesengräber* or, in popular parlance, *Hünengräber*) seem to have displaced a more primitive pastoral and fishing population. Before the end of the millennium they appear to have come into contact, and subsequently to have merged, with a people from the south, who buried their dead in single graves with fine stone battle-axes and pottery decorated with impressed cord ('corded ware' or *Schnurkeramik*). The culture which resulted from this merger between the builders of the megalith graves and the warlike people from the south (*die Streitaxtleute*) may be termed Germanic, and its bearers regarded as the ancestors of the numerous tribes known later to the Romans by the collective name *Germani*.

The language spoken by this Germanic people was likewise the ancestor of the various Germanic dialects attested later. We have no records of this language, which we may call Proto-Germanic or Primitive Germanic. (We must distinguish between this completely inaccessible *real* Proto-Germanic and the *reconstructed* Proto-Germanic which comparative linguists extrapolate from the data of the later dialects.) The Germanic languages belong to the wider family of Indo-European languages, to which most of the languages of Europe (the exceptions today being Finnish, Esthonian, Lappish, Turkish, Hungarian, Basque, and Maltese) and some in Asia also belong. It is reasonable to assume that the Indo-European basis of Germanic was provided by the Battle-Axe People from the south, and that its peculiarly 'Germanic' characteristics (such as its consonantism, its accentual patterns, part of its verbal system, and the greater part of its vocabulary) resulted from its acquisition by the autochthonous population, who originally spoke a different tongue. It would therefore be justifiable to speak of the newcomers from the south as 'Indo-Europeans' in the sense that they were bearers of an Indo-European culture of which their language was part. It would, however, be improper to attach any ethnic sense to the designation. In view of the frequency with which, in historical times, once discrete communities have merged or diversified, and of man's capacity for acquiring and imposing languages, together with other components of culture, it seems unlikely that there ever was a pure Indo-European race.

'Indo-European' is therefore primarily a linguistic designation. We can, of course, extrapolate from the linguistic data and accredit to ancient Indo-European culture some shared aspects of religion, social organization, and the like. Thus, we can detect Indo-European elements in Germanic religion: for instance, the Germanic god whose name appears in Old English as *Tīw* and in Old Norse as *Týr*, can be linguistically identified with *Zeus* (IE base-form *$d\underset{.}{i}\bar{e}u$-). Since mythology may often reflect lost history, it is possible to conjecture that the Norse account of the defeat of one race of gods, the *Vanir*, by another, the *Æsir*, may owe its genesis to the supersession of an ancient cult by a newer one of Indo-European provenance. Apart from the common Indo-European vocabulary found in the Germanic languages, there is one proper name common to Germanic, Celtic, and Indian which may be regarded therefore as Indo-European, viz. OHG *Purgunt*, Irish *Brigid*, Sanskrit *Br̥hatī* (IE base *bhr̥ghn̥t*-).

Between 1000 and 500 B.C. the Germanic people extended their territory southwards to occupy much of northern Europe. During this expansion they came into contact with other peoples, notably their neighbours the Celts. From the Celts they seem to have learnt about iron-working (the word *iron* is of Celtic origin) and some aspects of legal and administrative organization (reflected by the originally Celtic words *Amt* and *Reich* among others). With this expansion there came a certain measure of linguistic diversification, though we may assume that this did not hamper intercommunication. After this period of expansion, which was no doubt due to the need for land to support the growing population, there came another in which different Germanic tribes began to migrate individually or in groups away from the common homeland, and to seek their fortunes amongst alien peoples. In the second century before Christ some of the tribes who were moving southwards came into conflict with the Romans and won a number of victories against them, but the superior military organization of the Romans ensured that the southward progress of the barbarians was arrested for several centuries. The Consul Marius inflicted annihilating defeats on them at Aquae Sextiae in 102 B.C. and at Vercellae in 101. Large numbers of German prisoners were brought to Rome as slaves or gladiators. Their descendants were prominent in the Spartacus risings of 73–71 B.C.

Although the southward progress of the tribes had been arrested, there were not more than a few years of peace in the west. In 73 B.C. the Suevi led by Ariovistus crossed the Rhine into Gaul and sub-jugated the Celts, who appealed to Rome for protection. At Mühl-hausen (Mulhouse) in Alsace, Julius Caesar inflicted a decisive defeat on the Germans in 58 B.C. Gaul was henceforth Roman, and now Gauls and Germans formed divisions of the Roman army. Under Augustus (died A.D. 14) and Tiberius (A.D. 14–37) the Romans, led by Drusus and Germanicus, penetrated as far as the Elbe, in spite of such set-backs as the defeat of Varus by Arminius and his Cherusci near Detmold in A.D. 9. Holstein and Schleswig were never Roman. The cities of Mainz, Trier, and Xanten date from this period, and Cologne (Colonia Agrippinensis) was founded by the Emperor Claudius (41–54). The annexation and romaniza-tion of Germany continued under Vespasian (69–79), Domitian (81–96), and Hadrian (117–38), but the Romans gave up the hope of controlling the northern part. They sought to consolidate their conquests and protect their territory from the northern barbarians by building a system of fortifications known as the *limes*. The *limes* ran in a generally south-easterly direction, following a zigzag course from a point on the Rhine north of Andernach to the Danube near Regensburg. Until the third century the Rhine, the *limes*, and the Danube provided effective barriers against the en-croachments of the northern tribes, but about 260 the Franks crossed the Rhine in the north, and the Alemanni breached the *limes* further to the south-east. The Roman Empire was now in decline, crumbling bit by bit and increasingly controlled by the barbarians; in 476 the last Emperor of the West was deposed by the Germanic chieftain Odoacer, a member of the tribe of the Sciri.

The movements of the Germanic tribes were given a fresh impetus in the fourth and fifth centuries by the pressure of the Huns from the east. This Asiatic tribe, which had long been moving westwards, came into conflict with the Ostrogoths in 375 and set in motion 'Migrations of the Peoples' which led to rapid shifts of population throughout Europe. The advance of the Huns was finally halted by the combined forces of the Romans and Visigoths under the Roman general Aetius at the Battle of the Catalaunian Plains, sometimes called the Battle of Châlons (Châlons-sur-Marne) in 451. When their leader Attila died in 453 the empire of the Huns soon collapsed, and they settled down in what is now Hungary.

Most of our information about the Germanic peoples during their early contacts with the Mediterranean world is supplied by Tacitus and other classical authors. A large number of tribal names and other data are preserved by them, but the interpretation of these data is extremely problematical, and in many instances we are not sure how reliable they are. We also have the evidence of archaeological finds, but it is often difficult to relate these to other evidence. The probable groupings of the Germanic tribes prior to their migrations from northern Europe, that is to say the early connections between them, are reconstructed primarily on the basis of the linguistic affinities between the later dialects, but for many of the Germanic peoples, even those, like the Vandals, who played an important role in history, we have little but personal names to go on. Even where we have connected texts, opinions often differ considerably on the interpretation of the linguistic affinities they exhibit.

The view that at present seems to command most support is that there were five principal groups of Germanic peoples. The first of these (the *Nordgermanen*) remained in their northern homeland and were the ancestors of the Scandinavian peoples; it was not till the Viking Age that they began to migrate in large numbers, colonizing Iceland from Norway, parts of Britain and France from Denmark, and later (as Normans) conquering England and Sicily from France. The second group (the *Nordseegermanen*) settled along the North Sea coast of the Continent and were the ancestors of the Frisians, Angles, and Saxons. The third group (the *Weser-Rhein-Germanen*) occupied the land between the Weser and Rhine and comprised a number of tribes, including the ancestors of the Franks and the Hessians. The fourth group (the *Elbgermanen*) occupied an area on both banks of the middle and upper Elbe; to this group may be reckoned the ancestors of the Thuringians, Swabians, Swiss, and Bavarians, as well as of the Lombards, who later settled in Italy. The fifth group (the *Ostgermanen* or *Oder-Weichsel-Germanen*) settled along the Baltic coast and its hinterland between the Oder and the Vistula; among them were the ancestors of the Goths, Burgundians, Gepids, Vandals, and others. It will be seen that the 'German' nation, as it emerged during the course of the Middle Ages, was made up largely of peoples belonging to the third and fourth of these groups, though after the conquest of the Saxons by Charlemagne the second group was also involved. This second group, through the emigration of the Angles and Saxons to Britain in the fifth century, provided the dominant ethnic component of the English nation. These three groups together traditionally make up the 'West Germanic' family, though it is now no longer generally held that there was once a unified West Germanic people or language.

It is important to remember that not all the peoples whom we encounter in later history represent original ancient tribes. The Franks, who appear late, were a confederacy of small tribes; the same is true of the Alemanni. One people in particular, the Bavarians, who emerge into history only in the sixth century, are of mysterious provenance, though they may contain elements of older tribes known to the Romans by different names.

In the brief survey that follows we shall be concerned only with those Germanic peoples who played an important role in the politics of Europe before or during the Old High German period and whose culture in some way contributed to early German literature, as well as with those who made up the later German nation—the Franks, Thuringians, Alemanni, Bavarians, and Saxons.

* * *

The Goths were the first of the Germanic tribes to leave their northern homeland. At first, having crossed the Baltic, they settled near the mouth of the Vistula. In the early centuries of the Christian era they pressed south-eastwards into what is now Russia, and in the fourth century they controlled a vast empire extending from the Black Sea to the Pripet Marshes. At this stage the tribe split into two parts: those who occupied the area between the

Dniester and the Don were known as Ostrogoths (East Goths), while those who dwelt to the west of them were called Visigoths. The Ostrogoths were driven westwards by the Huns in the fourth century and settled in Pannonia, a territory corresponding roughly to present-day Hungary, becoming federates of the Romans. However, a few seem to have remained behind, for a Germanic language (known as Crimean Gothic) was still being spoken in the Crimea in the sixteenth century.

After the collapse of the Hunnish empire in 455 the Ostrogoths moved into Moesia (which corresponds roughly to modern Serbia and Bulgaria) and harried the whole of the Balkans, now as enemies and now as allies of the Eastern Roman Empire. In 489, under their great king Theodoric and with the permission of the Emperor Zeno, they invaded Italy. Theodoric defeated the armies of Odoacer, the Germanic ruler of Italy who in 476 had deposed the last Emperor of the West, and drove him back upon Ravenna. After a long siege Ravenna fell in March 493. Ten days later Theodoric murdered Odoacer and ruled Italy until his death in 526. After the death of their great king the fortunes of the Goths declined. In 535 the Emperor Justinian sent forces into Italy to oust them, first under his great general Belisarius, and later under the eunuch Narses. At first the imperial forces met with great success, driving the Goths into the north of Italy, but later, under Baduila (sometimes called Totila), the Goths recovered for a time most of what they had lost. Ultimately, however, they were defeated and Baduila killed at the battle of Taginae (probably Gualdo Tadino in Umbria) in 552. Their last king, Teia, continued the hopeless struggle, but was defeated and fell in the following year. The remnants of the Goths withdrew northwards over the Alps and played no further part in history. Some may have been absorbed into the native population of Italy.

Meanwhile the Visigoths were still a powerful people. In the third century they had inhabited Dacia (which corresponds roughly to Romania). It was during this period that their bishop Wulfila or Ulfilas (died 383) translated the Bible into Gothic. He was consecrated bishop in 341. How Christianity spread among the Goths we do not know, but we read of Christians being persecuted during this period. In 376 they were attacked by the Huns and sought refuge across the Danube within the bounds of the Roman Empire, though relations with the Romans were at first hostile; in 378 they defeated and killed the Emperor Valens. In 382 the Romans settled them as federates in Moesia, where they remained until 395. Then their leader Alaric led them southwards into Greece. From 401 onwards they repeatedly invaded Italy; the year 410 saw the great sack of Rome. Under Alaric's successor Ataulph they migrated northwards and settled in southern Gaul and Spain with their capital at Toulouse, where they remained as federates of the Romans until 475, when their leader Euric declared himself an independent king. They fought alongside the Romans at Châlons in 451. They lost most of their territory north of the Pyrenees to Clovis the Frank in 507, and were never able to secure a firm hold on it again. Though a minority among the Romano-Hispanic population of Spain, the Goths maintained their sway in spite of the hostility of the Basques and Suevi[1] in the north and north-west of the peninsula and the invasions of the Imperial forces in the south, until 711. In that year their kingdom was utterly destroyed by the Saracens.

To the cultural climate of the Roman-Gothic state established by Theodoric the Great we owe the most influential secular book of the Middle Ages, the *Consolation of Philosophy*, written by the Roman consul Boethius when he was awaiting execution, and translated by Notker of St. Gall four and a half centuries later. We also owe to Gothic legend some of the great figures in medieval literature. The Gothic king Ermanaric, who is reported by the Gothic historian Jordanes to have died at the age of 109 in the year 375 as the result of a conspiracy while the Hunnish hordes overran his kingdom, became the legendary Jǫrmunrekr of one of the finest lays of the Edda, the *Hamðismál*. This figure also appears as the evil Ermrich in the Middle High German Dietrich epics. Much more important, however, is the figure of the great Theodoric himself, who became the Dietrich von Bern (i.e. of Verona) of the medieval heroic epic, and whose struggle with Odoacer provides the background for the incident recounted in the *Hildebrandslied*. The legendary founder of the Gothic dynasty was called Amal, and after him their kings were known as Amales. In medieval German legend the name of the people is lost, but the name of the dynasty survives in the designation of Dietrich's followers as 'Amelunge'.

The Visigoths provided German literature with no complete

[1] These Suevi had migrated to north-western Spain in the fifth century.

legend, but one of their princesses, Brunichildis, who married the Frankish king Sigibert in 567, may have been the historical prototype of the Brünhilt of the *Nibelungenlied* and even, as one scholar has maintained, of the vengeful Kriemhilt.

Another powerful tribe, the Vandals, having originated in the north, seem to have taken the land route southwards and southwestwards through the Rhineland, Gaul, and Spain, whence, between 429 and 441, they invaded and conquered North Africa, making Carthage their capital. Their powerful fleets controlled the Mediterranean during the fifth century and enabled them in 455 to occupy Rome. An echo of their mastery of the sea is no doubt to be heard in the poetic name *wentilseo* by which the Mediterranean was known to the poet of the *Hildebrandslied*, and which was used in a less specific sense by the author of *Beowulf*. The Vandals were defeated and their kingdom destroyed by the forces of East Rome under Belisarius in 533.

A less important tribe from the historical point of view was that of the Burgundians (whose name is probably related to the OHG personal name *Purgunt* mentioned above and may have meant 'the hill-people' or some such). Their original home may have been the island of Bornholm in the Baltic, whence they migrated, like the Goths, to the region of the Vistula. In the fourth century, however, they turned westwards, settling on the west bank of the Rhine around Worms, where the *Nibelungenlied* places their capital. They became federates of the Romans, and in the early fifth century some of the tribe settled in Gaul. In 435 they tried to extend their dominions and were in the following year attacked by the Huns with Roman collusion. This led to the battle in which their king Gundicarius (a latinized form of *Gundahari*), and his brothers Gislaharius and Godomarus perished. This was the historical basis of the fall of the Burgundians recounted by the *Nibelungenlied*. In 443 the Romans settled the tribe in the vicinity of Lake Geneva, and in 451 Burgundians were among the forces that fought on the Catalaunian Plains under Aetius. About 470 a prince called Sigismer is mentioned among them; soon other names with the first element *Sigis-* appear. Since such names were common among the Franks, this may indicate a dynastic connection between the two peoples comparable to that which arises in the *Nibelungenlied* between Burgonden and Niderlant when Kriemhilt marries Sivrit. Under their king Gundobad (died 516) they occupied the valleys of the Rhône and the Saône. The independent Burgundian kingdom ceased to exist in 534 when it was conquered by the Franks, who inherited the Burgundian legends. It seems that the Burgundian language was still being used in the seventh century, though it was eventually replaced by a Romance dialect.

After the Goths had been driven out of Italy by the Imperial forces under Narses, their place was soon taken by another Germanic people, the Lombards or Langobardi. Their original home had probably been in southern Sweden, whence they had migrated through Jutland to the upper reaches of the Elbe and had settled, by the sixth century, in the land on the middle Danube which is now Lower Austria and Moravia. There they had contacts not only with the Ostrogoths, Saxons, and Franks, but also with the Eastern Empire. In 552 they aided the Imperial forces against the Goths. In 568, under their king Alboin, they invaded Italy in force and soon conquered it, making Pavia their capital. They had strong contacts with the Bavarians north of the Alps, and it may be that the marriage of their king Authari, who came to the throne in 584, to a Bavarian princess is remembered in the German story of King Rother, though the hero no doubt owes his name to the king and law-giver of the next century, Rothari. The Lombard kingdom survived until Charlemagne, acting upon a complaint from the Pope against the Lombard king Desiderius, invaded Italy, defeated the Lombard armies, occupied Pavia, and made himself king of the Lombards in 774. After the Frankish conquest the Lombards long retained their sense of national identity and caused much trouble for Charlemagne's successors, but they forgot their Germanic language; no continuous texts in it have survived. The world of learning in Charlemagne's empire owed much to such Lombards as Paul the Deacon and Peter of Pisa, whom Charlemagne brought to Germany; it is from the former's *Historia Langobardorum* that we know most of the events of Lombard history. Apart from the story of King Rother, German literature perhaps owes to this people that of Hildebrand and Hadubrand, whose names appear to be Lombardic, though, as we have seen, the political background of their encounter derives from Gothic history. It may even be that the whole of the Gothic material entered Germany not directly through contact between the Goths and the Bavarians, but indirectly through Lombard transmission.

The most successful of the Germanic peoples who remained

on the continent of Europe were the Franks, for they were the founders not only of France, which is named after them, but of Germany. They were not an ancient Germanic tribe, but a confederacy of small tribes which inhabited the area of the lower Rhine and came together to pursue common territorial objectives. When they first appear in history they are ruled by a number of kings, each with his own territory. The tribe which was to prove the most influential was that of the Salians, who may have taken their name from the 'salt sea' (probably the Zuider Zee) by which they lived; the area on the lower Yssel round Deventer is still called Salland. The Salians furnished the first race of Frankish kings, the Merovingians, and were to constitute one of the two main divisions of the Frankish people. The first king of all the Franks, the great Chlodowech—or Clovis, as he is usually called by the French and the English—was the grandson of one Merowech, who flourished about 460, but the name of the dynasty may go back to an unknown prince of earlier times.[1]

The Franks (whose name probably meant 'free men') are first mentioned in the third century, when they came into conflict with the Romans. About the middle of that century they crossed the Rhine, probably near Cologne. Some of them, taken prisoner by the Romans, were settled by the Black Sea, whence, having obtained ships, they returned to their homeland. This remarkable voyage may have given rise to the fiction that traced the origin of the race back to ancient Troy. Throughout the fourth century they were in conflict with the Romans, though from time to time the Romans employed them as auxiliaries against the more powerful Alemanni, and they seem to have settled some of them in Gaul. In 406 the Roman legions were withdrawn from the Rhine, and this gave the Franks the opportunity to move southwards into Guelders and Brabant, which was Empire territory, and into northern and eastern France. Their advance was made easier because the whole of the Roman Empire was under attack from other Germanic tribes, to which was added, in the middle of the century, the invasion of Gaul by the Huns. At the battle of the Catalaunian Plains Frankish loyalties seem to have been divided between the two sides, though a Frankish king Merovaeus is credited with having fought on the side of the Romans and Visigoths. When the

---

[1] See G. Baesecke, *GRM* 24 (1936) 161–81: 'Es muß einen einstämmigen Namen *Mero* gegeben haben . . . Seine Bedeutung wissen wir nicht' (p. 177).

Huns retired, the Franks took possession of much of northern Gaul. About 460 the Franks gained permanent possession of Cologne, having held it once a century earlier.

The Franks who settled along the Rhine from the Lippe to the Lahn and along the Meuse (Maas), on the land around Cologne, Trier, Mainz, and Metz, were known as Ripuarians, i.e. inhabitants of the river-banks. (The name Ripuarii is first recorded in 727, though it is probably much older.) The Salian Franks, who have already been mentioned, held the land between the Scheldt and the Somme, and between the Meuse and the Straits of Dover, their principal cities being Cambrai, Arras, Tournay, and Tongres.

Early associates of the Franks were the Hessians, who, unlike most of the Germanic tribes of the Continent, have remained in their ancestral homeland since Roman times, if the customary identification of the tribe with the ancient Chatti is correct (though it is phonologically difficult). Occupying land on the east bank of the Rhine north of the Main, they were comparatively untouched by Roman civilization, and they retained their pagan faith until the eighth century. In 723 Boniface felled their sacred oak dedicated to Wodan during his missionary work among them.

When Clovis came to the throne in 481 or 482, the south of Gaul was the territory of the Visigoths. To their east, in the valleys of the Rhône and the Saône, lay the newly established Burgundian kingdom of Gundobad. To the north of these two Germanic kingdoms there lay a remnant of Roman Gaul, which extended over the valley of the Seine and the central plain of France as far as Orleans and Troyes. It was ruled from Soissons by the patrician Syagrius, whom the Franks called the king of the Romans. In 486 Clovis, in league with his kinsman the king of Cambrai, invaded this territory and defeated Syagrius. In the course of the next three years it was incorporated into the Frankish dominions. Clovis then, by a combination of force and treachery, set about eliminating all his rivals of the Merovingian house. He next turned his attention to the Ripuarians and subjected them all to himself save King Sigibert of Cologne, who was his ally. In the year of his death, 511, Clovis succeeded in annexing this last Frankish kingdom: Sigibert was murdered by his own son at the instigation of Clovis, and Clovis then punished this son with death.

In 492 Clovis had married the Burgundian princess Chrotechildis or Clotilda. This marriage was to be of immeasurable importance for the future of the Franks, indeed of the whole of Germany and even Europe. Clovis and his people were largely heathen, though there were undoubtedly some Christians among them. His queen, however, was not only a Christian, but a Catholic Christian, and succeeded in converting him to her faith. Clovis's christening is traditionally said to have taken place at Reims on Christmas Day 496. Alone among the Germanic tribes of the Continent the Franks became Roman Catholics. The Goths and the Lombards were converted from paganism to Arian Christianity.[1] Thus, while these peoples were continually in conflict with the Catholic Church, Clovis secured for himself and his successors the valuable support both of the clergy within the realm and of the Pope without.

Clovis defeated the Alemanni in 496, and in 507 he won Aquitaine from the Visigoths, thus depriving them of most of their land north of the Pyrenees. However, Theodoric the Great (who had incidentally married Clovis's sister Audefleda) came to their aid and regained much, though not all, of the lost territory for them. It was nevertheless only a matter of time before the Franks had permanent possession of the whole of what is now France.

Clovis's successors continued his policy of territorial aggrandizement. In 531 his sons Theuderich and Chlothar, aided by the Saxons, destroyed the Thuringian kingdom, and his grandson Theudbert in 534 conquered Burgundy (Clovis himself had made a treacherous but unsuccessful attack on his father-in-law's kingdom over thirty years earlier). Theudbert also invaded Italy in 535, the same year as the Imperial army under Belisarius. At first the Franks took all before them, but their army was struck down by the plague, and they had to retire. A later Frankish attempt to gain territory in Italy was thwarted by Narses. It was to be another two and a quarter centuries before such ambitions could be realized. Theudbert's last territorial achievement was the subjugation of the Bavarians, probably in 543.

After Clovis's death the Frankish dominions were partitioned among his sons, and it was not until 558 that they were reunited

---

[1] Arius (Ἄρειος) was a native of Alexandria. He was excommunicated about 323 for preaching that Jesus Christ had been *homoiousios* 'of like being', that is to say created by God the Father and by Him filled with the Holy Spirit, whereas the orthodox doctrine is that God the Father and God the Son are *homoousios* 'of the same being'; Jesus Christ was, therefore, not a later creation but coeternal with the Father.

under the rule of his last surviving son Chlothar; but after Chlothar's death in 561 another partition was made, by which his son Sigibert obtained the Frankish heartland to the east of the Meuse and Scheldt. His brother Chilperich got the western territory roughly corresponding to the old Roman area conquered by Clovis nearly a century before. In the seventh century we first find the western Frankish territory called Neustria, a name which contains the Frankish equivalent of the word *new* (Gmc. **neuja-*) and seems to have arisen because this was new, colonial territory where the Franks were a ruling aristocracy among a Gallo-Roman population. Unlike the Roman overlords whom they superseded, however, they did not impose their language on the native population, but gradually forgot it in favour of Gallo-Roman Latin, which they spoke in their own way. This 'Latein in fränkischem Munde', as one philologist has called it, developed into French. Meanwhile that part of the old 'Francia' to the east came to be known as Austrasia or Austria, in which is to be discerned the word for 'east' (Gmc. **austra-*).

When the split in the Frankish dominions became permanent in the ninth century, the West Franks began more and more to use the old name Francia for the whole of their territory and to restrict the name Neustria to the area between the Somme and the Loire, later to Brittany or Normandy. Likewise the name Austrasia in the ninth century came to denote the area to the east of the Meuse. Its vernacular equivalent, *Ostarrichi*, was used for the realm of Louis the German. Finally this German name was applied to the extreme south-east of the Empire, where in 1156 Barbarossa established the duchy of Austria.

The history of the Franks under the Carolingians will be referred to in relation to the literary documents of the Old High German period, for it is with this people that the development of German—as distinct from Germanic—culture may be considered to begin. We must first, however, pay some attention to the early history of those peoples who, as we have already seen, were conquered by the Franks, namely the Alemanni, the Thuringians, and the Bavarians, together with their powerful northern neighbours, the Saxons, who resisted them until the reign of Charlemagne.

The Alemanni were in the third century a powerful confederacy of tribes, among which were apparently some of the ancient Suevi (whose name survives in Germany as 'Schwaben').

The name Alemanni, meaning quite simply 'all men', clearly points to the composite ethnic character of the people. In 260 or thereabouts they pushed south-westwards across the *limes* and established themselves in the valley of the Neckar. In the next century, under the Emperor Julian, they were temporarily pushed back to the *limes* (in 359), but this did not permanently check their expansion. They became rivals of the Burgundians; this may have forced them to extend their territory to the west and south, where they occupied Alsace (*Alisaz* meant 'foreign domain') and what is now Switzerland. In the fifth century they began to expand into the area west of the middle Rhine, and in 480 they occupied Trier. This inevitably brought them into conflict with the Franks, by whose powerful king Clovis they were resoundingly defeated in 496. This defeat forced them to give up their westward expansion, and in 507 some of them placed themselves under the protection of the Ostrogoths. In 552, when the Ostrogothic power in Italy was spent, their dukes Leuthari and Butelin led an army into Italy, but it was smitten by the plague and achieved nothing. When Frankish power weakened in the later Merovingian period, the Alemanni, who still had their own dukes, began once more to assert themselves. They rebelled against the Franks under their duke Lantfrid in 730 and were quelled by the army of Charles Martel. Their duke was killed in battle, and the Alemannic dukedom was not revived until 911, when the duchy of Swabia was created. They rose against the Franks once more in 742, but were put down by Pippin the Short.

Behind the Alemanni, as they swarmed across the *limes* in the third century, lay the Thuringians, whose name in this form first appears about the year 400, but who may well have been descendants of the Hermunduri of earlier times. (This may be explained linguistically if we take *Thur-* or *Dur-* to be the nucleus of the two names and *Hermun-* (perhaps from Gmc. **ermana-*, **ermuna-*) to be the first element of a compound as in *Ermanaric* etc. The suffix *-ing-* is familiar to us from other tribal and dynastic names, e.g. *Merovingi* etc.). They may have absorbed elements of other tribes during their early migrations from the middle Elbe. Following the Alemanni, they seem to have moved into the area of the Harz mountains, though they are later found farther south, in the region of the Main. They achieved considerable power in the fifth century under their king Bisin and were on good terms with the

Langobards, whose duke Wacho married Bisin's daughter Rade-
gunde. Bisin's son Herminafrid married Amalaberga, the daughter
of Theodoric the Great. They came into conflict with the Franks
during the third decade of the sixth century, and in 531 their
kingdom was utterly destroyed by the Franks; Herminafrid was
murdered, and his queen and their children fled south, where they
were taken prisoner by the Imperial forces. In the war the Franks
had been aided by the Saxons, who took the northern part of the
Thuringian territory, while the southern part, the land on the
Werra and the Unstrut, became tributary to the Franks. Being
an outlying tribe, the Thuringians were able to neglect their
allegiance to the Franks when Frankish power declined during the
seventh century. In the eighth century, however, they were once
more brought under Frankish control and converted to Christianity. The area round Würzburg which they inhabited was later
to become an integral part of the eastern Frankish realm.

The Bavarians or Baiuvarii, who were later to man the south-
eastern marches of Germany, are a people of mysterious origin.
They appear on the political scene in the sixth century. One
hypothesis sees in them the descendants of the Marcomanni, who
had dealings with the Romans in the first century of the Christian
era, and who later moved eastwards into what is now Bohemia.
The name *Boihaemum* (Gmc. **Baihaima-*, later German *Bēhaim*,
Böhmen) is probably connected with the Celtic tribe called the
Boii: Tacitus makes this connection (*Germania* 28) and states
(ibid. 42) that the Boii were ousted by the Marcomanni. Now the
Marcomanni are last heard of in Pannonia at the end of the fourth
century, where they presumably became subjects of the Huns, who
occupied Pannonia in 433. It seems that, after leaving Bohemia, the
Boii too had settled in parts of Pannonia. The anonymous geographer of the seventh century who is known as 'the Geographer
of Ravenna' mentions a region called *Baias* which might be identified with an area to the south of Lake Balaton. A tribal name
*Bajōwarjōz, later *Bajuwari*, could well mean 'inhabitants of
Baia(s)', and its bearers could be taken to have come from that
area. We may, therefore, conjecture that the Bavarians moved into
their later territory from the east, whether or not we identify them
with the Marcomanni. It is quite probable that elements of other
tribes were absorbed by the Bavarians. Place-name evidence suggests that the Sciri, Odoacer's tribe, may have been involved.

The area settled by the Bavarians is roughly bounded by the Lech and the Vienna Woods; the time of the settlement may have been the end of the fifth century or the first decades of the sixth. Friendly relations with the Huns are indicated by the favourable picture of Attila preserved in the Etzel of the *Nibelungenlied*, which goes back in part to a Bavarian account of the Fall of the Burgundians.

About 543 they were subjugated by the Franks under Clovis's grandson Theudbert, but during the following century they became virtually independent again. They maintained on the whole friendly relations with the Germanic rulers of Italy, first with the Goths, whose national legend they preserved, and later with the Lombards. They were converted to Christianity by the seventh century. The overlordship of the Franks was restored during the eighth century by Charles Martel, but they were an unruly people, and their duke Tassilo rose up several times against Pippin the Short and Charlemagne. He was finally deposed in 788 and confined to a monastery.

To the north of the Franks lay the powerful and independent tribe of the Saxons, whose land was bounded in the north by the Eider and in the east by the Elbe and Saale. Their name, which is probably taken from the Germanic word *sahs*, denoting a single-edged sword, is first mentioned by Ptolemy in the second century, and in historical times they occupied an area formerly inhabited by tribes whose names seem to be continued in some of the Saxon regional names (e.g. Engern, which may stem from the name of the Angrivarii mentioned by Tacitus). Whether this circumstance points to the supplanting of the earlier tribes by the Saxons or to an ethnic union is difficult to decide. Some scholars would like to believe that the ancient Cherusci of Arminius were ancestors of some of the Ostfalahi of later times (Eastphalia corresponds geographically with the area of the Cherusci). It is also possible that the Chauci, whom Tacitus places near the sea to the west of the Elbe, were absorbed into the Saxon people and were the ancestors of those Saxons who sailed across the North Sea to colonize parts of southern Britain in the fifth century. By comparison with the Franks they were a primitive people with no urban life, no sophisticated military organization, and a tenacious adherence to their pagan religion. On the other hand, they organized themselves politically as an aristocratic republic; traces of this political organization may be found in the Old Saxon *Heliand*.

From the sixth century onwards we read of conflicts between the Saxons and the Franks. The two peoples collaborated in 531 to destroy the Thuringians, but in 555 the Franks attacked the Saxons, only to be soundly defeated. In the eighth century they clashed several times with Charles Martel and Pippin the Short, under whom the first attempts at Christianization were made. Their ancient religion, under which they worshipped not only Thuner and Wodan, but also their national god Saxnot, came to symbolize their national independence. It was left to Charlemagne, with his zeal for extending the bounds of Christendom and his own dominions, to subdue this proud race and make them part of the Christian German nation, but even he had to mount five costly campaigns before this was achieved. In later times it was the Saxons, especially under the Saxon Emperors, who protected Germany from the Slavonic tribes to the east and made it possible for the Germans to colonize the land beyond the Elbe and Saale. This process, which began towards the end of the Old High German period and led to the establishment, in the late fifteenth century, of the electorate of Saxony, based on the Margravate of Meissen and the Landgravate of Thuringia, became an abiding feature of German history until recent times.

There was one people whom the Franks managed to subdue by military force under Charles Martel and whose land became part of Frankish territory, but who have retained their national identity and their language until today. These are the Frisians, who occupy the area to the east of the Zuider Zee together with the Frisian islands, and who once held the land on its western side, as well as the area of Germany which is now called Ostfriesland. They were converted to Christianity with great difficulty in the eighth century: it was among them that Boniface met his martyr's death in 754. 'The free Frisians', say their laws, were charged by Charlemagne with defending the coast against 'the salt sea and the wild Viking'. These ancient laws, which are preserved in manuscripts of the thirteenth century and later, present a social and legal organization which had its origins in very early times. The 'North Frisian' dialects of the east coast of Schleswig–Holstein, the Halligen, and the islands of Sylt, Föhr, Amrum, and Heligoland, which were first recorded in fairly recent times, are probably due to colonization from Frisia proper. (The name Amrum is perhaps connected with that of the ancient tribe called the Ambrones.)

The Germanic-speaking tribes of central and northern Europe had been known to the Romans collectively as Germani; the origin of this name is obscure, and it was to remain a foreign or learned name among those tribes to whom it was applied. They may have felt some common bond between them, especially when pitted against Rome, but the powerful Germanic peoples who emerged during the Dark Ages regarded themselves as Franks or Saxons or Bavarians, and even those who lost their political independence early, like the Hessians, retained a large measure of national identity. The ninth-century Otfrid regarded himself as a Frank, and he wrote *in frenkisgun*. He praised his king as a noble Frank who ruled over *Ostarrichi*. He could probably have expressed only in Latin the idea that he was a German subject of a German king ruling over Germany. Since, however, Frankish was the language of the people (OHG *theota, thiota, diota*) in contrast with Latin, the language of learning, he felt the need to explain to his readers 'cur scriptor hunc librum theotisce dictaverit'. Three centuries or so later we find Walther von der Vogelweide speaking of *uns tiuschen*. This ethnic sense of the word developed out of the linguistic, as we can observe when Walther addresses the Germans as *tiuschiu zunge*; the contrast now is not with Latin, but with the people and language of the *Walhen*, the 'foreigners' within the Empire, that is the Italians. The Germans acquired a sense of nationhood much later than the French or the English, but it is clear that by Walther's time they had a sense of nationality, a sense of belonging to a supranational community whose cohesion was due in large measure to the fact that the constituent 'nations', the Bavarians, Swabians, Thuringians, and others, all spoke varieties of the 'same language', even though they were to have to wait centuries yet for the emergence of a unified 'national language'.

In the Old High German period there is little, if any, trace of such a sense of nationality, yet it was during this period that the bond uniting the Germans was being forged. The Germanic part of the Frankish Empire, except for the newest accessions—Frisia and Saxony—was peopled by descendants of either the *Weser-Rhein-Germanen* or the *Elbgermanen*; the Lombards, though usually reckoned among the latter group, were fast losing their inherited tongue when they were conquered by the Franks in 774, and in any case they had been separated by the Alps from the other Germanic peoples of Europe since 568. The transalpine territories conquered by the Merovingians formed a continuous area. The later Empire, whether Charlemagne's or Otto the Great's, provided furthermore a political framework within which intercourse between the constituent nations (represented politically by the national duchies) could be fostered, and it may well have retarded linguistic diversification. The peoples of the different parts of Germany, while retaining their regional allegiances, were thus induced, willy-nilly, to recognize a supra-regional nationality manifested in large measure by the degree of linguistic inter-communication possible between them. It was not long after Charlemagne's Saxon wars that the Saxons too began to partake of this German nationality, and, in spite of their divergent language, in the tenth century they took over the hegemony within the Empire from the Franks. The sense of nationality was certainly strengthened too by the split between the 'old' and the 'new' parts of the Frankish dominions. The old Frankish nation ceased to be a reality during our period: the conquerors of Gaul founded a new Frankish nation on a non-Germanic linguistic basis, while those Franks who had stayed behind in the East soon found themselves to be just one nation among several of German nationality.

III

The Charms

THE only German texts that can possibly be relics of pagan poetry are the two charms preserved by a fortunate chance in the same ninth-century manuscript which contains the *Frankish Baptismal Vow*.[1] As the manuscript belongs to the Cathedral Library of Merseburg, near Halle, they are known as the **Merseburger Zaubersprüche**.[2] Most scholars hold that they are of genuine pagan origin, although some maintain that they were originally Christian charms which have been transposed into pagan form. They were entered, probably copied, into the Merseburg manuscript in the tenth century.

The dialect is Middle German, with *d* retained in *idisi, uuodan*, etc., *g* in *biguolen*, but with the spirant *z* in *sazun* etc. There is a possibility that the manuscript may have come from Fulda, which would be reconcilable with the linguistic form: the letters *uuo* in *uuodan* may represent *wō* with undiphthongized *ō*, the proper name having retained an archaic form longer than other words did; on the other hand they may represent *wuo*, with the later diphthongized vowel.

There are many obscurities in the texts, and each charm presents difficulties peculiar to itself which will be examined separately. Both charms, however, are in the alliterative metre, although the first may have rhyme also, and both are of the same type, that is to say each has two parts; the first part describes in narrative a situation similar to the one with which the charm is to deal, and the second part is the magic formula expressed in the form of a command. This form is natural to charms as to prayers, for magic is an inverted religion and a charm is an inverted prayer. Instead of appealing humbly to God in prayer for aid, the magician claims

---

[1] See pp. 109 f., below.

[2] MS. 136, f. 85ʳ. Text: *MSD* IV; *Ahd. Lb.* XXXI. 1; *Kl. ahd. Spdmr.* LXII; *Schrifttafeln* 16a.

to be able to bend spirits to his will by means of the power inherent in the formula. (The Middle Ages believed, of course, in
a host of minor and minimal spirits endowed with supernatural
powers.) Prayer is communication from man to God involving
spiritual communion, and before such communion can be established, it is necessary to free the mind from restrictive and ob-
structive earthly contacts. That is the function of the hymns or
psalms which precede prayer in Divine Service or of the words of
praise commonly used in opening sentences of the prayer itself.
Similarly the magician collects and concentrates his powers by
reciting the narrative part of the charm in which he recalls a
similar case, and then he pronounces the magic formula. Sometimes, especially in medical charms, a course of action (bathing,
rubbing, treading on the foot, etc.) is prescribed to follow the use
of the formula, but that is probably characteristic of a later period
when faith in the power of the will had weakened. No such action
is ordered[1] in the *Merseburg Charms*, but we find it in some of the
later charms for curing diseases of men and animals. Both the
Merseburg Charms have, as we shall see later, the characterisitic
of antiquity or 'authenticity' that they contain no inconsistencies
such as are introduced when an old charm is reshaped by a later
generation. This distinguishes them from the *Trier Charm*, which
is obviously a later and Christian composition.

The first Charm runs:[2]

> Eiris sazun idisi,   sazun hera duoder,
> suma hapt heptidun,   suma heri lezidun,
> suma clubodun   umbi cuoniouuidi.
> insprinc haptbandun,   inuar uigandun. H.

The exact meaning of the words has been much disputed, but
they may be roughly translated:[3]

Once[4] (the) women were seated[5] on the ground, here and there,[6] one

---

[1] But see below, p. 28, n. 2.

[2] Punctuation has been inserted and the spelling slightly normalized.

[3] See esp. Th. von Grienberger, *ZfdPh* 27 (1895) 433 ff. and *PBB* 45 (1921)
231–2.

[4] *Eiris*, either an adverb formed from *êr* and the genitive termination -*es* (*ei*
for *ê* occurs elsewhere), or perhaps *eines* should be read.

[5] Or 'settled', then *hera duoder* could be 'hither and thither', 'on this side
and on that'.

[6] The translation given for *hera duoder* is that most commonly adopted, but it
does not satisfy. *Hera* is attested in the sense of 'here, hither', but *duoder* is not

company fastened bonds,[1] one company hindered the host, one company picked at fetters: 'Leap from the fetters, escape from the foes.'[2]

Although A. Schirokauer[3] holds that it is a medical charm to cure paralysis of a limb, it is ostensibly a charm to effect the escape of a prisoner of war. It is immaterial whether it is intended to be spoken by the prisoner or by his friends; the details of the situation envisaged are obscure. A battle is presumably proceeding and three groups of women are intervening, but what women are they, and are the groups part of one company with a common purpose, or are they independent and opposing? It is most probable that all the groups have a common purpose friendly to the prisoner, for in a charm concentration and accumulation of force is desired, and that can best be achieved by internal harmony. If the women were at cross purposes, one group releasing the prisoners bound by another, the cumulative effect would be lost and the concentration of will impaired. The first two groups, therefore, are probably to be regarded as binding enemy prisoners and hampering the enemy, perhaps by means of magic fetters, while the third group is behind the enemy lines, setting prisoners free. There are no charms sufficiently resembling this one to enable any more certain or detailed deductions to be made.

There is no real evidence to establish the origin of this charm. It may be an ancient survival of Germanic paganism, or it may have been composed shortly before it was entered into the manuscript, possibly by a cleric who dabbled in magic. No pagan gods are mentioned, and nothing about the nature of the 'women' can be inferred from the word *idis* (standard OHG *itis*), for, although

otherwise attested and the meaning given is only conjectural. One would expect to find a noun in the half-line to alliterate with *idisi*, but there is none. Many conjectures, some of them fanciful, have been, and are still being, made, but none has proved satisfactory. On the analogy of an Old English charm, it is thought possible that *hera* is a spelling with an inorganic prothetic *h* for *era* ('earth'), but the difficulty still remains that even then the authenticity of *era*, without the medial dental, in the sense of 'Erde' is dubious (see under *Wessobrunn Prayer* below).

[1] *hapt* is more usually taken as the acc. pl. of a neuter noun meaning 'fetter', but it could be the acc. sg. of a masculine noun meaning 'prisoner', as in Otfrid IV. 22. 10. The spelling *pt* for *ft* is also found in the OHG *Psalm 138*, l. 23; *pht* also occurs. See *Ahd. Gr.*, § 139, n. 7.

[2] The 'H' has not been satisfactorily explained. It has been suggested that it might be a sign for *ter*, meaning '(repeat) three times', which commonly occurs. An isolated 'H' occurs in a letter from Notker (ed. Piper, 1. 859, l. 21).

[3] *ZfdPh* 73 (1954) 360–1.

it is very rarely found in OHG, it is used in OE and OS as a normal word for a woman, particularly a woman of distinction (e.g. the wife of Herod in the *Heliand* and the Virgin Mary in Otfrid and the *Heliand*).[1] Unconvincing attempts have been made to prove that the charm was derived from Christian charms founded on the anointing and wrapping of Christ's body by the three Marys.[2] In favour of ancient origin are the alliterative metre, though it may be contaminated with rhyme in the formula, and the reliance on the concentration of will-power in the formula unsupported by actions. As there are no indications of discrepancies and confusion such as would be introduced by popular remodelling over a long period, we may conclude that the original form of the charm has been well preserved.

The second Merseburg text, more complex in form than the other, is a charm to cure sprains. The text is:[3]

> Phol ende Uuodan   uuorun zi holza.
> du uuart demo balderes uolon   sin uuoz birenkit.
> thu biguolen Sinthgunt,   Sunna era suister,
> thu biguolen Friia,   Uolla era suister,
> thu biguolen Uuodan   so he uuola conda:
> sose benrenki,   sose bluotrenki,   sose lidirenki—
> ben zi bena,   bluot zi bluoda,
> lid zi geliden,   sose gelimida sin.

The meaning of the words is fairly clear:

Phol and Wodan went to the forest. Then Balder's[4] horse sprained its foot. Then Sinthgunt the sister of Sunna[5] charmed it, then Frija[6] the sister of Volla[7] charmed it, then Wodan charmed it, as he was well

---

[1] See J. de Vries, *Altgermanische Religionsgeschichte*, i, pp. 210 f. and 264.

[2] See J. Schwietering, *ZfdA* 55 (1917) 148–56. Mary Magdalene and Mary the mother of James are mentioned with Salome (Mark 16:1), for whom Mary the Mother of Jesus, who stood by the Cross (John 19:25, 20:16) was substituted in medieval tradition. See also W. H. Vogt, *ZfdA* 65 (1928) 97 ff.

[3] The spelling has been slightly normalized. In *Phol* the *h* has been inserted in the manuscript above the line. *birenkict* MS.; *sinhtgunt* MS. (such metathesis of *th* is common).

[4] Or possibly 'the chief's'. *vole* (NHG 'Fohlen') occurs in MHG also in the sense 'war-horse'.

[5] Or: 'and Sunna her sister'.

[6] It has been proposed to transpose *Friia* and *Volla* on the ground that if Volla represents the Norse Fylla, she was a servant of Frija (Norse *Frigg*), and that, in any case, as Volla 'Copia' was an aspect of Frija, the change would make the order parallel to that of the previous line, as Sinthgunt is an aspect of Sunna.

[7] Or: 'and Volla her sister'.

able to do.[1] Be it sprain of the bone, be it sprain of the blood, be it sprain of the limb: Bone to bone, blood to blood, limb to limbs, as if they were stuck together (or: thus be they fitted together).[2]

There is a very great number of variants of this charm in all the Germanic languages and also in Indian languages, but not, apparently, in the Romance languages. In some variations two persons are present, in others there is only one. The Merseburg variant alone has such a large number of names. In some forms the owner of the horse heals it himself, in others it is healed by another person. Sometimes it is a horse's foot, sometimes it is a human foot that is injured and healed. In some of the Germanic charms the names are pagan, in most they are Christian; in a few, Greek and Roman names are mingled with Christian and Germanic pagan names. The Merseburg text is the oldest, and in it all the names are pagan. The questions that arise are, therefore: was the variant preserved in the Merseburg text of pagan or of Christian origin, and, if it was pagan, can we conclude that the Germanic tribes in the 'pre-literary period' possessed charms of a conventional form as exemplified in this text, or was this text an isolated phenomenon? Opinion is sharply divided, and as the pagan German poetry is entirely lost, it is impossible to give a definite answer.

Taking first the magic formula, there are parallels in the Indian languages which are so close that no doubt is possible that this part at least is extremely ancient. It may have been carried by the Germanic tribes on their migrations, or it may have found its way into northern Europe later from the east. There is little doubt that the Lettish and Finnish variants are of German origin.[3]

[1] A formal phrase, found also in Otfrid 1. 27, 31. Th. von Grienberger compares *so he* with *so se* in l. 34 of the *Hildebrandslied* and interprets it as a relative clause, meaning 'he, who . . .' *PBB* 45 (1921) 233.

[2] Ehrismann, *PBB* 32 (1907) 283 n. 1, takes *sose* to be *sô si* and thus interprets 'as if they were . . .'; Th. von Grienberger, *PBB* 45 (1921) 234, takes it to mean 'thus' and interprets 'thus be they joined'. A basic problem of interpretation is involved here, which is not always clearly brought out: whether the action ordered is the putting together of two severed parts (against which it must be pointed out that the injury is a sprain, not a break) or the juxtaposing of the injured limb and the healthy limb of the person effecting the cure. In the latter case the obvious meaning of *gelimid* is 'placed as close as if they were stuck'.

[3] For examples of texts and references to the very extensive literature of the subject see A. Kuhn, *Zeitschrift für vergleichende Sprachforschung* 13 (1864) 49–63, 151–7; Karle Krohn, *Z.f. finnisch-ugrische Forschungen* 1 (1901) 149 ff., 5 (1905) 128–38; and esp. R. Th. Christiansen, *Die finnischen und nordischen*

The first five lines, the narrative part, present a more complicated problem. The situation envisaged is only vaguely indicated. We are not told where the incident took place, or why Phol and Wodan were proceeding thither, or how it came about that the goddesses were present. Some scholars have imagined a hunting party,[1] others an expedition against hostile spirits, giants, or rebellious men, others again that all the gods and goddesses mentioned might be on the way to the Council at the Ash Yggdrasil.[2] It must, however, be borne in mind that we have no right to assume that any situation found elsewhere was contemplated here also. No accidents to Balder's horse and consequently no healing are recorded.

Of the seven names two, Phol and Sinthgunt, occur in no other document. The absence of OHG pagan poetry renders us dependent on ON sources, archaeological discoveries, and Latin historians for whatever knowledge we have of the ancient gods once worshipped in Germany. Such material must be used with very great caution, because the Latin historians were naturally neither completely informed nor wholly free from bias, and because German mythology developed and changed from period to period, just as, for example, Hebrew and Greek conceptions changed. What can be deduced concerning one period and one district is not necessarily applicable to other times and places.[3] Names of pagan gods are mentioned in only two other documents in the OHG language, namely the *Saxon Baptismal Vow* and perhaps the *Charm against Epilepsy*.[4]

The origin of the worship of each individual god and goddess and the traditions associated with their names present a series of

Varianten des zweiten Merseburger Spruches, Folklore Fellows Communications, no. 18 (1914), where an excellent account of the literature down to 1914 is given on pp. 1–17; see also the author's closely reasoned statement of his conclusions on pp. 195–217.

[1] The evidence of OHG does not permit a more precise translation of *zi holza* than 'to the woods', but in MHG the phrase is used for 'hunting'. See D. Dalby, *Lexicon of the Medieval German Hunt* (Berlin, 1965).

[2] F. Genzmer, *AfnF* 63 (1948) 64.

[3] In addition to the works by Betz and de Vries listed in the Bibliography (I), the following are convenient handbooks: K. Helm, *Altgermanische Religionsgeschichte* (Heidelberg, 1913–53); W. Golther, *Handbuch der germanischen Mythologie* (Leipzig, 1895); R. M. Meyer, *Altgermanische Religionsgeschichte* (Leipzig, 1910). It must be understood that many statements in all these works are admittedly controversial.

[4] *Kl. ahd. Spdmr.* LXX; *Ahd. Lb.* XXXI. 8.

complicated problems into which we cannot enter here. Some scholars hold that many of the divinities, including Wodan, Frija, and Balder, were imported from the East.

Wodan was the principal god and noted for his skill in magic, whence the words *so he uuola conda*, although it must be remarked that this is a formal phrase and found in Otfrid, and that the word *uuola* alliterates conveniently with *Wodan*. Frija (ON *Frigg*) was his wife. Sinthgunt is mentioned nowhere else. It is generally held that it is a name expressing one aspect of Sunna, and there is some evidence that there existed a cult of the sun among Germanic tribes.[1] In the same way Volla ('Copia' in the *interpretatio romana*, 'abundance') is regarded as an aspect of Frija. There was a Fylla in ON mythology, and she appears in a similar Swedish charm of a later date.[2] There are, therefore, two possible interpretations:

1. Two (or four)[3] goddesses tried in vain, and then Wodan, the skilful magician, worked the cure.

2. Sinthgunt and Volla (or Sinthgunt with Sunna, Volla with Frija)[4] and Wodan all pronounced the charm in succession, none being regarded as failing, but all as speaking with cumulative force.[5]

The second interpretation is to be preferred, for the reasons given in connection with the first charm. The advantage of the interpretation that Sinthgunt and Volla are aspects of Sunna and Frija respectively is that the number three, which is so notable a feature of Germanic charms, is retained.

Balder, who apparently rode the injured horse, was the son of Wodan and Frija.[6] He is mentioned without any explanation, but

---

[1] The reference by Caesar in *De Bello Gallico* 6. 21 is treated usually with some scepticism; some see behind the statement of Tacitus in *Germania*, ch. 45, an allusion to a sun-god. On the possible archaeological evidence, see K. Helm, *Altgermanische Religionsgeschichte* 1. 173–87. F. R. Schröder, *GRM* 34 (1953) 161–83, revived Sophus Bugge's interpretation of *Sinht-* as deriving from *sinnaht* 'dark night', and explained *gunt* as present participle stem of *gân*, hence 'walker by night', 'Moon', made feminine by analogy with *Sunna*. Th. von Grienberger held that Sinthgunt was the wife of Phol and parallel to Frija, the wife of Wodan (*ZfdPh* 27 (1895) 452). G. Ehrismann regarded Sinthgunt–Sunna as representing the heavens (*uphimil*) and Volla–Frija as representing the earth (Ehrismann, p. 103). See also F. Genzmer, loc. cit.   [2] See Christiansen, op. cit., p. 50.

[3] Assuming that there is asyndeton in ll. 3 and 4: 'Sinthgunt *and* Sunna her sister.'   [4] Assuming that the names Frija and Volla are transposed.

[5] See W. H. Vogt, *ZfdA* 65 (1928) 114; A. Schirokauer, *ZfdPh* 73 (1954) 362.

[6] On Balder see G. Neckel, *Die Überlieferung vom Gotte Balder* (Dortmund, 1920), esp. pp. 242–4.

he is presumably regarded as present, though he makes no attempt to heal the horse himself. Some scholars maintain that the word *balder* is not the name of a god at all, but an appellative noun meaning 'chief'; it would thus be the sole example in OHG of the word, of which traces are thought to exist in Old English.[1] The horse would then be the chief's, i.e. Wodan's. Others, however, consider that the god Balder is meant, although, as stated above, no accident to his horse is recorded elsewhere and his name does not appear in later charms of this type; nor, in fact, does his name occur anywhere else in German writings of this time.

Neckel's theory has the attraction of simplicity: the idea of the accident and the attempt to heal the foot arose naturally from the familiar tradition of Balder's tragic death in the presence of the assembled gods and goddesses. They had been warned of the threat to his life and they saw in this accident an evil omen; added to the desire to cure the injured horse was their fear and premonition that this injury presaged something worse.[2] One could then regard the narrative section as being a specifically Germanic preamble grafted on to an ancient, perhaps even Indo-European formula.

The deepest mystery in the text is the word *Phol*. Even the tenth-century scribe did not, apparently, understand it, for it was written at first without the *h*, which was added later, whether by the same scribe or by a corrector is uncertain. None of the attempts hitherto made to explain it has been universally accepted. It is widely held that the alteration in spelling was made in the interests of alliteration. *p* can alliterate with nothing in the second half of the line; *ph* in OHG usually represents the affricate (modern German *pf*) but the spelling is also found for the spirant *f*, in which case the word could alliterate with *vuorun*. It is perhaps best to agree that at the best an imperfect alliteration has been achieved.[3] In any case no god or goddess *Pol*, or *Phol* or *Vol* is known, and it is said to be unusual for a minor god or a goddess to precede the

[1] See especially K. Helm, *PBB* 67 (1945) 216–22; id., 'Erfundene Götter' in *Studien zur Philologie des Mittelalters, Festgabe für F. Panzer*, ed. R. Kienast (Heidelberg, 1950), pp. 1–11; H. Kuhn, 'Es gibt kein balder "Herr"' in *Erbe der Vergangenheit, Festgabe für K. Helm* (Tübingen, 1951), pp. 37–47.

[2] Neckel, loc. cit.

[3] Th. von Grienberger, *PBB* 45 (1921) 232: 'Die Alliteration *pf*:*f* (phol: vuorun) ist unvollkommen, bedingt jedoch keine Lesung oder Herstellung von *f* für *pf*.'

major god, although metrical convenience might suffice to account for it here. Phol is held by some to be a name for Balder, and the word is associated by them with place-names compounded with *Pol-* in England and northern Germany or *Pfol-* in southern Germany,[1] in order to demonstrate that a cult of Balder existed in England and Germany as well as in Scandinavia. More recently a sceptical attitude has been gaining acceptance.[2]

As literally nothing is known about a cult of Balder in Germany and very little is known about it as practised elsewhere, attempts have been made to connect the god with Indian and Greek myths of the Sun-god, with Indian gods of the morning twilight, and with the Dioskuroi, and thus to deduce a Germanic tradition of Indo-European ancestry. The injury to Balder's horse, it is argued, symbolizes the normal setting of the sun, and the healing symbolizes its rising; if the horse were not healed it would be disastrous for the world. Such speculations are interesting, but they cannot be substantiated.[3] A revolutionary explanation of Phol and his prominent position in the line was offered by A. Schirokauer, namely that Balder is the name of the god in his human form, *Balderesvolo* is his name in his animal or totem form, and *Phol* is the name of the combined animal and human forms, a centaur-like conception which would take precedence over the major god Wodan in his merely human form.[4] The only evidence adduced in support of this remarkable theory is the Trundholm Bronze, ascribed to about 1500 B.C., which is commonly considered to be a model of a car used in processions connected with the cult of the sun-god. It consists of a frame on six wheels supporting the figure of a horse and a disc supposed to represent the sun.[5] Nothing definite is known about the meaning and purpose of this object, and it need hardly be said that it is a very insecure foundation for the new theory.

A vigorous slash at the Gordian knot was attempted by E. Wadstein who proposed to emend the text to *Folente Wodan vuor unti*

---

[1] Th. von Grienberger has made a detailed study of possible etymologies of *Phol* (*ZfdPh* 27 (1895) 452–62).

[2] See, e.g., A. Bach, *Deutsche Namenkunde* (Heidelberg, 1952–6), esp. II, § 358.

[3] See Kuhn, de Vries, and Neckel, opp. citt., and esp. F. Niedner, *ZfdA* 41 (1897) 305–34; 42 (1898) 229–58, esp. 253 ff.; 43 (1899) 101–12. On Frija in this connection see the old article by K. Müllenhoff, *ZfdA* 30 (1886) 217–60.

[4] *Corona, Studies in Celebration of the Eightieth Birthday of Samuel Singer*, ed. A. Schirokauer and W. Paulsen (Duke University Press, Durham, North Carolina, 1941), pp. 117–41.

[5] See the illustrations in Helm and de Vries, opp. citt.

holta 'On horseback Wodan rode to the forest'.[1] O. Warnatsch proposed *Volende* as a verb from *Vâlant* 'demon'.[2] W. Krogmann interpreted *Phol enti* as *vollenti* for **vollhendi* 'full-handed', i.e. 'helpful'.[3]

The German sources of evidence for Teutonic mythology are so scanty that it is only to be expected that the text, which seems at first sight to tell us so much, should be pressed for all the information it could produce. This has led to much speculation, some of it fanciful, for close examination reveals that few, if any, certain conclusions can be drawn. One could wish to know more about Balder. As R. Much says, 'wir sind über den Gott Balder sehr spärlich unterrichtet',[4] and most of what we do know is derived from Norse sources; it is tempting to regard the charm as evidence of the cult in Germany, but in view of the uncertainties in its interpretation, one is not justified in using it as evidence of anything not fully confirmed from outside it. It is inevitable that one should wish to know more about Phol, but his identity is likely to remain a mystery.[5] The text simply tells us that the party went into the forest but, apart from any conclusions that it may be possible to draw from the words *zi holza*, it gives no indication of their purpose. Suggestions of a moral behind the narrative, such as that of Th. von Grienberger that it enshrines the idea that only the God of War can heal an injury to the God of Peace— 'daß der Kriegsgott dem Unfall des Friedensgottes allein Remedur schaffen kann, daß der Krieg die Schäden des Friedens zu heilen weiß'[6]—are pure speculation.

Other scholars refuse to accept *Phol* as a name for Balder, or even as a Germanic god at all. Some regard the word as a corruption of *Apollo* (the *interpretatio romana* of Balder); this would imply that the initial *P* in the text is correct (the *h* having been added to produce a semblance of alliteration), for during the Old High German period *p* in a loan-word would remain unshifted or be represented by *b* (cf. *predigon, bredigon*), and an initial vowel might disappear (cf. *biscof* from *episcopus*).[7] Others have seen *Pol*

---

[1] *Stud. Neophil.* 12 (1939/40) 205–9.   [2] *ZfdPh* 64 (1939) 148–55.
[3] Ibid. 71 (1951) 152–62. Other suggestions also are discussed.
[4] *ZfdA* 61 (1924) 114.
[5] For a discussion of the problems raised by the charm see de Vries, op. cit. 1, pp. 228–32.   [6] *ZfdPh* 27 (1895) 462.
[7] See S. Bugge, *Studier over de nordiske Gude- og Heltesagns Oprindelse* 1 (Christiania, 1880), p. 288.

as representing *Pōl*, deriving from *Paul(us)*.[1] Both interpretations involve a totally different conception of the origin of the text. Instead of being a survival of an ancient pagan tradition, it would be a comparatively late composition from a period when paganism had been undermined by Roman and Christian influences. If *Pol* or *Phol* stands for St. Paul (or is a heathen name of unknown significance substituted for the saint's), then Wodan might be a substitution for Christ and the goddesses substitutions for saints. *Balderes volo* might then be the Lord's (i.e. Christ's) horse. The supporters of this syncretistic view rely on the numerous English and Scandinavian variants of the charm which are wholly Christian, as well as those Swedish variants which contain both Germanic heathen names and Latin names. Germanic pagan names occur only in this text and in the Swedish variants. We find there 'Ture' standing on a mountain talking to his mother Helena,[2] and also the trinity Odin, Thor, and Fregga.[3] In very many texts Jesus Christ, either riding or walking, either alone or accompanied by Peter or by non-contemporaries such as Paul and Stephen on the way to Jerusalem, or riding on the mountain, once even hunting, heals either his or his companion's horse's foot, or his own or his companion's foot. The ass, which also occurs, is usually called 'the mouse-grey horse'. Opinion is sharply divided.[4] Those who believe in the pagan origin of the text ask under what circumstances a Christian charm could have been adapted to suit an obsolete and forbidden faith, and point out that the *Trier Charm*, to which reference will be made later, is obviously not original in form. On the other hand, scholars like E. Schröder[5] and R. Much[6] reply that the names of pagan gods do appear in Norse texts which are of Christian origin, and that the same may have been the case in Germany at a period when the old religion was contending with the new, and also that pagan names and practices survived to some extent in popular superstition long after the religion had passed away, when the Wodan of popular superstition bore little

---

[1] See Christiansen, op. cit.   [2] Ibid., p. 56.   [3] Ibid., pp. 55 f.

[4] A clear summary of the controversial literature on the subject is given by R. Th. Christiansen, op. cit. The opposing opinions on either side are clearly set forth in K. Krohn's review of R. M. Meyer's *Altgermanische Religionsgeschichte* in *GGA* 174 (1912) 212–23, and by E. von Steinmeyer, *Kl. ahd. Spdm.*, pp. 368–70.

[5] *ZfdA* 52 (1910) 180. Cf. the reply by R. M. Meyer, ibid., pp. 390–6.

[6] *AfdA* 43 (1924) 37–8 on F. Ohrt, *De danske Besværgelser mod Vrid och Blod* (Copenhagen, 1922).

resemblance to, and had little connection with, the Wodan of the
skaldic poetry. As we have no German texts of the period, the
theory can be neither proved nor disproved. It can only be said
that the Merseburg text is the oldest of all, and conclusions drawn
from later documents are always of doubtful validity.

The comparative method can yield no definite conclusions about
the origin of the Merseburg text, because it is possible to discover resemblances and differences and to argue from them about
substitutions, omissions, and accretions indefinitely. A study of
the form, such as that attempted by W. H. Vogt, *ZfdA* 65 (1928)
117–30, offers better prospects of success, although the element of
subjectivity cannot be entirely eliminated. It must remain a matter
of opinion whether the verse is mere ornamentation and does not
rise above the level of prose, but there can be no doubt that the
Second Merseburg Charm is constructed in a strict form. It is, as
Vogt says, 'art', not a 'popular' version, even though, in contrast
to the more concise *First Merseburg Charm*, it is undeniably diffuse,
which may possibly be a sign of late date. This diffuseness appears
in the number of names mentioned and in the comprehensiveness
of the formula itself (*bên zi bêna* etc.) and in the introduction to it
(*sosê bênrenki* etc.). It is doubtful whether this diffuseness can be
reduced by excising any portion, as it is a feature of this style of
charm to work to climaxes, as already stated, and to form sets
of three. The first charm is certainly much terser.

A manuscript belonging to the Stadtbibliothek, Trier, contains two charms of Low German origin, commonly called the
Trierer Sprüche, which were copied into it in the tenth century
by a Rhenish Franconian scribe.[1] The second of these is headed
'Incantacio contra equorum egritudinem quam nos dicimus spurihalz'. *Spurihalz* (the word survives in MHG) means 'lameness'.[2]
The disease, called *daz antphangana* in the body of the charm, is
a kind of cramp. The Latin heading and the inversion in the first
sentence: *Quam Krist* (translating *Venit Christus*) are signs of
clerical influence. The charm may be translated:

Christ and St. Stephen came to the city of Saloniun; there St.
Stephen's horse developed a swelling. As Christ healed St. Stephen's

---

[1] *Kl. ahd. Spdmr.* LXIII; *Ahd. Lb.* XLV, B2. On the date and language see
W. Braune, *PBB* 36 (1910) 551–6.

[2] On the nature of the disease, or injury, in this and the following charms see
MSD vol. II, 302–4 and C. F. Groenewald, *ZfdPh* 47 (1918) 372–5.

horse of the cramp, so I heal this horse of it by the power of Christ.
[Say a] Pater Noster. Hail Christ, do thou deign to heal this horse of
the cramp or the lameness by thy grace as thou didst heal St. Stephen's
horse at the city of Saloniun. Amen.

The late date of this charm is obvious. It does not rely on the
will-power of the sorcerer, but enlists the aid of Jesus Christ.
Instead of the magic formula there is a prayer. The technique
of a narrative section preceding the application of the charm is,
however, retained, and it would be possible to argue that the
magic three is discernible in the structure: first the narrative, in
the first sentence, then the actual application, or charm proper,
then the entirely Christian element of prayer in the third section.
This prayer section is subdivided into a Pater Noster and the
sorcerer's own prayer. No directions for rubbing or other action
are given; in this respect, therefore, unless the directions have been
omitted owing to negligence by the scribe, the charm follows the
older type, and could be a Christian adaptation of the *Second
Merseburg Charm*. There is, however, no positive evidence of any
connection other than a common model for the first two parts,
and there is nothing to correspond to the magic formula of the
Merseburg Charm. Saloniun is usually thought to be a popular
distortion of the name Jerusalem or Sion.[1] St. Stephen is well
known in traditional beliefs as the patron saint of horses.[2]

A number of other charms for curing diseases of horses have
been preserved.[3] It is convenient to include them here, although
they date from the ninth to the twelfth century and are various
in form. All are obviously clerical. One, **De hoc quod spurihalz
dicunt,** is a prayer that Christ will cure the lameness of a horse
as he healed the fins of a fish. It begins with the Pater Noster, then
follows the narrative and then the prayer. The words 'quod dicunt'
in the title indicate the cleric referring to the customs of the people,
but it must be borne in mind that in a medieval manuscript the
title may be the addition of a scribe, and originally not connected
with the text to which it is prefixed. The text in its present form is a
mixture of verse and prose, with a trace of alliteration.[4] As the sense

---

[1] See, for example, Steinmeyer, p. 370, and Christiansen, op. cit., p. 205.

[2] See, for example, von Unwerth, *ZfdA* 54 (1913) 195–9.

[3] *Kl. ahd. Spdmr.* LXIV–LXVI.

[4] On the versification of the charms see Heusler, II, §§ 436–8. He holds that
alliteration lingered on in the 'Kleinkunst' after it had ceased to be used in
literature of a higher class.

is perfect, it may well be in its original form, although it may, of course, be a corrupted form of an original in pure alliteration.

Another, **Ad equum errehet** (for stiffness of a limb), is in three strophes of rough rhymed verse:[1] Christ met a man leading his horse, and asked him why he was not riding it. On being told that the horse was lame, Christ bade the man whisper into its right ear (what he was to say is not stated) and tread on its right foot. Then follow directions to say the Pater Noster, to rub its legs and feet, and to say: 'may this horse [mentioning the colour] be cured of stiffness as God [i.e. Christ] healed that horse'. The form is late and degenerate. The magic formula has disappeared, leaving as its sole trace the whispering into the horse's ear.

The charm **Contra rehin** has degenerated still farther.[2] A Pater Noster is to be said into the horse's right ear. Then the sense, as far as it can be ascertained, could be ' "Horse, move!" "I cannot!" "Muntwas Marhwas [perhaps nonsense words for the disease?]. Whence comest thou? Go into thy [?hills], into thy [?sea]. Let that heal thee!" [Repeat] thrice [and say a] Pater Noster.'

There were many charms against worms, which were believed to be the cause of many diseases and pains associated with rheumatism and toothache. Jesus cured Peter, whom he found holding both hands to his face, of worms in the teeth.[3] The charms are naturally directed to the expulsion of the worm. In **Contra vermes pecus edentes**[4] the sun is exhorted in the name of St. Germanus not to shine until the worm has left the animal [the colour to be mentioned]. There is no narrative here or in the worm-charms **Contra vermem edentem**[5] and **Contra vermes** (*Pro Nessia*) which exists in two slightly different forms, one Bavarian and the other Low German (evidence of its wide diffusion).[6] In the last-named the worm is ordered to leave with nine small worms, i.e. together with a host of other diseases, and to pass into an arrow which,

---

[1] *Kl. ahd. Spdmr.*, p. 373, cf. p. 369; *Ahd. Lb.* xxxi. 7.

[2] *MSD* vol. ii, 302; *Kl. ahd. Spdmr.* lxvi; Th. von Grienberger, *PBB* 45 (1921) 413–15.

[3] *MSD* vol. ii, 281. Cf. O. Cockayne, *Leechdoms* (London, 1864–6), iii. 64, § 100, and also a Latin charm of the late eleventh or twelfth century *AfdA* 15 (1889) 145. See also *Kaiserchronik* 690–882: Tiberius suffered from a ferocious worm in his head. When he touched his head with the *sudarium* possessed by Veronica, the worm fell out dead.

[4] *MSD* vol. ii, 305; *Kl. ahd. Spdmr.* lxvi. 3.

[5] *MSD* vol. ii, 281; *Kl. ahd. Spdmr.* lxvi. 4.

[6] *MSD* iv. 5; *Kl. ahd. Spdmr.* lxvii A and B; *Ahd. Lb.* xxxi. 4 and 4a.

we imagine, would be shot away into the distance. In the afore-
mentioned charm, *Contra vermem edentem*, the worm is simply
exorcized in the name of the Father, Son, and Holy Ghost, by
Jesus of Nazareth who was born at Bethlehem, baptized in
Jordan, martyred in Jerusalem, and who ascended into Heaven
on the Mount of Olives. At the end of this charm is added the
warning in Latin that if it is used on an animal first, it will not
be efficacious on a human being, and a similar warning is appended
to a charm in a Vatican manuscript that if it be applied to a dog,
it cannot aid any other animal.[1]

There are several charms to check bleeding. Nine lines of OHG
(Bavarian) were copied by G. H. Pertz from an eleventh-century
Strasbourg manuscript which is now lost.[2] It appears that in this
so-called **Straßburger Blutsegen** fragments of three charms have
been combined, but the confused spelling renders the interpretation very uncertain. In the first four lines the situation appears to
be that 'Genzan and Jordan went casting spears [*sôzzon*, i.e.
skôzzôn weak verb?] together, and Genzan struck Jordan in the
side'. Here there appears to be a gap, for the text continues without
explanation or motivation: 'Then the blood stopped. Let this blood
stop. Blood stop! Blood stop completely!' Possibly the key to the
situation and to the lacuna is the **Bamberger Blutsegen**.[3] Here
Christ and Judas were playing with spears; Christ was wounded
but stopped the blood with His thumb. The blood stopped as the
waters of Jordan stopped when Christ was baptized. Several motifs
are contaminated here, namely the soldier, later called Longinus,
who thrust the lance into Jesus' side (John 19:34), the Baptism in
Jordan (Matt. 3:13, Mark 1:9, Luke 3:21), the parting of the
waters of Jordan to allow the Ark of the Covenant to pass (Joshua 3
and 4), and an apochryphal legend that once, when Jesus and
Judas, being small boys, were playing, Judas struck Jesus in the
side, 'and that same side . . . the Jews pierced with a spear'.[4] The
same kind of contamination appears in other charms.[5] In one,
Ad fluxum sanguinis narium, Jesus is said to have stopped the
Jordan in order that He and John might pass.[6]

[1] *Kl. ahd. Spdmr.* LXIV. 2.

[2] *MSD* IV. 6; *Kl. ahd. Spdmr.* LXVIII; *Ahd. Lb.* XXXI. 6.

[3] *Kl. ahd. Spdmr.* LXIX; *Ahd. Lb.* XXXI. 6a.

[4] The First Gospel of the Infancy XIV. 7–10; see *The Apocryphal New Testament* (London: printed for W. Hone, 1820).

[5] *Kl. ahd. Spdmr.*, pp. 377–80.   [6] Ibid., p. 379.

The fifth line of the *Straßburger Blutsegen*, 'Vro unde Lazakere keiken molt petritto', is completely unintelligible.[1]

The last three lines are a distinct and separate charm for the use of women. The obscurity of them is resolved by reference to a Latin charm of the fourth or fifth century, in which the adjective *stupidus* and the verb *stupeo* are used in the concrete sense of coming, or being brought, to a halt (in this case of blood). *Tumbo*, in the German, translates another meaning of *stupidus*.[2]

The Bamberg charm mentioned above is the first of, apparently, three which are intended to check the flow of blood.[3] They are of late date. The first, though printed by Steinmeyer as prose, could be a confused jumble of alliteration, Otfridian verse, and prose.[4] The second is apparently intended to be Otfridian verse, although the last line, 'In nomine Ihesu Christi daz dir ze bvze', is written as prose. It is to be followed by three Pater Nosters and then by the third charm, which is to be said three times. This last is merely an exhortation by the five wounds of Christ; it may, in fact, be a conclusion to the second.

There were charms to cure epilepsy,[5] growths, swellings of the neck, gout, and diseases of the eyes,[6] to protect and control dogs and bees, and to aid travellers.[7]

A curious little charm **Ad signandum domum contra diabolum** is preserved in a tenth-century manuscript of the Cantonalbibliothek, Zürich.[8] It runs:

uuola uuiht taz tu uueist   taz tu uuiht heizist,
taz tu niuueist noch nechanst   cheden chnospinci.

The kobold is warned that it knows its own name, but does not know and cannot pronounce the charm *chnospinci*. The word is obscure. Karl Helm holds that the second line is not an extension of the first, but is the exorcism, and translates: '(Ich kenne deinen Namen und sage dir) daß du Wicht (nach meinem Willen) das

---

[1] Ibid., p. 375.

[2] For the details see Steinmeyer in *Kl. ahd. Spdmr.*, p. 376. See also F. Genzmer, *AfnF* 63 (1948) 70.

[3] *Kl. ahd. Spdmr.*, p. 377.

[4] See A. Heusler, *Deutsche Vergeschichte* I, §§ 436–8.

[5] *Kl. ahd. Spdmr.* LXX; *Ahd. Lb.* XXXI. 8. See G. Baesecke, *PBB* 62 (1938) 456–60; W. Krogmann, *Archiv*, 173 (1938) 1 ff.

[6] *Kl. ahd. Spdmr.* LXXI–LXXIV.

[7] Ibid. LXXVI–LXXVIII; *Ahd. Lb* XXXI. 2. 3.

[8] *MSD* vol. II, 305; *Kl. ahd. Spdmr.* LXXV; *Ahd. Lb.* XXXI. 5.

Wort *chnospinci* nicht (mehr) sollst wissen und aussprechen kön-
nen.' He takes the word *chnospinci* to be a magic formula by means
of which the kobold could harm the house, but now is rendered
unable to pronounce. The meaning of the word is unexplained.[1]

[1] See *Kl. ahd. Spdmr.*, loc. cit.; H. Harmjanz, *ZfdPh* 62 (1937) 124–7; K.
Helm, *PBB* 69 (1947) 358–60. On 'Wichte' see W. Golther, *Germanische
Mythologie*, p. 122.

IV

The Lay of Hildebrand

FROM references by Roman historians there is abundant evidence that there existed in Germany during the pagan era songs of religion and war, of merriment and mourning, and poetry of other types. Of this 'preliterary' production not a verse has survived in German, except perhaps the *Merseburg Charms*. That there existed a native heroic poetry similar to that preserved in Old Norse and Old English we cannot doubt, since it provided the sources for much of the heroic literature of the Middle High German period. The nature of this heroic poetry, which seems to have treated largely of themes and persons from the age of the Great Migrations, can be discussed profitably only on a Germanic, not on a purely German basis, and in connection with the German epics of the twelfth and thirteenth centuries. It will therefore be passed over here.

There is no German collection of lays like the Norse *Edda*, nor is there an alliterative epic like the Old English *Beowulf*. The sole representative of German heroic poetry from the Old High German period is the *Hildebrandslied*, a poem of less than seventy lines.[1]

---

[1] *MSD* II; *Kl. ahd. Spdmr.* I; *Ahd. Lb.* XXVIII. Facsimiles; *Schrifttafeln* 12–13; Enneccerus I–IV; also in E. Danielowski, *Das Hildebrandslied. Beitrag zur Überlieferungsgeschichte auf paläographischer Grundlage* (Berlin, 1919); J. Mansion, *Ahd. Lesebuch*; W. Traupel and W. Grothe, *Das Hildebrandslied. Volksausgabe* (Halle, 1938); G. Baesecke, *Das Hildebrandlied. Eine geschichtliches Einführung für Laien* (Halle, 1945).

The work by Baesecke provides a useful introduction to the problems surrounding the text, but must be used with caution. The same is true of F. Saran, *Das Hildebrandslied*, Bausteine zur Geschichte der deutschen Literatur XV (Halle, 1915).

The poem is discussed in all standard works on Old High German literature. Among these the following must be mentioned: Ehrismann, pp. 121–37, H. de Boor, pp. 65–73.

A very valuable commentary on the secondary literature is provided by

The *Hildebrandslied* belongs to the cycle of legends surrounding Dietrich von Bern, a figure who plays an important role in the heroic literature of the later Middle Ages, but the form in which this legendary material was current at the time when the *Hildebrandslied* was composed and performed can only be reconstructed. Some account of what can be ascertained about the place of the lay in the Dietrich cycle will be given later, but such second-hand knowledge of the legendary background has no bearing on the aesthetic or artistic value of the lay itself and contributes little to our understanding of the work beyond the clarification of certain allusions. The *Hildebrandslied* is self-contained and complete in itself, apart from the loss of the conclusion and, perhaps, some other lines. Although it must have made a more direct appeal to a generation more familiar than ours with stories of Dietrich and Hildebrand, neither the intelligibility nor the emotional effect of the narrative depends on knowing the tradition or understanding the allusions. Dietrich and his enemy Otacher are of no more significance in the lay than are the great historical figures in the stories of Conrad Ferdinand Meyer. They exist, as it were, merely to explain Hildebrand's exile and Hadubrand's fatherless childhood. Therefore, it is desirable to analyse the text of the lay itself as preserved in the manuscript before studying the historical, literary, and linguistic problems connected with it. The analysis requires great care in order that we may realize what the poet has said, and that we may not be misled by our own subjective interpretation of his words or by what commentators have imagined him to have said or implied. It will be useful first to give a translation of the lay:

This I have heard told, that warriors[1] met singly between two armies. Father and son[2] ordered their equipment, they made ready their battle-garments, girded their swords on, the fighting men, over their ring-mail, when they rode to the fight.   (ll. 1–6)

Hildebrand spoke, Heribrand's son.[3] He was the senior man, the more experienced in life. He began to ask with few words who his[4] father was

H. van der Kolk, *Das Hildebrandlied. Eine forschungsgeschichtliche Darstellung* (Amsterdam, 1967).

The most detailed treatment of the language is to be found in H. Pongs, *Das Hildebrandslied. Überlieferung und Lautstand im Rahmen der althochdeutschen Literatur* (Marburg dissertation, 1913).

[1] Or 'challengers', 'champions', but see below, pp. 49 f.
[2] Or 'between two armies of followers of father and son'.
[3] The second part of this formula is sometimes deleted *metri causa*.
[4] i.e. his opponent's.

in the host of men[1] . . . 'or to what family you belong. If you tell me one, I shall know the others, young man, in the kingdom. All the great people[2] are known to me'. (ll. 7–13)

Hadubrand spoke, Hildebrand's son: (l. 14)

'This I was told by our people, old and experienced men who lived in former times, that my father was called Hildebrand: I am called Hadubrand. (ll. 15–17)

'Long ago he went to the east, he fled Otacher's hatred, away with Dietrich and many of his[3] warriors. He left at home sitting in the dwelling a young wife [and] an ungrown[4] child bereft of inheritance. He rode away to the east. (ll. 18–22)

'Of him, my father, Dietrich was later deprived:[5] that was such a friendless man.[6] (ll. 23–4)

---

[1] Or 'what man his father was in the host'.

[2] i.e. either 'the whole nation' or 'all the great men' as opposed to what the *Heliand*, ll. 3901, 4226, calls *thiu smala thiod* 'the humble people'.

[3] 'his' probably refers to Dietrich, though it might refer to Hildebrand or even (so Norman thought) to Otacher.

[4] In the *Þiðrekssaga* the son is born after his father's departure.

[5] This translation presupposes that *d&* in the manuscript is due to a miscopying of *des* with a ligature of *e* and *s* such as is found elsewhere; see Heffner, *JEGPh* 39 (1940) 179 ff. and 465 ff., and Lehmann, *MLN* 74 (1959) 438 f. It also presupposes that *fatereres* in the manuscript is to be emended, as most scholars think, to *fateres*.

If we delete *d&* as mere dittography in anticipation of the first three letters of *detrihhe*, as is customary, the passage should be translated: 'Later Dietrich was deprived of (i.e. lost) my father' or (more literally) 'Later to Dietrich deprivations arose of my father'.

However, Lehmann, loc. cit., and, following him, Ebbinghaus in *Ahd. Lb.* (15th edn.) take *fatereres* to be the gen. sg. of **faterero* 'fatherland' (cf. *ero* 'earth' in l. 2 of the *Wessobrunner Gebet*). This somewhat dubious reading would give the sense: 'Of this, my fatherland, Dietrich was later deprived', i.e. 'Dietrich was later exiled from my fatherland'. This would then represent a topic shift in ll. 23–4 from Hildebrand to his master Dietrich, not, as is usually thought, the first mention of Hildebrand's supposed death (with a parenthetical reference to Dietrich's plight in l. 24*b*).

All these interpretations take into account the findings of E. Karg-Gasterstädt, *PBB* 67 (1945) 357 ff., that *darba*, if it is an OHG word, is unlikely to mean 'need'; according to her it must mean 'lack', 'deprivation', 'loss', or some such. So long as we hold fast to this view, we must take *sid* as an adverb ('later') and l. 22*b* as a complete sentence. If we disregarded this view, we might regard *sid* as a conjunction and translate: 'He rode away to the east, since need(s) of my father arose to Dietrich.' This would involve deleting *d&*, emending *fatereres* and interpreting *darba* contrary to the OHG evidence; it would, however, remove the exceedingly bald half-line sentence in l. 22*b* and provide a logical link between l. 24*b* and what precedes it.

The whole passage is difficult, and we shall never be sure of its meaning.

[6] This half-line is usually taken to refer to the plight of Dietrich; it would make poor sense in relation to Hildebrand. On its relation to what precedes see n. 5, above.

'He was exceedingly hostile to Otacher, the truest[1] of warriors with Dietrich.[2]　　　　　　　　　　　　　　　　　　　　(ll. 25–6)

'He was always in the forefront of the army; fighting was always too dear to him.[3] He was renowned among brave men. I do not expect he is still alive.'　　　　　　　　　　　　　　　　　　　(ll. 27–9)

'I call the great God', said Hildebrand, 'from heaven above [to witness] that you have none the less never held parley with a man so closely akin.'　　　　　　　　　　　　　　　　　　(ll. 30–2)

He then unwound from his arm spiral rings which the king had given him, the lord of the Huns: 'This, I give it you in token of favour.'
　　　　　　　　　　　　　　　　　　　　　　　　(ll. 33–5)

Hadubrand spoke, Hildebrand's son:　　　　　　　　　(l. 36)

'With the lance must a man[4] receive gifts, point against point. You are exceedingly crafty, old Hun: you entice me with your words, you want to hurl me with your spear.[5] You have reached such a great age by practising continual deception.　　　　　　　　　　(ll. 37–40)

'This I was told by mariners travelling westwards across the circling[6] sea that battle took him[7] off: dead is Hildebrand, Heribrand's son.'　(ll. 41–4)

Hildebrand spoke, Heribrand's son:　　　　　　　　　(l. 45)

'I perceive clearly from your armour that you have a good master at home, that you have not yet become an exile under this régime.[8] (ll. 46–8)

'Ah, now, mighty God!', said Hildebrand, 'a woeful fate is being enacted.[9] I have been wandering for thirty years[10] abroad, where I have always been assigned to the company of the spearmen. Whereas at no city has death been inflicted on me, now must my own child strike me with the sword, smite me with his blade, or I become his killer.　(ll. 49–54)

'Yet you now may easily—if your courage serves you—win the armour from so distinguished[11] a man, carry off the spoils, if you have any right on your side.　　　　　　　　　　　　　　　　(ll. 55–7)

---

[1] Or 'dearest' (if we take *dechisto* to be related to ON *þekkr*, a very dubious assumption).

[2] The manuscript reading would mean: 'until deprivations arose to Dietrich'. This is almost universally taken to be a corruption.

[3] Or 'greatly to his liking'.

[4] Or 'one', taking *man*, as in l. 51, to be a pronoun.

[5] Or 'hurl your spear at me'—taking the object of *werpan* to be the goal of the verbal activity, as in the NHG usage *mit Steinen werfen* 'to cast stones upon', 'to stone'.　　　　　　[6] Or 'the Vandal Sea', i.e. the Mediterranean.

[7] With the usual emendation of *man* to *inan*.

[8] *riche* may be from *rich* 'king' or *rihhi* 'kingdom', 'reign'.

[9] Or (future) 'is about to be enacted'.

[10] Literally 'of summers and winters sixty'.

[11] *hēr* in OHG (unlike its OE cognate *hār*) nearly always refers to rank and not to age. Hildebrand is probably referring to the prowess in battle he has just described rather than to his advanced age, on which his opponent has just commented.

'Yet let him now be the most despicable', said Hildebrand, 'of eastern folk, who now refuses you combat, since you are so eager for it, battle joined. Let the encounter discover[1] which man may today boast[2] both the suits of armour or be master of both these breastplates.   (ll. 58–62)

Then they first cast[3] spears of ash-wood, sharp weapons; these[4] stuck in the shields. Then they brought together their resounding[5] battle-boards,[6] struck fiercely at the white shields, until their shields of limewood became small, hacked by the weapons.   (ll. 63–8)

Here the text ends without any hint as to the outcome of the battle. It is almost universally assumed that the poem had a tragic ending—the death of either the father or the son, or possibly both.[7] It is true that most of the extraneous evidence suggests a reconciliation, as will be seen later, but this does not seem to accord with the tragic mood of the poem as it stands. It is impossible to decide, on internal evidence, how the encounter ended. If the father slew the son (and this is the most likely conclusion on the basis of such evidence as we have for a tragic outcome), it was a tragedy of frustrated hope, of happiness snatched away when it was almost within his grasp, and—worst of all—of a father

---

[1] This translation takes *de motti* to be a noun-phrase, subject of *niuse* and an abstract formed from the verb found in l. 2, *muotin*. It is sometimes taken to be the object of *niuse*, the subject being shared with *si* in l. 58, thus: 'let him try the encounter'. Alternatively, *motti* may be taken as the 3rd pers. sg. subj. of the auxiliary verb OHG *muozzan* and *de* as a demonstrative pronoun, thus: 'Let him who may, discover.' This last rendering makes *motti* a variant spelling of *muotti* (l. 61).

[2] Some scholars emend *hrumen* to *rumen*, which would mean 'vacate', but this reading is grammatically improbable and metrically repellent.

[3] Lit. 'let glide' with an instrumental dative.

[4] Some scholars would emend *stont* to *stontun*, thus making *dat* into a conjunction meaning 'so that'.

[5] This translation takes *stoptun* to be the past tense of a causative verb and *chludun* to be a postposed adjective (OHG *hlūtun*). If *stoptun* is taken to be an intransitive verb ('they stepped'), *chludun* has to be taken as a verb, thus: 'They stepped together; the battle-boards resounded.' Some scholars prefer to emend *chludun* to *chlubun* and translate: 'They cleft the battle-boards.'

[6] This is a bipartite metaphor or 'kenning' for 'shields'. The first element *staim* is a rare word found in MHG as *steim* 'Kampfgewühl'.

[7] Although it is always presumed that the text is incomplete and that the original poem told of the outcome of the fight, it is conceivable, in view of the near-perfect symmetry of the extant text, that nothing is lost, and that the poem treated an episode in a well-known story. Such episodic lays are found in the *Edda*. The way in which the poem alludes to the destinies of Dietrich and Otacher compels the presumption that it belonged to a rich heroic tradition and that the audience was not dependent on any single work for its knowledge of the underlying fable.

compelled by circumstances to destroy his own creation. If Hadubrand slew his father, it was a tragedy of helpless ignorance, of Man at the mercy of Fate. If both were slain, it was a double tragedy, the complete extinction of a line of warriors. One critic has imagined that the father killed the son and then took his own life.[1]

This tragic situation is the essence of the lay. The poet has not inserted any moralizing or general reflections, and it is open to any hearer or any reader of any period to form his own impression of the moral—if there is one—which lies behind the story, but we must beware of attributing to the poet any meaning we think we discern in it. The only legitimate foundation for conjectures is our knowledge of the life and thought of the poet's period. We must be very careful in our choice of material for comparison, as it is hazardous to draw conclusions from even slightly later periods of German literature, and still more dangerous to base our interpretation on material drawn from non-Germanic sources. Combats and clashes between close relatives are a very common literary theme and occur in works of many periods and cultures. There are striking resemblances between the *Hildebrandslied* and similar stories in Persian, Russian, and Irish sources. It has been held that there is a genetic relationship between our lay and its Persian, Russian, and Irish analogues. Some scholars speak of an 'Urfabel' which was passed down (as 'Erbgut') from ancient times to these various literatures, or migrated (as 'Wandergut') from people to people. If one is convinced of the 'monogenesis' of the story, then similarities and divergences between its supposed variants become significant. On the other hand, there is abundant evidence of 'polygenesis', i.e. the emergence of identical fables independently of one another in often quite unrelated cultures, and it must be admitted that the notion of a fight between father and son could have occurred to any poet at any time or in any place. It must be left to the folk-lorist to investigate such matters; we must confine our attention to the poem and its Germanic analogues.[2]

[1] F. Maurer, *DU* 9. 2 (1957) 9 f.

[2] See W. Hoffmann, 'Das Hildebrandslied und die indogermanischen Vater–Sohn–Kampf–Dichtungen', *PBB* 92 (1970) 26–42. This study examines the various views that have been held on the affinities of the *Hildebrandslied* with other father–son contests and concludes that it arose independently. Full bibliographical references to the controversial literature are given. For a comparison of the lay with its analogues in Persian, Russian and Irish, see A. T. Hatto, 'On the excellence of the "Hildebrandslied": a comparative study in dynamics', *MLR* 68 (1973) 820–38.

The poet is sparing of detail, and all that we learn is allowed to emerge from the conversation between the two characters and the brief account of their actions. The special background of the lay is Germanic feudal society. Hildebrand had been the vassal of Dietrich (l. 26). He had held land (*arbi*, l. 22). He had a wife and young child (ll. 20 f.). We are, therefore, left to infer that he had been about twenty-five or not more than thirty when he had left all to follow Dietrich into exile thirty years ago, so he must now be fifty-five to sixty years of age. He has been in the East among the Huns, where he has found favour. From the past tense of *wallota* (l. 50) it appears that he has returned from exile,[1] and from his undertaking to cap name with name (ll. 8–13) we may gather that he is either in or near his own country. (On the other hand, it is relevant to point out that the near-omniscient warrior is a stock type in heroic literature: in the *Nibelungenlied*, Hagen knows all about Sivrit without having seen him, and Sivrit is a reliable informant about people and places he is never stated to have visited.) No place is named, but we gather that it is west of the sea (l. 43), which in connection with Dietrich (as we shall see later) implies the eastern part of Italy, and more especially the neighbourhood of Ravenna. Hadubrand's position is left vague. The poet does not tell us who his overlord is or how he is situated.[2] We are left to imagine him just over thirty, for his father has been in exile for thirty years, so he is not so youthful as some critics imply. We are not told what has happened to his mother, but it is noteworthy that he has had to rely on old people of his clan (ll. 15–17) for knowledge of his father's name and qualities.

Of the size and composition of the two opposing armies and of the occasion for the encounter we are told nothing; the poet merely hints that Hildebrand's followers appear to be Huns, and it is by no means certain (though knowledge of the historical and legendary background might suggest it) that he intends Hadubrand to be a Goth. Furthermore, the circumstances in which the two men meet are by no means as clear from the text as some commentators have assumed. It is customary to take the word *urhettun* as meaning 'challengers' or 'champions' and to see the protagonists as the chosen representatives of their respective armies; the phrase *untar*

---

[1] This point should not be unduly pressed, since the OHG preterite may have a perfect sense: 'I wandered' or 'I have been wandering'.

[2] Possibly the audience knew; we shall therefore return to this point.

heriun tuem is then taken to indicate that the two armies are ranged on either side, looking on, while the altercation between the representatives takes place. This interpretation has enabled critics to see Hadubrand's insulting words as a public affront to his father's honour which can be countered only by fighting. The case for regarding the contest as a public encounter between champions is forcefully presented by Norman,[1] who adduces evidence for the custom among the Lombards. It was not, apparently, a Germanic custom, but one that the Lombards had taken over from the Romans.[2] According to Norman, a Lombard poet of the seventh century adapted the international motif of the father–son conflict to the situation of the contest between champions and grafted the resulting fable on to the Dietrich legend: in this way the original *Hildebrandslied* was born.

Yet it is not at all certain that this reading of the opening lines is correct. The word *urhettun* may, like its Old English cognate *ōrettan*, be a poetic word for 'warriors' and no more specific than *helidos*, with which it appears in variation, and the phrase *untar heriun tuem* is open to different interpretations. The encounter could take place in the course of a general battle: there are many examples of such meetings between individuals in the later heroic epic. On the other hand, this might be a lone encounter between men whose armies are encamped in the vicinity; in the thirteenth-century epic *Dietrichs Flucht* there is a parallel to this situation, in which Hildebrand conducts a mounted patrol.[3] It could be a meeting in no-man's-land.[4] The poet has, it seems, deliberately withheld the details from us because they would be irrelevant.[5]

---

[1] F. Norman, 'Das Lied vom alten Hildebrand', *Studi germanici* I (1963) 19–44. This article and those cited on pp. 51, 61, and 78 are reprinted in F. Norman, *Three Essays on the* Hildebrandslied (Publications of the Institute of Germanic Studies 16, London, 1973).

[2] Tacitus, *Germania* 10, records a Germanic custom of pitting a chosen champion against a captured enemy warrior in order to discover the outcome of a future battle: 'est et alia observatio auspiciorum, qua gravium bellorum eventus explorant. eius gentis, cum qua bellum est, captivum quoquo modo interceptum cum electo popularium suorum, patriis quemque armis, committunt: victoria huius vel illius pro praeiudicio accipitur.' This is obviously a different situation from the one usually imagined for the lay.   [3] See de Boor, p. 68.

[4] See J. de Vries, *Heldenlied und Heldensage* (Berne/Munich, 1961), p. 68.

[5] See Hugo Kuhn, 'Stoffgeschichte, Tragik und formaler Aufbau im Hildebrandslied' in id., *Text und Theorie* (Munich, 1969), pp. 118 ff., esp. p. 122: 'Das Lied will es so: es blendet aus der Handlung eine einzige Szene heraus, das Gegenüber von Vater und Sohn im tragisch gespannten Dialog. Alles andere bleibt absichtlich im Dunkel: irgendwie, irgendwann, irgendwo.'

The *Hildebrandslied* is not an epic description of an episode in Hildebrand's Odyssey, nor is it a lyrical account of a personal experience or emotion. It is a tragic drama of conflicting personalities in a situation which evokes sympathy for both parties. It is a not uncommon error to blame Hadubrand too severely. He is clearly proud of the father he never knew, and his taste for fighting is inherited: the phrase *imo was eo fehta ti leop*, used by the young man of his father, might be applied equally aptly to himself. He has no reason to accept the unsupported claim of his adversary, whom he takes for a Hun, to be his long-lost father. It has been remarked that his tone changes from politeness in his first speech to angry scorn in his second. This *volte-face* has been explained by supposing that Hadubrand construes his opponent's claim as a misuse of the information he himself has just imparted, and his invocation of the Almighty (l. 30) as a monstrous blasphemy.[1] The sympathy of the hearer or reader is apt to incline towards Hildebrand, because he is the more active: he speaks first and does most of the talking (assuming always that the text is reasonably accurate), and he has to face a subtler conflict, for he knows that Hadubrand is his son, whereas Hadubrand does not recognize his father.[2] Hildebrand is shown trying hard to escape his tragic dilemma, and the lyrical climax of the lay is contained in his lament (ll. 49–54). While the son goes into battle eagerly and in ignorance of his opponent's identity, Hildebrand accepts the challenge reluctantly, knowing the enormity of the crime he is being forced to commit. We, the audience, know from the beginning (*sunufatarungo*, l. 4) that the two men are father and son, and there is double irony when Hildebrand learns of the relationship. Yet, although we have used the word 'drama', the lay contains no action in the customary dramatic sense. The situation is clear to the audience from the beginning, and it becomes clear to Hildebrand during Hadubrand's first speech. He makes an attempt, by proffering the arm-rings, to change it, but when his offer of peace is rejected, he knows that there is no escaping the contest. The characters do not determine the outcome by their decisions; the situation is unfolded, but not shaped, in the course of their dialogue.[3]

---

[1] F. Norman, 'Some Problems of the *Hildebrandslied*', *London Medieval Studies* 1 (1937) 17.

[2] See Werner Schröder, 'Hadubrands tragische Blindheit und der Schluß des Hildebrandslieds', *DVjs* 37 (1963) 481–97.

[3] See Hugo Kuhn, op. cit., p. 123.

The language of the lay is appropriate to the concentrated simplicity of the treatment, for it is terse, simple and direct. There is no moralizing such as we find in *Beowulf*, and there are no similes, antitheses,[1] or other elaborations of style. The epic variations are severely restricted, being confined to the introductory and closing narrative and to Hildebrand's final words. There is only one expression, namely *staimbort* (l. 66), which might be regarded as a 'kenning', i.e. a conventional bipartite metaphor of the type represented by OE *beadulēoma* 'sword' (literally 'battle-light').[2]

Unlike the heroic lays of Scandinavia, with which it is inevitably compared, this lay concentrates the action into one scene. The poet employs five and a half lines to introduce the situation and the characters, and an equal number are allotted to the description of the battle. This circumstance is perhaps fortuitous, but it is unlikely that much is missing, since the warriors' shields are already hacked to pieces when the text breaks off.[3] Heusler assumed that a long conclusion and several speeches between l. 45 and l. 62 were lost.[4] Kienast believed that the original poem contained just over a hundred lines.[5] Rieger thought it might have been almost twice as long as the surviving fragment.[6] Although the action is clearly incomplete, it is difficult to imagine that much could be added which would not produce an anticlimax, and although there are difficulties in the passage extending from l. 45 to l. 62 which some have sought to remove by presuming lacunae, it is pointless to try to reconstruct portions of the text which are either irretrievably lost or perhaps never even existed. Comparisons with the *Battle of Maldon*, an English poem composed at least two centuries after the *Hildebrandslied*, or with some of the lays of the Norse *Edda*, reveal similarities of diction and ethos which allow us to place the *Hildebrandslied* in a wider literary context, but these resemblances

---

[1] The one possible instance of antithesis is contained in ll. 61–2 if we emend *hrumen* to *rumen*, but see above, p. 47 n. 2.

[2] See I. Reiffenstein, 'Zu Stil und Aufbau des Hildebrandsliedes', *Sprachkunst als Weltgestaltung. Festschrift H. Seidler* (Salzburg/Munich, 1966), pp. 229–54, esp. 249.

[3] It is not entirely true to say that the scribe stopped writing for lack of space: there is a little room left, though not much. Norman conjectured that, unless the work was interrupted and never resumed, the text from which the scribe was copying was itself a fragment.

[4] *ZfdA* 46 (1902) 199.

[5] *Archiv* 144 (1922) 166.

[6] *ZfdA* 48 (1904) 9.

must not obscure the uniqueness of this sole surviving German lay, with its one tense scene made up almost entirely of dialogue and with its masterly exploitation of dramatic irony.

In spite of the claim made above that the poem is self-contained, there are some difficulties in the narrative which cannot easily be overlooked. It may appear strange that the older man never clearly informs his son that he is Hildebrand, son of Heribrand, but only makes the allusive statement that Hadubrand has never had dealings with a man so closely akin, proceeding then to proffer arm-rings as a token of goodwill (ll. 30–5). It may be that there really is a small lacuna here; on the other hand, one might argue that Hadubrand appears to understand what is meant, and that this allusive style is appropriate to the studied brevity and simplicity of the lay. Moreover, the climax of pathos is attained in Hildebrand's lament, when he cries (ll. 53–4):

> nu scal mih suasat chind   suertu hauwan,
> breton mit sinu billiu   eddo ih imo ti banin werdan.

An earlier announcement in so many words—'I am your long lost father'—might, therefore, have been a premature climax and have distracted attention from the father's lament, which is the kernel of of the poem.

Some have discerned an inconsistency between l. 29, in which Hadubrand says that he believes his father is dead, and ll. 42–4, in which he declares, on the evidence of seafarers' reports, that Hildebrand fell in battle. This supposed inconsistency has been explained as doubt prevailing over hope in the younger man's mind. Such subtleties, however, are unnecessary: OHG *wānen* implies greater conviction than NHG *wähnen*, and the second passage is spoken angrily in answer to Hildebrand's seemingly preposterous pretension.

Lines 45–62 also cause difficulty to commentators and are generally thought to be imperfectly preserved.[1] Although the scribe (l. 45) assigns the succeeding seventeen lines to Hildebrand, it is generally believed that ll. 46–8 are misplaced. There are two grounds for this view: the first is that they seem to have no connection with Hadubrand's foregoing assertion that his father is dead; the second is that a monologue of seventeen lines, with

---

[1] See W. Schröder, op. cit., p. 482, for an account of the controversy and references to the controversial literature.

pauses and resumptions, is inordinately long for this kind of composition, and that it should properly be broken up into dialogue, which is the normal medium of the heroic lay.[1] It has further been observed that in ll. 46–8 and ll. 55–62 the speaker is addressing his opponent, and that in ll. 49 and 58 the words *quad Hiltibrant* are inserted (probably not by the poet, since they are hypermetric, but by a copyist at some stage) in the middle of what are ostensibly Hildebrand's words. This has led some critics[2] to postulate lost passages, namely insulting replies by Hadubrand after ll. 48, 54, and 57. The most attractive (though in our view unnecessary) suggestion is Baesecke's, that l. 58, containing the word *argosto*, followed upon a speech of Hadubrand employing the attested Lombardic insult *arga*, 'coward!'[3]

It has seemed preferable to the majority of critics to assume, not

---

[1] A. Heusler *ZfdA* 46 (1902) 233.

[2] Notably Saran, op. cit., p. 162, and Baesecke, op. cit., p. 25.

[3] Paulus Diaconus, in his *Historia Langobardorum*, written during the reign of Charles the Great, tells the story of one Argait, whose unfortunate name led to an insult which cost him and the offender their lives. Returning from an unsuccessful pursuit of some Slav marauders, Argait is met by a certain duke Ferdulfus who asks him what has happened to the Slavs. He replies that they have fled. The narrative continues: 'Tunc ei Ferdulfus indignans ita locutus est: "Quando tu aliquid fortiter facere poteras, qui Argait ab arga nomen deductum habes?" Cui ille maxima stimulatus ira, ut erat vir fortis, ita respondit: "Sic velit Deus, ut non antea ego et tu, dux Ferdulfe, exeamus de hac vita, quam cognoscant alii, quis ex nobis magis est arga." Haec cum sibi invicem vulgaria verba locuti fuissent, contigit non post multos dies, ut exercitus Sclavorum, pro quorum adventu dux Ferdulfus praemia dederat, cum magnis viribus adventaret. Qui cum castra in summo montis vertice posuissent, et pene ex omni parte difficile esset ad eos accedere, Ferdulfus dux cum exercitu superveniens, coepit eundem montem circuire, ut per loca planiora super eos possit inruere. Tunc Argait, de quo praemisimus, ita Ferdulfo dixit: "Memento, dux Ferdulfe, quod me esse inertem et inutilem dixeris et vulgari verbo arga vocaveris. Nunc autem ira Dei veniat super illum, qui posterior e nobis ad hos Sclavos accesserit." Et haec dicens, verso equo, per asperitatem montis, unde gravis erat ascensus, ad castra contendere coepit Sclavorum. Ferdulfus vero opprobrium ducens, si non ipse per eadem difficilia loca super Sclavos inruerit, eum per aspera quaeque et difficilia inviaque loca secutus est. Quem suus exercitus, turpe ducens ducem non sequi, subsequi et ipse coepit. Videntes itaque Sclavi eos per devexa loca super se venire, praeparaverunt se viriliter, et magis lapidibus ac securibus quam armis contra eos pugnantes, pene omnes deiectos equis perimerunt. Sicque victoriam non viribus sed casu adepti sunt. Ibi omnis nobilitas periit Foroiulianorum; ibi Ferdulfus dux cecidit; ibi et ille qui eum provocaverat extinctus est.' (*MGH, Scriptores Rerum Langobardicarum et Italicarum Saec. vi–ix* (Hanover, 1878), p. 173.)

There is further evidence in the *Edictus Rothari*, where the use of the word *arga* is seen to be a serious offence.

that a number of lines is missing, but that some have been displaced in the course of transmission.

It is quite clear that ll. 49–54 and 58–62 are correctly assigned to Hildebrand, and it is reasonably certain, in view of the use of the word *heremo*, that ll. 55–7 too belong to the father. The majority of critics hold, however, that ll. 46–8 are wrongly given to Hildebrand. From his lips, it is felt, they could only be weakly sentimental, contrasting the lot of the exile with the more comfortable life of his stay-at-home son. Even if we accept their attribution to Hildebrand, it is thought, they must be misplaced, since they show no clear connection with the son's foregoing assertion that his father is dead. There is extraneous support in the *Jüngeres Hildebrandslied* for the contention that they are spoken by Hadubrand; this will be touched upon later, but here it will suffice to remark that any interpretation that invokes evidence from later texts (in this case at least four centuries later) is, at the least, somewhat dubious.

Although most critics agree that ll. 46–8 belong to Hadubrand, there is disagreement about their proper location. Some would place them after either l. 38 or l. 41. This would add the insult 'liar' to that of 'cheat' contained in ll. 39–41. It would also extend Hadubrand's speech from eight to eleven lines and reduce Hildebrand's final words from seventeen lines to fourteen. If one is intent on adding to the element of dialogue, one might favour an earlier location, say after l. 32.[1] The majority, however, would prefer to place the disputed passage after l. 57, making it Hadubrand's rejection of his father's claim to have been in exile and the final insult that forces Hildebrand to accept the challenge. It would, of course, make better sense if it could be placed after l. 54, immediately after Hildebrand's account of his exile, but this is impossible, since Hildebrand's lines 55–7 would then be unconnected with what preceded them. It can justifiably be objected that an insult from Hadubrand in these terms at such a late stage would be weak and pointless, but this is the solution which has commended itself to the majority of scholars.

There is, however, a very serious objection to any such rearrangement of the text, namely that the scribes who wrote it knew the poem, however imperfectly, and that we who read it know it only through them. There is no other manuscript of the

---

[1] This is de Boor's solution, op. cit., p. 68.

work, and therefore we cannot subject it to normal textual criticism. Let us for a moment assume that their knowledge is more trust-worthy than our speculation,[1] and try to make sense of what they wrote down. Are ll. 46–8, if assigned to Hildebrand, really nothing more than an embittered contrast between his own exile and his son's agreeable life at home? Hildebrand has just revealed his identity; admittedly he has done so in an indirect manner, but Hadubrand has understood him. His offer of the Hunnish rings as a token of goodwill has been scornfully rejected. It seems that now, rightly or wrongly, he concludes that his opponent, whom he knows to be his son, is a man of the enemy.[2] He reproaches him for having stayed at home with his 'good master'—unlike his father, who went into exile out of loyalty to Dietrich's cause. He can see from his son's armour (not from its brightness—this is mentioned in the *Jüngeres Hildebrandslied*, but not here—but pre-sumably from its design) that he is not one of the Eastern folk. The bitter comparison between his own thirty years' exile and what he now assumes to be his son's shameful allegiance leads to his lament (ll. 49–54): combat is now inevitable, and all his pre-vious escapes from death have merely spared him for this, the most outrageous contest of all. His reference to his prowess as a warrior in l. 52 provides the link with his next words (ll. 55–7),[3] which, we should note, begin with the adversative *doh*. Although no enemy has yet succeeded in killing him, his present opponent might defeat him, distinguished warrior though he is. Yet there are two conditions for victory: his opponent must have sufficient valour (or strength), and he must have right on his side. The second of these conditions, which is the rationale of all trials by combat—cf. the opinion of the *uueroltrehtuuison* in the *Muspilli*—is unlikely to be fulfilled, since Hildebrand knows that his is the just cause.[4] The final lines of the speech (ll. 58–62) follow on logically from this admission of possible defeat: although this contest might at last bring him the defeat he has never known,

[1] F. Norman, *Studi germanici* I (1963) 27, remarks: '. . . und doch ist auf die Schreiber mehr Verlaß als auf moderne Gelehrte.' Yet in the article where this remark appears he goes back on his earlier conviction (*London Medieval Studies* I. 17) that the lines in question are correctly assigned by the scribe.

[2] See Hugo Kuhn, op. cit., pp. 132 f.

[3] On the meaning of *heremo* in l. 56, see above, p. 46, n. 11.

[4] In other words, ll. 55–7 are to be understood, as S. Beyschlag, 'Hiltibrant enti Hadubrant untar heriun tuem', *Festgabe für L. L. Hammerich* (Copenhagen, 1962), pp. 13–28, observes, as a warning to the opponent.

nevertheless (note again the adversative *doh*) only the most cowardly Eastern warrior would now (note the thrice repeated *nu*) refuse to do battle with a man who was so eager to fight. Hildebrand accepts the inescapable challenge.

It is possible, then, to trace a clear logical thread through this passage without tampering with the text that the scribe wrote, and it is arguably better sense than that produced by any of the emendations and rearrangements discussed above. Furthermore, there are good structural grounds for leaving the text as it stands: in the first half of the lay, Hadubrand has a long speech of fifteen lines (ll. 15–29) which nobody has wished to break up into dialogue; this is balanced, unless we interfere with the received text, by Hildebrand's speech of seventeen lines (ll. 46–62) in the second half. Indeed, there is a remarkable balance in the extant text: apart from the introductory and concluding narrative, each comprising five and a half lines, there is only one narrative passage of two and a half lines in the middle (ll. 32–4a), describing the proffering of the rings.[1] One might regard the first part (up to l. 29) as being concerned with Hildebrand's past as it was known to his son, while the second part (beginning at l. 45) is devoted to Hildebrand's reflections on the present situation in the light of his own knowledge of the past. The intervening fifteen lines (30–44), which contain the father's declaration of kinship, his gesture of reconciliation, and its rejection, might then be regarded as the axis of the poem. However, since the conclusion of the work seems to be lost, there can be no certainty about its structure. The foregoing remarks are intended simply to suggest that what has been preserved is probably not as corrupt as has sometimes been thought.

It will have been perceived that our reading of ll. 45–62 removes all Hadubrand's supposed insults except the one contained in

---

[1] If we accept Ebbinghaus's interpretation of the metre of ll. 46–7, we may reduce Hildebrand's final-speech to sixteen lines and arrive at an almost perfect equation of the two principal speeches. According to Ebbinghaus these two lines form one over-long line alliterating on *h* (*hrustim–(habes)–heme–herron*) of a type found occasionally in the *Heliand* (e.g. *Hel.* 1144, 3062). See E. A. Ebbinghaus, 'Some Heretical Remarks on The Lay of Hiltibrant', *Festschrift Taylor Starck* (The Hague, 1964), pp. 140 ff., esp. p. 145. Perhaps this over-long line is paralleled by l. 17 in Hadubrand's speech, which likewise has possibly four staves on *h* (*hiltibrant–hætti–heittu–hadubrant*) and apparently more than the normal quota of lifts. If this were so, Hadubrant's speech would still be two lines shorter, but since it is obviously less well preserved, we might presume that a little had been lost.

ll. 39–41. If the received text is left unemended, one cannot maintain that Hildebrand is goaded into fighting by repeated affronts to his honour which can be wiped out only in blood, and yet the common interpretation of the lay places great emphasis on the compulsion felt by the father to defend his martial honour. This compulsion is felt to have been the stronger for its having been exerted before witnesses, *untar heriun tuem*. It has, however, already been shown that this is by no means the only possible construction of this phrase. We must therefore approach the ethic of the work with great care.

Every work of art is founded upon an ethic, or at least upon an outlook on life conditioned by the social circumstances of the author, and, although the poet does not moralize, it is necessary to reconstruct, as far as we can, the impression the poem would leave on the minds of his contemporaries. Though nothing is said about the two armies between which the warriors meet, it may be assumed that the audience would realize that a conflict of obligations had arisen for Hildebrand. He was not only a father with natural human feelings for his son, but a distinguished warrior in the service of his rightful master. He could not remain true to his lord without violating the ties of kinship. Hadubrand similarly had to uphold the cause of his master, whoever this was. Such conflicts of loyalty are a common theme in heroic literature: for example, in the *Waltharius*, Hagen has conflicting obligations to Gunther, his king, and to Walther, his blood brother; and in the *Nibelungenlied* Rüdiger has to choose between fealty to Etzel and Kriemhilt and loyalty to his friends, the Burgundians. In these instances, as in the *Hildebrandslied*, the warrior's prime loyalty is to his master. Though the lay does not emphasize this, but concentrates on the paternal feelings of Hildebrand and the scepticism of Hadubrand, it may be assumed that the listeners would appreciate the father's dilemma.

Yet what makes the tragedy inevitable? It is generally held that the motive that drives Hildebrand into battle is his sense of honour as a Germanic warrior. This indeed accords well with the view that the confrontation takes place in public and that the younger man's insults suffice to make reconciliation impossible. We must recall, however, that the only insult recorded by the text is that contained in ll. 39–41, and that all the others are conjectured. We are bound to ask whether this insult, with or without others supplied by scholarly ingenuity, is sufficient to drive a father, even if he is a Germanic warrior, into deadly combat with his own son.[1] There is certainly no parallel, but it might be maintained that this is the extreme case of the very dilemma that faces Hagen and Rüdiger in the instances just cited. Yet neither Hagen nor Rüdiger is stung by insults into fighting; indeed, Rüdiger has the sympathy of the friends whom he must attack. The circumstance common to all three situations—Hagen's, Rüdiger's, and Hildebrand's—is the military or political necessity of fighting. If Hildebrand were not pitted against his son, this contest would be like any other of the many he has fought in the past thirty years; the tragedy for him lies not in the fact that he must avenge his honour against his own son, but in the fact that this son insists on fighting. We are not told who is Hadubrand's master; the audience may or may not have known. It is clear, however, that Hildebrand takes him to be an enemy. This may be a misconception: it is hard to imagine that a son who was so proud of his illustrious father should have taken service with Otacher, his father's deadly enemy. Perhaps there is a tragic error on both sides.[2] Only the most cowardly Eastern warrior would avoid battle in these circumstances. Such an interpretation, which dispenses with the commonly assumed insults, does not invalidate the concept of the Germanic warrior's honour. Hildebrand could, as he hints in ll. 58–9, refuse to fight, but this would make him the most despicable (or cowardly) of Eastern folk; similarly Rüdiger (*Nib.* 2154) is aware of the possibility of contracting out of the battle—and of its consequence, universal condemnation (*mich schiltet elliu diet*). The Germanic warrior must do his duty, for only thus can he safeguard his reputation. Ultimately, Hildebrand's dilemma is not specifically

---

[1] The question is raised by A. T. Hatto, 'Ine weiz', *German Studies presented to Leonard Ashley Willoughby* (Oxford, 1952), p. 100. It is pursued by Hugo Kuhn, op. cit., who thinks that the notion of Germanic martial honour, as commonly understood, is perhaps 'ein gefährliches germanisches Klischee'.

[2] This is suggested by the course of events narrated in the *Þiðrekssaga*, where Alibrand is loyal to Þiðrek's cause and is said to have sent men 'north into Hunland' to summon him back after the death of Erminrik. It seems unlikely that Hildebrand had a renegade son whose loyalty a later writer decided to rehabilitate. Perhaps his son represented the resistance at home, while he himself belonged to the government in exile. One thing seems clear: the 'test fight' devised by the father in the late versions must have grown out of the obscurity of the situation in the intermediate stages of the fable. See D. R. McLintock, 'The Politics of the *Hildebrandslied*', *New German Studies* 2 (1974), 61–81.

Germanic: it arises from the universal obligation of the soldier to fight when required, whatever the circumstances.[1]

Ehrismann was undoubtedly right in holding that the form of the lay was influenced by the conventional form of a trial by combat.[2] The parties to the dispute state their names, the elder speaking first; an attempt at reconciliation is made and rejected, and then the combat begins. The equipment of the vanquished becomes the spoil of the victor. It is assumed in such trials by combat that God will defend the right. In our poem God is twice invoked by Hildebrand (*irmingot*, l. 30, *waltant got*, l. 49), but it is not clear that God is regarded as defending the right, nor even where the right is supposed to lie. Even though fighting a kinsman was an evil deed, Beyschlag is probably right in supposing that the audience would regard both men as acting correctly in the circumstances.[3]

The problem of the ethic of the lay is sometimes stated in the misleading form of the question: Is the work pagan or Christian? Thus Saran rejects Ehrismann's moral interpretation and argues that it is a tragedy of frustrated hope and unrequited faith in God.[4] Neither the poet nor Hildebrand could understand how a good God could allow such things to be. The objection is obvious: there is no question of Hildebrand's humbling his pride and turning the other cheek to a normal opponent, and there is nothing specifically Christian in avoiding battle with one's own son; in fact, as we have already stated, fighting a kinsman was regarded as an unnatural act, and therefore as an offence against Germanic law and custom. Saran tries to show, in effect, that the lay is concerned with the problem of evil (which in a certain fundamental sense is, of course, true, although not in any specifically Christian sense). He sees a connection between the lay and the Old Testament material in the body of the manuscript and, supporting his contention with

---

[1] W. Hoffmann, op. cit., p. 42, speaks of 'jene Grenzsituation, jene ausweglose tragische Zuspitzung eines Konflikts, die er [der Dichter] als eine erschütternde Grunderfahrung des heroischen Menschen aufzeigen wollte'.

[2] *PBB* 32 (1907) 260–92. The idea is pursued by K. J. Northcott, *MLR* 56 (1961) 342–8.

[3] S. Beyschlag, op. cit., p. 24. Ehrismann, op. cit., clearly goes too far in attributing the whole of the tragic guilt to Hadubrand and comparing him with the young Helmbrecht in the thirteenth-century poem *Meier Helmbrecht* by Wernher der Gärtner. Young Helmbrecht knew that he was defying his father, whereas Hadubrand has no reason to accept the apparently preposterous claim of the stranger who looks like a Hun.

[4] 'Gott, der ja das Regiment der Welt führt, hat den tapferen, treuen, frommen Mann innerlich zerschmettert.' Saran, op. cit., p. 176.

remarkable philological ingenuity, he postulates a rather sceptical court poet who, like his own Hildebrand, found it difficult to believe in a just and merciful God. Saran's argument is almost a caricature of the method of study which endeavours to relate a work of art to its social and cultural background. The simple fact is that no more can be deduced from the ethic concerning the poet's purpose, the origin of the poem, and the reasons for its preservation than can be inferred from the story itself, namely nothing at all.

The lay is probably Christian since the historical Dietrich was a Christian, and so Hildebrand and Hadubrand must have been Christians too. Unless the composer was a Saxon who lived before the conversion by Charles the Great (which appears on linguistic grounds to be impossible), he too is likely to have been a Christian. The word *irmingot* may be a rendering of the Latin Christian formula 'deus universalis', or it may be an antiquated survival of obsolete pagan vocabulary.[1] The spirit of the lay is pagan in the sense that it reflects the pessimistic pagan conception of a merciless and arbitrary fate.[2] The unnatural combat is forced on Hildebrand; he cannot choose. Why the gods allow such evil things, no man knows to this day; the question has exercised the minds of pagans and Christians alike, and the poet of the *Hildebrandslied* suggests no answer. It is noteworthy that Hildebrand, addressing the *waltant got*, describes the impending combat by the word

---

[1] See W. Braune, *PBB* 21 (1896) 1–7. The element *irmin-* is found not only in this word, but in *irmindeot* (l. 13), which has cognates in other languages (OS *irminthiod*, OE *eormenþēod*), and in other compounds where it seems to mean 'great'. It probably had a religious significance in pagan times. In ON the serpent of Midgard is called *jǫrmungandr* and the simplex *Jǫrmunr* is one of the names of Óðinn. The Saxons venerated a great column *irminsūl*, which a contemporary Latin writer interpreted as 'quod latine dicitur universalis columna quasi sustinens omnia'. If this element (Gmc. **ermana-, *ermuna-*) is to be discerned in the tribal names *(H)erminones* and *(H)ermunduri*, we may compare it with Gmc. **Ingwa-*, found in *Inguaeones* (Tacitus writes *Ingaeuones*); this too seems to have been the name of a god. See J. de Vries, *Altgermanische Religionsgeschichte* I, pp. 214–15 and 239–41.

As has been seen already, Norman's interpretation requires Hadubrand to react to his father's claim as to a blasphemous perjury. Hugo Kuhn ('Hildebrand, Dietrich von Bern und die Nibelungen', *Text und Theorie*, pp. 127 ff.) sees a striking resemblance between Hildebrand's twofold invocation of God and comparable appeals by Rüdiger and Dietrich in the *Nibelungenlied*. See below, pp. 66 f.

[2] On Germanic pessimism see G. Ehrismann, *PBB* 35 (1909) 209–39, esp. 235 ff.

wewurt (l. 49). It is fate to which both father and son are subject. There is nothing here of God's mercy or love. (It is, of course, true that anyone who had studied Boethius' *Consolation of Philosophy*, a work written during the historical Theodoric's reign, would have known how the notions of fate and providence might be reconciled.) It would have been open to a preacher of the period to use the lay as an example of what happens when men act according to human standards unguided by the Church, but no such deduction appears in the text of the lay. Perhaps it is best to say that, while the poet was most probably a Christian, he subscribed, like most Christians, to a worldly morality, and that he admired those qualities of defiance and self-reliant fortitude which characterized the Germanic hero. The Christian warrior, like King Louis in the *Ludwigslied*, put his trust in God and relied on Him for his strength: the Germanic warrior, like Hildebrand, might call upon God as a witness or address a bitter complaint to Him, but he put his trust in his own prowess and drew his strength from his own will.

Up to this point we have confined our attention to the lay itself. We have seen that the poet, being concerned with the tragic situation, gave no detailed descriptions of persons, actions, or scenes, because these would have distracted attention from his main purpose. Consequently there have been attempts to reconstruct the Dietrich legend as it was at the period by comparing the *Hildebrandslied* with the facts recorded by historians and with later literary fictions.

Like many of the legends in German heroic literature, those concerning Dietrich have their ultimate source in historical events. The figure of Dietrich (known in Middle High German literature as Dietrich von Bern after the city of Verona) grew out of the historical king of the Ostrogoths, Theodoric the Great, who ruled Italy from 493 until his death in 526. The Otacher of the lay is to be identified with the Germanic chieftain Odoacer (or Odovacar), whom he supplanted. In 476 Odoacer, a member of the tribe of the Sciri, had deposed the last Emperor of the West, the boy Romulus Augustulus, and the Roman Senate had petitioned the eastern Emperor Zeno to appoint Odoacer as vice-regent. Theodoric meanwhile was plundering Greece. Odoacer was too powerful in Italy to suit Zeno's purpose, so he got rid of Theodoric by authorizing him to invade Italy and displace Odoacer. Theodoric entered

Italy at the head of his people in 489 and laid siege to Ravenna (MHG *Rabene*). The city at last fell in March 493, and after treating with Odoacer for some days, Theodoric murdered him.[1] During his long reign Theodoric, aided by able ministers, notably by Boethius (whom he later imprisoned and executed) and Cassiodorus, tried to restore the Western Empire as a Romano-Gothic state, but one of the obstacles to his success was the hostility of the Catholic Church, which had the political support of the Eastern Empire. The Goths had been converted to Christianity in the fourth century but, as adherents of the Arian heresy, they were at odds with the Church, and one of Theodoric's last acts was to have Pope John I killed. The Ostrogothic kingdom in Italy, seemingly so secure under Theodoric, survived his death by a mere generation. The country was soon laid waste by wars between the Goths and the Empire under the Emperor Justinian I (527–65), the compiler of the famous code of law. The Ostrogothic kingdom in Italy came to an end in 553.

It may be that the legend of Dietrich grew up within a few decades of his death.[2] At all events, enough time must have elapsed for memories of historical events to dim and for the historical usurper to be transformed into the innocent victim of tyranny that we find in the legend. Such a distortion of history, which proceeds from national wishful thinking, is a common phenomenon in the growth of legends. It seems as though later generations came to look upon Theodoric's early life in the Balkans as a time of enforced exile, and his victory at Ravenna as a reconquest of his rightful kingdom. Accordingly Odoacer, historically the legitimate ruler of Italy, came to be regarded as a usurper. Legend also appropriates famous

---

[1] A hint that Theodoric might have had a personal motive for this murder is given by the sixth-century John of Antioch, who credits him with having replied to Odoacer's cry 'Why in God's name?' by saying: 'This is what you too did to mine'; it is not clear whether this refers to Theodoric's men or members of his family. (. . . Θεοδώριχος προσδραμὼν παίει τῷ ξίφει αὐτὸν κατὰ τὴν κλεῖδα, εἰπόντα δὲ "ποῦ ὁ θεός;" ἀμείβεται "τοῦτό ἐστιν ὃ καὶ σὺ τοὺς ἐμοὺς ἔδρασας.") Quoted by G. Sotiriadis, 'Zur Kritik des Iohannes von Antioch', *Jahrbücher für classische Philologie*, *Supplementband* 16 (1887–8) from *Hermes* 6, 332. See also G. T. Gillespie, *A Catalogue of Persons named in German Heroic Literature* (Oxford, 1973), pp. 26–31 and 103–4.

[2] On the Dietrich legend see H. Schneider, *Germanische Heldensage* (*Grundriß*), 2nd edn. by W. Betz (Berlin, 1962) I, *Deutsche Heldensage*, pp. 214 ff.; G. Zink, 'Heldensage', in *Kz. Grundriß* I. 25 ff.; id., *Les Légendes héroïques de Dietrich et d'Ermrich dans les littératures germaniques* (Lyon and Paris, 1950); W. Betz, 'Die deutsche Heldensage', *DPA* III (1st edn.) 1459 ff., (2nd edn.) 1871 ff.

and familiar names with sovereign disregard of fact and chronology. In legend Dietrich was befriended in exile by Etzel (Attila)
the Hun, though the historical Attila died before Theodoric was
born; there was, however, a historical link between Attila and the
fathers of both Theodoric and Odoacer. Among the legendary
sources only our lay and the Quedlinburg Annals of the tenth
century[1] have preserved the name of Odoacer. In all other works
that embody the legend, such as the thirteenth-century Norse
þiðrekssaga (a prose compilation, based largely on North German
sources, of many traditions concerning Dietrich)[2] and the Middle
High German epics known as *Dietrichs Flucht* and *Die Rabenschlacht*, the role of the usurper has been transferred to a figure
called Erminrik or Ermrich, who is to be identified ultimately with
the early Gothic king Ermanaric. This king, who died in 376, became the subject of other legends which are preserved in Old Norse
literature.[3] In the later Dietrich legend Ermrich is the hero's uncle.

Owing to the close connection there has always been between the
south of Germany and Italy, Dietrich became the dominant hero
of southern German legend, just as Siegfried became the hero of
the West, the territory of the Rhineland. The Bavarians received
the Gothic tradition of Etzel as the merciful protector, whereas the
West remembered him as the ruthless invader, even ascribing to
him (falsely) the annihilation of the Burgundian army of Gundicarius in 437.

As for Hildebrand, he is in all probability not a historical personage. The attempts that have been made to identify him with

---

[1] Annales Quedlinburgenses, *MGH Script*. III. 22–90, esp. 31. 'Eo tempore
Ermanricus super omnes Gothos regnavit, astutior in dolo, largior in dono; qui
post mortem Friderici unici filii sui, sua perpetratam volunte, patrueles suos
Embricam et Fritlam patibulo suspendit. Theodoricum similiter patruelem
suum, instimulante Odoacro patruele suo, de Verona pulsum apud Attilam
exulare coegit . . . Amulung Theoderic dicitur; proavus suus Amul vocabatur,
qui Gothorum potissimus censebatur. Et iste fuit Thideric de Berne, de quo
cantabant rustici olim. Theodoricus Attilae regis auxilio in regnum Gothorum
reductus, suum patruelem Odoacrum in Ravenna civitate expugnatum, inter-
veniente Attila, ne occideretur, exilio deputatum, paucis villis iuxta confluentiam
Albiae et Salae fluminum donavit.'

[2] The standard edition of the saga is *þiðriks Saga af Bern*, ed. H. Bertelsen
(Copenhagen, 1905–11). There is a convenient translation by F. Erichsen,
Die Geschichte Thidreks von Bern (Sammlung Thule 22), 3rd edn. (Düsseldorf–
Cologne, 1967). This contains a useful account by H. Voigt of the history and
manuscript tradition of the text (pp. 464 ff.).

[3] The Quedlinburg Annals, loc. cit., though mentioning Odoacer, already
make Ermanric the antagonist of Theodoric; Odoacer is his nephew and

recorded servants of Theodoric and of other princes whose names and roles were different are unconvincing. In other heroic works he is merely the companion of Dietrich, appearing as the old and experienced master-at-arms, who advises the young prince and sees to it that princely dignity is maintained. The story of his encounter with his son is the only one in which he plays an independent role. We cannot be sure whether this was accredited to an already existing Hildebrand, or whether the figure was invented for the purpose of the story. In later works, viz. the *þiðrekssaga* and the younger *Hildebrandslied*, the son's name is Alibrand or Alebrand. In the Middle High German epic *Biterolf und Dietleip* there is a character called Hadebrant von Stire, but apart from being a follower of Dietrich he seems to have no connection with Hildebrand. Although we cannot know how and when the figure of Hildebrand was created, one thing appears reasonably certain: names ending in *-brand* were common among various Germanic tribes, including the Lombards, but not, it seems, among the Goths. This suggests that Hildebrand entered the Dietrich cycle after the Gothic period, and that our story was composed by a Lombard who knew the Gothic legends.[1] The view that the origin of the poem was Lombardic, first mooted by Heusler,[2] is now generally accepted, though it is impossible to reconstruct its original form.[3] This process is analogous to the adoption and adaptation by the Franks of the story of the Fall of the Burgundians. A later instance is afforded by the twelfth-century epic *König Rother*: the story it tells is commonly thought to have arisen out of historical events concerning the Lombard king Authari and his wife Theudelinda; the king was renamed after a more illustrious successor, Rothari, and was later, by a Frankish poet, transformed into an ancestor of Charles the Great.

counsellor. Odoacer is defeated at Ravenna but spared on the intervention of Attila and exiled by Theodoric. It is uncertain whether this stage of the legend, or an earlier one in which Odoacer was the chief antagonist, underlies the *Hildebrandslied*. Since the lay does not mention Ermanric, it is usually assumed that by the time when it was composed he had not yet supplanted Odoacer; thus the lay is taken to represent an earlier stage in the legend than the Annals. In the Middle High German epics, the role of the evil counsellor is filled by Sibeche (Sifka in the *Þiðrekssaga*).

[1] On the Hildebrand legend, see Schneider, op. cit., pp. 315 ff.

[2] *Preußische Jahrbücher* 208 (1927) 145 f.

[3] F. Norman, *GLL* 11 (1957–8) 333, asserts: 'There is no convincing reason why we should not assume that the whole of the Gothic—and later—Theodoric material passed through Langobard versions.'

In the thirteenth-century epic commonly called *Dietrichs Flucht* the hero chooses exile in order to save eight loyal followers who have been imprisoned and threatened with death by the tyrant Ermrich. He flees into exile and seeks hospitality with Etzel, who provides him with the military aid necessary to regain his kingdom. Having defeated Ermrich, Dietrich unaccountably returns to the Huns. In the approximately contemporary *Rabenschlacht* Dietrich is again provided with an army of Huns, and he again defeats Ermrich at the Battle of Ravenna. In the course of the expedition, however, Dietrich's only brother Diether and, what is worse, Etzel's two sons, whose safety Dietrich has guaranteed, are killed by the traitor Witege. Witege escapes the vengeance of Dietrich, who, instead of resuming control of his kingdom, once more returns to Etzel in order to seek his forgiveness. The work concludes with Dietrich once again in exile. In the *Nibelungenlied* Dietrich loses all his men except Hildebrand in the battle against the Burgundians. In the slightly later *Klage*, he decides to return to his kingdom. He and his wife Herrat, a niece of Etzel's first wife Helche, pack up as much as they can carry of the treasure given by Helche to Herrat, and ride away, accompanied only by Hildebrand and a menial. When the poem ends, they are at Bechelaren.

It has been assumed[1] that in an earlier phase of the legend Dietrich returned in triumph to his kingdom, but that this ending was marred by his being introduced into the Nibelung cycle: he now had to remain in exile until well after Etzel's second marriage in order to take part in the battle with the Burgundians. In the *þiðrekssaga* he does return to his kingdom, but he regains it only after the usurper has died.[2]

If we accept the possibility that the version we know from thirteenth-century sources was already current at the time when the *Hildebrandslied* was composed, we may be inclined to favour the interpretation recently advanced by Hugo Kuhn.[3] While it is customary to say that the story of Hildebrand was linked to the Dietrich cycle as an episode (much like *Alpharts Tod* at a later

---

[1] See G. Zink, 'Heldensage', pp. 25 ff., and id., *Les Légendes héroïques*, pp. 127 and 266.

[2] On his return he raises an army and defeats his uncle's successor Sifka (MHG Sibeche), but this is probably a late invention, see Zink, *Les Légendes héroïques*, pp. 130 f.

[3] 'Hildebrand, Dietrich von Bern und die Nibelungen', *Text und Theorie*, pp. 127 ff.

stage), Kuhn sees a more intimate connection. For him Dietrich is the type of the eternal exile, the embodiment of the most poignant theme in heroic literature. He characterizes Dietrich's triumph in the Battle of Ravenna as one bought at a price so high as to render the victory futile. In the same way Hildebrand's return home is bought at too high a price, the death of his only son. Kuhn thus sees the story of Hildebrand not as a casual accretion to the Dietrich legend, but as a 'contrafacture' of the fate of the master in that of the servant. This attractive theory depends, as we have already said, on the assumption that what is usually taken to be a late version of the Dietrich legend was current in the eighth century.[1]

Whether or not we are convinced by Kuhn's theory, it remains true that the background of the *Hildebrandslied* is the warrior's return from exile. Exile is a common theme in Germanic literature: Wolfdietrich, Rüdiger, and Herzog Ernst are all driven into exile, and the Old English poet of *The Wanderer*, describing the tribulations of the *wineléas guma* (the OE equivalent of the *friuntlaos man*) gives the theme its most lyrical treatment. The exile's return and the high price he has to pay for it are central to the Walther tradition also.

We must now consider briefly the later medieval versions of the fight between Hildebrand and his son, namely those found in the *þiðrekssaga* and the *Jüngeres Hildebrandslied*, a German ballad preserved in manuscripts and prints of the fifteenth century and later, but probably of thirteenth-century origin.[2]

In the saga, þiðrek, accompanied by Hildibrand, is on his way back to Bern. Hildibrand, learning that his son Alibrand is count of Bern, rides out alone to seek him. Father and son meet and fight, without exchanging a word, until both are weary. Alibrand invites the old man to surrender and reveal his name (this being, in the thirteenth century, equivalent to surrender); if he will not, he will kill him. Hildibrand defies Alibrand, and they fight again until they are weary. Alibrand again demands Hildibrand's

---

[1] A further parallel from the *Rabenschlacht* might be added: Etzel's sons and Dietrich's brother are killed by the Witege, who had formerly been a follower of Dietrich; it is only with extreme reluctance and shame that he fights them, but they are insistent and he cannot do otherwise.

[2] A critical text of the *Jüngeres Hildebrandslied* is given by Steinmeyer in *MSD* vol. II. 26–30 and by G. Zink, *Le Cycle de Dietrich, morceaux choisis* (Paris, 1953), pp. 231–5, who also provides on pp. 235–7 a French translation of the relevant part of the *þiðrekssaga*.

surrender, which is again refused. They fight a third time until both are exhausted. Hildibrand now asks whether Alibrand is one of the *Ylfingar* (this corresponds to MHG *Wölfinge*, the name of Hildebrand's clan); if he is, he will make peace. Alibrand denies that he is and demands his opponent's surrender with threats. In the fourth encounter Alibrand is wounded so severely in the leg that he can fight no longer. He offers his sword in token of surrender, but when Hildibrand puts out his hand to take it, Alibrand treacherously attempts to strike off his hand. Hildibrand draws his sword, saying that his opponent's wife, not his father, must have taught him such a blow. He knocks Alibrand down and demands that he reveal his name, but the other refuses since he no longer values his life after being defeated by so old a man. Hildibrand then asks him if he is Alibrand, for in that case he himself is his father. The two are at once reconciled, and Hildibrand is (strangely) well pleased with his son. They ride home together and a joyful reunion takes place between Hildibrand and his wife.

The German ballad tells how Hildebrand and Dietrich are in the Rosengarten, in the latter's territory. Hildebrand announces his intention of going home to Bern, for he has not seen his wife Ute for thirty years. A certain Duke Abelon (in some versions Amelon)[1] warns him that he will be challenged by his son, Her Alebrand. Hildebrand retorts that he will deal him blows which he will remember for a year. Dietrich bids Hildebrand seek peace, for he himself likes Alebrand. Hildebrand is in due course challenged by Alebrand and they fight. The father wins, but not before the son has dealt him a grievous blow, of which the poet says:

> Ich weiss nicht wie der junge dem alten gap ein schlag,
> das sich der alte Hildebrant von herzen sēr erschrack.
> Er sprang hinder sich zu rücke wol siben clafter wīt.
> 'Nun sag, du vil junger, den streich lert dich ein wīb.'

The son denies that he is a Wölfing, as in the saga, but mention of his mother Ute brings about a reconciliation. The two men go home to Bern, and Alebrand places Hildebrand at the head of the table—greatly to his mother's surprise until the identity of the stranger is revealed.

[1] The name rhymes with *jung* and probably stands for *Amelung*: in the saga Þiðrek first learns of conditions in his kingdom from a young warrior called *Aumlung*.

The version in the saga has the appearance of an attempt to substitute a happy ending for a tragic one, and the repeated resumptions of the fighting are characteristic of later narrative technique. In the German ballad tragedy has become farce. Both may preserve some ancient details, but it is impossible to identify them with any confidence. It has often been inferred that the treacherous blow, explicit in the saga and implicit in the ballad, derives from the lost ending of the old lay. The proponents of this view argue that, while insults might be enough to make Hildebrand do battle with his son, only treachery could justify his killing him.[1] There is logic in this view, and it cannot be disproved; however, it might be held that it introduces into the old lay an unnecessary (and unheroic) complication which would mar the simple directness of the tragedy. Another element which has been thought to derive from the old lay is Alebrand's comment on Hildebrand's shining armour and the latter's reply (str. 6 ff.):

'Du fürest dîn harnesch lûter und clâr reht wie du sîst eins küniges kint,
du wilt mich jungen helden mit gesehenden ougen machen blint.
Du soltest da heimen blîben und haben gut hûsgemach
ob einer heissen glûte.' Der alte lachet und sprach:

'Solt ich da heimen blîben und haben gut hûsgemach?
Mir ist bî allen mînen tagen zu reisen ûfgesatzt,
zu reisen und zu fechten bis ûf mîn hinefart.
Das sag ich dir, vil junger, darumb grawet mir mîn bart.'

These strophes have been compared with ll. 46–8 and 50–2 of the old lay and used in support of the attribution of the former passage to Hadubrand. The parallel is admittedly striking, but it must be treated with caution. It is noteworthy, for instance, that in the younger lay the son compares his father's armour to that of *eins küniges kint*; this would surely have been more appropriate in the mouth of an older man. One should also observe that the mood of the younger lay is humorous, and that the humour relies to a large extent on the cut and thrust of dialogue, while the old lay (on the evidence of Hadubrand's first speech and what the editors allow to be Hildebrand's last) relies, like *Beowulf*, on a more measured form of dialogue. We cannot doubt that the later poet, or a predecessor, found the remarks about the armour in his source (though

---

[1] See A. T. Hatto, op. cit., for a discussion of what constituted foul fighting at different periods.

we have no evidence that its brightness was mentioned); we may, however, surmise that he adapted them to his humorous purpose by converting them into one more taunt from the son, to be followed by the inevitable riposte from the father. It seems not unlikely, then, that the critics have on this occasion stood tradition on its head, taking the thirteenth-century adaptation of the text as original and the ninth-century version as a corruption.

There is some evidence that the tragic version of the story survived in Germany into the thirteenth century; the poet Der Marner knew a poem about 'des jungen Albrandes tot'.[1] The two versions may have co-existed for a time. Our chief evidence for a tragic ending, however, comes from Scandinavia. In the fourteenth-century Icelandic saga *Ásmundar Saga Kappabana*, Hildebrand dies in a fight with his half-brother Ásmund who is leading an enemy army. As he lies dying, he utters some verses, probably composed in the twelfth century, describing his shield, on which are painted pictures of eighty warriors whom he has killed; at his head is the picture of his own son, whom he had slain unwillingly:

> Liggr þar inn svási   sonr at hǫfði
> eptirerfingi   er ec eiga gat;
> óviliandi   aldrs syniðag.[2]

Critics have been impressed by the similarity between the phrase *inn svási sonr* and the *suasat chint* of *Hildebrandslied*, l. 53. The story is told two centuries earlier by the Danish historian Saxo Grammaticus in Book VII of his *Gesta Danorum*, though there the father is called Hildigerus and his half-brother Haldanus. Saxo too makes the dying father refer to the fact that he had once killed his own son.[3] A third Norse source is a Faroese ballad called

---

[1] See H. Schneider, op. cit., p. 319.

[2] 'There lies my own dear son at my head, the heir that I begot to be my own. Against my will I took his life.' The saga is edited by F. Detter, *Zwei Fornaldarsögur* (Halle, 1891), pp. 79 ff. The Death Song is printed by G. Neckel and H. Kuhn, *Edda* I (3rd edn., Heidelberg, 1962), p. 314.

[3] See *Saxonis Grammatici Gesta Danorum*, ed. J. Olrik and H. Ræder (Copenhagen, 1931), p. 204. Saxo gives the death song in Latin hexameters. The killing of the son is referred to in the following lines:

> Ad caput affixus clipeus mihi Sueticus astat,
> quem specular vernens varii cælaminis ornat
> et miris laqueata modis tabulata coronant.
> Illic confectos proceres pugilesque subactos
> bella quoque et nostræ facinus spectabile dextræ
> multicolor pictura notat; medioxima nati

Snjólvskvæði (after one of its heroes, Snjólvur, who is the brother-in-law of Hildebrand), in which Hildebrand is tricked by Ásmund into killing his son (here called Grímur). When the father learns what he has done he dies of grief.[1]

The presentation of the story in the Old High German poem is characteristic of Germanic heroic poetry. The almost exclusive use of dialogue concentrates the hearer's interest on situations and the psychological problems arising out of them. The course of events which has led to the present conflict and the course of action after the men meet are revealed in the speeches of Hildebrand and Hadubrand. It has been held (though, as we showed above, this view is not necessarily true) that the long passage ll. 46–62, which the manuscript attributes to Hildebrand, should be broken up into dialogue. If it is to remain as a monologue, this might, though not necessarily should, be regarded as late technique. The transition from narrative to direct speech in l. 35*b* is unparalleled. Similarly, while transitions from direct to indirect speech and vice versa are common form in heroic poetry, the mixture of the two in l. 11 (with the second person *du* and the subjunctive *sis*) is unique and probably ungrammatical. Here it seems most probable that there is a lacuna in which a verb of saying once stood. It is often impossible to distinguish between copyists' mistakes and unusual features in the poet's technique.

The lay is composed in alliterative verse. The technique deviates at a number of points from that employed in Old English, Old

> illita conspicuo species cælamine constat,
> cui manus hæc cursum metæ vitalis ademit.
> Unicus hic nobis heres erat, una paterni
> cura animi superoque datus solamine matri.

('Close to my head stands my Swedish shield which is adorned by a bright mirror variously chased and encircled by a wondrously wrought border. There a many-coloured picture depicts the nobles I have slain and the champions I have conquered, wars too and the notable deed of my right hand; in the very middle there stands painted in clear relief the picture of my son, whom this hand robbed of the span of his life. He was our only heir, the only concern of his father's mind and given to his mother for solace from above.') For a translation of the relevant part of Saxo's account, see *The First Nine Books of the Danish History of Saxo Grammaticus*, transl. by O. Elton (London, 1894).

[1] The text of *Snjólvskvæði* is preserved in a Copenhagen manuscript of Faroese songs, *Corpus carminum færoensium*. The Norse tradition of the Hildebrand material, together with its German analogues, is discussed fully by H. de Boor, 'Die nordische und die deutsche Hildebrandsage', *ZfdPh* 49 (1923) 149–81 and ibid. 50 (1924) 175–210. Somewhat different conclusions from the same data are drawn by Werner Schröder, op. cit.

Norse, and Old Saxon verse.[1] It is tempting to regard such divergences, especially when they seem to flout the basic principles of
alliterative verse, as defects due to faulty transmission, and to try
to emend the text accordingly. However, the position of the would-
be emenders is weak, because so little Old High German alliptera-
tive verse has survived, and, moreover, it seems not unlikely that
Old High German, having a different accentual pattern, had also
different rules of versification. Recently it has been argued that
the technique was late and permitted liberties not found in the
more 'classical' verse composed in other languages.[2] On the other
hand, if the poem really comes from the Lombards, it no doubt
represents technique evolved on a very different soil. One piece of
evidence in support of this last supposition is the use of 'Hakenreim',[3] which Krogmann took to be an 'East Germanic' feature of
the verse. Even if one is prepared to explain some of the metrical
anomalies as due to a different verse technique, others should no
doubt be ascribed to faulty transmission; it is difficult to avoid the
impression, for instance, that something has gone wrong in those
passages (e.g. ll. 31 f.) where the alliteration breaks down, and the
apparently hypermetric formula *quad Hiltibrant* in ll. 49 and 58
(perhaps also in l. 30) has all the appearance of a 'stage direction'
inserted by a copyist.

How the lay was performed we can only guess. There is evidence
in *Beowulf* for the use of the harp as an accompaniment to song,
though it is clear that we must not imagine a regular tune such as
we find in modern songs. The poem can be divided into sections,
the end of a section coinciding with the end of a line. It is possible
to see here an irregular strophic pattern.[4]

The manuscript text of the poem is characterized by a baffling
mixture of opposing elements which makes it difficult, if not impossible, to form a clear opinion about its origin. Even if we were

[1] For an account of the verse-form, see Appendix.

[2] See W. P. Lehmann, 'Das Hildebrandslied ein Spätzeitwerk', *ZfdPh* 81
(1962) 24–9. A spirited defence of the extant text is given by E. A. Ebbinghaus,
op. cit. For a survey of opinions on the verse, see van der Kolk, op. cit., pp. 42 ff.

[3] See W. Perrett, *MLR* 31 (1936) 532 ff., and W. Krogmann, *Das Hildebrandslied in der langobardischen Urfassung hergestellt* (Berlin, 1950), p. 19. By
carrying through the principle of 'Hakenreim' Krogmann succeeded, to his own
satisfaction, in rewriting the poem in what he supposed to be its original
Lombardic form.

[4] See C. Minis, *Handschrift, Form und Sprache des Muspilli* (Philologische
Studien und Quellen 35) (Berlin, 1966), pp. 26–34.

able to establish the origin of the language of the extant text, this would tell us nothing about the origin of the work itself. Beside a number of erasures and normal scribal errors we find in the script a mixture of the insular (i.e. Anglo-Saxon) and the Carolingian minuscules, and in the text we find what appears to be a mixture of High and Low German forms. We find this mixture in the phonology and in the morphology. Some of the vocabulary is unusual, but this could be due to the nature of the subject matter, which is unique in German. As in the case of other poems, the text is written continuously across the page as if it were prose, but there are frequent punctuation marks which may have a metrical function. There are no gaps in the text as it stands, but it is thought by many that there are some omissions. This view is based on considerations of content, syntax, and metre; most of the lines fall readily into the pattern of alliterative metre, but some do not. All these problems have been subjected to the most minute scrutiny and, although much of the argument has been inconclusive, some of its results have found wide acceptance.

We must first consider the origin of the script and the peculiar form of the language in which the text has been preserved.

It is now generally accepted that there were two scribes, and that the manuscript text is not the poet's original. From this arise two further questions. In the first place, was it copied from another manuscript, taken down from dictation, or written from memory? In the second place, what light do our conclusions on these problems throw on that of the script, the apparent mixture of High and Low German, and the date of the exemplar from which the extant text may derive? If we can offer even a tentative answer to these questions, we may then ask, thirdly, what can be deduced from all this and from the literary form of the lay concerning the language and the date of the original poem.

The text of the poem was entered on the first and last leaves of a parchment manuscript which was preserved in the Landes-bibliothek in Kassel. It disappeared either during or soon after the Second World War from an underground store near Bad Wildungen, but both leaves have since reappeared and are now back in Kassel.[1] Many manuscripts in the Kassel library, including this

---

[1] For detailed descriptions of the manuscript see Saran, op. cit., pp. 3–7, and Pongs, op. cit., pp. 1–23. On the recovery of the second leaf see C. Selmer, *WW* 6 (1955) 122–4.

one, are known to have been formerly the property of the monastery of Fulda, because either the ancient pressmarks or the titles or both agree with the details recorded in the ancient Fulda catalogue. It has been inferred for this reason, and for others which will appear later, that the manuscript was written at Fulda. The body of the manuscript contains matter from the Old Testament, and both the Carolingian and insular scripts are used; it was probably written in the third decade of the ninth century. The text of the *Hildebrandslied* was entered later, probably in the fourth decade; older opinion dated the text some twenty years earlier.[1] It is usually held that the first page and all but the first seven and a half lines of the second were written by one scribe, and the rest by a second; the smaller writing of the seven and a half lines accredited to the second scribe is clearly distinguishable in the facsimiles; differences in the formation of individual letters can also be detected. Both scribes wrote firm, clear hands, and it is noteworthy that none of the controversial spellings to which reference will be made later occurs on an erasure.

The script of the *Hildebrandslied* is mainly the Carolingian minuscule, but there is one open Merovingian *a* in *uuas* (l. 7);[2] there may be others in *dat* and *gihorta* in the partly obliterated line above the first line of the text and in *ubar* (l. 6). There are also insular traits, namely the shape of the *f* in *feh&a* (l. 27), the frequent use of the wynn-rune p for *w*, the occurrence of the letter *đ* in the first few lines, and possibly the error *min* for *mir* (l. 13).[3] With the exception of the rune, which occurs in only one other Old High German text, the *Lex Salica*, these traits are not uncommon in German manuscripts of the period. In the *Hildebrandslied* a stroke like an acute accent has been placed over most of the wynn-runes; the rune appears a few times without this diacritic mark, and once (in *wer*, l. 9) it is corrected from p. In addition, we note *puas* for *was* in l. 27 and *puortun* for *wortun* in l. 40. From these errors it appears that the rune was unfamiliar to the scribes, and that an attempt was being made to produce an accurate copy of a text which contained it. In initial position *uu* is found a few times beside p; as part of a consonantal combination *w* is represented by *u* (*tuem, suert, suertu, quad, huitte̜*). The isolated

---

[1] See *Schrifttafeln*, p. 20*, where the opinion of B. Bischoff is reported.

[2] Line numbers refer to the edited text, not the manuscript.

[3] A continental scribe could have taken an insular *r* for an *n*.

Merovingian *a* is merely an indication of the early date. It is clear that some insular influence has been at work, but it is difficult to infer anything precise. The supposition that the text was written at the abbey of Fulda, an English foundation with continuing English connections, would suffice to explain the mixture of insular and continental traits.

The *n*-stroke abbreviation occurs twice (*stoptū*, l. 65; *wabnū*, l. 68). Also used are the continental *st*-ligature and the *et*-ligature. The latter appears in *hera&*, l. 22, *d&sid*, l. 23, *feh&a*, l. 27, and *gialt&*, l. 41.[1] The *e* is occasionally run together with *r*.

The names of the two men appear in two forms, *hiltibraht hadubraht* and *hiltibrant hadubrant*. This variation occurs in Fulda charters, and very elaborate conclusions have been drawn from its presence in the manuscript of the lay. The names ending in *-braht* are Frankish and may have been more familiar to the scribes than those ending in *-brant*.

Certain errors suggest that the text was not written down from memory or dictation, but copied. The repetition of the phrase *darba gistontun* in l. 26 after the scribe had already written *darba gistuontum* in l. 23 is probably due to the scribe's having allowed his eyes to wander backwards; it should be noted that *gistontun* is a grammatically correct form, while *gistuontum* has an incorrect ending, due perhaps to false archaism. Conversely, *ar arme*, l. 33 may be a mistake for *ab arme* by anticipation of the second word. Other errors which suggest bad copying are *min* for *mir*, l. 13, either by anticipation of the *min* in *irmindeot* or (as already suggested) by misreading of an insular *r*; *man* for *inan*, l. 43, and *unti* for *miti*, l. 26. Nevertheless, the evidence is not conclusive, and psychological reasons could be urged in favour of dictation or writing from memory. In *gihueit*, l. 18, and *bihrahanen*, l. 57, the scribe has inserted a spurious *h* (the first *h* in the second word); the same is often held to be true of *hrumen*, l. 61;[2] on the other hand, he has omitted a historically justified *h* in *ringa*, l. 4, *wer*, l. 9, *welihhes*, l. 11, *werdar*, l. 61.[3] This might indicate that the

---

[1] For & as a miscopying of an *es*-ligature, see p. 45 n. 5, above.

[2] But see p. 47, n. 2, above.

[3] Even if l. 4 originally had three staves (*helidos–hringa–hiltiu*), it is still a perfectly good line without the second. The *h* need be restored in *werdar* (l. 61) only if *hrumen* is rejected in favour of *rumen*; it should be noted that if we accept alliteration on *hiutu–hregilo–hrumen* for this line, the third stave is indispensable.

scribe did not pronounce initial *h* before consonants, but was aware that the alliteration required it.

The consonantism of the text agrees partly with Old Saxon and partly with Old High German. Gmc. *þ* usually appears as *d* (e.g. *dero*, *du*, *degano*), but once as *th* in the proper name *theotrihhe* and four times in the first five lines as *đ* (*đat* twice, *hađubrant*, *guđhamun*). The voiced dental stop, WGmc. *d*, is always shifted to *t* (*hiltiu*, *ritun*, *lintun*, etc.) as in East Franconian and Upper German, except perhaps in *chludun*, l. 65, if this is an aberrant spelling for *hlutun*. On the other hand, Gmc. *t* is unshifted in all positions (*ti*, *to*, *dat*, *uuet*, *luttila*, *sitten*, etc.) as in Old Saxon. A curious and much discussed feature of the spelling, however, is the use of *tt* in intervocalic position where Old Saxon would have *t* and early Old High German *zz* (*heittu*, *hætti*, *lettun*—OS *hētu*, *hēti*, *lētun*; OHG *heizzu*, *hiezzi*, *liezzun*). The only apparent exception to this practice is the form *sceotantero*, l. 51, unless, as Krogmann believed,[1] this belongs to an unattested verb **skeotan* 'to rush' (cognate with OE *scūdan*, as OHG *beogan* is cognate with OE *būgan*). The Gmc. voiced labial appears initially and medially when single as *b* (*barn*, *gibu*). However, it appears twice initially as *p* (*prut* 21; *pist* 41) as in Upper German, once medially as *u* (*heuane*, l. 30) as in Old Saxon and Middle Franconian. In final position there are two instances of its devoicing (*leop*, l. 27; *gap*, l. 34); here Old Saxon and Middle Franconian would have *f*. In gemination it is represented by *pp* (*sippan*, l. 31) as in Upper German. The voiceless labial *p* is unshifted (*werpan*, *scarpen*) as in Old Saxon and Middle Franconian; it appears once as *b* (*wabnū*, l. 68). The voiced guttural appears regularly as *g* (*gibu*, *bauga*, etc.) except when devoiced in final position (*chunincriche*, *dinc*). The Gmc. voiceless stop *k* regularly appears as *ch* in initial position (*chind*, *chunincriche*, *chud*, etc.) but once as *c* (*cnuosles*, l. 11); *ch* is used also in post-consonantal position (*folches* etc.), and in gemination (*otachres*) beside *cch* (*reccheo*). For the final post-vocalic *k* which is shifted to a fricative in Old High German, the text uses *k* and *h* (*ik*, ll. 1, 12, beside *ih*, *mih*, *dih*, *sih*). Intervocalic *k* is rendered by *cc* (*harmlicco*, l. 66), *hh* (*aodlihho*, l. 55; *detrihhe*, l. 23), *ch* (*riche*, l. 48) and *cch* (*deotricche*, l. 26). There is uniform loss of nasal, as in Old Saxon, before Gmc. *þ* and *s* (*guđhamun*, *odre*, *chud*, *gudea*, *usere*) except in *chind*, which was originally a southern word and retains its *n* even in Old Saxon.

[1] *Archiv* 174 (1938) 10–24.

The same perplexing mixture is found in the vocalism. Gmc. *ō* appears both undiphthongized (as in early Bavarian and some varieties of Old Saxon) and diphthongized (as in East Franconian and other varieties of Old Saxon): thus we have *frote, chonnem, stont*, beside *muotin, cnuosles, gistuont*. Gmc. *ē* is represented by *ae* (*furlaet*), *æ* (*hætti*), and *ę* (*lęttun*). Gmc. *au* appears in its oldest form (*bauga, rauba, hauwan*); there are three instances of the apparently Bavarian *ao* before dentals (*laosa*, l. 22; *friuntlaos*, l. 24; *aodlihho*, l. 55) where other dialects have the monophthong *ō*, and once this spelling is used for the common Old High German diphthong (*taoc*, l. 55). The *a*-mutation of Gmc. *eu* is found in its old form *eo* (*theotrihhe, leop*), but once in the rare early Bavarian form *e* (*detrihhe*); before *w* the first element of the diphthong remains unraised (*heuwun*, l. 66) as in Old Saxon and the earliest High German.

Of the phonology as a whole one can observe that only the most striking features (unshifted *t*, sporadically unshifted *k*, loss of *n* before fricatives) are peculiar to Old Saxon, and there appears to be a strong Upper German (more specifically Bavarian) element present. This is equally true of the morphology. Although *usere*, l. 15, has the Low German loss of *n* before *s*, the suffixal *-er-* is High German. Similarly the nominative endings of the adjectives *alter, spaher, suasat*, would be absent in Old Saxon.[1] The dative plural endings *-im* (*hrustim, scurim, sciltim*) and *-em, -en* (*chonnem, dinem, scarpen*) belong to Old High German, but not to Old Saxon (e.g. *scarpen scurim* cf. OS *scarpon scuron*). The alternation of *-un* and *-in* in the weak declension (*banun*: *banin*) is High German, and more particularly Upper German: Old Saxon has no alternation and Franconian normally has *-on*: *-en*. The conjunction *ibu* is High German, its Old Saxon equivalent being *ef* or *of*; and the conjunction *eddo, erdo* would normally appear in Old Saxon as *eftha, eftho*. The preposition *to*, l. 6, has the appearance of being Old Saxon, though this language uses the form only adverbially, the preposition being *ti*. The only features of the morphology that seem unequivocally Old Saxon are the nominative plural ending *-os* in *helidos*, l. 6, and the suffix *-tic* for OHG *-zuc* in *sehstic*, l. 50.

---

[1] It is inaccurate to say that *suasat* is an 'incorrect' form. The ending *-at* is attested four times in manuscript P of Otfrid's *Evangelienbuch*, each time with the *t* corrected to *z*; it may, therefore, be an archaic western form. Furthermore, it is pointed out by A. C. Bouman, *Neophilologus* 40 (1956) 324, that Middle and Modern Dutch dialects preserve remnants of neuter adjectival endings in *-t*.

As we have already observed, the vocabulary allows no certain conclusions about the origin of the work, since there is no other comparable poetry in Old High German, and therefore the absence of some words from all other Old High German texts proves nothing.

It was thought by some early scholars such as Grimm, Müllenhoff, and Franck, that the apparent mixture of High and Low German pointed to a border dialect, perhaps Hessian or Thuringian. This theory is now discarded, since no dialect exhibits the same mixture of forms as is found in the *Hildebrandslied*. Kluge seems to have been alone in thinking the text pure Old High German: he believed that it represented the ninth-century dialect of Trier (or at least Moselle Franconian) at a period when the High German Sound-Shift was in process, and that *both* the apparently Low German *and* the apparently Bavarian features were illusory.[1] Wadstein, on the other hand, believed that the dialect was East Low Franconian.[2] Collitz argued that it represented a conventional literary language used by epic poets.[3] He supported his hypothesis by means of analogies with Homer and Heinrich von Veldeke.

It is almost universally agreed now that the manuscript version represents an attempt to convert a text from one dialect into another. It was formerly thought by many scholars that a Low German text had been incompletely converted into High German; but now the opposite view is generally held. It is commonly believed, as already stated, that our text was copied from another manuscript, but there must have been oral tradition before the first written version was made. The efforts of scholars to devise a scheme of evolution which would afford a logical explanation of all the details have led to elaborate constructions, some of which reflect more credit on the ingenuity than on the common sense of their authors.

[1] F. Kluge, 'Die Heimat des Hildebrandslieds', *PBB* 43 (1918) 500–16.
[2] *Göteborgs Högskolas Årskrift* 26 (1920) 154–67.
[3] *PMLA* 16 (1901) 123 ff., esp. 134–6. A similar view has recently been advanced by D. R. McLintock, 'The Language of the Hildebrandslied', *OGS* 1 (1966) 1 ff., who regards the orthography as an attempt to reproduce an ancient pronunciation surviving in heroic poetry after the High German Sound-Shift. If such a view can be sustained, it is possible to describe the language of the extant text as 'ein vollkommen unmögliches sprachliches Kauderwelsch' (Norman, *Studi germanici* 1. 28) only for those, like ourselves, who stand outside the supposed tradition.

Amid all the confusion one thing is absolutely certain, namely that the original lay was composed in High German (which for our purpose must be understood to include Lombardic). This is proved by the alliteration *riche:reccheo* in l. 48, because the Low German forms of these words at this period would have been *rīke:wrekkio* and consequently would not have alliterated, and by the necessity for the dissyllabic form *suasat* in l. 53, because the monosyllabic Old Saxon *suās* would not suffice to fill the line. We can therefore reject the once popular view that the original poem was composed in Old Saxon. This view was popular, as Neckel observed,[1] because it allowed us to assume an oral tradition immediately preceding the manuscript text. If we postulate a manuscript stage prior to the extant text, then what we have must be at least one stage removed from the supposed oral tradition.

Two examples of theories which have been developed with great erudition will serve to illustrate the nature of the problems involved.

Saran[2] argued that a Bavarian who had connections with Fulda composed the poem about 800 for a Saxon patron. He endeavoured to compose in the Saxon dialect, but did not succeed. His poem was spread by oral tradition, whence the lacunae and confusions. A second poet, inferior to the first and entirely under his influence in matters of form, tried to correct the text. A grammatically trained monk wrote it down, and this archetype was copied by the two Fulda scribes.

Baesecke[3] saw a striking parallel to the story of Hildebrand in that of the Lombard Ansbrand, which is recounted in the *Historia Langobardorum* of Paulus Diaconus. Ansbrand, a 'vir sapiens et illustris', was entrusted with the guardianship of a young prince called Liutbert, who was murdered by his cousin, the tyrannical king Aribert. Ansbrand fled into exile among the Bavarians. Ten years later he returned to Lombardy with military aid provided by Thiutbert, Duke of Bavaria, and on the death of the tyrant became king himself in 712. He founded a dynasty in which names compounded with -*brand* were common, but reigned for only three months. On his death he was succeeded by his son Liutbrand, who

[1] *PBB* 42 (1917) 97 ff. Neckel concluded that the scribes wished to do no more than make the High German text comprehensible to a Saxon reader, while retaining the 'flavour' of the original. In other words, the superficiality of the rendering was due, not to ignorance, but to design.

[2] Op. cit., p. 208.   [3] Op. cit., pp. 45 ff.

reigned until his death in 744 and in his old age made his nephew Hildibrand co-regent. Baesecke believed that the first version of our lay was composed by a Lombard poet at the court of Liutbrand to celebrate the brave but tragic career of his sovereign's father. Cultural contacts with Bavaria, perhaps through Arbeo, bishop of Freising from 764 to 784, soon brought the lay to Bavaria, where a Bavarian redaction was made. Further transmission of the lay was ensured by the close connection between Bavaria and Fulda, where a Frankish version was produced. In Fulda, which had an important role in the conversion of the Saxons, an attempt was made to render the lay into Saxon. It is this version which has come down to us. According to Baesecke, then, an original Lombardic lay was submitted to three successive redactions, though he refrains from attempting to reconstruct any but the penultimate one. He observes that the much discussed alliteration of *riche* and *reccheo* would probably not have been possible in Frankish until well on in the eighth century, since there is evidence for fairly late retention of initial *wr-*, but it would have been possible in Bavarian at least as early as 765 (the supposed date of the *Abrogans*), and of course in Lombardic.

Baesecke's is the most ingenious of all the reconstructions of the lay's prehistory, but it is almost entirely speculative. The only solid evidence in its favour is provided by the probably Lombardic names, and these do not prove that the poem was composed in Lombardy, for heroic matter was international. The similarity between the careers of Hildebrand and his supposed historical prototype is not compelling. On the other hand, there is overwhelming evidence that much legendary material did migrate from south to north, and such transmission must have been effected by translation and partial recomposition. A new redaction may in some cases (such as the Norse *Vǫlundarkviða*, based on a North German lay) retain linguistic traces of its source. All that one can say of Baesecke's theory is that it could be correct, but the evidence for proving or disproving it is lacking. The danger of such speculation is that it might incline us to view the lay as a kind of patchwork and distract our attention from its artistic unity, which we have been at pains to underline.

It may well be that the spelling of the *Hildebrandslied* rests on a basis of an archaic Fulda–Mainz orthography. Fulda belonged to the archdiocese of Mainz, and we know that the Fulda charters were to a large extent written in Mainz.[1] Apart from the loss of *n* before fricatives and the use of *t* or *tt* for OHG *z* or *zz*, the outstanding phonological details of our text are to be found in the Fulda charters of the second half of the eighth century. The spellings *ao* for *ō* and *o* for *uo* need not be Bavarian, but could be archaic Franconian spellings (open to confusion with Bavarian, which is conservative in its vocalism); *ch* need not represent the Upper German affricate, but could be the old Franconian spelling for *k* (*c* being used at this date for the affricate *z*). On the other hand, it must be borne in mind that Fulda had close associations with Bavarian foundations, and that its early orthography owed much to this connection, just as the Anglo-Saxon features were due to the house's English connections. It is incidentally worth repeating here Kluge's observation[2] that the use of *d* for normal Franconian *th* need not be taken, as it commonly is, as evidence of Bavarian provenance, since the first scribe also used *đ* and *th* and doubtless intended a fricative. Alternation of *p* and *b*, especially before *r* (cf. *prut*, l. 21) is also found in the charters. Even the use of *cc* in *harmlicco*, l. 65, could be compared (though less convincingly) with the use of seemingly unshifted consonants in Latinized names.

It may be seen, therefore, that the postulation of a Bavarian stage in the transmission of the lay rests upon literary considerations, since the apparently Bavarian features of the spelling may all be archaisms or the orthographical product of Fulda's early cultural links with Bavaria. It is now almost universally held that the text was transposed superficially into Old Saxon, probably at Fulda: hence the apparently Low German forms *ik*, *helidos*, *gudhamun*, *chud*, *mi*, *heuane* and the consistently unshifted *t* or *tt*. We can do no more then speculate about the motives behind this transposition.

The *Hildebrandslied* is the only surviving heroic lay recorded in German. Moreover, it is the only specimen of the genre from the whole of southern Germania, and the manuscript text is older than that of any other work of Germanic heroic literature. The first version of the poem was perhaps composed in Lombardy in the seventh or eighth century and grafted on to the Dietrich legend. In construction, style, and metre it represents a distinct type of

---

[1] See H. Kletschke, *Die Sprache der Mainzer Kanzlei nach den Namen der Fuldaer Urkunden* (Hermaea 29) (Halle, 1933).

[2] Kluge, op. cit.

composition, differing in a number of important respects from its English and Norse counterparts. It may have been inspired by historical events or personages no longer identifiable, and it may owe its genesis to the international motif of the father–son conflict. It may have existed in a Bavarian version, of which some scholars believe they can discern evidence in the linguistic form of the surviving text. From Bavaria it may have found its way northwards, probably to Fulda—or at all events to a place of learning in Frankish territory where English scribal influence was at work. It is generally believed that by this stage it had already been committed to parchment. It was now copied by two monks whose interests extended beyond the clerical pursuits of most of their literate brothers. Why they should have taken the work in hand we can only guess. Since heroic poetry relied on oral transmission, and since the Church appears to have been ill disposed to worldly song, it is remarkable that even this fragment was recorded.

This unique poem has come down to us in a form which is almost universally regarded as corrupt, though there is no agreement on the extent of the corruption. A century and a half of scholarly endeavour has produced a few agreed emendations of the text, but although there have been many attempts to rewrite it, scholars have of late become more modest in their pretensions, recognizing that the extant text is as near as we shall ever get to the poem which the unknown genius composed. Perhaps the two worldly monks to whom we owe its preservation did not know it as well as we might wish, but we cannot know it any better.[1]

---

[1] For a recent discussion of the textual problems of the work and a translation see U. Pretzel, 'Zum Hildebrandslied', *PBB* (Tübingen) 95 (1973) 272–88.

V

The Franks to the Beginning of
the Reign of Charles the Great

To the Merovingians Germany owed the beginning of the feudal
system and the Salic Law. The **Lex Salica** is now generally
thought to have been drawn up by Clovis between 507 and 511;
it is still completely free of Christian influences and consists of
sixty-five titles, or headings. The original underwent alteration
and numerous additions were made, including Christian interpolations, and these, combined with scribal liberties, distort the
original recension almost out of recognition. Charles Martel is
thought to have produced a new redaction which became standard.
Later, a text with a hundred titles was prepared by, or under,
Pippin in 763/4 with an altered arrangement and sequence, and
later still, now generally held to be in 798, an emended form
(*Lex Emendata*) of this was made. The *Lex Salica Karolina* of
802/3 reverted to the old arrangement of Charles Martel and
comprised seventy titles.

The *Lex Salica* is the earliest first-hand piece of written evidence
of the daily life of the Franks that has survived and is thus a document of the utmost importance. We can only conjecture whether
there once existed a form of it in the vernacular, either oral or
written, which was then written down in Latin when the Franks
came into contact with Latin civilization; but it is clear that vernacular vocabulary was used and that we have in this document
a direct link with the language and life of the sixth century, however corrupted the words may be.[1]

[1] The text of this (ed. by K. A. Eckhardt) and other codes of Germanic law
are available in the series *Germanenrechte. Texte und Übersetzungen* and others
in *Schriften d. Akademie für deutsches Recht. Gruppe Rechtsgeschichte*, under the
general editorship of the Historisches Institut des Werralandes, published by
Böhlau, Weimar. See reviews by E. Schröder, *AfdA* 53 (1934) 221 ff.; 54 (1935)
68 f., 100–2; 56 (1937) 60–2; 57 (1938) 179–81. The old edition, *Lex Salica*. The
ten texts with the Glosses synoptically edited by J. H. Hessels, with notes on the

The recensions preceding the *Emendata* contain some ancient and often barely intelligible Germanic words known as the Malberg Glosses, so called because the Germanic words are preceded by *mab*, *malb*, or *mallobergo*, which is taken to mean 'in the language of the court, i.e. in legal language'). The word *Malberg* means 'Hill of Assembly' (Gothic *mapljan*, OHG *mahalen* 'to speak', *mahal* 'meeting place', 'place of judgement'). It was taken into later Latin as the verb *mallare* and the noun *mallum*, and the root survives in modern German 'Gemahl', 'Mahlstatt', 'Detmold' ('the meeting-place of the people'). Whether these words were introduced as catchwords or titles, or whether they are used because there was no known Latin equivalent is uncertain. They are by far the oldest words in 'German' that have been preserved—they are much earlier than the High German sound-shift—but owing to the circumstances of their transmission they are often so distorted as to be unintelligible. The scribe who originally incorporated them in the Latin text may well not have understood them; certainly, subsequent scribes reproduced some of them in barely recognizable forms. We are, therefore, in many cases unable to say what the original form of the word was. One example will suffice. In the section *De furtis porcorum* in the sixty-five-title text the first sentence reads: 'Si quis porcellum lactantem furaverit . . . mallobergo chramnechaltium hoc est . . .'; other manuscripts have *charcalcio*, *charcalio*, *chranne calcium*, *dirani*, and even other variations. Kern interprets *chran* as 'enclosure' and *calcium* as a Latinized form of a Frankish word **galti*, meaning 'hog', the whole thus meaning a 'sty-porker' (in contrast to one running free), an interpretation which is now generally accepted. *Dirani* is a scribe's misreading of *chrani*, an error which is easily comprehensible to anyone familiar with the Merovingian script.

The sections deal with particular offences, and state the punishment. The first section deals with failure to attend at the court when summoned. Then follow sections dealing with theft of pigs, cattle, sheep, goats, dogs, birds (in the longer versions, trees), bees. The scale of fines is precisely stated, according to the type

Frankish words by H. Kern (Murray and Trübner, London, 1880), gives all the texts in parallel columns. Studies on the Law include W. van Helten, *PBB* 25 (1900) 224–542; Th. von Grienberger, ibid. 48 (1924) 25–36; W. Kaspers, 'Wort und Namenstudien zur Lex Salica', *ZfdA* 82 (1948–50) 291–335.

and age of the animal. Other sections deal with theft of servants, of women, with arson, wounding, horse-stealing (evidently a very serious offence), digging up and plundering the bodies of the dead, false witness (burning and plundering churches, in the longer versions).

There exists a fragment of a translation made into Old High German from the *Karolina* in about 830.[1]

Under the Frankish kings the christianization of Germany continued. The spread of the new religion among the tribes was a gradual and lengthy process. Irenaeus of Lyon refers before 200 to Christians in the neighbourhood of the Rhine; many of the Roman soldiers were Christians and so were some of the Greeks who came with the Romans, as is attested by inscriptions which have been found, and after the baptism of Constantine in 337 Christianity became the official religion of the Empire, which meant, as far as Germany was concerned, the Rhineland and the area south of the Danube. Bishoprics on the Rhine and Moselle are attested from the end of the third century. The invading Teutonic tribes destroyed much of this Roman Christian civilization, but not all. Before the migrations proper started there were Teutons in the Roman army and some probably accepted Christianity and, although there is plenty of evidence of large-scale destruction by the migrating Teutons, there is also much evidence of rapid restoration and continuity of the civilization. As already stated, the Franks formally accepted Christianity when their king, Clovis, was received into the Church of Rome on Christmas Day 496. Other Teutonic tribes had adopted Christianity before this, but it was the Christianity represented by Arius of Alexandria and it was rejected by Rome as heretical. Chief among these tribes were the Goths who brought their Arianism with them when they moved from the Balkans westwards into Gaul and Spain. They influenced many, and there resulted bitter conflicts between them and the orthodox Roman Catholics. Clovis extended his realm by conquest, first over Roman Gaul as far as the Loire, then over the Alemannic territory of the Main and Neckar, and then, in the name of the true Church, over the Visigothic lands in Aquitaine and Provence. There he was checked by the Goth Theodoric the Great (493–526). When Clovis died in 511 his realm was divided among his sons in

---

[1] *MSD* LXV; *Kl. ahd. Spdmr.* X; and *Ahd. Lb.* XVIII, with the corresponding sections of the *Lex Emendata*.

accordance with the prevailing Frankish custom; years of ruinous internecine strife followed. Throughout the sixth century the history of the Merovingian dynasty is a catalogue of sordid murders for personal ambition.

The efforts of Brunichildis, the strong-minded daughter of the Visigothic king Athanagild and wife of King Sigibert, Clovis's grandson, to avenge her sister Gailswintha, who had been murdered in 567 by her husband, King Chilperich, a brother of Sigibert, for the sake of her dowry and to please his mistress Fredegunda, have very possibly contributed to form the historical background of the MHG *Nibelungenlied*. The ruthless Hagen may have been drawn from the high officials of the court, the mayors of the palace who steadily usurped the royal power as the stamina of the Merovingians decayed and the kings degenerated into figureheads. As the authority passed from the king to the great officials, the feudal system developed. From two of these officials, Arnulf, bishop of Metz (died about 635), and Count Pippin the Elder (died 639), whose land lay somewhere between the Meuse and the Moselle, were descended the great mayors who were destined to found a new royal (Carolingian) dynasty. Arnulf's son Ansegisel married Pippin's daughter Begga. Their son Pippin the Younger (died 714) did much to restore the strength of the kingdom, by re-establishing Frankish authority in the east of his realm and by fighting the Frisians in the north. He re-established the fortress town of Utrecht and encouraged the missionary work of the Englishman Willibrord both there and at Echternach. He also gave encouragement to another English missionary, Suitbert, between the Lippe and the Ruhr.

The period of Pippin's rule saw the beginning of the really systematic conversion of the neighbouring tribes to Christianity and the foundation of monasteries in the areas thus affected. Previous activity had been sporadic and had lacked organization and the full backing of the established power. Monastic settlements had been spreading through Gaul throughout the fifth century, but it is not until the coming of the Irish at the end of the sixth century that we have certain evidence of such settlements further eastwards. The best known is that which resulted from the expedition of Columbanus and Gallus; when they were driven out of Gaul (Luxeuil) through the enmity of Brunichildis, they passed into what is now Switzerland on their way to Italy.

Gallus remained behind and settled at a remote spot on the river Steinach, south of Lake Constance, in 612; on the site of this monk's cell the Benedictine monastery of St. Gall was formally constituted by St. Otmar in 719.[1] The Anglo-Saxon monks, who began to come in the late seventh century, worked in closer association with the temporal power and also secured for themselves the support of the Pope. Willibrord did so, as did Boniface shortly afterwards. Charles Martel, who died in 741, actively pursued his father's, Pippin's, policy and gave much support to the Church. He supported Pirminius in the foundation, in 724, of the monastery on the island in Lake Constance named originally 'Sintleozes augia', after a person, and then, descriptively, Reichenau. Within a few years Pirminius had founded another monastery, at Murbach in Alsace, as well as others. Although he was active, and very effectively, at the same time as Boniface, the two do not seem to have had any association with one another, and it is not certain that they even met. Pirminius's provenance is unknown, but it is now usually held that he came from Spain.[2]

While Pirminius was active in the south-west, Winfrith of Wessex, later consecrated as Bishop Bonifatius, was reorganizing the diocesan system in Bavaria, founding monasteries in Hesse, of which Fulda, founded in 744, was to be of the first importance for the development of German letters in the following century, and following in the wake of Willibrord in trying to complete the conversion of the Frisians. He met his death at Dokkum, on the Frisian coast, in 754. He had also founded the bishopric of Würzburg in 742, and in 732 Pope Gregory III had raised him to the rank of archbishop.[3]

On the death of the mayor Charles Martel in 741, the kingdom

---

[1] The history of the Abbey of St. Gall and of its members is fairly well known from contemporary sources. J. M. Clark, *The Abbey of St. Gall as a Centre of Literature and Art* (Cambridge University Press, 1926), gives a comprehensive account of the contribution of the monastery to letters, calligraphy, painting, and music, with a summary sketch of its history. See also pp. 281 ff. below.

[2] On the foundation of Reichenau in general, see *Die Kultur der Abtei Reichenau*, ed. K. Beyerle (Munich, 1925), I. 10–18, on the history of the abbey, loc. cit. 55 ff., on Pirminius, loc. cit. 19–36, and Pater G. Jecker, *Die Heimat des hl. Pirmin* (Münster, 1927).

[3] The best account of Bonifatius is Th. Schieffer, *Winfrid-Bonifatius und die christliche Grundlegung Europas* (Freiburg i. B., 1954).

was divided among his sons, and there followed the usual tedious wars. Pippin, called the Short, and Carloman prevailed and ruled jointly for a short time. Carloman suddenly decided to become a monk, so that from 747 to 768 Pippin the Short ruled alone over the undivided kingdom; in 751 he had himself elected king of the Franks in place of the imbecile Childerich III with the approval of Pope Zacharias. At the Frankish assembly at Soissons he was anointed by St. Boniface. Soon afterwards Pippin was faced with the important decision whether to intervene in the political affairs of Italy. Pope Stephen was in danger of subjection to the Lombards and appealed to Pippin for help; he asked to be invited to Francia to arrange the details of Pippin's hoped-for intervention. The invitation was arranged, and in January 754 Pippin greeted his guest by dismounting and leading his horse like a groom, in accordance with the terms of the famous forgery concocted at this time, the *Donation of Constantine*. This incident marks the beginning of the political connection between Germany and the Papacy which was to become such a serious problem later, particularly in the Hohenstaufen period. The Pope rewarded Pippin by anointing him and his two sons, confirming them as kings of the Franks and, under penalty of excommunication and interdict, forbidding the Franks ever to elect a king not descended from them. This was the beginning of the Carolingian dynasty.

The period which elapsed between the beginnings of the Irish mission and the death of Charles the Great, about two hundred years, was one in which the religious and cultural situation in the German lands underwent a fundamental change. The connections across the Alps with Italy had never been entirely severed since the days of the Roman Empire and continued to play an important part; to this was now added the stimulating influences of the Irish and then of the English. The English worked in conjunction with the temporal power and the Papacy and in many cases there is direct and visible evidence of their work, while that of the Irish is much more difficult to identify; they had, however, much in common and the useful term 'insular', which is used particularly by the paleographers, can be used here too. This insular influence is found in the style of handwriting, of book-illustration, in the choice of reading matter and, at least in the case of English, in the language itself, as well as in liturgical matters and the whole organization of the Church. The upsurge in glossing activity, dealt with in the next chapter, is almost certainly a result of insular influence.[1]

[1] An outstandingly good account of the insular influence is by W. Levison, *England and the Continent in the Eighth Century* (Oxford, 1946). Two illuminating contributions on the Irish contribution in particular are: id., 'Die Iren und die fränkische Kirche' *Historische Zeitschrift* 109 (1912) 1–22, repr. in *Aus rheinischer und fränkischer Frühzeit* (Düsseldorf, 1948), pp. 247–63, and the chapter 'The Irish in the Carolingian Empire' in L. Bieler, *Ireland Harbinger of the Middle Ages* (London, New York, Toronto, 1963), pp. 115–36. On the influence of the English language, see W. Braune, *PBB* 43 (1918) 361–445.

VI

Early Translations from Latin

THE introduction of the Roman culture and the Christian religion made it necessary for educated men to understand the Latin language. For this purpose glossaries were produced in large numbers. The standard edition of the OHG glossaries and glosses is now *Die althochdeutschen Glossen* by Elias Steinmeyer and Eduard Sievers (abbreviated *Ahd. Gl.*).[1] It should be borne in mind that, although this work reproduces the texts faithfully, it does not reproduce the appearance of the manuscripts. It is therefore important that, if the manuscripts cannot be consulted, reference be made to the facsimiles which will be mentioned below. The quantity of glossaries compiled during the Middle Ages must have been immense. After fifty years of study, although his own collection of OHG glosses filled some 4,000 large pages, Steinmeyer recorded his opinion that there were still many left for others to discover.[2] Fragments of glossaries and odd words appear in unexpected places, scribbled in the margins and on blank pages of manuscripts. Sometimes they elude the eye, because the lemmata only are written in ink, while the glosses are merely impressed on the parchment with a dry point.[3] In some of these cases the first or the last syllable of the gloss has been entered in ink as an indicator, a practice which may have something to do with the peculiar condition of the OHG *Benediktinerregel*. Sometimes the lemma is written normally while the gloss is written in a crude cipher, the vowels being replaced by the following consonant of the alphabet

---

[1] Five vols. (Berlin, 1879–1922). Many of them had been collated by E. G. Graff for his *Althochdeutscher Sprachschatz* (see p. 330). Some texts were published by H. Hattemer in *Denkmahle des Mittelalters, St. Gallen's altteutsche Sprachschätze* (3 vols., St. Gallen, 1844–9). The article 'Glossen, althochdeutsche', in the 2nd edn. of Merker–Stammler, *Reallexikon*, gives later information. Selections, *Ahd. Lb.* i.   [2] *Ahd. Gl.* iv, p. vi.
[3] See, for example, *Ahd. Gl.* ii. 163; v. 27. B. Bischoff and P. Lehmann, 'Nachträge zu den althochdeutschen Glossen', *PBB* 52 (1928) 153–70.

or by the next consonant but one, e.g. 'moleste' *xngfmbchp* for *ungemacho*,[1] 'congeminatio' *gfzxxkfbldxngb* for *gezuuifaldunga*,[2] 'amplius' *mfrb* for *mera*,[3] 'anus' *brslph* for *arsloh*,[4] among glosses normally spelt.

The influence of the glossaries on literary production was probably much greater than is generally realized. Even the author of the *Heliand* has been shown to have used a glossary.[5] Now they are of great value as records of the OHG language, preserving many words which are otherwise unknown.[6]

Glosses are entered on the pages in three ways: above (or even below) the word they translate, in which case one speaks of inter-linear glosses; in the margins (marginal glosses); or in the line of text immediately after the word they translate (context glosses). Glossaries, i.e. collections of glosses, are in outward appearance usually of two types: interlinear and parallel, that is to say some-times the German words have been entered in the manuscript im-mediately above the original Latin, and sometimes the Latin and the German are in parallel columns, as in a modern vocabulary. In some manuscripts the scribe has copied the whole text, Latin and German, in a way which makes it look like continuous prose: a Latin word followed by its German translation, followed by the next Latin word and so on.[7] In either type of glossary the words may either be alphabetically arranged (alphabetical glossaries), or they may be grouped according to subject-matter (class glossaries), for example words found in the Book of Genesis or words denoting parts of the body. There are complete texts glossed in the inter-linear style, such as the OHG *Benediktinerregel* and the *Murbach Hymns*. There are also glossaries which appear to have been de-signed as travellers' guides. Even a fairly adequate study of the OHG glossaries with the intricate problems of their derivation and interrelationship would fill a large volume. Only the briefest ac-count can be attempted here, and only a few of the most notable

---

[1] *Ahd. Gl.* II. 62, l. 49.
[2] Ibid., p. 48, l. 16.
[3] Ibid., l. 38.
[4] Ibid. III. 642, l. 46. See G. Baesecke, *ZfdA* 58 (1921) 271. In one manu-script the scribe substituted *altzwip* (= Lat. *anus* f.).
[5] See p. 179.
[6] On the value of the glosses as linguistic evidence see E. Karg-Gasterstädt, 'Untergegangene althochdeutsche Wörter', *PBB* 63 (1939) 119–34; E. Ochs, ibid. 44 (1920) 315–21.
[7] An example can be seen in Baesecke, *Abrogans*, plate X; *Schrifttafeln* 1a.

can be mentioned. The material for further study can be obtained from the works of G. Baesecke which will be cited below.

Of the OHG alphabetical glossaries the *Kero* or *Abrogans* and the *Hrabanus* are the oldest and the most notable. As the latter is only a shortened and revised version of the former, they are known collectively as the **Kero-Rhabanus Family** (*die Keronisch-Hrabanische Sippe*). The titles have no historical justification. It was a common practice of medieval scribes to affix a well-known name to passages they were copying,[1] so a scribe appropriated the name of the famous teacher Rhabanus Maurus for the shorter text, unaware or regardless of the fact that Rhabanus was born about the date when the glossary had been compiled. The name Kero is applied to the older glossary because a monk of St. Gall of that name was once thought to be the author and to have written the St. Gall manuscript of it (K).[2]

The *Kero* glossary is now usually called *Abrogans*, according to the present practice of designating glossaries by the first word, which in this case is 'Abrogans', 'humilis' *aotmoat, samftmoati*.[3]

The OHG *Abrogans* has been preserved in three manuscripts, Pa, Ra, and K, and seven fragments.[4]

Pa, Manuscript 7640 of the Bibliothèque nationale, Paris, is a folio of the late eighth or the early ninth century. It contains a Latin alphabetical glossary known as the *Abavus minor* and, on fols. 124–32, the OHG *Abrogans* down to the word '*Infandum*', '*nec dicendum*'[5] *za fardakenne, ni za q;danne.*[6] The two glossaries were entered by different scribes. The script of both the Latin and the German portions of the *Abrogans* is a good Carolingian minuscule.[7]

---

[1] See, for example, B.M. Add. MS. 16581, in which familiar sayings are attributed to Wolfram von Eschenbach, Walther von der Vogelweide, and others.

[2] See Ehrismann, p. 255.

[3] i.e. in the dialect of Tatian *ôtmuot, samftmuoti* 'humility', 'gentle'. The word *abrogans* is the opposite of *adrogans* 'arrogant'.

[4] For a full description of the manuscripts see Baesecke, *Abrogans*, ch. I.

[5] The manuscript was once in the possession of Christina of Sweden. On her death her books were in Rome, so the lost portion of the *Abrogans* may be lying unidentified in the Vatican Library, or it may have been lost in Stockholm. See G. Baesecke, 'Über die verschollene Hälfte von Pa', *Festschrift für Strauch* (Hermaea 31, Halle, 1932), pp. 48–52.

[6] *q;* was a common scribal abbreviation for *que* both in Latin and in German.

[7] For a complete facsimile see G. Baesecke, *Lichtdrucke nach althochdeutschen Handschriften* (Halle, 1926), plates 1–20. See also R. Priebsch, *MLR* 22 (1927) 480–1.

It has always been agreed that the dialect of *Pa* is Bavarian, but there are certain peculiarities in the orthography which are significant, not merely from the linguistic point of view, but also because they give some indication of the way in which such texts were distributed. The Bavarian initial *p* for Germanic *b* occurs 256 times beside only five examples of *b*, all of which are on the first three leaves. Medially after a consonant there are 70 *p* and 17 *b*, medially after a vowel there are 169 *p* to 35 *b*, but on the first three leaves the proportions are 10 to 13 and 32 to 24. The proportion of unshifted *g* to the Bavarian *k* rapidly decreases: initially *g* remains unshifted on p. 1 four times out of five, on p. 4 nine times out of thirteen, on p. 6 once out of eight, in all fifty-three times out of 206. These figures suggest that a non-Bavarian scribe was accustoming himself to the Bavarian dialect of his original. There are even a few examples of *g* in place of Germanic *k* (e.g. *kadringum* (for Franconian *gidrinkum*) 'conuiuiis')[1] and the double error *glati* (for Bavarian *chalti*) 'algor'.[2] The letter *g* also occurs where *z* should be (*z* was probably written *c* in the original), e.g. *dag* for *daz*, *zaslagan* for *gaslagan*, and as the scribe had corrected the error by writing *z* above the *g*, the non-Bavarian *g* may reasonably be attributed to him. Germanic *d* occurs both shifted to *t* and unshifted initially, and also medially after vowels, throughout the manuscript.

Steinmeyer and Ehrismann held that the scribe was Alemannic, but Baesecke noted that the further development of *f* for OHG *pf* which took place in Alemannic does not occur here, and argued that the combination of *pf* with unshifted *b d g* and the weak preterite ending *-tôn* is the Franconian–Alemannic mixture found in documents written at Murbach in Alsace, a prominent example of which is, he thinks, the OHG *Isidor*.[3] *Pa* would, therefore, be a copy made at Murbach, or at least by a Murbach-trained scribe, of a Bavarian original. In any case the text is clearly making its way westwards.[4]

Though the script in which the Latin text of *Pa* is written is a Carolingian minuscule resembling that of the *Frankish Prayer* of

---

[1] *Ahd. Gl.* I. 76, l. 11. Baesecke, *Abrogans*, p. 3.

[2] *Ahd. Gl.* I. 6, l. 6.

[3] This view has been challenged. See pp. 121 ff. below.

[4] The view expressed by R. Koegel, *Geschichte der deutschen Litteratur bis zum Ausgang des Mittelalters* (Strasbourg, 1894–7), II. 429, and *PBB* 9 (1884) 357, that the original had been Rhenish-Franconian, has never been accepted.

the year 821,[1] some of the forms of the German language are much older, probably dating as far back as 765,[2] so the text is clearly a careful copy.

Ra, a folio manuscript formerly at Reichenau, but now, like all Reichenau manuscripts, in the Landesbibliothek, Karlsruhe,[3] has on fols. 76a–90a a text of the *Abrogans* which was formerly an independent manuscript. The dialect is Alemannic with only traces of Bavarian. Steinmeyer, followed by Ehrismann, assigns the manuscript to the tenth century, but Preisendanz and Baesecke[4] hold that it belongs to the early ninth century, possibly as early as 802. The latter base their opinion on entries in certain contemporary catalogues of the Reichenau library and on the resemblance of the script to that of another Reichenau manuscript. The former arguments are unconvincing, and the latter could not be criticized without a detailed examination of the manuscripts.

K, a quarto of the late eighth century, is now, as it always has been, in the library of the monastery of St. Gall.[5] The volume consists of three manuscripts bound together, the first of which, pp. 4–289 of the whole, contains the *Abrogans*. The other manuscripts contain Latin theological matter and on pp. 319–22 the *St. Gall Paternoster and Credo*.[6] The letters vary greatly in form. Baesecke professes to have identified as many as sixty divisions and twenty scribes; fol. 120, he thinks, shows four hands.[7] He admits, however, that his twenty scribes display a certain amount of uniformity due to the tradition of the scriptorium, and not all readers will be convinced that so many can be distinguished.

Though it is the oldest of the manuscripts, *K* has diverged farthest from the original, for the dialect is in one part pure

---

[1] See Petzet–Glauning, i. 4.

[2] See G. Baesecke, *PBB* 55 (1931) 321–76.

[3] Cod. Aug. cxi (Augiensis because the ancient name of the island of Reichenau was 'Sintleozes Augia', see p. 87). For a history of the monastery of Reichenau and its literary production see *Die Kultur der Abtei Reichenau*, ed. K. Beyerle (Munich, 1925). *Ra* is described *Ahd. Gl.* iv. 401 ff., and Baesecke, *Abrogans*, pp. 15 ff. Facsimiles: G. Baesecke, *Lichtdrucke*, plates 24 and 25 of fols. 76a and 90a, and Beyerle, op. cit., p. 687 of fol. 84.

[4] *Abrogans*, pp. 15–20. The earlier dating had been accepted by Längin in *Kultur der Abtei Reichenau*, pp. 684 ff.

[5] Cod. S. Gall. 911. Text: *Ahd. Gl.* i. 2 ff. Description: ibid. iv. 459; Baesecke, *Abrogans*, pp. 11–15. Facsimiles: Baesecke, *Lichtdrucke*, plates 21–3; id. *Abrogans*, plate X; F. Steffens, *Lateinische Paläographie*, plate 43b.

[6] See p. 111 below.

[7] *Abrogans*, plate X.

Alemannic and in the other Alemannic with Franconian influences. The three manuscripts afford, therefore, circumstantial evidence of a Bavarian text making its way quickly westwards to Alemannia and north-westwards to Franconia.

It is argued that the orthography of the archetype from which the three manuscripts were derived resembled that of the German names in certain charters and records written at Freising, while Arbeo was bishop (764–84).[1] Certain errors in *Pa* such as *s* for *r* in *eslidit* (*erlidit* 'erleidet') and *uuost* (*wort*) suggest that the archetype had the insular *r*, and certain others, e.g. *u* for *c* in *uesacit* (for *casacit* 'gesagt') and *di* for *cl* in *dilepenti* (for *clepenti* 'klebend') suggest the older type of script with open *a* and *d* with curved shaft, a combination found in Clm. 6298, which contains a work of Korbinian, bishop of Freising (died about 730). This also establishes a connection with Bishop Arbeo, for he wrote lives of Korbinian and of St. Emmeram in a peculiar Latin which corresponds to certain forms in the *Abrogans* which could not have originated on German soil. Thus the loss of final *s* and *t* (e.g. *alia*(*s*), *ciuita*(*s*), *genera*(*t*), *honora*(*t*)) and the adding of *s* (e.g. *turbas* for *turba*) together with the loss of *c* before *t* (*Artus* for *Arctus*) are italianisms. Also *conuescit* for *congessit* points to north Italian *sc* for *ss*, and the *v* for *gw* which arose from Germanic *w* is specially Lombard or Venetian spelling. Even the German words sometimes show Italian influence, for the rendering of *militum* by *herimanno* (*Ahd. Gl.* I, p. 87, l. 25) suggests the Lombard term *hariman* (a soldier peasant settled on frontier territory in ancient Roman fashion), which was unknown in Germany proper. This specially Lombardic Latin, the italianized German, and the Lombardic word produce the impression that the translator had at least had an Italian training. Arbeo was born about 724 near Meran, then a Bavarian settlement under Lombard rule. He appears in various capacities, and from 764 to his death in 784 he was bishop of Freising.[2] Though there is no positive evidence to connect him with the *Abrogans*, he fulfils the conditions required of at least the author of the archetype of the three manuscripts, and he may well have been responsible for the inception of the Glossary itself, in which case it represents the Italian (Lombard) culture in South Germany which was superseded by the Anglo-Saxon influences

---

[1] Baesecke, *Abrogans*, pp. 78–102.
[2] See ibid., esp. p. 117, and id., *PBB* 68 (1945) 75–134.

under Charles the Great and Alcuin. The *Abrogans*, therefore, the first book in the German language, would date back to shortly after the middle of the eighth century, when Pippin the Short was reigning. Though the Anglo-Irish monks had been earlier in the field, as we see from the insular script in so many manuscripts and in Arbeo's own charters, their written literature at this time was Latin, and it was Arbeo's German *Abrogans* that began literature in the German tongue.

The quotations which follow will suffice to give an idea of the nature of the glossary and of the skill of those who prepared and those who copied the OHG portion. In the original Latin text the words were arranged in alphabetical order which has often been disturbed in the manuscripts. Each word is followed by a synonym. The intention can hardly have been to explain the meaning, but must rather have been to provide a list of alternative words and expressions which could be used to render one's style more elegant. The Latin glossary was, therefore, intended to be a dictionary of synonyms to assist composition. The compiler of the Latin text never contemplated that it would be used as the basis of a Latin–German dictionary. His work was appropriated by the compiler of the OHG glossary who simply inserted German words above the Latin, a procedure which saved both the trouble of collecting new material and the expense of new parchment, provided for the German reader a rendering of several Latin words at once, and also suggested to him several Latin and German synonyms. The *Abrogans* does not appear to have circulated in Italy, so it was not intended to teach German to Italians.

The Latin text in these manuscripts is far from accurate, e.g. 'Agere, strata siue uia puplica' *toan, ardhanit, so sama castrauuit*.[1] A scribe had misunderstood 'Agger' as 'Agere', and the glossator rendered it correctly *toan* (Franconian *tuon* 'tun'). The German glossator took 'strata' for the past participle of *sterno*, and, ignoring the explanation 'uia publica', rendered it by the past participles of *ardhennen* 'erdehnen' *strawen* 'streuen'. The German glossators were neither learned nor discerning. They render, for example, 'Arrogantia, petulantia, jactantia, superbia' by *hrom, sohenti, gelf, ubarmoti*, not knowing the meaning of 'petulantia' nor guessing that, standing where it does, it must be a synonym for the preced-

---

[1] *Ahd. Gl.* I. 26, ll. 26 ff. For convenience of printing the interlinear arrangement has been ignored here and later.

ing word.[1] With misguided ingenuity they connected it with *peto*. Similarly, in the following example: 'Adamans, lapis ferro durior, id est genus gemme' *Minneonti, stein isarne hardiro, daz ist chunni gimmono*, they assume, in spite of the definition, that *Adamans* 'diamond' is connected with *amans* 'loving'. The definition is translated word for word, although the syntax is un-German. Nevertheless, the Latin genitive singular has been made plural in the German. Even *aut* 'or' and *haud* 'not' are confused in 'Haut procul, non longe' *edo fona, nalles rumo* and 'Haut aliter, non aliter' *edo anderuuis, nalles anderuuis*.

It must always be remembered, however, that the manuscripts we have are copies of something older, and in some cases the German has almost certainly been copied into the manuscript we have from another, in which the Latin reading was different. The last entry in the glossary is an example of this: 'Zarda, alienatus' *irscopan, irfremidid*. 'Zarda' is not a known Latin word and could not have led a German monk to translate it by 'driven out'. The original word, whatever it was (perhaps something like *ex(s)arta*) was translated by *irscopan*, and the synonym 'alienatus' by *irfremidid*. The scribe of the *Abrogans* miscopied the first word as 'zarda' but the rest correctly.

The **Rhabanus Glossary** is a shortened and revised version of the *Abrogans* generally agreed to have been made about 790 in Bavaria, possibly at the monastery of St. Emmeram in Regensburg. As stated above, there is no evidence to connect it with Rhabanus Maurus; the oldest recorded and accurate title is *Samanunga uuorto fona deru niuuiun anti deru altun euu* ('Collection of words from the New and the Old Testament'), and it is called for brevity *Samanunga*. The text has been preserved complete in one ninth-century manuscript, now in Vienna (R), and there are seven fragments. All are Bavarian in dialect.[2] Many errors have eluded the revisers.

Whereas Rhabanus's name has been wrongly attached to the *Samanunga*, it seems likely that he was associated with what are known as the Old High German **Isidor Glosses**.[3] These are some

---

[1] Op. cit., p. 4, ll. 39 ff.

[2] Codex Vindobonensis 162, fols. 10*a*–43*a*. Text: *Ahd. Gl.* I. 3–270 where it is printed parallel to the *Abrogans*. Description: ibid. IV. 628 (no. 162). See G. Baesecke, *Abrogans*, p. 41, and id., *PBB* 46 (1922) 456–94, esp. 491.

[3] For the text and a discussion of the problems see G. Baesecke, *ZfdA* 58 (1921) 241–73.

sixty or seventy words denoting parts of the body; they occur in a Latin text, where they are given as the equivalent of the corresponding Latin words, which has been identified as an extract from the *Liber Etymologiarum* of Isidor, bishop of Seville 600–36. Melchior Goldast, who published the work in his *Rerum Alamannicarum Scriptores* in 1606, attributed it to Rhabanus Maurus and his pupil Walahfrid Strabo, whose notes this glossed text represents. Goldast did not give his reasons for this identification. Rhabanus is, however, known for his glosses—they are referred to by Notker Balbulus (died 912)[1]—and for his sedulous copying activity, and the relevant part of Isidor appears in Rhabanus's *De rerum naturis*, which was begun in 844. What appears here, however, is not the complete Isidor text and, further, Walahfrid was no longer at Fulda in 844, having already been abbot of Reichenau for two years. Recent scholarship is inclined to a view which only slightly modifies the statement of Goldast, namely that the glosses were the work of Walahfrid long before he went to the Reichenau and that they are in fact notes taken by him from Rhabanus's lectures. The date would be between 820 and 830.

Walahfrid has been credited with more independent glossing activity. A St. Gall manuscript (no. 283) with German glosses to some Old Testament books contains a statement of Walahfrid that they are based on notes taken by him at Rhabanus's lectures. They show, however, certain similarities with some Reichenau glosses, and it seems that Walahfrid had worked up his notes taken at Fulda and incorporated material from Reichenau glosses after he had gone there. The language shows an element of compromise between East Franconian and Alemannic features and has been shown to be very similar to that of the scribe of the St. Gall *Tatian* manuscript known as γ. It is argued that Walahfrid was in fact responsible for this section of the *Tatian* translation.[2]

A prominent collection of biblical glossaries is contained in another Reichenau manuscript, Cod. Aug. IC;[3] they are referred

---

[1] See R. v. Raumer, *Die Einwirkung des Christentums auf die althochdeutsche Sprache* (Stuttgart, 1845), pp. 82 ff.

[2] E. Schröter, *Walahfrids deutsche Glossierung zu den biblischen Büchern Genesis bis Regum II und der althochdeutsche Tatian* (Hermaea 16, Halle, 1926), esp. pp. 52 f.; 68–73; 140 f. See also G. Baesecke, 'Die deutschen Genesisglossen der Familie *Rz', *ZfdA* 61 (1924) 222 ff.

[3] Described in *Ahd. Gl.* iv. 399 f. and by Th. Längin in *Kultur der Abtei Reichenau*, 688 ff. with facsimiles.

to by letter symbols (*Rb, Rd, Re, Rf, Rz*), the first letter standing for Reichenau, the second denoting the different collections in the same manuscript. *Rb* is a Latin–German dictionary of the Old Testament arranged, not alphabetically, but in the order of the words in the text; sometimes even whole sentences occur. The Latin words are written one below the other and the German equivalents in a parallel column, but the space here is often left blank. After a few pages produced in this way, there follow others where another dictionary, known as *Rd*,[1] is added, also in two parallel columns, so that there are now four columns on a page. *Rd-Jb* is also a glossary of books of the Old Testament, but arranged alphabetically. Sometimes the scribe has added words from yet another glossary (*Re*) in the blanks left in *Rb*. *Rb* is thought to be an original entry and to date from early in the ninth century; the others are copied and appear to be spread over the following hundred years.

Some very early biblical glosses are to be found on two leaves of a sixth- or seventh-century uncial manuscript of the Vulgate, now in the Benedictine monastery at St. Paul in Carinthia.[2] The manuscript was for a long time in St. Blasien in the Black Forest, but it bears a Reichenau mark.[3] The linguistic form of the German words is very archaic (Gmc. *ē* appears as *ea* in *keanc*, but *ai* as *ei* in *scein*, *ufsteic* beside *ai* in *ainluze*), and they were probably entered late in the eighth century. Sometimes odd words are glossed, sometimes whole sentences, but always word for word. They are called the *St. Pauler Lukas-Glossen*, because the portion of the text is St. Luke's Gospel, Chapters 1:64–2:51.

Besides the Bible glossaries there are glossaries of words used by the patristic writers, e.g. the **Glossae Salomonis** of the late ninth century, so called because they were attributed to Salomo III, bishop of Constance (890–922), a nephew of Salomo I, to whom Otfrid dedicated his *Evangelienbuch*.[4] They contain also words used by classical writers, including Cicero and Virgil, who were

---

[1] This glossary is also preserved in a manuscript now in the Bodleian Library, Oxford (Junius 25), but recorded in Murbach in the fifteenth century; the glossary forms section *b* of it and is now referred to as *Rd-Jb*.

[2] *Ahd. Gl.* I. 728–37, IV. 600. *Drei Reichenauer Denkmäler* ed. U. Daab, Altdeutsche Textbibliothek, No. 57 (Niemeyer, Tübingen, 1963). Extract: *Ahd. Lb.* I. 5. Facsimile: Baesecke, *Abrogans*, plate II.

[3] Längin, loc. cit., p. 688.

[4] *Ahd. Gl.* IV. 27–174.

regarded as semi-Christian. There are numerous Virgil glosses.[1]
A large part of the value of these glosses and glossaries is the indication they give us about what writings were read and considered
important at the time.

One of the most important of the glossaries arranged according
to subjects, and the best known, is the so-called **Vocabularius
Sancti Galli,** preserved on pp. 181–206 of MS. St. Gall. 913.
An entry in the manuscript refers to an ancient belief that it was
written by St. Gall himself, but this has not been accepted by
modern scholarship, although the name remains; it was, however,
long believed that it was written at St. Gall, but doubts about
even that have been expressed. Since the work of Baesecke it is
no longer believed that it was written there. The vocabulary itself
forms only a small part of the manuscript; it is of words of practical application: parts of the body, human qualities, the house and
land, natural phenomena, animals, etc. Much of the rest is scrappy
and in note form. The pages themselves are very small (less than
4 inches square and some even smaller), the parchment is poor
and dirty and worn, indicating much use. It has been suggested
that it served as a compendium and word-and-phrase book of
a missionary or that it was the notebook of a student, but this
can be no more than speculation. The source of the vocabulary
was formerly held to have been Isidor's *Liber Etymologiarum,* but
Baesecke found all the material in the *Hermeneumata* ('Interpretations'), a Greek–Latin glossary of the third century, which circulated freely in the Middle Ages in various forms with theological
interpolations from various sources.[2] Baesecke has subjected the
content of the whole manuscript, its style of writing, and the
linguistic features of the German to a minute analysis and come
to the conclusion that it was most probably written at Murbach
about 790. From the content of the manuscript and from some
palaeographical features Baesecke argues that the original was a
work of the Anglo-Saxon mission to Germany; it could date from
about the middle of the eighth century, but proof is lacking.

A manuscript now at Kassel, formerly at Fulda, contains among
miscellaneous theological matter the OHG *Exhortatio ad Plebem*

---

[1] *Ahd. Gl.* ii. 625–727. See E. Steinmeyer, *ZfdA* 15 (1872) 1–119; 16 (1873)
110–11.

[2] Facsimile: *Schrifttafeln* 1b. See *Voc. St. Galli, passim,* esp. p. 31, and G.
Goetz, *Corpus Glossariorum Latinorum* (Leipzig, 1888–), i. 12–23. For the
Latin texts see ibid. iii.

Christianam[1] and, on the next two leaves, but in a different hand, the **Kassel Glosses** (*Die Kasseler Glossen*).[2] These are fragments of a Latin–German glossary arranged, like the *Vocabularius St. Galli*, according to subjects. The dialect of the German words is Bavarian and the date about 800. As in the *Vocabularius St. Galli* there are groups of words denoting parts of the body and animals, and in these cases the similarity is so close that a common source seems certain. Other sections deal with articles of clothing, household equipment, and parts of the house. There are also some short sentences. The latter are interesting because they relate to everyday affairs, e.g. 'Indica mih' *sage mir* 'unde estu' *uuanna pistdu*, 'de quale patria' *fone uueliheru lantskeffi*; 'sapiens homo' *spaher man*, 'stultus' *toler*. The words and sentences are in the tradition of the *Hermeneumata*. One passage, which does not belong to the Hermeneumata tradition, is of sufficient interest to be quoted in full: 'stulti sunt' *tole sint* 'romani' *uualha*, 'sapienti sunt' *spahe sint*, 'paioari' *peigira*; 'modica est' *luzic ist* 'sapienti' *spahe* 'in romana' *in uualhum*; 'plus habent' *mera hapent* 'stultitia' *tolaheiti* 'quam sapientia' *denne spahi*. This is an ancient example of the familiar popular gibe of the South Germans at the Italians, another instance of which occurs in Wolfram von Eschenbach's *Parzival* 121, ll. 7–10:

> Ein pris den wir Beier tragen
> muoz ih von Waleisen sagen:
> si sint tœrischer denne beierisch her,
> und doch ze manlicher wer.

The *Kassel Glosses* are Latin–German. The collection of words and phrases known as **Die altdeutschen Gespräche** are German–Latin.[3] The Vatican manuscript Reg. 566 has bound in it one leaf (No. 50) which was formerly the first leaf of MS. Lat. 7641 of the Bibliothèque nationale, Paris. The latter unites in one binding two manuscripts, one of the tenth and the other of the twelfth century. The tenth-century manuscript contains the *Abavus Glossary*, into which some German words have been inserted (fols.

[1] See pp. 111 f.
[2] *Ahd. Gl.* iii. 9–13. Selections: *Ahd. Lb.* i. 3. See G. Baesecke, *Voc. St. Galli*, pp. 36 ff. Facsimile with transcription: W. Grimm, *Exhortatio ad Plebem Christianam Glossae Cassellanae* (Berlin, 1848).
[3] *Ahd. Gl.* v. 517 ff. *Ahd. Lb.* v. For a full discussion of the problems raised by this text see J. A. Huisman, 'Die Pariser Gespräche', *RhVB* 33 (1969) pp. 272–96.

1–74*a*), and some other Latin matter. The *Altdeutsche Gespräche* were entered by a tenth-century hand on the margins of the Vatican leaf and on three leaves (1*a*–3*a*) of the Paris manuscript. Some sentences of the *Tatian* (known as fragment P) are also written in the margins of the same manuscript, working backwards from fols. 16*a* to 4*b*.[1]

As may be seen from the examples quoted below, the spelling of the German words, such as the omission of initial *h* and *gu* for *w*, indicates clearly that the scribe was a Frenchman and that he was spelling them as he, a foreigner, would pronounce them. This distortion of the German makes it difficult to determine the place of origin, but certain features, such as *b* for *m* in *bit*, combined perhaps with *o* (instead of *uo*) in *got* and *e* instead of *ie* in *enschlepfen*, might indicate Middle Franconian; the pronoun *ger* 'vos' seems to be a combination of OLG *ge* and OHG *ir*. On the other hand, it has been held that the language may be West Frankish.[2] The words which interested the scribe include parts of the body and articles of clothing, e.g. *Ob&e* 'cap(ut)', *An* 'manus', *Follo guanbe* 'plenus venter', *Ansco* 'guanti'.[3] There are phrases for the master demanding from his servant his horse, spear, shield, gloves, and other articles, e.g. *Gimer min schelt* .i. 'scutum', and for such simple daily needs as *Buozze mine sco* 'emenda meam cabattam'. His servant (*isnel canet* (i.e. *snel kneht*) 'velox vasallus') was troublesome at times and quarrels arose between persons who are not specified, for we read: *Guaz queten ger erra?* (for *waz quedet ir herro?*) 'quid dicitis vos?', *Coorestu narra?* (for *Gihorestu narro?*) .i. 'Ausculta fol', and *Scla en sin als* (for *slah ime sin hals*) .i. 'da illi in collo'; *Vndes ars in tine naso* .i. 'canis culum in tuo naso'. The servant is reproached for his wicked ways: *Quandi næ guarin ger za metina?* (for *Wanta ni wârut ir* (or *wâri tu*) *zi metine?*) .i. 'quare non fuisti ad matutinas?', *en ualde* (for *ih ni wolta*) .i. 'ego nolui'. *Ger ensclephen bitte uuip in ore bette* .i. 'tu jacuisti ad feminam in tuo lecto'; *Guez or erre az pe de semauda ger ensclephen pe dez uip sesterai rebulgan* (i.e. *Wessi iuwer herro pî dia smâhî dâ ir insliefut bi demo uuîbe sô ist er iu erbolgan*) .i. 'si sciverit hoc senior tuus iratus erit tibi per meum caput'. There are obvious close similarities with the Kassel glosses, in the classes of words and in some of the questions, such as on the origin of the journey and on

<hr/>

[1] See p. 160.   [2] See Huisman, op. cit.
[3] In normal East Franconian spelling: *houbit, hant, folliu wamba, hantscuoh*.

the mother country; Baesecke[1] has drawn attention to the dependence of both, as well as the *Vocabularius St. Galli*, on the *Hermeneumata*, but the *Gespräche* have a character of their own, based on the interesting adventures or lively imagination, or both, of the writer. Most of the OHG literature that has survived is soberly clerical. The *Gespräche*, like the verses on the matrimonial misadventure of Liubene's daughter[2] and the Latin *Ruodlieb*[3] are taken from life, although there is literary tradition behind them.

The technique of the interlinear glossary was applied to the translation of whole texts word for word or even syllable for syllable; these are known as 'interlinear versions'. A notable example is the OHG translation of the **Benedictine Rule.**

Benedictine monasticism was introduced into Germany at the beginning of the eighth century and soon became, under the influence of the English missionaries, the only order in the area. The Rule of the order was composed by its founder, Benedict of Nursia, early in the sixth century; the traditional date for its composition and the founding of the monastery of Montecassino is 529, but it cannot be confirmed with accuracy. The Rule consists of seventy-three chapters prescribing in detail how a monk must live. As part of his policy of strengthening discipline in the Church, Charles the Great had a copy made in 787 of the genuine Montecassino manuscript of the Rule; a very careful, annotated copy of this was made at Aachen in 817 by two monks from the Reichenau and sent by them to the librarian of that monastery. MS. St. Gall 914, upon which all modern editions of the Rule are based, is thought to be this copy, or a faithful transcript of it. Charles also ordered that all monks should know and understand the Rule and, as far as possible, know it by heart, an order which was codified at the Synod of Aachen in 802. Entered between the lines of MS. St. Gall 916, of the early ninth century, but belonging to a less reliable branch of the textual tradition, is the translation into German;[4] as the language shows, this translation must have been made also at the beginning of the ninth century, and it may

---

[1] *Voc. St. Galli*, pp. 44 ff.
[2] See pp. 211 f.   [3] See pp. 270 ff.
[4] Full text *Kl. ahd. Spdmr.* xxxvi; Ursula Daab, *Die althochdeutschen Benediktinerregel des Cod. Sang. 916*. Altdeutsche Textbibliothek, No. 50 (Niemeyer, Tübingen, 1959); extract: *Ahd. Lb.* vii. Facsimile: *Schrifttafeln* 3; Baesecke, *Abrogans*, plates III–V.

well be the result of Charles's order. The language is Alemannic, and could be either that of St. Gall or the Reichenau: Gmc. *ai* appears as *ei*, though *au* is still unchanged; *hl, hr, hw, hn* are still common; final *-m* has become *-n*; there are numerous glide vowels. An interesting orthographical feature is that vowel length is indicated by doubling. Two other manuscripts containing copies of the translation, which also belonged to the St. Gall library, have perished.[1]

The OHG version preserved in MS. St. Gall 916 is an interlinear translation from the Latin, which it follows word for word, sometimes even syllable for syllable. A few examples will suffice to illustrate the technique and the quality of the work: 'Hecque mandavit suis servare alumnis' *indi desv kepot sinem haltan chindun* (*Kl. ahd. Spdmr.*, p. 191, ll. 20–1); 'deo auxiliante' *cote helfantemv* (p. 196, ll. 23–4); 'inquieto' *unstillemv* (p. 198, l. 24); 'Ne aliis predicans ipse reprobus inveniatur' *ni andreem forasagenti er farchoraneer si fundan* (p. 199, ll. 12–14) (*predicare* 'preach' and *predicere* 'prophesy' have been confused); 'apud deum' *mit cotan* (p. 200, l. 4) beside 'apud ipsum' *mit imo* (p. 200, l. 6); 'Cum de monitionibus suis emendacionem aliis subministrat, ipse efficitur a vitiis emendatus' *denne fona manungoom sineem puazza andres vntarambahte er ist ketaan fona achustim kipuasteer* (p. 202, ll. 16–19); 'Cum discordante ante solis occasum in pace redire' *mit vngaherzamv er dera sunnuun sedalkange in fridu huurban* (p. 206, ll. 8–9); 'Mox matutini qui incipiente luce agendi sunt subsequantur' *sareo morganlob demv pikinantemv leohte ze tuanne sint untar sin kafolget* (p. 218, ll 26–8).

The literal translation, word for word and syllable for syllable, practised in the interlinear versions is not necessarily a sign of ignorance of Latin, nor does it prove that the German language had not yet developed an independent prose style. It is true that Latin was taken to be the standard language, by Otfrid for example, who accepted the Latin gender as 'correct' when it differed from the German gender of the equivalent word, but it is improbable that the prose of the OHG *Isidor* was as unique and as isolated as it appears to be today. Word-for-word translations

---

[1] Seven other manuscripts contain fragmentary German glosses of the Benedictine Rule; four are of the ninth century, two are of the eleventh, and one is of the fourteenth; all are printed in *Ahd. Gl.* See U. Daab, *Studien zur althochdeutschen Benediktinerregel* (Hermaea 24, Halle, 1929).

of the Greek and Latin Classics were published even in the eighteenth and nineteenth centuries, and word-for-word translations are still used for instructional purposes. When the translator of the *Benediktinerregel* rendered *subsequantur* by *untar sin kafolget* and *discordante* by *vngaherzamv*, or made the German prepositions govern the cases of their Latin equivalents, his object was in all probability to instruct his fellow countrymen in the peculiarities of the Latin language, or at least to reproduce as exactly as possible the appearance of the 'noble' tongue.[1] A translator so ignorant of elementary grammar would have made more mistakes of vocabulary, and there are in the *Benediktinerregel* some signs of independence of style; nevertheless, he cannot be acquitted of carelessness or indifference, for example when he renders 'Monachorum quattuor esse genera manifestum est' by *municho fioreo vvesan chunni chund ist*, i.e. 'There are kinds of four monks' instead of 'There are four kinds of monks' (p. 196, ll. 7–8).

Numerous discrepancies between the German and the Latin above which it is written are due to neither of these causes, but to the fact that the OHG translation was clearly not made from the Latin of the manuscript into which it is copied. For example, (*qhui*)*du* (p. 225, l. 17) is written above 'dixit', but 'dixit' is a peculiar reading of St. Gall 916, whereas the correct reading, in other manuscripts, is 'dixi'.[2]

The vocabulary and the style do not vary, so the translation is the work of one man, but the hands of several scribes can be identified, which alternate regularly. Certain regularly alternating variations in the orthography, such as *za tuanne* beside *ze tuenne*, *ka-* beside *ke-*, loss or retention of initial *h* before consonants, are due to these alternations of the scribes,[3] and to the peculiar nature of their copy, in which, apparently, only the endings of many of the German words had been entered. Traces of this remain in the present manuscript: for example only *tin* (for *truhtin*) is written above the ending of 'dominus' (p. 192, l. 19) and *nan* above

---

[1] See N. Leibowitz, *PBB* 55 (1931) 377–463 esp. 377, 386. Detailed examinations of this translation and the technique used can be found in F. Seiler, *PBB* 1 (1874) 402–85; U. Daab, *Studien zur althochdeutschen Benediktinerregel* (Hermaea 24, Halle, 1929); H. Ibach, *PBB* (Halle) 78 (1956) 1–110, 79 (1957) 106–85, 80 (1958) 190–271, 81 (1959) 123–73, 82 (1960) 371–473.

[2] See Seiler, pp. 461–71; U. Daab, *PBB* (Halle) 78 (1956) 8–42; *Kl. ahd. Spdmr.*, p. 283. Some corrections in the Latin appear to have been made by the German scribes.

[3] See *Kl. ahd. Spdmr.*, pp. 284 f.

'dominum' (for *truhtinan*, p. 195, l. 34). There are many other examples, e.g. *uzzaan tres* (for *munistres*, p. 203, l. 17) 'foras monasterio', *n* (for *man*, p. 214, l. 23), 'homines', *to* (for *sehsto*, p. 215, l. 21) 'sextus', *lu* (for *allu*, p. 215, l. 24) 'omnia', *ti* (for *qhuedenti*, p. 215, l. 27) 'dicens', *gin* (for *wizzagin*, p. 215, l. 28) 'propheta' (ablative). The abbreviations become more and more numerous. It has been suggested that the scribes had to supply the body of the words from these indications. Sometimes the first and last syllables are given, e.g. *ke ti* for *kescrifti*. The eighth-century St. Paul Glosses to St. Luke are also severely abbreviated.[1]

Only the Prologue and the first fourteen chapters have been fully translated. At Chapter 15 gaps appear and grow larger in the later chapters, only odd words and phrases being translated, until the OHG text breaks off in the middle of Chapter 67, leaving 68 to 73 untranslated. Chapter 31, 'De cellarario monasterio qualis sit', and Chapter 49, 'De quadragesime observatione', however, have been translated in full.

It was formerly held that the *Benediktinerregel* was translated and copied at St. Gall, where the manuscript has been certainly since 1461, as it is mentioned in the catalogue of volumes in the library made in that year (Codex S. Gall 1399), and perhaps since the eleventh century, but more recently the translation has been attributed to the Reichenau on account of certain agreements with the Glossary *Rb* (Reichenau MS. Aug. IC).[2]

An interlinear version of twenty-six Ambrosian hymns, known as the **Murbach Hymns**, is also thought on grounds of the language and the translation technique to be Reichenau work;[3] it is contained in the same Murbach manuscript, now in Oxford, as the glossary *Rd-Jb* mentioned above. Its previous history is unknown. A list of books in the Reichenau library drawn up in 822 mentions *De carminibus theodiscae volumen I*, and another of about twenty years later mentions two books, one containing *XII carmina theodiscae*

---

[1] See p. 99 above.

[2] For the older view see R. Koegel, *Geschichte der deutschen Litteratur bis zum Ausgang des Mittelalters* (Strasbourg, 1894–7) I. ii, p. 465; M. Roth, 'Über den Wortschatz der Benediktinerregel' (unpublished Heidelberg dissertation, 1921); H. Brauer, *Die Bücherei von St. Gallen und das althochdeutsche Schrifttum* (Hermaea, 17, Halle, 1926), pp. 39 f. For the more recent view see Steinmeyer, *Kl. ahd. Spdmr.*, pp. 287 and 289; U. Daab, op. cit., *passim*. Ehrismann, in the 1st edn. of his *Geschichte der deutschen Literatur* (1918), supported the older view, but in the 2nd edn. (1932) he followed Steinmeyer.

[3] See U. Daab, *Studien*, pp. 29 ff.

linguae formata and another *Carmina diversa ad docendum theo-discam linguam,* but it cannot be assumed that these references are necessarily to this particular manuscript. They do, however, show that something at least comparable was available at the Reichenau at about the time when this version was made, and they give a hint of the didactic purpose, although the usual view is that the purpose of the glossing activity was to teach Latin, not German. The reference to *De carminibus theodisca lib. I* in a catalogue claimed to be from Murbach[1] has been held to show that in fact one of the Reichenau manuscripts did go to Murbach, but the attribution to Murbach has been challenged.[2] The translation is rather more accurate than that of the Benedictine Rule.[3]

---

[1] J. Senebier, *Catalogue raisonné des manuscrits de Genève* (Geneva, 1779), pp. 74 ff.

[2] H. Bloch, 'Ein karolingischer Bibliothekskatalog aus Kloster Murbach', *Straßburger Festschrift zur XLVI. Versammlung deutscher Philologen und Schulmänner* (Strasbourg, 1901), pp. 257–85. P. Lehmann describes it as a ninth-century copy of the 822 Reichenau catalogue (*Kultur der Abtei Reichenau,* p. 647).

[3] Extract *Ahd. Lb.* xi.

VII

Minor Theological, Legal, and Medical Documents of the Reign of Charles the Great

PIPPIN THE SHORT (741–68), following the usual Frankish custom, arranged that his kingdom should be divided after his death between his sons. The younger, Charles, known later as the Great, received the more important portion, namely the Frankish territory proper between the Main and the Channel. The elder son, Carloman, died in December 771, before the *solita fratribus odia* developed into open war. His subjects, ignoring his infant son, elected Charles king, so that the Frankish realm between the mouths of the Rhine and the Rhône, from the Main to the Bay of Biscay, was reunited under his rule. To this Charles added by conquest in 774 the Lombard kingdom in Italy, completing the destruction begun by Pippin and continuing the latter's policy of supporting the Papacy. His first expedition against the Saracens in Spain is remembered for the annihilation of his rearguard at Roncevalles, which is the foundation of the *Chanson de Roland* (*c.* 1100), from which is derived the MHG (Bavarian) *Rolandslied* of Pfaffe Konrad. Charles had to fight the Saracens again from 785 to 812. There is no contemporary German poem extant in his praise. On Christmas Day 800 he had been crowned Emperor by Pope Leo III and in 812 Michael Rhangabe, the Eastern Emperor, recognized him as Emperor of the West. Charles also warred successfully against the Slavonic tribes east of the Elbe (Mecklenburg was then Slavonic), and forced them to profess Christianity. The Saxons, who occupied what is now Westphalia, Hanover, Oldenburg, and Brunswick, and in the north Holstein, i.e. the land watered by the Lippe, the Ems, and the Weser with its tributaries the Aller and the Ocker, from Holland and Frisia eastwards to the Elbe and as far south as the Harz, resisted bitterly the encroachments of the Frankish king and the new religion. (By Saxony is meant at this period what is now called 'Niedersachsen'. 'Obersachsen' or Saxony in the modern sense of the word, derives its name from the Saxons who settled there in later times.) Charles had to undertake five great campaigns before their famous leader Widukind was forced to submit and be baptized in 785. Even then the Saxons were not resigned to their defeat and continued to rebel until 804. German literature has no account of this grim struggle. The Saxon clerical poet who, in the reign of Arnulf (887–99), wrote in Latin hexameters the annals of Charles's achievements, was proud of his ancestors, but the best that he could (or dared to) say was that the courage of the Saxons exceeded their virtues.[1] In German literature there are merely allusions to the traditional ferocity of the Saxons, such as the Saxon attack on the Burgundian Gunther in the Fourth Aventiure of the MHG *Nibelungenlied*, and in the thirteenth-century Bavarian *Meier Helmbrecht*, ll. 422–3:

> Vater, einen Sahsen
> züget ir lîhter danne mich.

The only direct reflection of the campaign is the little document called **The Saxon Baptismal Vow** (*Das sächsische Taufgelöbnis*).[2] It is written in Old Saxon with some High German traces, which could derive from the scribe, and is regarded as the official catechismal formula for the newly converted Saxons. It cannot be dated precisely, but it is now generally thought likely that it would have been used after the conversion of Widukind in 785. The Saxons are clearly regarded as still heathen or newly converted, for they are required to renounce specifically and by name their gods Thunaer, Uuoden, and Saxnot. Apart from the second Merseburg Charm this is the only occurrence in OHG or OS writings of the god Wodan. **The Frankish Baptismal Vow** (*Das fränkische Taufgelöbnis*),[3] being intended for a nation in which the Church

---

[1] See *Poetae Saxonis Annalium de Gestis Caroli Magni Imperatoris Libri V*, in *MGH, Poetae Latini Aevi Carolini* iv. i (1899), Bk. ii, l. 110.

[2] *Kl. ahd. Spdmr.* iii; *MSD* li; *Ahd. Lb.* xvi. 2. Facsimile: G. Könnecke, *Bilderatlas zur Geschichte der deutschen Nationallitteratur* (Marburg, 1898), p. 8. See A. Leitzmann, *PBB* 25 (1900) 567–86; 26 (1901) 573–4; J. Meier, ibid. 317–18; Th. von Grienberger, ibid. 47 (1923) 450–2.

[3] *MSD* lii; *Kl. ahd. Spdmr.* iv; *Ahd. Lb.* xvi. i. Facsimiles: *Schrifttafehln* 8; Enneccerus 6.

was already established, does not mention the names, though there is a reference to heathen practices.[1] The language of the Saxon vow has been explained by Agathe Lasch as a translation from the Latin formula made by an English missionary, with the assistance of a High German model, who was attempting to write in the language of the Saxons among whom he had been commissioned to work.[2]

Both texts as preserved in the manuscripts are later copies. The Saxon vow is preserved in an early ninth-century manuscript, Palatinus 577 of the Vatican Library, which contains a collection of theological excerpts. The Frankish vow is preserved in the ninth-century theological manuscript of the Merseburg Cathedral Library which also contains the *Merseburg Charms* (no. 136) and in a marginal entry in a copy of M. Goldast's *Alemannicarum Rerum Scriptores*, which is now in the Bayerische Staatsbibliothek in Munich, and was made shortly after 1607 by one Dionysius Campius from a Speyer manuscript now lost. Steinmeyer holds that the original dialect was Rhenish Franconian.

Another Saxon baptismal vow recorded by a seventeenth-century scholar of Cologne concludes as though it were a charm with the direction: 'Suffla in faciem et dic hanc orationem: Exi ab eo immunde spiritus et redde honorem deo vivo et vero.' The heathen gods are not mentioned.[3]

Charles the Great issued regulations for the training of the clergy and also instructions to guide them in the performance of their duties. His edicts are called *Capitula* or *Capitularia* because of the division into chapters or sections. Ehrismann, *Litg.* 1, § 54, prints extracts from some of these, including one known as the *Admonitio Generalis* of 23 March 789 (March was the traditional time for the national assembly), and there exists an OHG text known as the **Exhortatio ad Plebem Christianam,** a sermon or exhortation connected, no doubt, with Charles's legislation of the

---

[1] Two poems printed in *MGH Poetae Latini Aevi Carolini* 1. 50–2 are interesting in this connection. No. xiii, *Versus Petri*, refers to the proposed baptism of a heathen, 'pompiferi Sigifrit . . . / Impia pestiferi nunc regni sceptra tenentis' (ll. 17–18), and no. xiv, *Versus Pauli Diaconi*, refers to the heathen gods: 'Si satagam Sigifrid truculentum cernere vultum, / Vix perpendo aliquod utilitatis opus' (ll. 17–18), 'Sin minus, adveniat manibus post terga revinctis / Nec illi auxilio Thonar et Waten erunt' (ll. 35–6).

[2] *Neuphil. Mitt.* 36 (1935) 92–133.

[3] *Ahd. Lb.* xvi. 2. i; G. Frenken, *ZfdA* 71 (1934) 125–7.

years 802–12.[1] The People of the congregation (*ir chindo liupostun*) are solemnly warned that it is their duty to be familiar with the articles of the Christian faith, which contain a great mystery in a few simple words, and with the prayers, and to see that their children receive instruction therein. If they fail to do so, they must answer for it at the Day of Judgement.

There are two manuscripts, one of which is in Kassel[2] and the other in Munich,[3] both of the ninth century, Bavarian in dialect and based on the same faulty archetype. The Old High German text is translated from a Latin original which accompanies it in both manuscripts, in the Kassel manuscript in parallel columns and in the Munich manuscript on the opposite page. The translation is close but not slavish.

A result, perhaps, of the order in the *Admonitio Generalis* of 789 that the congregations were to be taught to understand the Lord's Prayer and the Creed, is the Alemannic translation preserved on some leaves bound up with the St. Gall manuscript of the OHG *Abrogans*, and therefore known as the **St. Galler Paternoster und Credo.**[4] The hand is of the late eighth century, almost contemporary, therefore, with the text. Some unintelligent mistranslations (*kiscaft himiles ende erda*, i.e. 'creatorem' read as 'creaturam'; 'Pontio Pilato' read as 'potentia Pilati', which gave rise to *in kiuualtiu Pilates*; *urlaz suntikero* for *sunteono*) show that the full benefit of the reforms had not yet manifested itself.

Another translation of the Lord's Prayer accompanied by an explanation is preserved in two Bavarian manuscripts of the ninth century, both of which are now in Munich.[5] It is called the **Freisinger Paternoster**[6] from the monastery where the older and better manuscript was discovered (the other came from St. Emmeram in Regensburg). The Freising manuscript has some older forms (*intfengun, o* beside *uo* for Gmc. $\bar{o}$) which suggest that it was copied from an original written about 800–20, and the script is not later than 825. The St. Emmeram manuscript is of

---

[1] *MSD* LIV; *Kl. ahd. Spdmr.* IX; *Ahd. Lb.* X; Enneccerus 32 and 33; Petzet–Glauning 2; Könnecke, p. 9.
[2] MS. Theol. 4°; 24 of the Landesbibliothek.
[3] Clm. 6244.
[4] *MSD* LVII; *Kl. ahd. Spdmr.* V; *Ahd. Lb.* VI. Facsimiles: *Schrifttafeln* 2, Enneccerus 18–20.
[5] Clm. 6330 and Clm. 14510.
[6] *MSD* lv; *Kl. ahd. Spdmr.* VIII; *Ahd. Lb.* XII; Enneccerus, 29 and 30; Petzet–Glauning, 3a and 3b.

the late ninth or even early tenth century. The technique of the translation is reminiscent of the glosses. Each sentence of the Latin is followed by a translation and a short commentary in German, as though it were being expounded by a teacher. The translation follows closely the Latin order of the words, but this is not necessarily a sign of incompetence, as the explanation, though undistinguished in style, is written in quite normal German. The text in the St. Emmeram manuscript is a shortened and modernized, but inferior version.

A volume of 175 leaves now in Wolfenbüttel,[1] formerly in Weissenburg (Wissembourg in Alsace), which unites in one binding five, or six, ninth-century manuscripts of miscellaneous Latin theological matter, has preserved also a few lines of the *Georgics*, and, on fols. 149*b* and 152*b*, some OHG texts in a language which may have been that of the monastery of Weissenburg as it was before the modernizing reforms of Otfrid, who wrote his *Evangelienbuch* there between 865 and 870. These are the German text of the Lord's Prayer followed by an interpretation sentence by sentence; then comes a list of deadly sins in Latin with a word-for-word German translation,[2] the German texts of the Apostles' Creed, the Athanasian Creed, and the Gloria in Excelsis. The five texts are known collectively as the **Weissenburg Catechism**.[3] All the pieces are written by the same hand, but there are several instances of differences of spelling and of variety of grammatical forms, as well as of different translations of the same expressions. Steinmeyer has listed some of the differences between different sections, and it is now thought that the copyist used translations by different individuals, united them, and made some attempt at ironing out the differences.[4] Examples are the diphthong *uo* beside the *ua* characteristic of the area, the first person plural ending -*em* besides -*mes*, the spellings *heilogo* and *heilago*. There are also differences of style, but these could be, at least in part, due to the nature of the subject matter. The translation of the Lord's Prayer and the commentary read smoothly, but in the Athanasian Creed,

---

[1] Herzogliche Bibliothek. Codex Wissenburgensis 91.

[2] Lists of deadly sins are based ultimately on the Epistle to the Galatians 5: 19–21.

[3] *MSD* LVI; *Kl. ahd. Spdmr.* VI; *Ahd. Lb.* XIII. Facsimiles: *Schrifttafeln*, Enneccerus 21–8. See R.-M. S. Heffner, *JEGPh* 40 (1941) 545–54 and 41 (1942) 194–200.

[4] *Kl. ahd. Spdmr.*, p. 36.

where the thought is more esoteric, there is more slavish adherence to the Latin model, e.g. *untaruuesenter* for 'subsistens' and *ungiscaffan fater, ungiscaffan sun, ungiscaffan endi ther heilogo geist* for 'increatus pater, increatus filius, increatus et spiritus sanctus', where the emphatic 'et' is rendered *endi*.

Several linguistic features, such as the retention of the diphthong *au*, of the initial *h* before consonant, final *-m* in inflexional endings, retention of the post-consonantal *j* as *e* in such words as *willeo*, indicate a period at the beginning of the ninth century. Certain features in the *Catechism* have appeared to some scholars to indicate that it was a direct result of the *Admonitio Generalis* of 789; in particular Scherer[1] drew attention to the common omission of 'impudicitia' from the list of deadly sins, but against that, the Catechism has in addition two adjectives 'obstinatus' *einuuillig*, and 'anxius' *angustenter*, following 'inuidia' *abunst*, and 'homicidia' *manslagon*, which are neither in the *Admonitio* nor in the Epistle to the Galatians (5:19-21), which is the ultimate source. Further, the *Admonitio* ordains the use of the Gloria Patri, but the *Catechism* substitutes the Gloria in Excelsis. In view, however, of the clearly early date of the work and its general conformity to the requirements of the *Admonitio*, there can be little doubt that it was inspired by that or similar ordinances of about A.D. 800. The work as a whole is greatly superior to the almost contemporary St. Gall *Paternoster and Credo*. It is worthy of note that both of the current translations of 'spiritus sanctus' are used: *heilago geist* is used exclusively in the Athanasian Creed, where it occurs frequently, *wiho adum* in the Gloria, and both in the Apostles' Creed.[2]

All the king's orders to the clergy would have been in vain had he not provided the Church with financial support. Two charters preserved in the Reichsarchiv in Munich record a gift of land at Hamelburg in Bavaria to the monastery of Fulda on 7 January 777. One is entirely in Latin, the other, a unique document, called **Die Hamelburger Markbeschreibung** is written partly in Latin and partly in German.[3] The style of writing in the document, a Carolingian minuscule of the time of Louis the Pious, and the linguistic

---

[1] *MSD* vol. II. 340.

[2] On the substitution under Anglo-Saxon influence of *heilag* and *geist* for *wih* and *âtum* see W. Braune, *PBB* 43 (1918) 398–409.

[3] *MSD* LXIII; *Kl. ahd. Spdmr.* XII; *Ahd. Lb.* II. 3; E. E. Stengel, *Urkundenbuch des Klosters Fulda* I (Marburg 1913) 151–4, with detailed geographical description of the boundary and identification of some of the points.

forms (with the vowels *ou, eo, uo,* and the *p* in *Perenfirst*) would be consonant with its being a copy of the original made in Fulda about 820.[1]

The form is as follows: firstly, in Latin, the date with the name and style of the assignor, the name and style of the assignee, the names of the officials who carried out the transaction, and the names of the witnesses. It is dated the third year of the reign of the most pious King Charles. The Latin document has 'anno nono et tertio regni nostri' (the ninth year from 768, when, on the death of Pippin the Short he inherited part of the kingdom, and third year from 774, when he visited the Pope at Rome, though he was not crowned Emperor until 800). The assignee was the Abbot Sturmi, who took possession on 8 October 777, receiving the land from Counts Nidhart and Heimo and two royal vassals (*vasallos dominicos*), Finnold and Gunthram, in the presence of twenty-one witnesses: Hruodmunt, Fastolf, Uuesant, Uuigant, Sigibot, Suuid-beraht, Sigo, Hasmar, Suuidger, Elting, Egihelm, Geruuig, Attumar, Bruning, Engilberaht, Leidrat, Siginand, Adalman, Amalberaht, Lantfrid, Eggiolt. Then comes the body of the charter. After the nobles had sworn to render a true account of their wealth, the bounds were marked. The names of the boundary places are given in German, with descriptions such as *caput* (source of brook) sometimes in Latin, sometimes in German. The boundary ran past the sources of brooks, a deep pit, the Perenfirst, a stony hill, some hill streams, a lake surrounded by limes, the hill of oaks, and an elm which was presumably a familiar landmark.

A delimitation of the boundaries of Würzburg was made in the twelfth year of Charles's reign 'sub die II Idus Octobris' (14 October 779). It exists in two differing versions, known as **Die Würzburger Markbeschreibungen,** one in Latin with German words interpolated and many German names of witnesses, the other entirely in German. They have been entered by a good hand of the early eleventh century on the first and last pages of a very beautiful ninth-century manuscript of the Gospels, now at Würzburg. The Latin–German version is more elaborate than the other, but it includes only a portion of the boundary, namely that part west of the Main. The German version contains the whole boun-

---

[1] *Monumenta Paleographica. Denkmäler der Schreibkunst des Mittelalters,* ed. A. Chroust (Munich, 1902–), vol. I, fasc. 5, no. 7. See G. Baesecke, *ZfdA* 58 (1921) 275.

dary, but it is not possible to reconcile the whole of its version of the boundary west of the Main with that given in the Latin–German version. The German version contains no date, the names of the witnesses do not coincide, and the relationship of the two is not clear. Scherer suggested that the Latin–German version was an official correction of the other.[1] Among the names of witnesses may be noticed: Otfrid, Dancrat, Sigifrid, Ortwin, Ermanarich, Hiltiberaht, Folcger.[2]

To the economical practice of using every available blank space on the parchment we owe the preservation of such unique texts as the *Hildebrandslied*, the *Muspilli*, and the two prescriptions known as **Die Basler Rezepte** which were entered by three scribes in the middle of an eighth-century manuscript containing part of Isidor's *De Ordine Creaturarum*. The manuscript is in the University Library, Basle.[3] The script of the prescriptions is insular, with some early Carolingian minuscule features.

The first prescription is in Latin with an expanded German version (not a translation) following. Nine or ten ingredients including myrrh, sulphur, pepper, red and white incense, and fennel are to be rubbed down separately in wine, mixed, and allowed to stand fermenting for three nights. The patient is to fast for forty days. He is not to wash his eyes, nor is he to eat anything on the day on which it was gathered or cooked, or an egg on the day it is laid, or to drink water on the day it is drawn, nor is he to wash therein. He is to take a dose in the morning when the attack comes on, and another at night when he goes to bed. He is not to be alone by day or to sleep alone by night, and he shall do nothing except in the presence of the person who gives him the medicine and attends him. If he gets another attack when the first bottle is nearly finished, let a second be prepared. The purpose of the prescription is not clear. Koegel took it to be a cure for fever; Steinmeyer, seeing no reason why a fever patient, especially if allowed to get up during

---

[1] *MSD* vol. II³. 361. The course of the boundary had been studied in detail by K. Dinklage in 'Würzburg im Frühmittelalter' in *Vor- und Frühgeschichte der Stadt Würzburg*. Mainfränkische Heimatkunde 3 (Würzburg, 1951), pp. 119–32, with a map.

[2] *MSD* LXIV; *Kl. ahd. Spdmr.* XXIV; *Ahd. Lb.* II. 4; *Monumenta Paleographica* (see p. 114, n. 1, above), vol. I, fasc. 5, no. 10.

[3] *MSD* LXII; *Kl. ahd. Spdmr.* VII. Facsimile: Enneccerus. 17. See R. Koegel, *Litteraturgeschichte* II. 497–9; G. Baesecke, *ZfdA* 58 (1921) 277; Th. von Grienberger, *PBB* 45 (1921) 404 ff.; G. Baesecke, *Voc. St. Galli*, pp. 114 ff.; R.–M. S. Heffner, *JEGPh* 46 (1947) 248–353.

the day, should be constantly watched, suggested that it was meant for epileptics. Both the Latin and the German texts are in a bad condition, and the interpretation is uncertain at several points.

The second prescription is even more difficult to decipher and therefore to interpret. It is a remedy for cancer: salt, soap, and the slime (?) of oyster-shells have to be heated (?) and mixed together. After the wound has been rubbed with an old rag[1] until it bleeds freely, the mixture is to be applied, but apparently without letting the wound be wetted (perhaps as a poultice). Then the wound is to be anointed with white of egg and honey.

The text is in an even worse condition than that of the first prescription. The scribe has placed a full stop or a semicolon after almost every word. He has sometimes divided the words incorrectly (e.g. *alz. esamene*), and he has perpetrated some strange errors of spelling (*lot þet* from OE *oðþe it* = OHG *oddo iz*, *itzs* for *iz*, *daez* for *daz*, *hounog* for *honac*, etc.). From these errors and the insular script it has been argued that the writer was an Anglo-Saxon endeavouring without success to translate from his own tongue into High German, of which he had an imperfect knowledge. Others regard it as a copy made by an Anglo-Saxon from a High German original, on the grounds that the Anglo-Saxon features are only superficial: the reference to oyster-shells cannot necessarily be regarded as evidence of maritime origin. The date would appear to be about 800.

Though the basis of the new culture was necessarily Latin, Charles understood the value of local institutions and of the native language. One of the principal sources of our knowledge of his life is the **Vita Caroli Magni** written by Alcuin's friend Einhard between 814, the year of Charles's death, and 821, when a copy is recorded in the catalogue of the monastery of the Reichenau.[2] Einhard lived from about 770 to 14 March 840. He was educated at Fulda. Between 791 and 796 he was transferred to the palace, and spent his life in the service of Charles and his descendants. He writes as an admirer of Charles, discreetly ignoring what he cannot

[1] G. Baesecke, *Voc. St. Galli*, p. 116, compares this with a tenth-century OE prescription, and suggests that the word *uuaiffu* here rendered 'rag', which is unknown in German, is due to a misunderstanding of *sapan* 'soap', the *s* having been misread as the OE *w* rune.

[2] Some scholars believe that this is a later entry into the catalogue and date the *Vita* 830. A convenient edition is H. W. Garrod and R. B. Mowat, *Einhard's Life of Charlemagne* (Oxford, 1915).

praise. Einhard's *Vita* was used together with supplementary sources by the anonymous Saxon cleric, who, about 890, composed the **Annalium de Gestis Caroli Magni Imperatoris Libri V**.[1] Both Einhard in a much-quoted passage in Chapter 29, and the Saxon in a passage which supplements Einhard,[2] state that Charles had collected and committed to writing the local laws of his realms, that he began a grammar of the native language and gave native names to the months and the winds.[3] Of special interest are the words of Einhard: 'Item barbara et antiquissima carmina, quibus veterum regum actus et bella canebantur, scripsit memoriaeque mandavit', and of the Saxon:

> Necnon quae veterum depromunt proelia regum
> Barbara mandavit carmina litterulis.

The word *barbarus* meant 'native', 'vernacular', 'non-Latin', as in Classical Greek all the world outside Greece was βάρβαρος γῆ· It occurs several times in the poem in this sense, e.g.

in aula

Nomen Heristalli dederat cui barbara lingua   (l. 317)

Barbaricae nomen linguae sermone vetustum   (l. 334),

and v. 19, where he says that the *barbara lingua* is overbold in attempting with its feeble powers the great task of recounting the glory of Charles. It alternates with *patrius*: 'Hos Northalbingos patrio sermone vocamus' (III. 371).

It is often assumed that by *barbara carmina* are meant the heroic lays, of which the *Hildebrandslied* is the sole surviving example in German, and which are regarded as the ultimate literary source of the MHG 'heroic' or 'popular' epics, such as the *Nibelungenlied* and the Dietrich epics. The collection has perished. (It is not likely to have included songs about the pagan gods, as does the corresponding Scandinavian collection, the *Edda*, for it would have been contrary to Charles's political and religious policy to encourage such interests.) It is also possible that the reference is to the more factual type of encomiastic poetry, of which the OHG *Ludwigslied* is an example. There is no reason why it should not have included both.

---

[1] *Poetae Saxonis Annalium de Gestis Caroli Magni Imperatoris Libri V, MGH, Poetae Latini Aevi Carolini* IV. 1 (1899).

[2] Op. cit., Book V, ll. 539–62.

[3] *Ahd. Lb.* III.

VIII

The Old High German Isidor Translation and the Monsee–Vienna Fragments

A GREAT contrast to the mechanical glossaries is the translation of the treatise *De Fide Catholica contra Judaeos* of Bishop Isidor of Seville,[1] commonly called the OHG **Isidor**.[2] There are two manuscript texts, one in Paris and the other in Vienna.

The *Isidor* is a unique document in the German literature of its period, for its unknown author surpassed in his knowledge of Latin and his command of the German language any other writer earlier than Notker, who appeared some 200 years later. He was still to a large extent bound by the Latin, but it must be borne in mind that he was creating a language for his purpose, and could do so only on the Latin model. The carefully planned system of orthography in the Paris manuscript is worthy of the translation. Like the *Tatian*, and the works of Otfrid and Notker, the *Isidor* is one of the most valuable standards of comparison we possess, so that the correct localization both of the translator and of the scribe would be of supreme historical importance. The early date is

---

[1] Died 636. His works are to be found in Migne, *Patrologia Latina*, vols. 81–4. The *Liber Etymologiarum*, a vast encyclopedia of religious and useful learning, was one of the most popular and influential books of the Middle Ages.

[2] *Der althochdeutsche Isidor. Facsimileausgabe des Pariser Codex nebst kritischem Text der Pariser und Monseer Bruchstücke mit Einleitung, grammatischer Darstellung und einem ausführlichen Glossar*, ed. G. A. Hench (Quellen und Forschungen 72, Strasbourg, 1893). This edition shows a facsimile of each leaf with the transcription on the opposite page. The most convenient edition is that of H. Eggers, *Der althochdeutsche Isidor. Nach der Pariser Handschrift und den Monseer Fragmenten neu herausgegeben*, Altdeutsche Textbibliothek 63 (Tübingen, 1964). A complete Latin–OHG glossary to the text is provided by H. Eggers, *Vollständiges lateinisch-althochdeutsches Wörterbuch zur althochdeutschen Isidor-Übersetzung* (Berlin, 1960). Extract: *Ahd. Lb.* VIII; facsimiles: *Schrifttafeln* 4.

evident, but, unlike these works, the *Isidor* is written in a form of German which it has so far been impossible to date and locate precisely. It is, however, clearly of great antiquity.[1]

The Paris manuscript (Cod. 2326 of the Bibliothèque nationale) contains the Latin and the German texts in parallel columns. The Latin is complete, but for the first chapter, on fols. 1–79*a*, but the German breaks off prematurely on fol. 22*a*; the columns left for it on fols. 22*b*–33*b* are a melancholy blank, and on fols. 34*a*–79*a* the Latin occupies both columns. Such sudden terminations of German texts in manuscripts are not uncommon. The loss of the rest of the *Isidor* is one of many similar little disasters, the causes of which can only be conjectured. Both the Latin and the German texts are copies, and were written by the same scribe in a Carolingian script of the late eighth or early ninth century with traces of the older style. See especially plate XV, ed. cit., where the three types of *a* are present. Fragments of the *Isidor* (the German text only) have been preserved in what was once a very beautiful but is now a sadly mutilated manuscript of the early ninth century, some leaves of which were found in the monastery of Monsee near Salzburg, and others in the K. K. Hofbibliothek, Vienna. They are therefore known as the **Monsee–Vienna Fragments** (*Die Monsee–Wiener Bruchstücke*), for brevity M.[2]

That the translation was made early in the period is clear from the language, but it is less easy than some other writings to date precisely. The principal signs of age are the vowels. The Germanic diphthong *au*, which developed into *ou* in the ninth century, remains unchanged, apart from six cases; Gmc. *ē* appears as *ea*, which usually develops further to *ia* or *ie* in the ninth century; and similarly the diphthong *eu*, which is represented in the ninth century by *io*, appears in the earlier form *eo*. These features alone would permit a dating in the earliest period of OHG; others, however, such as the change from Gmc *ō* to *uo* beside a few instances of *oo* and of *ai* to *ei*, seem to conflict with a very early dating. As it is not known where the translation was made and com-

---

[1] For an exhaustive study of the *Isidor* and related texts, and for a discussion of all the problems connected with them, see Klaus Matzel, *Untersuchungen zur Verfasserschaft, Sprache und Herkunft der althochdeutschen Übersetzungen der Isidor-Sippe*, Rheinisches Archiv 75 (Bonn, 1970); W. Haubrichs, 'Zum Stand der Isidorforschung', *ZfdPh* 94 (1975) 1–15.

[2] The monastery of Monsee or Mondsee was founded in 748 and dissolved in 1787.

mitted to writing, it is not possible to determine its date exactly from these vowel changes; but it is generally accepted that a date very shortly before the end of the eighth century is the most likely.

One of the most immediately striking features of the translation is its orthography. It appears at first sight to be complicated, and it is indeed more elaborate than anything else from the period. Close examination reveals that its elaboration is the result of a well-considered system which is designed to indicate, much more subtly than any other contemporary writing does, the actual spoken sounds. This orthographical system is only fully present in the Paris manuscript. Its principal features are as follows. A clear distinction is made between the affricate and the spirant which develop from Gmc. *t*: the affricate is written *z* initially and finally, but *tz* medially, whereas the spirant is written *zss* medially, but *zs* finally. Gmc. *þ* is written *dh* initially; medially after a vowel it is usually written *dh* but occasionally *d*. Gmc. *g* is written *g* before the middle and back vowels *a, o,* and *u,* but *gh* before the front vowels *i* and *e,* and *ch* in the prefix *gi-* (i.e. *chigheban, ghibis, gab*). *qu* is written *quh*; *k* is written *ch*; *b* remains unshifted but *t* occurs beside *d* (for WGmc. *d*). Apart from *quh, chi,* and *ch* for *k*, the development of consonants represented by these spellings would be reconcilable with a Rhenish Franconian origin, possibly with Middle Franconian, although there is no evidence of the final *t* in *dat, wat, it,* which is a characteristic of that dialect. Usually the occurrence of *ch* for Gmc. *k* is taken as a sign of Upper German origin, and similarly *quh* for *qu*; but it is difficult to reconcile such apparently Upper German forms with the decidedly Franconian character of the other consonants, and it has been suggested that these spellings do not represent the Upper German affricate, but that they are part of the peculiar orthographical system of the text and do not represent anything other than the Franconian pronunciation. It is, however, in certain morphological features that the Upper German characteristics are most clearly marked; the ending *-in* in the dative and genitive singular of masculine and neuter weak nouns is typically Upper German, although it is found in Franconian too, but the *-ōm, -ōt, -ōn* endings of the preterite plural of the weak verbs are distinctly Alemannic. It is not uncommon to find dialect mixtures in OHG texts, but they can often be satisfactorily explained. In the case of the Isidor translation, however, the situation is different: the quality of the translation is unique, and the care and consistency with which the whole is spelt are unique; both of which circumstances demand that we accept the language in which it is written as the genuine product of one place or one person.

In addition to the features mentioned so far, which would allow us to characterize the language of the *Isidor* as one which has the phonological system of Rhenish Franconian and the morphological system of Alemannic, there are others which are found in no other OHG texts from either area. These are: the apparently short stem vowel in the preterite of those strong verbs of class VII whose stem contains a nasal, e.g. *chifenc, arhenc*; the short preterite form *hapta* in lieu of the normal OHG *habēta*; the use of the pronoun *er* for the second person plural and *ir* for the third person singular masculine, corresponding respectively to normal OHG *ir* and *er*. The first two of these features seem to point away from OHG altogether, since phonologically equivalent forms are normal in OE and OS. They might, however, be morphological archaisms, since the OHG forms which correspond to those cited may well be due to analogy. The third feature too may be ancient, for we may reconstruct the Pr. Gmc. forms of the pronouns concerned as **jez* (2nd person plural) and **iz* (3rd person singular masculine, cf. Goth. *is*, Lat. *is-te*). The former is continued in OE and OS *gē* and perhaps in the unique form *ger* of the *Altdeutsche Gespräche* (see p. 102 above); unlike the OHG form, that of the *Isidor* kept the original vowel *e*, since there was no occasion for realignment within the paradigm, as there was in OHG. (The OHG paradigm is *ir, iuwih, iuwer, iu*, while that of the *Isidor* is *er, euuuih, — , eu*.) The pronoun *ir* similarly keeps its original vowel, while OHG *er* shows the same lowering ('breaking') to *e* as we find in the interrogative *hwer* (cf. Lat. *quis*, Greek *tis*, Sanskrit *kis*); in the *Isidor* the interrogative pronoun, however, presents no problem.

These features for which there are no parallels in Old High German do not, therefore, justify us in speaking of 'Low German influence', even though there may be Low German or Old English parallels.

It has been argued that the scriptorium whose practice accorded most closely to the *Isidor*, and where we might expect to find Franconian and Alemannic features side by side was Murbach.[1]

---

[1] G. Nutzhorn, *ZfdPh* 44 (1912) 265 ff.

For a long time it was generally agreed that no other place was more likely, both on the ground that this was the only place likely to have such a linguistic mixture and because of the importance of its monastery at the time when the translation is believed to have been made and the favour in which it was held by Alcuin, who also wrote on the Trinity. Although this view was so widely accepted, and for so long, the arguments are inconclusive and other suggestions have been made. A recent full-scale study has revealed on what insecure foundations the Murbach theory is based.[1] A view which has received much support is that the place of origin should be sought outside the German-speaking area as known from OHG literature, namely in Neustria, in the area where French was already being spoken but in which the Frankish aristocracy probably still spoke German. Those who defend this origin point out that the apparently Upper German consonants mentioned above are, in fact, regular Franconian consonants spelt according to Romance practice. The spelling *ch* would thus not represent the Upper German affricate, but be a relic of the old Merovingian orthography which, under Romance influence, used it before *i* and *e* to indicate the plosive quality of the sound instead of *c* or *k* (*c* before *i* and *e* at that time was used in Latin for the affricate *ts*). The use of *gh* before front vowels and *g* before back vowels is also a feature of Romance orthography.[2] The *quh* has been claimed as specifically characteristic of Murbach, and taken to be a spelling for the Upper German affricate, but the supporters of the 'West Franconian' view point out that *qhu* would be the more appropriate sign for the affricate, explaining *quh* in relation to the Romance tendency to prefix *g* to the bilabial *w* in loan-words from the Germanic languages (*werra* > *guerra*, etc.) and pointing out that in Italian charters *h* is inserted in such names as *Albu(h)in*, *Landu-(h)in*, *Gero(h)in* in order, apparently, to indicate this particular sound more precisely. The *w* of *quedan*, it is maintained, was bilabial and therefore the *h* was inserted, whereas *h* was not inserted after the labio-dental *w* in *suuebal* or *chidhuuingu*. The consistent use of *chi-* in the prefix (i.e. *ch* for *g* instead of for *k*) has been explained also as a survival of old Merovingian spelling practice. It is further pointed out that a similar practice seems to have prevailed in Lombardy, for Paul the Deacon regularly uses

[1] B. Kirchstein, *PBB* (Tübingen) 84 (1962) 5–122.
[2] Both *ch* and *gh* are used in this way in Italian.

-chis for *-gis* in names ending with this syllable, e.g. *Ratchis,
Witichis, Anschis, Arichis,* although he retains the *g* in names like
Agilulfus, Sigiprandus, Herminigildus, and also in *Gisa* and *Giselpert.*

The characteristic and consistent use of *zss* medially and *zs*
finally presents no problems of pronunciation: the signs are for the
voiceless spirant sound which occurs throughout the High German
area for the Gmc. voiceless plosive *t.* The problem is: why did such
an excellent sign for the spirant not find acceptance in Germany
(most writings use the same sign *z* for affricate and spirant) and
what was its origin. The nearest parallel known is in Langobardic,
where the dental spirant is spelt *s* or occasionally *ss,* and thus distinct from the affricate *z,* and it has been suggested that the *Isidor*
spelling is a combination of the usual German *z* with these Langobardic signs. Langobardic influence on the Isidor translation would
also be consonant with West Franconian origin.[1]

One further feature of the spelling calls for comment, and that
is the indication of vowel length; the vowel is doubled as a sign of
length, but in closed syllables only. This can also be interpreted
as a sign of West Franconian origin, for in Old French the short
accented vowels had already been lengthened in open syllables
and there would, therefore, be no need for a Romance scribe to
indicate the length except in closed syllables.

The arguments presented above, with others, are to be found
in the article by W. Bruckner[2] in which he argued in detail in
favour of a West Franconian origin, thus following up a tentative
suggestion made a few years earlier by E. Sievers, using his own
very personal methods.[3] Bruckner argues that the quality of the
translation is comparable to that made by Ulfilas and that, like
Ulfilas, the translator must have been fully conversant with two
or—if one regards the early French of the time as a separate language—three languages, and have grown up in an area where they
were spoken. 'Der Verfasser hat sein Latein nicht mühsam gelernt,
wie die Mönche von St. Gallen oder Fulda, er kann's.' He does not
attempt to specify a place, except to say that it will have been

[1] It is worth noting that one other text, viz. the *Ludwigslied,* uses the graphy
zs (e.g. *heizsit*) though not *zss.* This is another text of probably West Frankish
provenance.
[2] 'Zur Orthographie der althochdeutschen Isidorübersetzung und zur Frage
nach der Heimat des Denkmals', in *Festschrift Gustav Binz* (Basle, 1935),
pp. 69–83.
[3] *PBB* 52 (1928) 171–208, esp. 197 and 203–8.

one of high cultural attainment—with which everyone has always agreed—and that it was probably one which was in close connection with the Palace School. This last view had been expressed by Müllenhoff many years earlier.[1] This West Franconian hypothesis has found favour, although it is open to the objection that nothing which is known for certain to be 'West Franconian' has been preserved, and that it is in any case a very nebulous conception. Agreement with the theory, combined with some scepticism, seems to be expressed by G. Nordmeyer:

> It seems futile to indulge in new speculations on localizing the *Isidor* dialect, classifying attempts might be content with saying that the *Isidor* differs from East Franconian as well as South Franconian (*T* and *O*), so that a very general term like West Franconian seems most appropriate, with boundaries relatively open to the south, west, and north.[2]

Others, while still rejecting Murbach, do not choose to go so far west, into completely unknown territory. Müllenhoff had thought of the 'court language' as being based on Rhenish Franconian, and now W. Mitzka has expressed the view that the language of the *Isidor* is that of the upper classes of Middle Franconian.[3] H. de Boor draws attention to the high quality of translation noticeable in the *Weissenburg Catechism* and adds a tentative word in support of the possibility suggested by R. Koegel that one should look to Lotharingia, in particular to Metz.[4]

The problem of the place of origin remains unsolved, except that no one has suggested a place other than in the Rhineland or to the west of it. Common to all suggestions is the view, either expressed or implied, that the translation must have been made in a place where the standard of scholarship was high, from which it is a small step to the assumption that that place was in close contact with the royal court. Alcuin himself wrote on the question of the nature of the Trinity, but there is no evidence to support a view that he was responsible for this translation; in fact, he expresses views which differ markedly from those of Isidor.[5] Discussions on these and related matters were taking place in

---

[1] *MSD*, p. xxiii.   [2] *PMLA* 73 (1958) 13–35.
[3] 'Mittelfränkische Denkmäler der althochdeutschen Literatur', *ZfMaf* 30 (1963) 31–6.
[4] See R. Koegel, *PBB* 9 (1884) 301 ff.; id., *AfdA* 19 (1893) 218–35; id., *Litg.* ii. 497–9; Matzel, op. cit., esp. pp. 469 ff.
[5] H. Kowalski-Fahrun, *PBB* 47 (1923) 312 ff.

Germany in the last years of the eighth century, and Alcuin's work was written in 802. The language of the Isidor translation points to its having been made in this period.

The above-mentioned *Monsee–Vienna Fragments* include in addition to the *Isidor* some portions of a translation of St. Matthew's Gospel and a number of minor pieces.[1] At the beginning they show some signs of the most characteristic features of the *Isidor*, namely *dh*, *gh*, *quh*; in addition, some of the vowel forms are the same: *ai* has become *ei*, but *au* is retained, as are also the inflexional ending *-m* and the initial *h* in the combinations *hl*, *hn*, *hr*, *hw*. In general, however, the linguistic picture is Bavarian: *d* has become *t*, *th* usually *d*, the *-in* endings of the genitive and dative singular of masculine and neuter weak nouns are, as would be expected in Bavaria, retained, while the Alemannic verb endings *-ōm*, *ōt*, *-ōn*, have been replaced by *-um*, *-ut*, *-un*; *b*, however, is generally retained and is only occasionally replaced by the Bavarian *p*. The manuscript was written in Carolingian minuscule early in the ninth century and it is always regarded as a Bavarian transcript made at that time of the older original. The *ʒss* and *ʒs* do not occur. It is impossible to determine the exact relationship between the *Isidor* and the *Fragments*, but it seems likely that they are very closely connected and may well have come from the same school. If one compares the Matthew translation with that in the *Tatian*, the higher quality of the former is evident; the order of the words shows the influence of the Latin, but the translator allowed himself more freedom in the choice of words and phrases, and did not hesitate to insert words in order to make the meaning clear.

It is true that the *Isidor*, which contains all the Old Testament evidence in favour of the divinity of Jesus, and the Gospel of St. Matthew, which gives His life and teaching, would together supply all that was needed for the instruction of those who were appointed to conduct a mission to the heathen, and so would go well together, and may therefore have been produced at the same time and place, perhaps at a centre for the training of missionaries or other instructors, but such speculations unsupported by documentary evidence must remain undemonstrable.[2]

[1] The fragments other than those of the *Isidor* have been printed by G. A. Hench in *The Monsee Fragments* (Strasbourg, 1890). See also *MSD* LIX–LX, and *Ahd. Lb.* IX, where parallel passages from the *Tatian* are given. Facsimile: *Schrifttafeln* 5. See also Ehrismann, 52.

[2] See G. Baesecke, *Abrogans*, pp. 51 f.

IX

The *Wessobrunn Prayer* and the *Muspilli*

B Y a remarkable chance there has been preserved in the literature of the Old High German period one example of each of several types. There is one theological treatise in prose, the *Isidor*; one gospel harmony in prose, the *Tatian*; one gospel narrative in alliterative verse, the *Heliand*; one gospel harmony with exegetical commentary in rhyming verse, the *Evangelienbuch*; one heroic lay in alliterative verse, the *Hildebrandslied*; one account of a historical event in rhyming verse, the *Ludwigslied*; and one life of a saint in rhyming verse, the *Georgslied*. In addition to these, there is one text, the *Wessobrunner Gebet*, which treats of the Creation, and another, the *Muspilli*, which describes the Last Things. Both these last are composed in alliterative verse, and it will be convenient to deal with them together, even though the former was composed probably more than half a century before the latter.

The mystery of the origin of the world has always been the subject of speculation. Minstrels sang of it before Dido and Aeneas,[1] and before Hrothgar when he feasted with his warriors on the mead-bench in Heorot.[2] Whatever pagan German hymns to the divine Orderer of the universe may have existed are lost. *Beowulf* cannot be cited as evidence, for it belongs to the Christian era in England. There may be Christian influence even in the Icelandic *Vǫluspá* ('The Sybil's Prophecy'), which is ostensibly a pagan account of the beginning and end of the world.[3] The Creation was

---

[1] *Aeneid* i. 742–6.   [2] *Beowulf* 90–8.
[3] Ed. G. Neckel, *Edda. Die Lieder des Codex Regius nebst verwandten Denkmälern*, 3rd edn. revised by Hans Kuhn (Heidelberg, 1962). See G. Turville-Petre, *Origins of Icelandic Literature* (Oxford, 1953), pp. 55–64. A convenient (though necessarily free) rendering into modern German alliterative verse is given in *Die Edda. Die wesentlichen Gesänge der altnordischen Götter- und Heldendichtung* (Düsseldorf/Cologne, 1956).

an important item in the teaching of the missionaries in heathen parts. Bishop Daniel of Winchester, writing to Boniface, warns him not to underrate the intelligence of the heathen, as he will find them not unskilled in controversy. The letter reveals two active missionaries planning a campaign, the older man advising the younger, from his experience, on the methods and the arguments to be used. Daniel stresses the importance of tact. He warns Boniface not to vex the natives by ridiculing or flatly denying their beliefs, but counsels him to meet them on their own ground, arguing courteously and seriously in order to convince them that their ideas are fallacious. With regard to the Creation, let Boniface ask them whom they believe to have controlled the world before the gods existed, if they think matter to be eternal and merely to have been arranged by the gods. Let him ask further whether they believe that gods and goddesses were begotten and born like men and women, and, if so, when and why did they cease to multiply, or, if they are still multiplying and immortal, how great do they imagine their number must be by now.

The Creation is the subject of a short Old High German text known as **Das Wessobrunner Gebet.** This title has been in general use since the text was edited by the brothers Grimm in 1812. It is found in a Latin codex which was once at Wessobrunn in Bavaria and is now in Munich.[1] The codex itself can be dated as belonging to the period about 800 on palaeographical evidence, but the German text appears to be a copy of something earlier. The original is thought to date from some time in the second half of the eighth century. The hand is a clearly legible Carolingian minuscule of the late eighth or early ninth century. The Tironian abbreviation which was widely used in Anglo-Saxon manuscripts for the copulative conjunction is found together with the English rune ⥇ ; since the word *forgāpi* appears as *for*⥇*pi* it is assumed that where the rune appears elsewhere for the verbal prefix beginning with *g*, the form intended is *ga-*, the vowel of which is characteristic of the early Bavarian dialect. Another Anglo-Saxon trait may be the 'e caudata' in *marẹo*, which would be more properly used for the *e* in the next word *seo*. The dialect of the text is clearly Bavarian in most respects: Gmc. *b-* and *-b-* appear as *p* (e.g. *pereg, galaupa* for E. Franc. *berg, giloubo*); Gmc. *g* appears as *c*

---

[1] Clm. 22053 (Wessobr. 53, Cim. 20) of the Staatsbibliothek, Munich. Printed *MSD* 1; *Kl. ahd. Spdmr.* 11; *Ahd. Lb.* xxix. Facsimile: *Schrifttafeln* 14.

or *k* (*cot, manake* for E. Franc. *got, manage*); Gmc. ō remains undiphthongized (*coot, uuistom* for E. Franc. *guot, uuistuom*). The
very early date is indicated by the fact that Gmc. *au* remains unchanged (*paum* for later Bavarian *poum*, E. Franc. *boum*). The fact
that the accusative singular masculine of the *n*-declension ends in
-*on* (usually taken to be the Middle German equivalent of Upper
German -*un*) in the word *uuilleon* might be adduced as evidence
of non-Bavarian provenance, but we know too little about OHG
morphology to be confident on this point. The word *dat*, which
does not appear to be Bavarian, will be discussed later.

The manuscript in which the German text is entered is a kind of
scrap-book or collection of fragments of useful knowledge in the
liberal arts. Our text is included in the section on *Arithmetica*, for
its subject, the Creation, had a bearing upon the calendar, which
was a province of that art. All the extracts have headings, and that
of our text is *De poeta*. This has usually been taken to mean 'by the
poet' or 'by a poet', indicating that what follows is, unlike everything else in the manuscript, composed in verse. It has, however,
been suggested[1] that this is most probably a Latinization of the
Greek ποιητής as used by Plato in the *Timaeus* to signify the
creator of the world. The title might therefore mean 'Concerning
the Creator'. Such Latinizations of Greek words were not uncommon, and the manuscript contains glosses showing that the
compilers had some knowledge of Greek.

The German text is written continuously as though it were prose,
but there are punctuation marks which seem to have metrical
significance. Even if these were absent, it would not be difficult to
recognize, in the first part of the text, the pairs of verses which
combine to make Germanic alliterative lines. It is equally clear
that not all the lines are complete, although there are no gaps in the
manuscript text; the indications of lacunae in modern editions
are based on the agreed requirements of alliterative verse (though
these, in turn, are derived from the study of Old English and Old
Norse usage, which may not be entirely relevant to the few fragments of verse preserved in High German).

The last section, beginning with the words *cot almahtico*, does
not obviously fall into alliterative lines and is usually held to be

---

[1] See W. Perrett, *London Medieval Studies* 1 (1938) 134 ff. See also
A. Schirokauer, *PMLA* 65 (1950) 317 f. where a similar suggestion is made,
apparently independently, with some additional supporting evidence.

composed in prose.[1] It is common practice to refer to the section concluding with the words *cot heilac* as Section A and to the rest, beginning with the words *cot almahtico* as Section B.

If we assume that some words have been omitted—and it is an assumption that has been challenged[2]—we can scan the first five lines satisfactorily according to what we think was Germanic technique. In the passage that follows (from *Do dar niuuiht niuuas* to *enti cot heilac*) we can find four alliterative lines, though some of the alliterating words are difficult to identify. Between the first five and the next four lines (after which the so-called 'prose' section, called B, begins) there is a further difference which may be loosely called one of style. In the first five lines each half-line (or 'verse') has a high degree of autonomy, whereas in the next four the half-lines show more dependence on one another. The scribe uses an uncial *D* for the first word (*Do*) of l. 6, and an uncial *C* for the first word of Section B (*Cot*), but it is doubtful whether this has great significance, since he uses an uncial *D* for the second *Dat* (l. 2).

The following literal translation may be taken to render the sense of Section A:

This I heard tell among men of marvels the greatest, that earth was not, nor sky above, nor tree . . . nor hill was; (there was) not any . . .[3] nor did the sun shine,[4] nor did the moon give light, nor the fair[5] sea. Then there was nought of ends or boundaries, and then was the one almighty God, the most generous (*or* mildest) of men, and there were also many with him, glorious spirits. And the holy God . . .

Here the 'verse' ends abruptly before what presumably would have been the act of creation. There now follows, without a break

---

[1] The brothers Grimm treated it as verse in their edition, and in recent years attempts have been made to identify an alliterative pattern. See E. R. Friesse, *MLR* 50 (1955) 317–19, L. Seiffert, *Med. Æv.* 31 (1962) 1–13, and, most recently, P. F. Ganz, 'Die Zeilenaufteilung im "Wessobrunner Gebet"', *Festschrift für Ingeborg Schröbler* (Tübingen, 1973). Ganz traces the history of the controversy and examines the implications of the punctuation; he concludes that the whole text is composed in verse.

[2] See Seiffert, op. cit.

[3] Normal OHG usage requires a verb in this half-line (4a) since *ni* is not used as a conjunction anywhere except (perhaps) here and in l. 6 of our text (in the phrase *enteo ni uuenteo*). The normal OHG conjunction meaning 'nor' is *noh*.

[4] The manuscript reading is *stein*, but this is usually emended to *scein* 'shone'.

[5] On this rendering of the difficult word *mareo* see below, p. 134.

in the manuscript text, the prayer to the Creator which has earned the whole text its traditional title and which may be rendered as follows:

God Almighty, who madest heaven and earth and didst grant so many boons to men, grant to me true faith in thy mercies, and goodwill, knowledge, and understanding, and power to resist devils and avoid evil and do Thy will.

It is generally accepted that there is a stylistic difference between the first five and the next four lines of verse, the terseness of the former contrasting with the relative syntactical complexity of the latter. It has also been maintained that this 'stylistic' difference corresponds with a difference in content. If it is really true that the Germans of the pre-Christian era believed that matter was eternal, it is difficult to reconcile the depiction of the primeval void found in the first five lines with the positive account of the existence of God and His glorious spirits in the next four. However, our knowledge of the heathen beliefs of the continental Germans is too uncertain to allow of even the most tentative opinion.

The strongest support for the view that the first five lines of our poem are based on pre-Christian beliefs is the close verbal similarity between them and strophes 3 and 4 of the Old Icelandic *Vǫluspá* ('The Sybil's Prophecy'):

Ár var alda,   þat er Ymir bygði,
vara sandr né sær   né svalar unnir;
iǫrð fannz æva   né upphiminn,
gap var ginnunga,   enn gras hvergi.

Áðr Burs synir   biǫðom um ypþo,
þeir er miðgarð,   mæran, scópo;
sól scein sunnan   á salar steina,
þá var grund gróin   grœnom lauki.

It was early in the ages that Ymir lived. There was neither sand nor sea, nor cool waves; there was no earth nor sky above. There was a great void, and grass nowhere, until the sons of Bur lifted the land, they who made the fair earth. The sun shone from the south on the stones of the edifice (i.e. the newly formed world) and the earth was covered with green plants.

Apart, however, from the fact that the Icelandic poem is thought to contain Christian influence and that therefore parallels found there are not necessarily heathen features, we need not go beyond the Bible in order to find a source for all the objects mentioned in the German text. In fact, all but one occur in Genesis 1: 1–16: *ero* 'earth' and *ufhimil* = 'caelum et terram' (v. 1), *der marₑo seo* = 'maria' (v. 10), *paum* = 'lignum pomiferum' (v. 11), *sunna* and *mano* = 'luminare maius et luminare minus' (v. 16). The one object not found in this passage of Genesis, namely *pereg*, occurs in Psalm 89 (A.V. 90): 2: 'Priusquam montes fierent aut formaretur terra et orbis a saeculo et usque in saeculum tu es deus'; moreover the word *berg* is conveniently associated in alliteration with *boum*, as for example in *Heliand*, l. 5534, and *Muspilli*, l. 51.

In the second sentence, ll. 6–9, we are told that there were with God many glorious spirits; these may be the angels, for in Psalm 103 (A.V. 104): 3 we read 'qui facis angelos tuos spiritus', which Notker rendered *du dîne geista machôst poten* 'who makest thy spirits messengers (angels)'. This reference to the spirits which were with God before the world was created probably arose from Genesis 1: 2: 'et spiritus Dei ferebatur super aquas'. The strangest phrase in this sentence is *manno miltisto* 'most merciful (*or* generous) of men', used in apposition to *der eino almahtico cot*. This phrase has an Old English equivalent, *manna mildust*, used at the end of *Beowulf* (l. 3181) in praise of the hero, the perfect king. This suggests an anthropomorphic conception of God the Creator which would have been appropriate to the Son. It seems as though here poetic licence has prevailed over theological accuracy. On the other hand, God was the Lord of the early German Christians as of all Christians—the word *druhtin*, like its Latin equivalent *dominus*, was originally a secular term—and it is not absurd that our poet should have described Him by a conventional poetic phrase proper to the ideal earthly king.[1] More relevant perhaps is the comparison with *guotero gomono* in l. 88 of *Muspilli* in variation with *engilo*. The same apparently conventional phrase is used in *Heliand*, l. 2135, for Abraham, Isaac, and Jacob. In view of the fact that one German poet could apply a

---

[1] Perrett, op. cit., suggests that the original poem, which he believes to have been in Old English, had *metod mildust* 'the most merciful God' (the word *metod*, originally 'fate', having acquired a Christian sense in OE); since there was no OHG word equivalent to *metod*, the inappropriate *manno* was substituted. L. Whitbread, *MLR* 34 (1939) 426 f., rejects Perrett's suggestion and takes the phrase to be an intensified superlative, 'most merciful possible'. Neither explanation convinces.

conventional phrase meaning 'good men' to the angels, it is perhaps not surprising that another should call God 'the most generous of men'.

It has been held that the text consists of not just two originally independent sections (the 'verse' and the 'prose'), but of three, the first five lines of the verse having been originally separate from the next four. There are undoubtedly differences of style, but unless one can identify a distinctly heathen element in the first five lines, the argument loses much of its credibility, for there is no contradiction between them and the rest. It is, of course, palaeographically possible: a scribe might leave a text uncompleted or enter fragments into a manuscript to which they did not belong; a later scribe might then copy the whole into a fresh manuscript and thus outwardly combine what was once unconnected. On the other hand, there is no compelling reason to deny that the nine lines all form part of a poem on the Creation. To that extent there is some justification for the view that we should call the poem 'The Wessobrunn Creation' and the whole text 'The Wessobrunn Creation and Prayer'. The act of creation, however, is not mentioned; at the point where it might have been, the verse apparently ceases in mid-sentence,[1] and the prayer begins. It begins with two words (*cot almahtico*) which were used in reverse order in l. 7 and are a variation of *cot heilac* with which the verse appears to end. This repetition could be fortuitous if the text were a compilation, but it might just as well be deliberate—whether it is a compilation or not. A number of prayers in Old High German have been preserved, but in no other is the prayer proper preceded, as it is here, by what could perhaps be called an encomium in verse; it must therefore be said that there is no external evidence for saying that the combination of narrative verse and prose prayer such as we appear to have here is original or conventional. There are no other poems on the Creation preserved in Old High German, and the Old English *Caedmon's Hymn* and the *Marvels of Creation*[2] are too unlike the Wessobrunn poem to permit of any surmise about how the 'verse' section might have continued.

Perhaps it is incorrect to say that the theme of the poem is the

---

[1] But see below, p. 133, n. 4.

[2] *Caedmon's Hymn* is edited by A. H. Smith in *Three Northumbrian Poems* (Methuen's Old English Library, London, 1933, 1968), and *The Marvels of Creation* (with translation) by W. S. Mackie in *The Exeter Book. Part II* (Early English Text Society 194, London, 1934).

Creation. It has been suggested[1] that it is about the Creator, and its form has been compared with that of the charms,[2] with, first, the narrative section and then the invocation proper.

The question of the place of origin of the *Wessobrunn Prayer* cannot be entirely separated from that of the content. If, as some contend, the subject matter is inspired by, or derived from, an Anglo-Saxon model, it is likely that it was composed at a place where Anglo-Saxon influence was strong. It does, in fact, contain unmistakable Anglo-Saxon features in the writing,[3] but these are unconnected with the content and tell us no more than that the scribe was familiar with insular conventions.[4] The language is clearly Bavarian, as already stated, except for the word *Dat*, which occurs at the beginning of the first two lines (and possibly the *-on* of *uuilleon*). The unshifted *t* of *Dat* is surprising in the Upper German area, for it is characteristic of Middle Franconian and Low German. However, in those areas at this time the initial consonant would be *th*, not *d*. It has been suggested, however, that this may be a relic form and therefore need not be evidence of northern provenance.[5]

The other allegedly anomalous features in the verse section are certain words which are either not found elsewhere in High German or occur in senses different from those required by the context of the poem.[6] Such words or senses may occur in Old English and are therefore held by some to point to Anglo-Saxon provenance.[7] An example is the verb *gafregin*, which is found nowhere else in High German but has congeners in Saxon and English. In the former it would be *gifragn* and in the latter *gefrægn* or

  [1] See Perrett, op. cit.
  [2] Ibid. See also Seiffert, op. cit.
  [3] See above, p. 127.
  [4] How he understood them is another matter. Ganz, op. cit., conjectures that the Tironian symbol rendered by *enti* in our editions may at times have indicated a pause, especially when following a full point. The only place in the text where it *must* represent the conjunction 'and' is the phrase *himil 7 erda*, where there is no full point. If this were established, the syntactical link between ll. 6 and 7 would become normal, and there would be no *enti* before *cot heilac*, which might then be in apposition to *Cot almahtico* and part of the prayer, though the uncial C of the second phrase would be unexplained.
  [5] See W. Krogmann, *ZfMaf* 13 (1937) 129 ff., esp. 145–9. Steinmeyer believed that this word belonged to the 'Rhapsodensprache'—which is presumably to be understood as meaning an archaic poetic diction.
  [6] These are conveniently collected and discussed by Krogmann, op. cit.
  [7] Perrett, op. cit., was so convinced of this that he reconstructed what he thought was the Old English original.

gefrang. The proponents of Anglo-Saxon provenance maintain that the *e* of *gafregin* is induced by the *æ* of the OE form. Those who favour German origin hold that the *e* is due to mutation by the following enclitic pronoun *ih* (there are numerous other examples of such mutation), and that the word belongs to a poetic diction used in works of which this is the only extant example. Another word which has been used in support of Anglo-Saxon provenance is the adjective *marẹo.* This word exists in OHG but with the meaning 'famous', 'glorious'. In OE it occurs in the sense 'bright', 'shining', which, it has been argued,[1] would be appropriate here as an epithet for the sea. This meaning may be accepted as suitable to the context, but again one might argue that its absence from other OHG texts is due simply to the paucity of comparable sources.[2]

Another difficulty is posed by the word *ero* in l. 2. No one has questioned the meaning 'earth', but all the Germanic languages, including OHG, have only forms with a dental, e.g. OHG *erda.* It has been held that it is a scribal error for *erda.* It has also been suggested that it is a uniquely attested word and various etymologies have been suggested.[3]

Attempts to fill the lacunae and restore a regular metre have been many and varied.[4] There are no gaps in the manuscript text, but editors have postulated lacunae on the basis of their knowledge of alliterative metre. Two examples will illustrate the problem. In l. 4 the sequence *ni nohheinig* suggests that there is something missing after *ni* and that it would have alliterated with *sunna* in the *b*-verse. The Grimms suggested *sterro* 'star', which has been rejected because *st-* cannot alliterate with *s-*. Another suggestion is *sant* (cf. *Vǫluspá*). Now, as early as 1797 Gräter had substituted *scein* for the manuscript *stein* in this line, and neither the Grimms nor any later scholars have challenged this emendation. Yet the *stein* which they rejected would have alliterated perfectly (albeit in the wrong position) with their *sterro*. In l. 6 the alliteration is

---

[1] Baesecke, *Voc. St. Galli* 120.

[2] In any case this sense is not confined to OE. Cf. the phrase *miðgarð mæran* in the passage from *Vǫluspá* quoted above. A. Schirokauer, *PMLA* 65 (1950) 313–18, interprets *der marẹo seo* as 'das Weltmeer der germanischen Mythologie', which could accord with the sense 'famous', 'glorious'.

[3] It has recently been held that its genitive form survives in the second part of the word *fatereres* (usually emended to *fateres*) of the *Hildebrandslied*, see p. 45, n. 5 above.

[4] Most of the suggestions are given by Steinmeyer, p. 16, and in *Ahd. Lb.*

faulty, and it has therefore been proposed to read *iuuiht* for *niuuiht* (scribal confusion of *ni* and *iu* would be very easy); we should then, however, have double alliteration in the line.

The predominantly Bavarian character of the language indicates that the manuscript was written in Bavaria.[1] Whether the original was composed in Bavaria is not easy to decide. Those who detect Anglo-Saxon influence suggest a place where Anglo-Saxon and Bavarian traditions met, and Fulda would be such a place. Others regard this as unnecessarily restrictive, for Anglo-Saxon influence was strong throughout Bavaria too.

About the motive behind the composition (or compilation) of the text we can only speculate. If we regard it as a presentation of the Christian doctrine of the Creation, couched partly in a traditional style deriving from pagan mythological poetry, we might interpret the work, like the *Heliand*, as a piece of conversion literature. This interpretation would, of course, favour a northern origin, since Christianity was well established in Bavaria at the supposed time of composition. (It would, of course, be possible to argue for a very early date during the early days of Bavarian Christianity.) If we accept the contention that it had a missionary purpose and link it with Daniel of Winchester's remarks about pagan notions of the beginning of the world, we might be inclined to see in the devils (*tiuflun*) of the prayer a reference to the heathen gods or their attendant spirits: in the Saxon Baptismal Vow *diobolgeld* presumably relates to heathen cults. On the other hand, Christians too have believed in devils, and nothing compels one to assume that the author was anything other than a pious Christian who put together, for his own or others' use, a hymn about God the Creator and a prayer to Him. There is nothing strange in the use of a hymn as a prelude to prayer, and hymns of any age are likely to employ traditional poetic diction.

The **Muspilli** has given rise to much controversy, and final agreement on all questions has not yet been achieved. The orthography of the manuscript text is not uniform; the form of the poem is peculiar; the progress of the thought is not clear; the theology appears to some to be unorthodox. In addition, a number of words are imperfectly legible, or not legible at all. Steinmeyer's

---

[1] B. Bischoff considers that a place in the diocese of Augsburg is the most likely; see id., *Die südostdeutschen Schreibschulen und Bibliotheken in der Karolingerzeit* I (1940, repr. Wiesbaden, 1960), 18 f.

description, 'das verzweifeltste Stück der althochdeutschen Literatur', has been quoted with approval by succeeding investigators.[1]

The *Muspilli*, like the *Hildebrandslied*, has been preserved only by chance. It was written in the margins and on three blank pages of a beautifully written ninth-century manuscript of the pseudo-Augustinian *Sermo de symbolis contra Judaeos*.[2] The manuscript, formerly in the monastery of St. Emmeram at Regensburg and now in the Staatsbibliothek, Munich, was a present from Adalram, bishop of Salzburg from 821 to 836, to Louis the German. Louis was born in 804 and came to Bavaria as duke in 825, when he was still a young man. As Adalram addresses him in his dedication as 'summe puer' while describing himself as 'Juvavensis pastor' (Juvavum or Juvavia was the ancient name for Salzburg) the presentation must have been made between 825 and 836, probably fairly early during this period. It has been suggested that the text of the *Muspilli* was entered by the duke himself, on the ground that no one else would have presumed to disfigure the royal property. This can be no more than conjecture, and it has been denied on the ground that the dialect of the text is predominantly Bavarian, whereas the duke's dialect should have been Franconian.[3] The *Muspilli* was entered by some unknown scribe who observed that it dealt with the same subject as the sermon. Parchment was costly. Even in the ninth century there were practical men who sacrificed beauty to utility, and such a one scribbled the *Muspilli* even over Adalram's dedication to the duke.

The language of the manuscript text is essentially Bavarian of the middle or late ninth century. It has *p* for *b*, as in *piqueme*, *pagant, kipannit*; *k* for *g* as in *kisindi, kotes* (l. 20) beside *gote* (ll. 27, 29); *kk* or *ck* for *gg* as in *likkan, huckan; kh* or *ch* for *k*, as in *khuninc, chunno*. The early Bavarian prefix *ga-* or *ka-* has been replaced by *ki-*, and early Bavarian *ō* has been diphthongized, as in *guot, kinuok, muot*, etc. There are, however, enough exceptions to what is usually taken to be Bavarian spelling to enjoin caution.

---

[1] *MSD* III; *Kl. ahd. Spdmr.* XIV; *Ahd. Lb.* XXX. Facsimile: *Schrifttafeln* 15.

[2] B. Bischoff, quoted by G. Baesecke, op. cit., p. 201, attributes the script of the *Muspilli* text to the middle of the ninth century, whereas Baesecke himself holds that certain orthographical details cannot be earlier than 882.

[3] W. Braune maintained that linguistically it was not impossible. The text was entered, he held, by a person who was not accustomed to, but was influenced by, the Bavarian dialect spoken at that time (*PBB* 40 (1915) 428 n.). This opinion was revived by R. van Delden (*PBB* 65 (1942) 303–29).

There are two certain cases of *ua* instead of *uo*, and two others which are uncertain, a spelling which is associated with Alemannic and the adjacent South Rhenish Franconian area; also several cases of *g* instead of *k* and *k* instead of *kh*.[1] The whole text was written by a single scribe, and the variations in the orthography show that it was copied, not written down from memory or from dictation.

The title was chosen for the poem by J. Schmeller, the first editor, from l. 57:

> *d*ar nimac denne mak andremo   helfan uora demo muspille

('there no kinsman may aid another in the face of the Muspilli'). The meaning and etymology of this word are still uncertain. This is the only example in OHG, and it is not found in any OE text. It occurs twice in the *Heliand*, at ll. 2591 and 4358. The contexts are as follows:

(2591)   anttat mudspelles megin   obar man ferid,
                     endi thesaro uueroldes

and

(4358)   Mutspelli cumit
               an thiustrea naht,   al so thiof ferid
               darno mid is dadiun,   so kumid the dag mannun,
               the lazto theses liohtes,   so it er these liudi ni uuitun . . .

In Old Norse there is a proper noun *Muspellr*, the name, apparently, of a giant who dwells in the land of fire.[2]

It will be seen that in l. 2591 of the *Heliand* it is the 'power of *mudspelli*' that will come upon men, and this phrase, *mudspelles megin*, is in apposition to *endi thesaro uueroldes* 'the end of this world'. The poet, therefore, seems to conceive of *mudspelli* here as a destructive force, possibly personified. In l. 4358 it is stated that '*mutspelli* will come in the dark night, as a thief goes stealthily about his deeds'. This simile is biblical (cf. Matt. 24: 43, 1 Thess. 5: 2, 2 Pet. 3: 10, and Rev. 3: 3), and in the biblical sources it is either the Son of Man (as in Matthew) or the day of the Lord (as in Paul and Peter) that is compared to the thief; St. John the Divine is reporting the words of him 'that hath the seven Spirits

---

[1] These and other anomalous forms are listed by van Delden, op. cit.

[2] See G. Neckel, 'Studien zu den germanischen Dichtungen vom Welt-untergang', *Sitzungsberichte der Heidelberger Akademie der Wissenschaften, Philosophisch-historische Klasse* (1918), Abh. 7.

of God'. The second passage goes on to compare the coming of the last day with the coming of the Flood, and of the fire that destroyed Sodom (as in the poet's sources Matt. 2: 37 f. and Luke 17: 26 ff.; Peter too mentions the fire that will consume the world in the passage just cited). A few lines further on mankind is reminded, in words strongly reminiscent of *Muspilli* 18 ff., to prepare for the *thing*, the assembly where the Judgement will take place:

> For thiu scal allaro liudio gehuilic
> thenkean fora themu thinge;   thes is tharf mikil
> manno gihuilikumu: bethiu latad an iuuan mod sorga.

In the OHG poem (ll. 55 ff.) *muspilli* is associated with the fire which will accompany the *stuatago*[1] when it goes into the land(s) to visit men. A careful study of these passages will make it clear that, while *muspilli* is clearly associated with the destruction of the world by fire, only the Old Saxon usage gives us a strong hint that it is a personal name, though this cannot be ruled out for the German. It is quite possible that the Saxon and the High German words, like the Norse, do denote a person, though the use of the definite article with the latter suggests an appellative rather than a proper name.[2] Indeed, the parallel between *uora demo muspille* (l. 57) and *uora demo rihcche* (l. 35), *fora demo khuninge* (l. 96) could be adduced in support of this contention.[3]

[1] This word is conjectured from the manuscript *tuatago* (the *s* is thought to have been lost, since the word occurs on the extreme left of the sheet: see plates III and IV in the work of C. Minis cited on p. 150, n. 3 below, and his discussion on pp. 66 ff.). The word is taken to mean 'Day of Judgement' (cf. Goth. *stojan* 'to judge', *staua* m. 'a judge', *staua* f. 'judgement'), with the *n*-declension of the second element as in the supposed synonym *suonetago*. The problem with the conjectured (*s*)*tuatago* is that it exists nowhere else in OHG, and on the evidence of OHG *stuēn* 'to atone' (cf. *Muspilli*, l. 25) it should mean 'day of atonement'. On this word, see G. Miller, *PBB* (Halle) 79 (1957) 308–21.

[2] At this point it is necessary to draw attention to a formal difference between the OS and OHG words. The former has the stem-vowel *e* in the second part of the compound, though the evidence of the geminate *ll* and the nominative termination -*i* proves it to be a *ja*-stem (masculine or neuter), whereas the latter has the stem-vowel *i*, which is what one would expect in a *ja*-stem. This would suggest that the OHG word is an older formation than the OS, and this might in turn imply that a pure *a*-stem, perhaps a proper name cognate with the Norse, had survived in Saxon longer than in High German, in fact until the time when *e* and *i* were in free distribution before *i* and *j*. The fact that the OHG word has every appearance of being older than the OS must be borne in mind whenever it is suggested that it might have been borrowed from OS.

[3] In this connection the morphology of OHG *rīhhi* n. 'regnum' is instructive. Unless *Muspilli*, l. 35, and *Hildebrandslied*, l. 48, have preserved the pure *a*-stem

The meaning of these words has been sought with the aid of etymology. It is best to start with the second element. This is connected either with the stem found in Engl. *spell* and *gospel* (OE *godspell*) or that found in Engl. *spill* (ON *spell* 'destruction', OE *spillan*, ON *spilla* 'to destroy'; there are also related words with a dental extension, OS *spildian*, OE *spildan*, OHG *spilden*, and similar meanings). The former etymology would suggest a meaning 'account', 'prophecy', 'pronouncement', or some such, while the latter would suggest 'destruction' or 'destroyer'.[1] The former etymology is associated with a Christian interpretation of the word, the latter with a pagan one, though this distinction is not essential. The first element is commonly connected either with the stem *mū-* found in OHG *mūwurf* 'mole' (literally 'earth-thrower' on account of the mole's most conspicuous activity) and with extensions in Engl. *mud*, OHG *molta* 'dust' (cf. l. 81 of our poem) or with the word for 'mouth', OS *mūth*, OE *mūþ*, OHG *mund*. (Other interpretations have been given, but we must confine ourselves here to the most popular and most probable.) The four combinations of these etymological interpretations would give the following possible meanings: (*a*) 'pronouncement about (the fate of) the earth'; (*b*) 'pronouncement from the mouth', i.e. 'judgement' or (appellative) 'judge'; (*c*) 'destruction of the earth' or (appellative) 'destroyer of the earth'; (*d*) 'destruction (or destroyer) of (or by) the mouth'. It is clear that the last of these is the least likely.[2] It should also be noted that (*b*) and (*d*), though phonologically possible in OS, where the first element has the dental *t* or *d* and where the nasal of Gmc. **munþa-* may once have stood, can be entertained for OHG *muspilli* only if we assume, as indeed some do, that the word (or the work itself) originated outside the High German area and lost its dental consonant before the *s* at some stage. (The origin is then more likely to have been Old Saxon than Old English, since the word is not attested in the

Gmc. **rīka-* 'king' (cf. Goth. *reiks*), otherwise found only in personal names, e.g. *Heinrih*, we must take the word to be the derivative *ja*-stem, Gmc. **rīkja-*, invested with the appellative sense 'king'. Thus, as *rīhhi* might mean 'kingdom' or 'king', so the element '*-spilli*, *-spelli*, if it is connected with the stem found in OE *spillan* 'to destroy', may have meant 'destruction' or 'destroyer'. A parallel case in English is the word *witness* with its two senses 'testimonium' and 'testis', the former being the older.

[1] See the preceding note.
[2] Unless one links it with Rev. 11 : 5 or Jer. 5 : 14 or takes it as a kenning meaning 'judge'.

latter language.) If we accept this hypothesis, we still have to explain the Norse form, which agrees with the OHG in having no dental. Phonological considerations thus seem to point to (*a*) and (*c*) as the most likely interpretations, and to the probability that the OHG and ON words were native and not borrowed. Opinion has fluctuated, but most scholars now agree with Braune,[1] that *muspilli* is an originally pagan word converted to Christian purposes. It belongs to the epic vocabulary of alliterative poetry and, like so many other words, it perished with that poetry. It disappeared from Old English and survived only here, in the *Heliand* and in Old Norse.

The theme of the poem is the fate of the soul after death; it deals with both the Particular Judgement and the Last Judgement, and it introduces too the cataclysm of the end of the world. The plan of the poem may be said to be as follows:

1. Lines 1–30 tell what happens to the soul immediately after death, when a man is rewarded according to his deserts. It describes how an army of angels and an army from hell contend for the soul, and contrasts the bliss of heaven with the pains of hell, warning men to do God's will and to take thought for their sins.

2. Lines 31–6 tell how the Almighty will summon all men to the Last Judgement, and how no one will be able to neglect the summons.[2]

3. Lines 37–62 describe the events preceding the Last Judgement. This section may be divided into ll. 37–49 (or 50), which describe the struggle between Elias and Antichrist. This is followed in ll. 50 (or 51)–62 by a vivid description of the frightening natural phenomena which will herald the end of the world, and it ends by bringing the audience's attention back to the main theme, the fate of the individual soul.

4. Lines 63–72 emphasize the advantage of proper behaviour, especially of avoiding corrupt judgement.

5. Lines 73 to the end deal with the Judgement itself. The Judge sets out for the Court, accompanied by an irresistible host of angels. (There is a parallel between the idea expressed in l. 76 and the conception of there being no defence against *muspilli* in l. 57.) At the Court all shall be revealed. No dissembling will avail. Only the

---

[1] *PBB* 40 (1915) 425–45.

[2] For an account of how contemporaries understood the Last Judgement, see Bede's *Ecclesiastical History* v. 12.

man who has made amends (*kipuazti*) by alms-giving and fasting can take heart. Finally the Cross of Christ will be carried forth, and He will show the wounds that He suffered for love of mankind.

It is possible, as this analysis shows, to trace a logical progression of thought throughout the poem, in spite of the obvious changes of emphasis which occur. On the other hand, some scholars have concentrated on what are here termed 'changes of emphasis' and maintained that the poem contains inconsistencies, not to say contradictions, which have arisen from a combination of elements of different origin. The argument has been conducted on the basis of both form and content.

The doctrine of the first section, that the soul shall be taken either to Heaven or Hell immediately after death, is founded on Jesus' promise to the malefactor, Luke 23:43: 'Verily I say unto thee, today shalt thou be with me in paradise', and on Luke 16:22: 'And it came to pass that the beggar died and was carried by angels into Abraham's bosom'. The alternative view, expressed in the Sections 3 and 5, is based on the account of the Last Judgement given by Jesus in Chapter 25 of Matthew's Gospel and on the belief in the coming of the Messiah represented in Revelation and numerous apocryphal writings. The two views were reconciled in the doctrine of Purgatory, first clearly formulated by Gregory the Great (*Dialogorum Liber* IV, caput xxxix, *P.L.* 77). The juxtaposition of these two views in one poem is not now considered a serious difficulty since Zarncke[1] showed that contemporary thinkers found it possible to reconcile and combine them. He quotes in support the vision reported by Bede in his *Ecclesiastical History*.

The part of the poem that has caused most controversy is that designated as Section 3 above. The account of the fight between Elias and Antichrist derives from the orthodox tradition which identified the two unnamed witnesses mentioned in Rev. 11:3 ff. with Elias and Enoch, and the Beast which comes up from the abyss with Antichrist. Elias and Enoch, alone among the saints, were taken up into Heaven before death and, since they possessed bodies, were able to contend with the Beast.[2] According to Rev.

---

[1] *Berichte d. Königl. sächs. Gesellsch. d. Wissensch., Phil.-hist. Kl.* 18 (1866) 191 ff.

[2] Gen. 5:24; IV Reg. (2 Kings in A.V.) 2:11; Eccl. 44:16; Heb. 11:5. The precise location of Elias and Enoch was a matter of controversy.

11: 3–12 the Witnesses will be defeated and slain by the Beast, but after three days and a half they will be restored to life and taken up into Heaven. Antichrist, according to tradition, is ultimately to be slain either by the Archangel Michael (Rev. 12: 7) or by Christ, 'Him that sat on the horse' (Rev. 19: 19–21). Our poem makes the war between the Beast and the Witnesses into a single combat, Enoch being omitted. In the OS *Genesis*[1] only Enoch is mentioned—understandably, since Elias belongs to a later book of the Bible.

The connection between ll. 50 and 51 (as printed in the editions) raises the problem of the source for the notion that the conflagration is caused by Elias' blood dripping into the earth. In Russian and Siberian legends first recorded in the last century Elias is wounded by Antichrist and his blood sets the earth on fire. This tradition is found nowhere in the West, except apparently in the *Muspilli*, and nowhere at all within a thousand years of the poem's composition. As Elias has displaced the local thunder-god in other Russian legends, it has been suggested that there might here be a trace of a lost South German legend akin to the stories told of battles between Germanic gods and various giants. This problem may well be totally unreal and occasioned by an erroneous reading of the manuscript text, which is very obscure at this point; the obscurity will be discussed below.

The meaning of the second part of the section (ll. 51–62) is clear enough apart from the line containing the word *muspille* (l. 57). The real difficulties of interpretation occur in the first part, which contain the crucial words *uueroltrehtuuison* and *gotmanno* and the apparently conflicting views concerning the outcome of the struggle between Elias and Antichrist. A paraphrase or an abstract of these lines would beg the questions arising. They follow, therefore, in full with a translation which is kept as literal as possible and in which no attempt is made to render the former of these problematical words:

37 Daz hortih rahhon   dia uueroltrehtuuison,
    daz sculi der Antichristo   mit *E*liase pagan.
    der uuarch ist kiuuafanit: denne uui*r*dit untar in uuic arhapan.
40 khenfun sin*t* so kreftic,   diu kosa ist so mihhil,
    *E*lias stritit   pi den euuigon lip,
    uuili den rehtkernon   daz rihhi kistarkan:

---

[1] See below, p. 184.

   pidiu scal imo helfan   der himilis kiuualtit.
   der antichristo   stet pi demo altfiante,
45 stet pi demo *S*atanase,   der inan uarsenkan scal:
   pidiu scal er in deru uu*ics*teti   uant piualla*n*
   enti in demo sinde   sigalos uuerdan.

I have heard the *uueroltrehtuuison* say that Antichrist shall contend
with Elias. The evil one will be armed; then the battle will be joined
between them. The champions will be so strong, the cause will be so
great. Elias will fight for the sake of eternal life; his purpose will be to
strengthen the kingdom for those who seek after righteousness. Therefore, He who rules heaven shall aid him. Antichrist will stand by the old
enemy, stand by Satan, who shall bring *him* down. Therefore, shall *he*
fall wounded in the place of battle and become victory-less in the encounter.[1]

It is not clear to whom the italicized pronouns refer, nor exactly
what actions are being described. It is difficult to believe that
Antichrist is struck down by Satan. On the other hand it would be
possible to understand the lines as follows: Elias shall win because
he is supported by God. Antichrist shall lose because he is supported by Satan and, in that sense, Satan will bring him down. Now
follow the lines

   doh uuanit des u*i*lo gotmanno
   daz *E*liaz in demo uuige   aruuartit *uuerde.*
50   *so daz* Eliases pluot   in erda kitriufit,
   so inprinnan*t* die perga . . .

Yet many men of God believe that Elias will be wounded (or slain)[2]
in the battle. When[3] the blood of Elias drips into the ground, the
mountains will take fire . . .

After this follow the Signs.

---

[1] The word *sind* 'journey', cf. ll. 2 and 74, is here taken to be a military term,
like the word *reise* which replaced it in MHG and means, among other senses,
'military expedition'.
[2] There is a tendency to assume that *aruuartit* means 'killed' here, but the
sense 'wounded' is certainly possible. Otfrid (iv. 17. 2) uses it in the latter sense.
[3] This translation follows the editions, making l. 50 a temporal clause which
opens a new section. Since, however, the words *so* in ll. 50 and 51 have been
supplied by editors, the manuscript being in a poor state at this point, it is
possible to take l. 51 as the beginning of a new section and l. 50 as either a main
clause or a consecutive clause completing the account of the battle. This would
remove the non-biblical notion that the fire is immediately consequent upon,
or even caused by, the shedding of Elias' blood.

There seem here to be two conflicting views about the outcome of the fight. The *uueroltrehtuuison* seem to be credited with the opinion that Elias, being aided by the Ruler of Heaven, must necessarily prevail—an idea which is contrary to all Western theological tradition, although it is found in Eastern sources—whereas men of God (though not all, it seems, if the manuscript *uula* really stands for *uilo* 'many') maintain the orthodox view that he will be defeated (slain or wounded, according to the uncertain sense of *aruuartit*). This interpretation has given rise to much erudite argument. Oriental texts have been produced in which the victory goes to Elias, and passages have been collected from Western theologians which resemble various passages in the German poem. It has been argued that there was actually a difference of opinion in the Western Church, and that by a remarkable chance, for which no certain explanation can be offered, the unorthodox view has been preserved only in the *Muspilli* among Western texts. If this were true, then this ninth-century Old High German smear on Adalram's elegant manuscript would indeed be a document of very great significance in the history of Western theology.[1]

Much depends, therefore, on the meaning of the word *uueroltrehtuuison*. If they represent a trend of opinion in the Church, we may be able to explain why the orthodox view is accredited only to many, and not to all, men of God. Since the word occurs nowhere else, we cannot be sure of its meaning. In OE *woruldwita* means 'philosopher', and this comes very close to the neutral rendering 'doctores', which could apply to ecclesiastical teachers. On the other hand, we may use the OE word *woruldriht* 'secular law' as a pointer; this would allow us to interpret *uueroltrehtuuison* as 'men learned in secular law' as opposed to 'priests' (*gotman*). We might then see the conflict of opinion as one existing not within the Church, but between the Church and the ignorant laymen, who import their warriors' and lawyers' ideas into their understanding of the Bible. This is the generally accepted interpretation of the

---

[1] See especially H. Schneider, *ZfdA* 73 (1936) 1–32 and G. Baesecke, ibid. 82 (1950) 199–239. On the uniqueness of the *Muspilli* Schneider says, op. cit., p. 11, 'Schritt vor Schritt nähert sich die Legendenbildung dem Ziel, das sie für uns auf westeuropäischem Boden nur einmal erreicht hat, im Muspilli. Das, was hier von Elias erzählt wird, ist also keine ausgefallene und einmalige Erfindung, auch sicherlich nicht auf den Osten beschränkt. Es haftet ihr auch nichts Unkirchliches an; der Zufall hat sie den uns überkommenen theologischen Schriften des Abendlandes ferngehalten.'

passage, and it is associated with the practice of trial by combat, on which the Church always frowned, and in which God was supposed to defend the right.

It is possible, in spite of all the erudition that has been expended on attempts to explain the contradictory views supposed to be expressed in this section, that the problem does not in fact exist (just as that of the connection between Elias' blood and the Fire may not exist). The *doh* in l. 48 is difficult only as long as it is taken to indicate a contrast of opinion. This need not be the case, for this line and the next could be detached from the group 37–47 and taken to introduce a new idea: 'Antichrist will stand by the Ancient Enemy, stand by Satan, who shall bring him down. Therefore he shall fall wounded in the place of battle and lose the victory in the encounter. And yet the men of God (or many of them) expect that Elias will be slain (or wounded) in the battle.'

As for the poet's sources for Section 3, it has been maintained that he drew not only upon the Bible and ecclesiastical tradition, but also upon secular, ultimately pagan, traditions. It has been held that these lines, or elements contained in them, were taken from a once quite independent poem which was interpolated into the main body of the *Muspilli* as we know it. Neckel[1] concentrated his attention chiefly on the content, in which he saw similarities with the Norse accounts of the 'Ragnarøk' or 'Twilight of the Gods'. Baesecke, starting at about the same time, was concerned more with the linguistic and metrical form of the text.[2] It will be preferable to consider the question of content first.

Just as speculation about the beginning of things has always exercised men's minds, so too there is a considerable literature on the End. It is referred to in the *Heliand* and in the OE *Christ*, but there are much fuller accounts in Old Norse. Neckel has considered all these, and in particular the Norse accounts; the references occur in the later strophes of *Vǫluspá*, in strophe 42 of *Lokasenna*, and in Chapters 4, 13, 51 of that part of *Snorra Edda*[3]

---

[1] Op. cit.

[2] His principal contributions are: 'Muspilli', *Sitzungsber. d. königl. preuß. Akad. d. Wiss., phil.-hist. Kl.* (11 Apr. 1918), pp. 414–29, and *ZfdA* 82 (1950) 199–239, where full references to the controversial literature are given. His arguments are ingenious and supported by immense erudition, but he himself admitted that he had erected 'eine etwas luftige Konstruktion'.

[3] German trans. by G. Neckel and F. Niedner, *Die jüngere Edda* (Thule, vol. 20, Jena, 1925).

known as *Gylfaginning*. Perhaps the most striking similarity to which Neckel draws attention is that between the wounding or slaying of Elias and the killing of the god Freyr by Surtr, who is connected with Muspellr and the sons of Muspellr. There are, of course, many similarities between these accounts and those in Revelation 6: 12–14; 8: 7–12; 11: 5–13; 12: 7–9; and Neckel is far from claiming that these lines of the *Muspilli* must be part of a heathen poem. His conclusion is that it is Christian, but coloured by traditional Germanic ideas.

At the same time, Baesecke had been examining the same problem and adduced very elaborate formal arguments in favour of different origins for ll. 37–62 and the rest of the poem. He claimed to be able to identify differences in the linguistic forms and in the spellings of the two parts. For instance, the main body of the text sometimes employs single *h*, *l*, and *n* for *hh*, *ll*, *nn*: *rihi*, l. 13, *rahono*, ll. 64, 69, *uelihemo*, ll. 19, 64, *kilihaz*, l. 32, *hela*, l. 21, *mano*, ll. 19, 81; though the normal geminates also appear. Such spellings are absent from ll. 37–62. The main body also uses *u* for *uu*: *uaz*, l. 93, *niueiz*, l. 66, *ueliha*, l. 64, *uerde*, l. 7, etc. beside the normal form, but ll. 37–62 do not. This middle section, however, is alone in using *uu* for *uui* (*uurdit*, l. 39, *uuhc*, ll. 39, 46, *uuze*, l. 62) and *ch* or *hc* for final *g* (*uuarch*, *uuhc*, l. 39, *(e)inihc*, l. 52, *piehc*, l. 60) while the main body alone omits *h* before *t* (*reto*, ll. 10, 64, *reta*, l. 67). The main body of the text prefers initial *f* to initial *u* in words like *finstri* (beside *uinstri*), while the middle section prefers *u* (though *f* appears in *arfurpit*, l. 59, and *farprunnan*, l. 61). The main body has *ia* for Gmc. *ē* (*hiar*, l. 30, *miaton*, l. 67, *miatun*, l. 72), but the middle section has *ie* (*piehc*, l. 60). Baesecke found some of the peculiarities of the main body of the text in St. Emmeram charters written by the scribe Ellinhart between 814 and 821 and concluded that their presence here indicated that the original from which it was copied had been written either by Ellinhart himself or by a scribe closely connected with him. Some of the peculiarities of the middle section (*ch* for *g*, *ie* for *ia*, and *-on* for *-un* in *-uuison*, l. 37, *euuigon*, l. 41) he found in Regensburg charters from the time of the scribe Anamot (890–906), and this, together with the spelling *ua* and the Otfridian ll. 61–2, which he associates with the Freising Otfrid manuscript, led him to date the manuscript text about the year 890.

In addition to the differences in orthography there are differences

in style and metre. The main body alone has the construction with
the genitive placed before the word it limits (*herio meista, allero
manno uuelihhemo*, etc.). It can also be divided into groups of lines
as though it were a strophic poem, whereas ll. 37–62 are stichic.
The middle section alone favours the rhetorical device of ana-
phora (*stet pi demo altfiante/stet pi demo Satanase*). None of the
arguments, taken in isolation, could be considered decisive, but
they must, taken together, be acknowledged as going a long way
towards supporting the contention that ll. 37–62 and the rest
were composed by different authors. Baesecke, however, goes
farther. The middle section is itself not uniform in prosody and
style, and Baesecke argues that it was an adaptation by the interpolator himself of an ancient lay on the destruction of the world
by fire. He considers that ll. 38–47 and 50–6 were taken from this
old lay and connected to the rest by means of lines of mediocre
quality composed entirely by the interpolator. Here he is on less
firm ground, although his argumentation is, as usual, based on
close observation. It is characteristic of good alliterative verse to
emphasize the third beat (i.e. the first beat of the second half-line)
by placing it on an alliterating noun. In the later period it could
fall on a verb, and the alliteration could even fall on the fourth
beat. Lines 38–47 and 50–6 are in his opinion good lines of the old
type, but the technique is faulty in ll. 48 and 49 and in ll. 58 and
59, in which the alliteration falls on the fourth beat. Lines 37, 61,
and 62 are rhyming lines of the Otfridian type. Baesecke regards
the metre of the middle section as a transition stage between
alliterative and rhyming verse.[1] Line 48 is either defective or not
verse at all (as is also l. 18). The repetition of *denne* in ll. 57, 58,
and 60 is weak. In l. 53, *muor uarsuilhit sih, suilizot lougiu der
himil*, the alliteration is borne by the verbs, three nouns being
ignored, and in the second half-line one noun is apparently not
even stressed; alternatively *suilizot*, which alliterates, stands in the
anacrusis.

The conception of the poem as consisting of two parts is, however, by no means universally held, and many scholars, like
Schneider,[2] have maintained that it is a unity. Ehrismann treats
the work as a unified conception. He divides it into two sections,
it is true, but according to the very obvious criterion of the two
types of Judgement (ll. 1–30 and 31 to the end). He includes the

[1] See also A. Heusler, *Deutsche Versgeschichte*, § 435.   [2] Op. cit.

passage about Elias as an 'episode' in the Last Judgement; he admits that this causes an interruption,[1] but makes the very valid point that this interweaving of the two ideas is original, and that there are no grounds for postulating an interpolation or rearrangement of lines. His conclusion that there are no features of Germanic mythology in the poem, apart perhaps from a vague reminiscence in the word *muspilli* itself, is consistent with his view of the formal structure of the poem.

The purpose of the author of *Muspilli* was to convey the Christian message, to encourage people to seek heaven and avoid hell; for that purpose he used a combination of direct admonition and colourful example. Elements of his colourful example are to be found in other Germanic literature, but they are also found in Christian sources; it is therefore just as likely that the account of the battle and the final conflagration represents an amalgamation of a number of features and incidents taken from various passages of Scripture as that they are drawn from heathen sources. Thus the *uueroltrehtuuison* may have been suggested by the 'viginti quattuor seniores', mentioned in Revelation 11 : 16 and 19 : 4, who sit in the sight of God and give thanks when the Kingdom of Christ has been proclaimed. The story told in Revelation 11 and 13 : 7 of the defeat of the Witnesses by the Beast is followed in 12 : 7–12 by the account of Michael's victory over the dragon: '. . . draco ille magnus, serpens antiquus, qui vocatur diabolus et satanas . . .' (Rev. 12:9) contains the material for *uuarch* (l. 39) *altfiante* (l. 44), and *Satanas* (l. 45). Rev. 13 : 4 '. . . draconem qui dedit potestatem bestiae . . .' could have inspired *stet pi demo altfiante*, and in v. 13 of the same chapter, another monster brings down fire from Heaven. There are references to fire and blood, flaming mountains, and the destruction of trees in Revelation 8:7–8:

Et primus Angelus tuba cecinit, et facta est grando et ignis mista in sanguine, et missum est in terram, et tertia pars terrae combusta est, et tertia pars arborum concremata est . . . Et secundus Angelus tuba cecinit, et temquam mons magnus igne ardens missus est in mare, et facta est tertia pars terrae sanguis.

Michael's victory was won 'propter sanguinem Agni' (Rev. 12: 11). The unorthodox statement that the moon shall fall[2] (*mano*

---

[1] Ehrismann, p. 145.

[2] Found also in a Norman poem of the twelfth century; see Nölle, *PBB* 6 (1879) 449, and in OE *Christ*, l. 939.

uallit, l. 54) could be a telescoping of Matt. 24: 29: 'sol obscurabitur et luna non dabit lumen suum, et stellae *cadent* de caelo', or it could have been inspired by Rev. 8:12: 'et percussa est . . . tertia pars lunae'.

No known work combines these features in a way which could have served as a direct source, but neither have the protagonists of a heathen origin of the poem been able to produce such a single, known source, though this is less surprising.

The situation, an encounter between two champions, is similar to the situation outlined in the opening verses of the *Hilde-brandslied*: *Muspilli*, l. 37, *Daz hortih rahhon dia uueroltrehtuuison*: *Hildebrandslied*, l. 1, *Ik gihorta đat seggen*; M, l. 38, *daz sculi der antichristo mit Eliase pagan*: H, ll. 2–3a, *đat sih urhettun ænon muotin/Hildebrant enti Hadubrant*; M, l. 39a, *der uuarch ist kiuuafanit*: H, ll. 4b–6a, *iro saro rihtun, / garutun iro guđhamun, gurtun iro suert ana, / helidos ubar hringa'*; M, l. 39b, *denne uuirdit untar in uuic arhapan*: H, l. 6b, *do sie to dero hiltiu ritun*. The *Muspilli* has none of the variations of the *Hildebrandslied*. Instead of the dialogue before the fight (H, ll. 7–62), there is an objective statement of the issue (M, ll. 41–2); in both there is the description of the opposing parties (M, ll. 40a, 43–45a: H, ll. 4a, 7b–8a and what emerges from the dialogue). There is no description of the battle as in H, ll. 63–8, but a brief forecast of the result (M ll. 45b–49) and a long account of subsequent events. Though the *Muspilli* makes obvious concessions to the Germanic literary convention, it is definitely clerical in substance and manner, and is no more primitively Germanic than is the passage in which Otfrid describes the victory of Christ over Satan (IV. 12. 61–4). Many of the phrases used in the *Muspilli* are, as Schneider has shown, Christian formulas.

The Battle between the Witnesses and Antichrist (the Beast) was a prelude to the Judgement. The two are linked in the *Muspilli* by the account of the Signs, which follow after the blood of Elias drips into the earth. After the Deluge God declared that never again would He curse the Earth or destroy it with water (Gen. 9: 11, Isa. 54: 9). It was foretold, nevertheless, that it would one day be destroyed with fire (2 Pet. 3: 10–12). Not only had the Judgement been prophesied (Matt. 25: 31–45), but certain Signs of the impending catastrophe had been promised: Et erunt signa in sole et luna et stellis' (Luke 21: 25). 4 Esdras 5, thought to have been written at about the end of the first century A.D., lists a number of such signs, and these are codified in the well-known Fifteen Signs of later medieval tradition. There are innumerable references to the signs in the writings of the Fathers and in later theological literature.[1]

The connection between the Battle, the Signs, and the Judgement was clear to the medieval mind, and so there is no incompatibility of content. The *Muspilli* is not pagan or even characteristically Germanic as opposed to Christian, except in a few details of the language and manner of expression. It is in the Christian tradition, and is based on one or more Latin commentaries, homilies, or sermons. No document has been discovered from which any part could have been directly translated or borrowed, for the resemblances to various Latin works,[2] to OE poems, and to the *Wessobrunn Prayer* merely prove that the composer was using familiar phraseology.

Significant arguments have been adduced to show that ll. 37–62 are of different origin from the rest, against which it has been convincingly shown that, apart from the word *muspilli*, there is nothing in them which cannot be found in Christian literature; thus there is no compelling reason for not regarding the whole poem as a unity. That there is more action in these lines than in the rest of the poem is natural in view of their content, but some critics will continue to maintain that the style is so different as to compel the assumption that the text is the work of more than one author.

A recent study of the *Muspilli*[3] arrives at the familiar conclusion that it contains interpolated lines, but these are not all to be found in the much discussed middle section, the bulk of which is held to belong to the original poem. According to the author of the study, the original *Muspilli* was a strophic poem (with strophes varying between five and eight lines) in alliterative verse, the subject of which was 'der Weg des Menschen zum ewigen Heil'. The ends

---

[1] See G. Nölle, *PBB* 6 (1879) 413–76.

[2] G. Grau, *Quellen und Verwandtschaften der älteren germanischen Darstellungen des jüngsten Gerichts* (Halle, 1908), is useful as a bibliography of theological writing, but many of the so-called parallels are manifestly absurd. See K. Guntermann, *ZfdPh* 41 (1909) 401–15; G. Ehrismann, *AfdA* 35 (1912) 184–96, esp. 188–96; *Kl. ahd. Spdmr.*, pp. 80 ff.

[3] Cola Minis, *Handschrift, Form und Sprache des Muspilli* (Philologische Studien und Quellen 35) (Berlin, 1966).

of the strophes are, he thinks, metrically indicated by the heavy *b*-verses in ll. 5, 10, 17, 60, and elsewhere; furthermore, the distribution of majuscule letters in the manuscript seems to support this analysis. He finds a similar strophic structure in the *Hildebrandslied*,[1] and claims that the heavy final *b*-verses belong to a technique which continued right down to the *Nibelungenlied*, with its extra-long half-line at the end of most strophes. This original strophic poem was then revised by a second poet of mediocre ability, who knew only the rudiments of alliterative technique and was also familiar with rhyming verse. From this second poet stem two moralizing passages, ll. 18–24, 63–72, and a few isolated lines which are either tautologous (l. 13, which does not alliterate) or feeble (ll. 61–2, which employ rhyme and provide a pedantic answer to the powerful rhetorical question in l. 60).[2]

It may be seen, then, that in a slightly different guise the old view persists that we have in the *Muspilli* an original poem which has been tampered with by a later interpolator. There have, however, been recent attempts to discern a consistent meaning in the poem. The most persuasive of these[3] concentrates on the views of justice contained in the poem. The words *hilfa* and *helfan* are prominent in the poem (ll. 17, 27, 43, 57). They are undoubtedly connected with the notion that, under the feudal system, a man expected help from his overlord and his kinsmen in times of trouble. In the context of the poem, man's overlord is God, just as He is in the conversation between Parzival and Trevrizent in Book IX of Wolfram's *Parzival*, where the same words (*helfe*, *helfen*) constitute a leitmotif. In forensic terms, however, 'help' had a more restricted meaning, viz. the help which under Germanic law a body of witnesses, friends of the accused, could supply by swearing on his behalf. It is to this practice that l. 57 alludes. Like Otfrid in his treatment of the Last Things,[4] the poet of the *Muspilli* contrasts the situation to which men are accustomed in society, when their fellows will aid them, either by oaths

---

[1] See p. 72, above.

[2] Other points made by Minis, such as his reading of the corrupt l. 55, carry less conviction.

[3] H. Kolb, 'Vora demo muspille. Versuch einer Interpretation', *ZfdPh* 83 (1964) 2–33. See also I. Reiffenstein, *Rechtsfragen in der deutschen Dichtung des Mittelalters* (Salzburger Universitätsreden, Heft 12. Antrittsvorlesung gehalten am 2. Feb. 1965, Salzburg/Münich 1966).

[4] See below, pp. 202 f.

(cf. l. 57) or by arms (cf. l. 60, where, according to this view, *mit* means 'side by side with' and not 'against') with his isolation in the face of God's judgement. Human justice, then, is imperfect, and under it crimes can be concealed both by false oaths and by bribery (ll. 63–72). Divine justice is perfect: before God all shall be revealed (ll. 90–6); only alms-giving and fasting (ll. 97–9) can avail one anything.

In connection with the words *kipuazti* (l. 98) and *gipuazzit* (l. 99) we should remark that in l. 62 the word *puaze* occurs, contrasted by the rhyme with the word *uuize* 'punishment'. Here we see a comparison between the 'amends' (*satisfactio*) required by the Church, namely alms-giving and fasting, and those required by the law, which laid down precise penalties for certain offences. If one could pay the required penalty one could escape all further consequences of one's misdeeds, but if one could not pay—and had no kinsmen to help—one was condemned to punishment (*uuizi*). The contrast between the earthly court of law and the divine tribunal seems to be pointed by linguistic means in the passage beginning with l. 63: there the former is called *mahal*, and the latter *suona* (l. 71).

It may be that the poem expresses clerical disapproval of the practice of trial by combat. The fight between Elias and the Antichrist should, according to those skilled in secular law (if this is the correct interpretation of the troublesome *uueroltrehtuuison*) lead to the immediate vindication of right, but the men of God, that is those familiar with the ways of God and with the lives of the saints and martyrs, know that right will be vindicated not in this world, but hereafter, when God's witnesses will receive 'the spirit of life from God' (Rev. 11:11). Certainly the poem offers no guarantee that right will triumph in the course of the combat. We may again compare the poem with the *Hildebrandslied*, where the father knows that his opponent needs to have right on his side in order to win (l. 57); it is this knowledge which crushes him, for he cannot but believe that Dietrich's is the just cause.

The view that the poet (or adaptor) of the *Muspilli* was particularly concerned to show the shortcomings of human justice and to contrast it with the perfect justice of God may lead one to ask whether he had in mind an audience specially involved in legal problems. One might argue that, since the poem deals with the Last Judgement, it is not surprising to find him using legal ter-

minology (*puaze, uuize, hilfa, kosa,* etc.) which any German would
have understood in the secular sense, but which he had to interpret in a religious sense. On the other hand, there is one passage
(ll. 63–72) which suggests that he was addressing himself to the
judiciary, as the clergy still does in assize sermons:

> Pidiu ist demo *m*anne so guot,   denner ze demo mahale quimit,
> da*z* er rahono u*u*eliha   re*h*to arteile.
> den*n*e ni darf er sorgen,   den*n*e er ze deru suonu qui*m*it.
> ni u*u*eiz der uuenago man   uuielihan uu*a*rtil er hab*et*,
> denner mit den miaton   marrit d*az* re*h*ta,
> d*az* der tiuval dar pi   kitar*n*it s*t*entit.
>
> . . .
>
> *n*i scolta sid manno *n*ohhein   miatun *intfahan.*

(Therefore it is so good for the man, when he comes to court, that
he should judge every cause justly. Then he need not be anxious when
he comes to the Judgement. The miserable man does not know what kind
of an observer he has when he perverts the right with rewards (and)
that the devil stands there in hiding. . . . It has been ordained that no
man shall receive rewards hereafter.)[1]

Here it is clear that the offence under discussion is not that of seeking to obtain, but of meting out, unjust judgement; not of offering,
but of taking, bribes. It has been pointed out that the fifth line of
the passage just quoted seems to echo a law of Charlemagne from
the year 802 (*Capitulare missorum generale*—the *missi*, 'Sendgrafen',
were the itinerant judges who represented the judicial power of the
sovereign, as the judges of assize do now), which contains the
words: 'ut nemo usum habeat pro cupiditate aliqua iustum iudicium marrire.' It seems that the phrase *daz rehta marren* was legal
phraseology, and that *iustum iudicium marrire* was a rendering into
Latin with adaptation of the vernacular verb.[2] This striking
parallel does not mean that the capitulary in question inspired the
Muspilli: the phrase may well have been in wide use. Nor does it
follow that the poem was composed with an audience of *missi* in
mind, since the passage may well, as has been argued, have been
interpolated. On the whole it seems best to characterize the work

---

[1] The translation of this last sentence takes account of the preterite indicative
form of the verb *scolta.* If we had the subjunctive *scolti* we could translate:
'No man should receive rewards from now on.'

[2] The parallel was mentioned by Koegel, p. 319, and discussed by R. van
Delden, op. cit., and C. Minis, op. cit., pp. 88 ff.

as a didactic piece which seeks to discourage vice by depicting the plight of the damned, the terror of the Last Things, and the majesty of the Last Judgement. In order to do this the poet, while basing himself on the Scriptures and patristic teaching, invoked conventional notions of justice and, perhaps, traditional conceptions of the end of the world. Yet the last word of the poet is not of judgement, but of mercy—of the Cross of Christ, which alone can save.

X

Louis the Pious (814–840)

CHARLES THE GREAT died at Aachen in January 814. As his two elder sons, Charles and Pippin, had predeceased him in 811 and 810 respectively, the whole realm passed, without suffering the usual partition, to his third son Louis, known as Louis the Pious. (He is regarded as Louis I by the French, who have given him the cognomen 'le Débonnaire' on account of his unpractical goodness.) Italy was given to Pippin's son Bernhard, to hold as Louis's vassal.

The Church was always nearer to Louis's heart than his royal duties. He would have preferred, in fact at one time intended, to enter a monastery. On ascending the throne he at once made large grants to the Church and freed many of the monasteries from their feudal obligations, thus dangerously weakening the royal power. He was averse from worldly pursuits and is reputed never to have smiled at the performances of professional entertainers. He has been credited, no doubt wrongly, with having discouraged the cultivation of native secular literature and having destroyed his father's collection of ancient songs mentioned by Einhard. His reign is marked by a succession of attempts to divide his realm among his future successors; these partitions were followed inevitably by civil wars fomented by the disappointed parties. The first to rebel was Bernhard of Italy, who was sentenced to blinding in 818 but died of shock during the execution of the sentence. For this act of cruelty Louis subsequently performed a humiliating act of public penance. Further discord in the realm was created by the fact that in 822 a son was born to him by his second wife, Judith, whom he had married in 819 after the death of his first wife, Irmengard. This child, later known as Charles the Bald (Charles II of France) was to spend much of his life contending with his half-brothers for control of the Frankish dominions after their father's death.

A law made by Louis in 818, authorizing any free man to dispose of his property ('res suas': *sachun sinu*) for the salvation of his soul, exists in Latin with an interlinear German translation in the Middle Franconian dialect. It is commonly called **Das Trierer Capitulare.**[1] The steps to be taken and the witnesses required to give the transaction legal force show how strong was the family claim to property. The manuscript, formerly in the Cathedral Library at Trier, disappeared in the seventeenth century, so the text is known only from *Antiquitates Trevirenses*, published by C. Brower in 1626 and itself a very rare book. The translation was apparently made in the tenth century. It contains a number of errors, and Steinmeyer went so far as to regard it as a private exercise in translation.

The oldest extant German 'Confessions', namely the **Fuldaer Beichte**[2] and the **Ältere bairische Beichte,**[3] were composed during Louis's reign. The manuscripts are later copies made in the tenth and eleventh centuries. There is a considerable number of other confession formulas, all going back ultimately to Latin texts, some of them being combined with a creed. The problems of their origin and interrelations are very complicated.[4] Some, such as the **Sächsische Beichte,**[5] are fuller than others, and the much later **Bamberger Glauben und Beichte,** together with the related Wessobrunn version (**Wessobrunner Glauben und Beichte I,**)[6] is a veritable encyclopedia of sin. The **Würzburger Beichte,**[7] entered by a tenth-century hand in a Würzburg manuscript of the ninth century, differs from the others in a number of respects. Among the sins it mentions are the worship of heathen gods (*heidangelt*), bestiality, sodomy, self-gratification, and the eating of flesh from beasts killed by other beasts (*in bluote gislizzenemo fona diorerun*).[8] Apart from its deviant content, this text is unique in exemplifying a dialect not otherwise attested in

[1] *MSD* LXVI; *Kl. ahd. Spdmr.* XL; *Ahd. Lb.* XIX.

[2] *MSD* XXIII; *Kl. ahd. Spdmr.* XLVIII.

[3] *MSD* LXXVIII A; *Kl. ahd. Spdmr.* XLI; *Ahd. Lb.* XXII. 1a.

[4] They are collected in *Kl. ahd. Spdmr.*, pp. 309–64. Confessions from Lorsch and Mainz, together with a later Bavarian formula and one in Low German are given in *Ahd. Lb.* XXII. For a discussion of the problems they present see Baesecke *PBB* 49 (1924–5) 268–355, and Eggers, *PBB* (Halle) 77 (1955) 89 ff.; 80 (1958) 372 ff.; 81 (1959) 78 ff.

[5] *MSD* LXXII; *Kl. ahd. Spdmr.* XLV; *Ahd. Lb.* XXII. 5.

[6] *MSD* XCI and XC; *Kl. ahd. Spdmr.* Further reference to this work will be made in Chapter 16.

[7] *MSD* LXXVI; *Kl. ahd. Spdmr.* XLIV.

[8] This last sin is mentioned in Exod. 22:31, Lev. 17:15, and 22:8.

the period. Its most striking linguistic features are the occurrence of infinitives with apocope of the final *n* (*uuasge*, *gihore*) beside others without apocope, and the use of the personal pronouns *mi* and *di* in the dative (but *mih* in the accusative). This latter feature might remind us of the morphology of the *Hildebrandslied*, where *mi* is used for the dative, but *mih* for the accusative (though in the second person the normal dative form *dir* is used in the lay).

The Old High German Tatian translation and the Old Saxon biblical epics *Heliand* and *Genesis* are usually considered to be literary products of Louis's reign, as the *Isidor* translation represents the age of his predecessor or perhaps that of Pippin the Short.

The Old High German **Tatian** is a translation of a Latin version of the *Diatessaron*, a gospel harmony (i.e. a narrative composed of excerpts from the four canonical Gospels) attributed to Tatian, a Syrian Christian of the second century. The German translation is found complete, side by side with a Latin version, in one manuscript, the Codex Sangallensis 56 (commonly referred to as G), which is preserved in the monastery library of St. Gall. It has lain there certainly since the end of the thirteenth century, and possibly since the tenth, when the word *hara* (the Alemannic form of *hera* 'huc') was entered in the text.

The modern scholarly edition was made by Eduard Sievers.[1] The text is reliable, and the grammatical introduction is full and accurate. Sievers' views on the history of the work, however, are no longer tenable, having been undermined by recent developments in Diatessaron scholarship. It will be necessary, therefore, to give some account of what is known or may reasonably be conjectured about Tatian's harmony.[2]

Tatian's original text, made about A.D. 170, is lost, and it is not even known whether it was written in Greek or Syriac. Opinion is divided on the question of whether Tatian made his own text,

---

[1] *Tatian. Lateinisch und altdeutsch mit ausführlichem Glossar* (Paderborn, 1872; rev. and enlarged edn. 1892, repr. 1960). Selections in *Ahd. Lb.* xx and also in footnotes to *Monsee–Wiener Bruchstücke*, ibid. ix. A valuable Latin–OHG glossary to the text is provided by Friedrich Köhler, *Lateinisch-althochdeutsches Glossar zur Tatianübersetzung* (Paderborn, 1914, repr. 1962). Facsimile *Schrifttafeln* 9.

[2] See articles on 'Tatian' and 'Diatessaron' in *Encyclopædia Britannica* and on 'Tatian' in Pauly–Wissowa, *Realencyclopädie der classischen Altertumswissenschaft*. More detailed treatment may be found in C. Peters, *Das Diatessaron Tatians* (Rome, 1939).

or whether he confined himself to harmonizing existing texts, modifications being consequent upon harmonization. His work was widely used in eastern Christendom until the fourth or fifth century, when it was ousted by the standard Syriac version of the Bible, the Peshitta. It can now only be reconstructed from later versions in Arabic, Persian, Latin, Italian, Dutch, and Middle English. A Latin version seems to have been current in the Western Church at an early date, coexisting with the 'Old Latin' ('Vetus Latina') versions of the separate Gospels, and there may have been mutual influence on the texts. When, in the fifth century, the new translation of the Scriptures commissioned by St. Jerome (the Vulgate) was adopted by the Church as the authoritative version of the Bible, Tatian's harmony lost much of its popularity, though in later centuries it provided a useful access to the Gospels, as is attested by the numerous vernacular translations.

In the sixth century Bishop Victor of Capua discovered a gospel harmony with no title which he conjectured to be the work of either Ammonius, whom he knew to have made a synopsis of the four Gospels ('unum ex quattuor euangelium' is Victor's phrase, of which the Greek τὸ διὰ τεσσάρων εὐαγγέλιον is the equivalent), or of Tatian, who had composed a harmony known by the perplexing name 'Diapente'.[1] Victor seems to have inclined to the view that Tatian was the author of the work, and in this view modern scholarship concurs. We do not know whether the text discovered by Victor was written in Greek or in Latin; if in Latin, we do not know whether it was an old Latin or Vulgate text. At Victor's behest the work was copied (or translated) and provided with gospel references in order to remove any doubt as to its authenticity. Victor's manuscript found its way at length to the Abbey of Fulda, where it may have been deposited by the founder, Boniface. This manuscript, the Codex Fuldensis Bonifatius I (commonly called F)[2] presents a thoroughly vulgatized text. Sievers, who believed it to be the parent manuscript of all Latin Diatessarons, including that found in G, described it has having been composed like a mosaic from the Vulgate Gospels. He seems to have hesitated over the question of which version of the Latin,

[1] This name has been taken to indicate that Tatian used a fifth source in addition to the canonical Gospels. It has, on the other hand, been understood as a musical term metaphorically used for 'harmony'.

[2] Ed. by E. Ranke, *Codex Fuldensis. Novum Testamentum latine interprete Hieronymo ex ms. Victoris Capuani* (Marburg/Leipzig, 1868).

that in F or that in G, had been used for the German translation (in his first edition he favoured F, in the second G), but for him this was hardly a matter of substance, since he considered the divergences trifling.

On Sievers' authority generations of students of Old High German have regarded the German version of G as a direct translation of either the accompanying Latin or the Fulda text. This assumption has led to judgements concerning the technique of translation and the syntax of ninth-century German prose, especially at those points where the translation appears relatively independent of the Latin. Such conclusions are now dubious, for it has been shown not only that the Latin of G is independent of F, but also that the German translation derives from neither. Sievers' view concerning the primacy of F had been challenged from time to time, notably by Baesecke,[1] but lack of contact between Germanists and biblical scholars ensured that it prevailed until the 1960s. The findings of Anton Baumstark, a Diatessaron scholar not primarily concerned with German, at last revealed the Old High German *Tatian* to be a text of far greater importance for Diatessaron studies than had formerly been imagined, since it could now be seen, together with other translations of the Harmony, as an independent witness to the form in which this was transmitted throughout the Middle Ages.[2]

A few examples will suffice to demonstrate the independence of the German version. At Tat. 15. 5 (Matt. 4: 8) both F and G read 'et ostendit ei omnia regna mundi', but the German of G reads *inti araugta imo allu thisu erdrichu*; this translation corresponds to the Old Latin readings 'regna mundi huius' and 'regna huius mundi'. For 'nunc dimittis servum tuum domine' (Tat. 7. 6, Luke 2 : 29) in F and G, the German translation reads *nu forlaz*

---

[1] G. Baesecke, *Die Überlieferung des althochdeutschen Tatian* (Hallische Monographien 4) (Halle, 1948), esp. pp. 4 ff.

[2] See A. Baumstark, *Die Vorlage des althochdeutschen Tatian*, Niederdeutsche Studien, 12 (Cologne/Graz, 1964). This important study appeared sixteen years after its author's death, revd. and ed. by J. Rathofer. Four years earlier W. Wissmann, unaware of its existence, had demonstrated the independence of the German version. See his article 'Zum althochdeutschen Tatian' in *Indogermanica, Festschrift für Wolfgang Krause* (Heidelberg, 1960), pp. 249–67. Baumstark discusses over 300 passages which illustrate the mutual independence of the two Latin versions and the German. Wissmann discusses a mere thirty-six, but only ten of these are even mentioned by Baumstark. These figures give some indication of the magnitude of the textual problem.

thu truhtin thinan scalc; here the imperative *forlaz* corresponds to an Old Latin reading 'dimitte', also found in some Vulgate manuscripts. At Tat. 4, 5 (Luke 1: 46) there is a similar divergence of mood: against the Latin 'magnificat anima mea dominum' the German reads *mihhiloso min sela truhtin*, where the first word, being either subjunctive or imperative, can correspond only to Latin 'magnificet' or 'magnifica'. A final example, and one which has earned the translator undeserved praise for his freedom of rendering is Tat. 6, 1 (Luke 2: 9), where the Latin 'et ecce angelus domini stetit iuxta illos'; the parallel German text reads: *quam thara gotes engil inti gistuont nah in*.[1]

There is evidence of several other German Tatian translations, but none has survived except for a few fragments[2] in a tenth-century Paris manuscript (which also contains the *Altdeutsche Gespräche*) and a seventeenth-century copy of an incomplete text now in the Bodleian Library, Oxford. The Paris fragments are too meagre to allow us to determine their textual affinities. The Bodleian copy was inspected by Sievers and declared to be derived from G. This view has recently been strongly challenged.[3] It was the Bodleian text which was used for the first printed editions (of 1706 and 1727).[4] The G text was referred to in 1538 by the Swiss historian Gilg Tschudi,[5] but it was not edited until 1841.[6]

Manuscript G dates from the mid-ninth century. Victor's Latin preface and the table of contents were entered by a typical Mainz

---

[1] Here 'ecce' is left untranslated, but it is omitted in some Latin texts too. The more striking divergence from the Latin is the addition of the words *quam thara*. That this is not a German invention is indicated by the corresponding passage in the Old Tuscan Diatessaron, which reads: 'e l'angelo di dio venne e stette allato a lloro'. (Quoted by Wissmann, op. cit., p. 258.)

[2] These are included in Sievers' edition.

[3] See P. F. Ganz, 'MS Junius 13 und die althochdeutsche Tatianübersetzung', *PBB* 91 (1969) 28 ff. Since the German of this version agrees with the corrected text of G (see below), Sievers believed it to have been copied from it. Ganz envisages the possibility that the corrector of G worked from a text which contained the 'correct' readings which are also found in B.

[4] *Tatiani Alexandrini Harmoniæ Evangelicæ antiquissima versio theotisca*, ed. J. Ph. Palthen (Greifswald, 1706). *Tatiani Syri Harmonia Evangelica e latina Victoris Capuani versione translata in linguam theodiscam antiquissimam, editio post primam Paltheniam nova emendatior* (Ulm, 1727). This formed part of Schilter's *Thesaurus Antiquitatum Teutonicarum*.

[5] Ægidius Tschudi, *Die vralt warhafftig Rhetia* (Basle, 1538).

[6] *Ammonii Alexandrini quæ et Tatiani dicitur Harmonia in linguam latinam et inde ante annos mille in francicam translata*, ed. J. A. Schmeller. This edition, while giving the German text of G, retains the Latin of B.

hand.[1] In the body of the work the hands of six scribes can be distinguished, known by the letters α, β, γ, δ, ε, and ζ. Scribes α, β, and δ wrote two portions each, the second portions being denoted respectively by α′, β′, and δ′. The Latin and the parallel German text were always entered by the same scribe. Scribe ζ seems to have been the ruling spirit, since he corrected the work of his colleagues throughout.[2]

The language of the German translation is commonly called 'Ostfränkisch' or, because of the supposed origin of the manuscript, 'Fuldisch'. There is considerable uniformity among the scribes in the representation of the consonants and the vowels of accented syllables. For Gmc. þ we usually find *th* in initial position and *d* medially and finally (though *d* is found initially in a number of monosyllables, and there are a few instances of medial *th*). Scribe α occasionally uses the Anglo-Saxon ð. For Gmc. ð we find *t* in all positions (though a few words show *d*). The fricative from Gmc. *t* is represented by *z* or *zz*; the affricate also appears as *z*, though sometimes as *c* before front vowels. The Gmc. voiced labials and gutturals appear as *b* and *g*, though γ has an occasional *p* for the former, and both *p* and *c* are common in final position. Gmc. *k* appears as *k* and *c*, but γ has a few instances of *ch*. For *sk* we sometimes find *sc* and in medial position *sg*. For Gmc. *au*, where it remains diphthongal in OHG, the normal representation is *ou* with occasional instances of *au*. Gmc. ō is usually diphthongized to *uo* (with one instance of *ua* in the work of γ). The *a*-Umlaut of Gmc. *eu* is represented regularly as *io* except by γ, who uses *eo*.[3]

Although there is such consistency in the text in spite of the number of scribes, each has his own peculiarities. Scribe γ has been singled out for much attention because of his apparently Alemannic characteristics. The chief of these is his use of *f* and *ff* beside *ph* for the labial afficate. Other possibly Alemannic features are the termination -*u* for the first person singular present indicative of weak verbs of Class III (a feature shared with ε), and the termination -*nt* for the second person plural of all verbs (a feature

---

[1] This is the opinion of B. Bischoff, cited in *Schrifttafeln*, p. 12*.

[2] It should be noted that Sievers' edition and the *Ahd. Lb.* give as far as possible the uncorrected text, the corrections appearing in the apparatus, where erasures are also noted. The result is therefore rather less uniform than either the individual scribe or the corrector intended.

[3] For a full account of the phonology see the introduction to Sievers' edition.

occurring also in the work of β and δ). This scribe's language is further characterized by the co-existence of certain apparently archaic traits, such as the pronominal forms *the* and *he* for the usual *ther* and *her*, and a relatively advanced phonology of inflectional vowels, exemplified by the apparent merger of *-e* with *-a* and *-ēn* with *-an*, and by the regular coalescence of the genitive and dative singular feminine of the pronominal declension in *-ro*.[1]

Although each scribe had linguistic peculiarities, these are largely confined, except in the portion of the text written by γ, to the accidence, and it must be borne in mind that this part of German grammar was at the time undergoing rapid changes everywhere. It is not unthinkable that such variety could be tolerated within one speech community, and even if it does reflect dialect variation, it should be remembered that each monastery drew its monks from far and wide. The relative uniformity to be observed in all other aspects of the language clearly points to one scriptorium. We must now consider which this is most likely to have been.

Although Victor's famous manuscript may now be discounted as the source of the Old High German translation, it is clear that the monastery which possessed such a treasure and which enjoyed such scholarly prestige at the time in question has a strong claim to be regarded as the centre of learning most likely to have produced the translation. The language is a Middle German type differing from the West Middle German of Otfrid. It is the closest of all the Old High German dialects to the modern standard language and is consequently used as the Old High German norm by Braune in his Grammar and the glossary of the *Ahd. Lesebuch*. It is commonly believed to be the language of the Fulda scriptorium. It is a well-known fact that its uniformly shifted *p* does not correspond to the phonology of the modern dialect of the

---

[1] W. G. Moulton, *PMLA* 59 (1944) 307–34, endeavoured to prove that this scribe's peculiarities need not have been Alemannic, but probably represented an old Franconian orthography. At least it can be asserted that his language, if it was Alemannic, cannot have been an older stage of that found in the works of Notker, where final *-e* and *-a* are kept distinct and where long vowels in inflectional syllables are on the whole preserved. For a detailed discussion of the inflectional systems found in the work of the individual scribes see D. R. McLintock, 'Morphological Syncretism in Old High German', *TPS* (1965), 1–14, and id. 'Medial and Inflectional Vowels in Early Frankish', *ArL* N.S. 1 (1970) 1–32.

Fulda area, but dialect boundaries are not static and, as has already been observed, monasteries were not peopled by local monks.[1] Boniface founded the abbey of Fulda in 744. In the early years there were many English monks at Fulda and also many Bavarians, especially under Sturmi, the first Abbot (744–80). During the first four decades of the ninth century the dominant figure at Fulda was Rhabanus Maurus (*c.* 784–856). Rhabanus was a pupil of the English scholar Alcuin and master of the monastery school from 804 to 822, when he became abbot. He remained abbot for twenty years; then, after a period of retreat, he became archbishop of Mainz in 847. He was famous as a learned theologian, diligently copying and rearranging the works of the fathers, and he was probably the most influential teacher of his day in Germany. One of his pupils was Walahfrid Strabo, who has been associated with the *Isidor Glosses*.[2] Walahfrid, one of the most accomplished Latinists of the period, was abbot of the Reichenau from 842 until his death in 849. He is known to have been in Fulda from 827 to 829, and it may have been during these years that he made the Glosses.[3] He has also been identified with scribe γ of the *Tatian*.[4] This identification is certainly erroneous, as Bischoff has shown.[5] It has also been held that scribe ζ was the great Rhabanus himself. This theory, though attractive, is undemonstrable. Of this scribe it may be observed, not only that he corrected the work of the others, but that in the matter of accidence his language is the most conservative.

If it is correct to localize the *Tatian* translation at Fulda, and if the *Isidor Glosses* and certain other texts (the *Basle Prescriptions*, the *Hildebrandslied*, and the *Hamelburger Markbeschreibung*) also issued from the same scriptorium, one may tentatively trace a linguistic development from the earliest Fulda charters to the

---

[1] Differences between the language of *Tatian* and the local dialect have been explained by reference to the isolated position of the foundation. Pope Zacharius, writing to Boniface in 751, speaks of its standing 'in vastissima solitudine' (*MGH Epistolae Merovingici et Karolini Aevi* 1. 370). See F. Wrede, 'Fuldisch und Hochfränkisch', *ZfdA* 36 (1892), 135 f.

[2] See above, pp. 97 f.

[3] See G. Baesecke, *ZfdA* 58 (1920–1) 241–79.

[4] See E. Schröter, *Walahfrids deutsche Glossierung zu den biblischen Büchern Genesis bis Regum II und der althochdeutsche Tatian*, Hermaea 16 (Halle, 1926).

[5] B. Bischoff, 'Eine Sammelhandschrift Walahfrid Strabos (Cod. Sang. 878)', *Aus der Welt des Buches, Festgabe zum 70. Geburtstag von Georg Leyh* (Leipzig, 1950), cited by Wissmann, op. cit., p. 266.

German of manuscript G. The early charters show traces of Bavarian spelling (*ao* for Gmc. *au*, *p* for *b*, and *d* for Gmc. *þ*). These Bavarian features are present in the *Basle Prescriptions* and the *Hildebrandslied*, mingled with Anglo-Saxon traits and elements of the older Franconian orthography. These texts may represent the earliest Fulda style. The orthography of the *Isidor Glosses* corresponds to that of charters written between 826 and 829 by Hruodolf, who succeeded Rhabanus as master of the abbey school. In this orthography we find examples of the apparently Bavarian *pr-* for *br-*, the Merovingian *ch* for *k*, and the diphthongs *au* and *eo* for later *ou* and *io*. These glosses, then, together with the *Hamelburger Markbeschreibung*, may represent the orthography in use before Rhabanus made his reforms. The German of manuscript G, which still exhibits some of these older features (e.g. *au* beside *ou*, *eo* beside *io*) together with residual traces of Anglo-Saxon influence such as *a*'s use of *ð* and the open shape of the *a*, may be the result of his reforms.[1] All such conclusions are uncertain, since no original Fulda charters of the period exist, and the problems of dating the various Fulda documents depend on the value assignable to the copies made at later dates. If we are right in believing G to be a copy, it was no doubt made a few years after the original text. If the translation was made about 830, the copy may be dated between 840 and 850 (which would agree with Bischoff's dating).[2] Its orthography would then appear to be a later stage of that represented by the *Isidor Glosses*, perhaps the final development of the Fulda style.

In judging the quality of the translation we cannot rely on certain knowledge of the actual Latin text that underlies it. Much discussion has centred upon the rendering of such particles as *aut*, *autem*, and *enim* or upon the means employed for dealing with present participles or the ablative absolute; obviously any conclusions derived from such material are dubious. However, it may be observed that certain parts of the translation are so close to the Latin as to resemble an interlinear gloss (for example Chapters 77–82), while others (such as the first seventeen chapters) undoubtedly

---

[1] Baesecke, op. cit., dates the *Isidor Glosses* around 830, but G. Kossinna, 'Über die älteren hochfränkischen Sprachdenkmäler', *QuF* 46 (1881) 93, dates them between 841 and 850 on account of the use of *t* for Gmc. *ð*, not found in Fulda charters until after 841. See also H. Kletschke, *Die Sprache der Mainzer Kanzlei nach den Namen der Fuldaer Urkunden*, Hermaea 19 (Halle, 1933).

[2] See above, p. 161, n. 1.

show a certain independence and skill which cannot be explained by different readings in the original. An instance of word-for-word rendering is afforded by the opening words of the Prologue (Luke 1: 1), where the Latin 'Quoniam quidem multi conati sunt ordinare narrationem quæ in nobis completæ sunt rerum' is translated *Bithiu uuanta manage zilotun ordinon saga thio in ûns gifulta sint rahhono*. Here, quite contrary to German usage, the relative clause is set before its antecedent. On the other hand, the translator some-times endeavours to reproduce the sense, as when he renders 'ut incensum poneret' (Tat. 2, 3, Luke 1: 9) by *thaz her uuihrouh branti* or 'ut profiterentur' (Tat. 5. 11, Luke 2: 5) by *thaz biiahin thionost*. In this last example the first two German words are a literal translation of the Latin, but *thionost* is added, presumably to clarify, in contemporary feudal terms, the sense of the verse. One Latin word may be given a variety of renderings according to context. Thus 'incensum' in the passage cited above is rendered by the concrete noun *uuihrouh*, but later in the same section a gerund is used ('in tempore incensi': *in thero ziti thes rouhhennes*); in the next verse the same word is rendered by an abstract noun ('altari incensi': *thes altares thero uuihrouhbrunsti*). When 'con-vertere' has a personal object (Tat. 2, 6, Luke 1: 16) it is translated by *giuuerben*, but when its object is 'corda' the translator chooses the rendering *giuuenten* (Tat. 2, 7, Luke 1: 17). The word 'mundus' is translated by *uueralt* at Tat. 13, 5, but the phrase 'regna mundi' corresponds to the German compound *erdrihhu* (15, 5) and 'peccata mundi' to *sunta mittiligartes*.

While such variations in the rendering of Latin words suggest thoughtful translation, others may be dialectal. It is to be observed, for instance, that four different verbs are used for 'respondere': they are *antlingen* (used ninety times), *antlingon* (used ten times), *antalengen* (used five times), and *antwurten* (used forty-nine times). The first three derive from the same root, and of these only the third appears elsewhere in Old High German; it is likely that each belonged to a certain area. The last occurs beside the others throughout the text, but it is noteworthy that it alone is used in Chapters 80-103, which includes the portion written by scribe γ.[1] The explanation may be that the translator responsible for this part of the text was unfamiliar with the synonyms.

[1] It is true that *antlingita* is found at 87, 3, but the first seven letters are entered by the corrector on an erasure.

It is commonly held that the translation, like the scribal activity, was the work of more than one man. Possibly a Latin manuscript of the *Tatian* was divided into its component quires or leaves and distributed among a number of translators in order to hasten the completion of the work. The number and extent of the divisions have been variously assessed. Whereas L. Kramp[1] postulated fourteen divisions without insisting on more than seven or eight translators, Arens[2] emphasized the essential unity of the whole, and Wunderlich[3] considered the variations no greater than those found in Notker's translation of Boethius, the unity of which has never been challenged. Baesecke[4] similarly rejected such attempts to identify divisions in the translation; however, he was inclined to regard that part of the text written by scribe γ as a special case. (It should be remembered that Baesecke, believing G to be an original and not a copy, could envisage such an association between translator and scribe.)

It is clear, then, that conflicting views may be held on the question of the technique employed in the translation. No less difficult are the problems posed by the vocabulary of the work as a whole. This shows that the *Tatian* occupies a special place among High German, and more particularly Middle German, texts.[5] Of the approximately 2,030 words in the text, about 280 are unusual in Old High German. Some are found only in a limited number of other High German texts; *antalengen*, discussed above, is one such. A surprising number (over seventy) are found only in the *Tatian* and Old English; *gifehan* 'gaudire' (OE *gefēon*), *gifeho* 'gaudium' (OE *gefēa*) belong to this group. This led early scholars to regard the *Tatian* translation as having been produced under the influence of Anglo-Saxon missionary activities and the Anglo-Saxon gospel-translations.[6] This view is no longer favoured. It is to be noted, for instance, that, while such words as *landeri* 'latro' and *gikeuuen* 'vocare' have equivalents only in OE *hlōðere* and *cīegan*, it is in-

---

[1] *ZfdPh* 47 (1918) 322–60. [2] Ibid. 29 (1897) 510–31.

[3] Ibid. 26 (1894) 269–72, in a review of Sievers' second edition.

[4] *Die Überlieferung des ahd. Tatian*, p. 18.

[5] See the indispensable collection of material made by E. Gutmacher, 'Der Wortschatz des althochdeutschen Tatian', *PBB* 39 (1914) 1–83 and 229–89, together with a word-index, ibid. 571–7. Gutmacher viewed the question in terms of dialect geography, but he drew no general conclusions. His findings were discussed by W. Braune, 'Althochdeutsch und Angelsächsisch', ibid. 43 (1918) 361–77, and placed in a wider context, ibid. 377–445.

[6] For references to the older literature see W. Braune, op. cit.

conceivable that they could have been borrowed from Old English and given their phonologically correct form. Furthermore, there are about eleven words which in Old High German are peculiar to *Tatian* but have equivalents not only in Old English, but also in other West Germanic languages. There are even eighteen such words which have no Old English congeners; one of these is *biril* 'cophinus', which occurs only in the *Tatian* and the *Heliand*. The obvious conclusion to be drawn from these facts is that the vocabulary of the *Tatian* has stronger affinities with the north than with the south; no question of borrowing need arise.

Further light is shed on the vocabulary by the observation that some words, for instance *hansa* 'cohors', while unique in Old High German, have cognates not only in Old English (in this case OE *hōs*), but also in Gothic (Goth. *hansa*). These must be survivals from common Germanic vocabulary which have been replaced elsewhere in Old High German. This view of the *Tatian* as a conservative text in the matter of vocabulary is fortified by the circumstance that it shares with the *Abrogans* a number of words having cognates in other languages but not occurring elsewhere in Old High German: examples are *fagar* 'speciosus' (with cognates in several languages) and *bruogo* 'terror', *bruogen* 'terrere' (with cognates only in Old English).

Not only does the *Tatian* preserve a number of words lost or uncommon elsewhere in High German; it also lacks some which occur frequently in other sources, including some texts of Middle German provenance, words such as *gināda*, *trōst*, *freuuen*, *trūrēn*, *clagōn*. Even more surprisingly, such common words as the verb *kunnan* and the preposition *āno* are wanting, their places being occupied by *uuizzan* and *ūzzan*.

On the evidence of the vocabulary, then, we can conclude that the text represents a conservative variety of Middle German which has strong affinities with the north. This conclusion is supported by some morphological features: we find the northern form of the personal pronoun *hē* beside the southern *er*, together with the intermediate Middle German form *her*,[1] and the pronominal adjectives based on the dissyllabic stems *unser-*, *iuwer-* beside the characteristically Middle German forms based on *uns-* and *iuw-*.[2]

We cannot be sure where such a language was in use, but there is nothing that contradicts and much that inconclusively supports

---

[1] *Ahd. Gr.*, § 283 n. 1 (a).   [2] Ibid., § 286.

the commonly held opinion that the text represents the culmina-
tion of a scholarly tradition which arose in Fulda, and was fostered
by that monastery's great abbot. No other important manuscript
is known to have been produced there, and it must be emphasized
that the main foundation of this opinion is linguistic, since we can
no longer be confident, as earlier generations were, that the non-
linguistic evidence points unequivocally to Fulda.

Tatian's harmony was the chief source of another, almost contemporary work of a very different kind, the Old Saxon religious
epic in alliterative verse known as the **Heliand**.[1] Of this poetic
treatment of the life of Christ 5,983 lines have been preserved. The
conclusion is missing, but the number of lines lost is unlikely to be
very great.

The text of the *Heliand* has been preserved in two major manuscripts, one in Munich (Cgm. 25, known as M or Monacensis), the
other in the British Museum (Cotton Caligula A VII, known as
C or Cotton after its former owner, Sir Robert Cotton). Portions
have survived in two others, one a single leaf preserved in the
University Library of Prague (P), the other a Vatican manuscript
(Codex Palatinus Latinus 1447, known as V).[2] This last contains

---

[1] The title, which is the Old Saxon word for 'Saviour', was given to the poem
by its first modern editor, J. A. Schmeller. His edition, *Heliand. Poema Saxoni-
cum sæculi noni* (Munich/Stuttgart/Tübingen, 1830), has only historical interest.
The most convenient edition is that of O. Behaghel, *Heliand und Genesis*
(Altdeutsche Textbibliothek 4). Behaghel's text is based on manuscript M, sup-
plemented by C. There is some regularization of spelling. It has a simple
critical apparatus, introduction, bibliography, references to Tatian and Otfrid,
and a simple glossary. The edition by H. Rückert (Deutsche Dichtungen des
Mittelalters IV (Leipzig, 1876)) is now out of date, but the commentary may still
be used with profit. The edition by E. Sievers (Germanistische Handbibliothek
IV) is essential for detailed study. It prints the texts of manuscripts C and M
on facing pages wherever both are extant, and there is a minimum of emendation.
Parallel passages from the Latin Tatian and relevant excerpts from the gospel
commentaries are given in the apparatus. There are over forty pages of notes
and a valuable list of poetic formulas used in the work. The Prague and Vatican
fragments were added as a supplement by E. Schröder when the edition was
reprinted in 1935. An important work of reference is the dictionary compiled by
E. H. Sehrt, *Vollständiges Wörterbuch zum Heliand und zur altsächsischen Genesis*,
Hesperia 14 (Göttingen/Baltimore, 1925). A reliable translation is provided by
W. Stapel, *Der Heliand* (Munich, 1953). Extracts: *Ahd. Lb.* XLIV and Holthausen,
Altsächsisches Elementarbuch. Facsimile: *Schrifttafeln* 17.

[2] For details of the manuscripts see Sievers' edition, pp. xi ff., and the
supplement, pp. 1 f. A full description of C is provided by R. Priebsch, *The
Heliand Manuscript Cotton Caligula A VII in the British Museum* (Oxford,
1925).

also the three fragments of the Old Saxon *Genesis*, which will be discussed later.

The Munich manuscript is the best, in spite of errors and lacunae, some of which are large, for there are fewer scribal errors than in the Cotton manuscript, and it belongs to the ninth century, whereas C belongs to the tenth century, and its text, though more complete than that of M, is less reliable. Its language, at least superficially, is closer to the Franconian dialects, though, as will be seen below, this does not necessarily mean that the language of M, which appears to be a purer form of Saxon, is that of the poet.

The origin of the manuscripts is unknown. Many scholars have held on palaeographical grounds that C was written in England. R. Priebsch[1] maintained that it was produced at Winchester, either by an Englishman who had learned the Carolingian script, or by a continental scribe who had been in England long enough for his hand to have acquired some insular characteristics, notably the *st*-ligature. Manuscript V, which contains also the three fragments of the *Genesis*, includes matter relating to Mainz and Magdeburg and belongs to the ninth century. M and C are derived from the same archetype, but P and V are independent both of that and of each other.

The *Heliand* is usually held to have been designed to make the Christian religion more easily acceptable to the Saxons, who were newly and reluctantly converted or even still unconverted. The author not only used the traditional Germanic alliterative verse and worked in familiar formal phrases of the worldly epic style, but, as far as possible, he adapted the Gospel narrative and the oriental milieu to Germanic conditions and taste. Thus, Jesus Christ is described frequently as the Ruler or the Child of the Ruler (*uualdand, uualdandes barn, uualdandes sunu*), 'the Lord of the peoples' (*thiodo drohtin, liudio drohtin*), 'the Lord of many' (*managoro drohtin*), 'the guardian of the land' (*landes uuard*), 'the protector of many', 'the protector of men', 'the mighty protector', 'the generous protector' (*managoro mundboro, manno mundboro, mahtig mundboro, mildi mundboro*). The Wise Men tell Herod that they seek 'a wise king, renowned and powerful, of the finest lineage' (*en uuiscuning, mari endi mahtig . . . thes bezton giburdies*, ll. 582–4) who will be 'courageous and powerful' (*bald endi strang*, l. 599), 'the shepherd of the cities, the beloved guardian of the

[1] Op. cit.

land, the powerful counsellor' (*burgo hirdi, liof landes uuard* . . .
riki radgebo, ll. 625-6).[1] The Virgin Mary is 'the loveliest of ladies'
(*frio sconiosta, idiseo sconiost*), 'a woman of noble lineage' (*adalcnosles
uuif, adalcunnies uuif*). The disciples are 'free-born men' (*erlos
adalborana*), Christ's companions (*gisidos*), His 'retinue' (*gisidi*),
'the loyalest men on earth' (*triuuistun man obar erdu*, l. 3517). Even
the Canaanite woman is nobly born (*adaligiburdeo*, l. 2985). The
tax-collector of Capernaum who demands tribute from Peter is
called 'a warrior of the king, a proud man among the people, a
highly placed representative of the noble Emperor' (*enan kuninges
thegn, uulankan undar themu uuerode* . . . *giuueldig bodo adalkesures*,
ll. 3184-6). The Jews, though as Jesus' enemies they are 'the fierce
Jews' (*thea grimmon Iudeon*, l. 4939), 'the hostile people' (*nithfolc*,
l. 5749), the evil-doers (*menscadon*, l. 3834), are 'the noble people
of Israel' (*Israhelo edilifolc*, l. 3318), 'renowned for courage' (*ellean-
ruoua*, l. 69). Herod is an alien ruler imposed on the Jews by the
mighty lord of *Rumuburg*. He is not of the noble race of Israel, but
commands the warriors only by the grace of Rome (ll. 54-72).
To his followers, however, he is the 'ring-giver' (*boggebo*, l. 2738)
and they are his 'ring-friends' (*bogwini*, l. 2756). He is called *folctogo*
(l. 5266), *folccuning* (l. 5276), *thiedcuning* (l. 5280), *uueroldcuning*
(l. 5284), *thegan kesures* (l. 5313), *hard heritogo* (l. 5314).

Nevertheless, the extent to which the personalities and events of
the Gospel narrative have been Germanized must not be exaggerated. Often the expressions used are mere formal phrases.
Above all, Jesus is never described as a warrior king, not even in
the account of the Cleansing of the Temple, which afforded an
excellent opportunity. The expulsion of the profaners is dismissed
in two expressively terse half-lines: *dref sie ut thanen | rumo fan
themu rakude* (ll. 3741 f.).[2] The ancient lineage attributed to Mary
and Joseph is in accordance with Germanic custom, but it is also
warranted by the first chapter of St. Matthew's Gospel and by
St. Luke, Ch. 1, vv. 5 and 36. With all his Germanic trimming the
poet remains true to the Christian doctrine taught by the Church
of his day.[3] The apparently Germanic military ethos of many

---

[1] This may echo Isa. 9: 6.

[2] 'He drove them out from there, far away from the Temple.'

[3] See H. Göhler, 'Das Christusbild in Otfrids Evangelienbuch und im
Heliand', *ZfdPh* 59 (1935) 1-52. This detailed study is valuable for its references
to the theological works of the period, although the passages quoted from the
Heliand do not always support the writer's view. The view of Christ as the King

passages should be seen not as the invention of the poet, but as a development of the Pauline view of the faithful as 'soldiers of Christ'. Recently scholars have been reluctant to accept the view that the poet deliberately (or even unwittingly) Germanized the Gospel story. Rathofer[1] has amply vindicated the poet's orthodoxy by reference to ninth-century theological thought. According to Rathofer one should speak of the poet's having 'accommodated' his source to the understanding of his public. Such 'accommodation' had an authoritative model in the Hellenizing tendency to be observed in St. Luke's Gospel, written for a Greek public unfamiliar with the Palestinian background.

This accommodation process can be seen both in the poet's omissions and his additions. Jesus is shown entering Jerusalem not on an ass, but apparently (ll. 3671 ff.) on foot. The omission of the ass has an interesting parallel in Rhabanus's comment on the passage of Scripture. He does not seem to believe that Jesus rode on such an unclean, ignoble, and stupid beast, and he interprets the 'impossible' and 'disgraceful' story allegorically: the ass represents the Synagogue! Though he does not intentionally falsify, the poet eagerly develops anything in the Gospel which will appeal to the tastes of his public. Thus the emphasis laid on loyalty was both good Christian doctrine and intelligible to German warriors: Matthew the publican is to the poet the trusted servant of noble men, who left all the gold and silver, great gifts and treasures, to become 'our Lord's man'; the king's warrior chose Christ as his Master, a more generous rewarder than his former lord had been; he chose the better part, the more enduring advantage (ll. 1189–202). The Matthew of the *Heliand* does not expect rewards during his life. More wordly are Thomas's words (ll. 3994–4001):

> Thuo en thero tuelifio,
> Thuomas gimalda — uuas im githungan mann,

who triumphs over His enemy but suffers for His people in doing so is Christian as well as Germanic (cf. Beowulf). Parallels between the depiction of events in the text, especially the Crucifixion, and that found in medieval art are drawn by F. P. Pickering, 'Christlicher Erzählstoff bei Otfrid und im Heliand', *ZfdA* 85 (1954) 262 ff. Valuable contributions to our understanding of the poem's religious vocabulary are made by M. Ohly-Steimer, '*Huldi* im Heliand', *ZfdA* 86 (1955) 81 ff., and H. Rupp, 'Leid und Sünde im Heliand und in Otfrids Evangelienbuch', *PBB* (Halle) 78 (1956) 421 ff. and ibid. 79 (1957) 336 ff.

[1] J. Rathofer, *Der Heliand. Theologischer Sinn als tektonische Form*, Niederdeutsche Studien 9 (Cologne/Graz, 1962), esp. pp. 1–194.

diurlic drohtines thegan —:   'Ni sculun uui im thia dad lahan'
                                             quathie,
'ni uuernian uui im thes uuillien,   ac uuita im uuonian mid,
thuoloian mid uus*on* thiodne: that ist thegnes cust,
that hie mid is frahon samad   fasto gistande,
doie im thar an duome.   Duan us alla so,
folgon im te thero ferdi: ni latan use fera uuid thiu
uuihtes uuirdig,   neba uui an them uuerode mid im
doian mid uson drohtine.   Than lebot us thoh duom after,
guod uuord for gumon.'[1]

Such sentiments are proper to a Germanic warrior, but they are not unchristian. Judas is a *treulos man* (l. 4828), who after bitter repentance is doomed to hell, the deep vale of death, because he failed his Lord (*huand he umbi is drohtin suek*, l. 5170); he forfeited God's help, as all men do who change masters (*herron uuehslon*, l. 4627). Peter made a strong appeal to the poet as a man, and the possibilities latent in his character were such as Germanic warriors could understand. The famous words 'Get thee behind me, Satan' are replaced by a mild rebuke (ll. 3098–4001). The poet eloquently expands Peter's vow at the Last Supper that he will never desert Jesus (ll. 4673 ff.). Jesus warns Peter that, although he has the feelings of a warrior and good intentions, yet shall he turn coward. When Jesus is taken in the garden, Peter is so full of anger that he cannot speak. The poet takes advantage of this one opportunity offered by the Gospel narrative to describe warlike deeds. The source, John 18:10, states simply: 'Simon ergo Petrus habens gladium eduxit eum et percussit pontificis servum et amputavit auriculam eius dextram; erat autem nomen servo Malchus.' This verse is expanded into a dozen lines (ll. 4869 ff.):

                              Tho he gibolgan geng,
suido thristmod thegan   for is thiodan standen
hard for is herron: ni uuas imu is hugi tuifli,
bloth an is breostun,   ac he is bil atoh,

---

[1] 'Then spoke one of the twelve, Thomas (he was an excellent man, a worthy warrior of the Lord): "We must not criticize what he does," he said, "let us not thwart His will, but let us stay by Him and suffer with our Lord: that is a warrior's choice, that he should stand firm beside his master and die there when the time comes. Let us all do likewise and follow Him on the journey: let us not count our life as anything worth, but die with Him, our Lord, as a warrior band. Then our fame will yet remain after us, renown among men."' In this passage the first use of *duom* probably refers to the judgement that awaits Christ in Jerusalem; the second to the judgement of one's fellow men. At this point the source reads simply: 'Dixit ergo Thomas . . .: Eamus et nos, ut moriamur cum eo.'

```
suerd bi sidu,      slog imu tegegnes
an thene furiston fiund      folmo crafto,
that tho Malchus uuard      makeas eggiun
an thea suidaron half      suerdu gimalod:
thiu hlust uuard imu farhauuan:      he uuard an that hobid uund,
that imu herudrorag      hlear endi ore
beniuundun brast;      blod aftar sprang,
uuell fan uundun.      Tho uuas an is uuangun scard
the furisto thero fiundo.¹
```

When Peter denies his Lord, the poet comments that he had no control over his words; it was destined so by Him who watches over mankind. The biblical statement that Peter wept bitterly is expanded into twenty-two lines, nine and a half of them being a monologue expressing Peter's remorse. After this the poet explains that there is no cause for surprise; it was the will of God, for He intended to raise Peter up to the highest place, and it is thus that he trains all mankind.²

Much has been made, by those who emphasize the essentially Germanic ethos of the work, of the poet's frequent use of terms denoting 'fate'. Such words are *gilagu, metod, metod(o)giscapu, metodigiskaft, regan(o)giscapu, uurd, uurd(i)giscapu, uurdigiskefti*. It has been held that he was unable to discard a pagan view of the world ruled by impersonal forces, a view supposedly irreconcilable with a belief in divine providence. It might, for instance, be maintained that an uneasy compromise is embodied in the following

---

¹ 'Then the courageous warrior in his anger went and stood staunchly in front of his King and Lord: his spirit did not waver or flinch in his breast, but he drew his weapon, the sword by his side; he struck out at the enemy leader with the power of his hands, so that Malchus was marked by the sword, the edges of the weapon, on his right side. His ear was hewn off: he was wounded in the head, so that his cheek and his ear, bloody from the sword-blow, burst as a result of the wounds. The blood spurted forth, pouring from the wounds. Then was the enemy leader injured in the cheek.' A translation cannot do justice to the epic variation in a passage like this: four different words are used for 'sword' (*bil, suerd, maki, heru*), two for 'ear' (*hlust, ore*), two for 'cheek' (*hlear, uuanga*), and two for 'blood' (*blod* and *dror*).

² Much discussion has centred upon the role assigned to Peter. It has for instance been noted that the poet writes (ll. 3071 f.): 'ni mugun uuid them thinun suideun crafte / anthebbien hellie portun', while the *Tatian* reads: 'et portae inferi non praevalebunt adversum eam' (referring to the preceding 'ecclesiam'. However, the substitution of Peter's power for the Church is paralleled in the Middle English and in two Dutch Diatessarons and may therefore have been in the version used by the poet. See Weringha, *Heliand und Diatessaron* (Assen, 1965), pp. 106 f.

words spoken by the angel to Zacharias concerning John the
Baptist (ll. 127 f.):

> so habed im uurdgiscapu,
> metod gimarcod   endi maht godes.

Similarly, when Jesus says to Judas at the Last Supper (ll. 4617 ff.):

> 'Frumi so thu thenkis,' quad he,
> 'do that thu duan scalt: thu ni maht bidernien leng
> uuilleon thinan.   Thiu uurd is at handun,
> thea tidi sind nu ginahid'

one might imagine an intrusive notion of fate. However, it must
be emphasized that the poet presents the Passion in a perfectly
orthodox manner as part of God's design. It might even be argued
that the first sentence of this passage makes the providential nature
of the events more explicit than the biblical 'quid facis fac citius',
and that the second is merely a poetic rendering of the words
'venit hora' or 'appropinquavit hora'.[1]

Germanization of details is common: the shepherds who hear
the Christmas message become horse-herds (*ehuscalcos*, l. 388); the
Magi follow the star 'along tracks and sometimes through forests'
(*uuegos endi uualdos huuilon*, l. 603); and the Temptation takes
place in the great forest.[2] A short statement is often developed
into a scene of action with elaborate and striking detail: the family
gathering to name the child of Zacharias and Elizabeth is am-
plified into an assembly of the clan. A difference of opinion arises
between 'a senior man who knew the ritual' and 'an over-bold man'
who protests at the choice of name. Herod feasts like a chieftain
among the lesser chiefs; the menials hasten with clear wine in
golden vessels; there is loud acclaim in the hall as the heroes drink
(ll. 2733–42). A similar scene of celebration is the marriage feast
at Cana (ll. 1194–2076), in which eleven biblical verses are expanded to over eighty lines describing a grand carousal in the no
doubt contemporary Saxon style. The repentance of Judas (ll.
5144–70), the grief of the widow of Naim (ll. 2183 ff.), the lamenta-
tions of the women at the massacre of the Innocents (ll. 736 ff.)

---

[1] For a full discussion of this problem and references to the controversial
literature, see J. Rathofer, op. cit., pp. 129–69.

[2] The word *uuald* is not altogether clear. In Old High German it frequently
glosses *eremus* 'desert' (the normal word for 'wood, forest' being *holz*), and its
English cognates are *weald* and *wold*. As for the rendering *ehuscalcos* for 'pastores',
it should be noted that the source does not explicitly mention sheep.

are other examples. The poet had a strong sense of literary effect, for the horrid scene of the massacre is followed at once by the Flight to Egypt and the peaceful life of the Holy Family there, a most effective antithesis.

Many little details which fire the imagination are quietly introduced in appropriate places. Before the birth of John the Baptist the winter advances, the year passes. The fate of the house built upon sand is graphically described (ll. 1818 ff.). The wall and the noble buildings of Jerusalem shine as Jesus enters the city (ll. 3683–7). The murky nocturnal deeds of Barrabas are touched upon (ll. 5415 ff.). The beauty of nature is real to the poet, as may be seen in the description of the trees putting forth leaves and blossom (ll. 4340 f.), and there are powerful descriptions of the storm on the Sea of Galilee (ll. 2238–60, 2906–19).[1]

With all its detail and the formal variation which is an essential feature of Germanic alliterative poetry, the *Heliand* is not diffuse. The poet expanded some scenes and omitted others; he condensed and combined passages from Tatian, and he did not hesitate to rearrange the matter.[2] As a literary artist he is a master of his theme and his medium. As a Christian teacher he remains true to the ideas of the Church of his time. The most that can be said against his orthodoxy is that he emphasizes the conceptions of Christ as King and Teacher, rather than as Sacrifice and Judge.

Various attempts have been made to determine the principle of composition which dictated the form of the work. Since the end is lost, no solution can carry entire conviction. However, certain obvious breaks in the narrative can be observed, notably after the twelfth, thirty-first, and fifty-third sections or 'fitts',[3] where the

---

[1] These passages could have been inspired by similar descriptions in Christian Latin poetry. Cf., for example, Juvencus, *Liber Evangeliorum* (4th cent., *P.L.* 19) ii. 25 ff.:

> 'Conscendunt navem, ventoque inflata tumescunt
> Vela suo, fluctuque volat stridente carina.
> Postquam altum tenuit puppis, consurgere in iras
> Pontus, et immensis hinc inde tumescere ventis
> Instat, et ad caelum rabidos sustollere montes.
> Et nunc mole ferit puppim, nunc turbine proram,
> Illisosque super laterum tabulata receptant
> Fluctus, disiectoque aperitur terra profundo.'

[2] For details see C. A. Weber, 'Der Dichter des Heliand im Verhältnis zu seinen Quellen', *ZfdA* 64 (1927) 1–76.

[3] On the meaning and use of this term, see below, p. 183.

poet continues his narrative with the epic formula *So gifragn ik.*
The last of these breaks is further signalled in C by the heading
Passio Domini, and in M by a descending marginal entry *Passio*.
Rathofer,[1] following Foerste, regards these breaks as indicating
the major divisions in the work, and he concludes that it consists
of four books, the first comprising twelve sections, the second
nineteen, the third twenty-two, and the fourth (as the work now
stands) eighteen. He also accepts Stapel's deduction[2] that the
complete work comprised seventy-five sections; thus the last book
must have been made up, like the third, of twenty-two. Unfortunately, Rathofer's extremely detailed analysis, which makes
use of medieval number symbolism, is vitiated by his reliance on
the division into 'fitts' which is peculiar to the Cotton manuscript.
Since such a division is an English scribal habit, and since the
Cotton manuscript is at least a century younger than the work
itself, it is very unlikely that the fitt-divisions derive from the
Saxon original. The probability is that they were introduced into
the text by an English copyist.

The *Heliand* was probably intended for the guidance of those
who were to instruct the Saxons, possibly to be read aloud in
sections on appropriate occasions. The verbose variations were in
the conventional epic style, and typical of the preacher or orator
are the formal phrases asking for the patience of the listeners (e.g.
ll. 3619 f.). The poet's command of the traditional style and metre
has given rise to the view that he was a professional bard or *scop*,
who had been converted to the new religion, and the words 'non
ignobilis vates' of the Latin Preface[3] have been cited in support of
this theory. It would be possible to reply that converts, in their
enthusiasm, are apt to fly to the opposite extreme rather than to
compromise with their former ways of thought and life, and that
the author of the *Heliand* is therefore more likely to have been
a monk who had adopted the old style as an artifice of war; but
such speculations are barren. The homily based on the parable
of the labourers in the vineyard, especially ll. 3493–515, has been
quoted to support the view that he was one of the newly converted,

---

[1] For a full account of earlier analyses of the poem's structure, see J. Rathofer,
op. cit., pp. 224–63. Rathofer's own analysis occupies the rest of his long and
detailed work. He provided a further justification of his views in *ZfdA* 93 (1964)
239 ff.

[2] See p. 174 of the edition of Stapel's translation cited above.

[3] See below, pp. 181 ff.

but without justification. He does indeed describe in vigorous terms the distress of the sinner who repents late, and expressly states that those who receive the faith late in life are taken into the same Heaven as the others, but he does not use the word 'we', even though Rhabanus wrote 'nos autem qui ad undecimam horam venimus', and he might equally well be reassuring a Saxon audience, not speaking for himself. The same applies to the sermon on the miraculous healing of the two blind men (ll. 3588 ff.), which has been the subject of much discussion.[1]

The *Heliand* seems to stand at the end of a literary movement. It is a book epic of a type developed in England, and it carries to an extreme certain traits which are characteristic of that class of poem. The 'Hakenstil' is more prevalent than in any other epic or lay; long sentences, elaborate periods, and indirect speech are common; the masses of unstressed syllables, the numerous 'Schwellverse', and the extensive use of epic variation may well be signs of late technique. It is commonly held that the *Heliand* is not the first stage in the development of a local Saxon form which arose in the ninth century, but the climax of a tradition which originated in Northumbria, and had been current in England for over a hundred years.[2]

Both the style and the manner of the poem incline us to the view that the author was a cleric, that is to say a man of some education. On the other hand, it has been said that he displays such ignorance of the Scriptures that he could not have been able to read them himself, but must have composed his poem from his confused recollection of what some trained theologian had read to him. He must have had, according to this opinion, a clerical

---

[1] This exegetical excursus is unique in that it occupies a whole fitt (44). W. Krogmann, *Nddʒb* 78 (1955) 1–27, considered it to be an interpolation by another poet. Rathofer, op. cit., esp. pp. 341–8, 444–7, rejects this view, arguing that it embodies an essential element in the theology of the work, viz. the salvation from sin by the illumination of divine teaching.

[2] See A. Heusler, *Deutsche Versgeschichte mit Einschluß des altenglischen und altnordischen Stabreimverses* (Grundriß 8) 2nd edn. (Berlin, 1956), vol. i, *passim* and *ZfdA* 57 (1919–20) 1–49. Against this view see D. Hofmann, 'Die altsächsische Bibelepik ein Ableger der angelsächsischen geistlichen Epik?', *ZfdA* 89 (1959) 173–90. It is undeniable that cultural links between England and Northern Germany were strong, but it does not necessarily follow that the poetic form of the *Heliand* was borrowed. Peculiarities of technique in Old Saxon (and Old High German) alliterative works may be signs not of degeneration, but of an autochthonous tradition, and the impulse to compose a long work on a biblical theme employing the native idiom may have come from within.

adviser.[1] In ll. 358–65 he says that David reigned at Bethlehem, and we are asked by those who maintain that the poet was a layman whether we believe that a cleric of the ninth century could have perpetrated such a blunder. We do believe it, for, in the first place, the location of David's capital is of no importance to the narrative, as the connection of Christ and David is all that matters, and the alteration may therefore have been deliberate; in the second place, a preacher of the twelfth century could speak of Cana as a street in the city of Galilee. In l. 641 the Magi travel home westwards (as did the voyagers who brought Hadubrand the false news of his father's death), probably because that would be the direction taken by pilgrims returning from the East to Europe. In ll. 2381 ff. Jesus and His disciples embark in the ship to avoid the multitude, but in l. 2538 Jesus is again surrounded by the crowd. The inconsistency is perhaps one of the poet's harmless Germanizations, for the chief spoke to his followers in the ring; they did not stand in rows. Many other passages of a similar nature have been cited. Some of these apparent blunders have been explained away. It has been claimed that the good disposition of the poem could not have been achieved by anyone who was unable to read or had not studied the Bible for himself, whereas other investigators have held that the clerical adviser selected and arranged the material, the poet being responsible only for the composition and the blunders. Such a division of labour appears highly improbable.

It remains to consider the sources on which the poet or his clerical adviser drew, and for this purpose it does not matter which view is accepted. It is almost universally thought that the author did not collect his material independently from the Scriptures, but relied on Tatian. We do not know which version of Tatian's harmony he used, but we can assert with confidence that it was not the Latin version of Fulda.[2] He may well have referred to the individual Gospels in addition, for not all his matter is to be found in Tatian. For his interpretation of the text he seems to have made extensive use of Rhabanus's Commentary on St. Matthew. He is also indebted to the Commentaries of Bede on St. Luke and, to

---

[1] See F. Jostes *ZfdA* 40 (1896) 341–68; W. Bruckner, *Der Helianddichter ein Laie* (Basle, 1904), and the reply by G. Ehrismann, *Engl. Studien* 37 (1907) 279–86. Also Weber and Göhler, opp. citt., *passim*.

[2] This has been established by recent scholarship. See J. fon Weringha, *Heliand and Diatessaron*, Studia Germanica v (Assen, 1965), and Rathofer's introduction to A. Baumstark, op. cit., pp. xii ff.

a lesser extent, of Alcuin on St. John. He knew also apocryphal legends of Jesus' childhood, and he followed legendary tradition against both Scripture and Bede in his statement that Pilate was punished both in this life and after death for yielding to the demands of the mob.[1]

Like the Irish geographer Dicuil he correctly makes the Nile flow northwards (l. 759), not southwards, as do Isidor and other early writers. As Dicuil dedicated one of his works to Louis the Pious, he may well be the source of this piece of knowledge. He displays his etymological knowledge at ll. 5462 f., when he renders 'in loco qui dicitur Lithostrotos, hebraice autem Gabbatha' (John 19:13) by *an them stenuuege, thar thiu strata uuas | felison gifuogid*. He may have gleaned this information from some glossary based on the *Hermeneumata*, a Greek–Latin glossary much used and freely adapted during the Middle Ages, one of the ultimate sources of the *Vocabularius Sancti Galli*.[2] However, Rathofer[3] draws attention to the fact that Rhabanus in *De Universo* devotes a chapter to the word in question. The poet's knowledge is therefore no indication of special erudition.

Many and widely divergent views have been expressed about the home of the author of the *Heliand*. None has been proved to be correct, for no certainty is possible. The monastery of Welanao (Münsterdorf in Holstein, founded in 823 in connection with the Danish mission of Louis the Pious), Corvey on the Weser, Werden on the Ruhr, Utrecht, Mainz, even Normandy and the estuary of the Loire have been suggested and rejected.[4]

Like the heroic epic, the *Heliand* is impersonal. There are no references to the author, nor are there allusions to persons or events known to history. Attempts to locate the poem by the reference to the salt of the earth (l. 1370, Matt. 7: 7),[5] the use of the term

---

[1] See C. A. Weber, op. cit. This careful and detailed study gives the clearest and best-documented account of the sources and contains much bibliographical matter. On apocryphal sources, see F. P. Pickering, 'Christlicher Erzählstoff bei Otfrid und im Heliand', *ZfdA* 85 (1954) 262 ff.

[2] See Weber, op. cit., pp. 66 f., and Baesecke, *Voc. St. Galli*, pp. 34 and 121.

[3] Op. cit., p. 382 n.

[4] For the controversial literature see Ehrismann, loc. cit.; F. Jostes, *ZfdA* 40 (1896) 129–92; F. Wrede, ibid. 43 (1899) 333–60; W. Krogmann, *Die Heimatfrage des Heliand im Lichte des Wortschatzes* (Wismar, 1937); A. Bretschneider, *ZfMaf* 14 (1938) 129–39. On the boundaries of the Old Saxon language see Gallée, *Altsächsische Grammatik*, and Holthausen, *Altsächsisches Elementarbuch*.

[5] See F. Jostes, loc. cit.; O. Behaghel, *PBB* 39 (1914) 225–7; E. Schröder, *ZfdA* 61 (1924) 35 f.

ehuscalcos for the shepherds to whom the angels appeared (l. 388),[1] and the allusion to the weed *durth* (l. 2545)[2] have failed. The vigorous descriptions of the storms on the Sea of Galilee (ll. 2241 ff., 2906 ff.), being common form in Latin religious poetry (which acquired such descriptions from Virgil), do not prove that the poet came from a maritime province. Wrede[3] attached great importance to the combination of alliteration of *g* with *j* (proving that the poet's *g* was a fricative),[4] the use of *-burg* to form names of towns, e.g. *Rumuburg*, *Nazarethburg*, and the forms *drokno*, *drucno* ('dry') *druknide* ('dried') with a voiceless plosive for the expected voiced fricative *g*. The most closely argued case is that of Krogmann,[5] who rejected all the evidence except for the words *leia* and *pascha*. The former word (meaning 'stone' in the poem) is native to the Rhenish Slate Mountains and thus sets the northern limit. The latter (used for 'Easter' instead of the normal southern word *ostaron*) is characteristic of the archdiocese of Cologne; it therefore sets the southern and eastern limits, ruling out Fulda, Corvey, and Paderborn, which belonged to the archdiocese of Mainz. The evidence of these two words, Krogmann maintains, points to a restricted area roughly within the angle made by the Rhine and the Ruhr. The most likely origin of the poem is therefore the monastery of Werden on the Ruhr which, though lying just out-side the area thus delimited, held lands within it and was a centre of missionary activity. Krogmann further attaches importance to the use of the letter *ƀ* for the voiced labial fricative; this unusual letter appears to have been characteristic of Werden documents.

No definite conclusions can be drawn from the language of the manuscripts, because they are copies, and because no adequate standards of comparison exist. The Low Franconian area can probably be eliminated by the almost complete absence of the characteristic *-ht* for *-ft* (found once in C: *craht* for *craft* l. 38). Rooth[6] attempted to determine the characteristics of the language

---

[1] F. Wrede, *ZfdA* 44 (1900) 320.

[2] F. Jostes, loc. cit., F. Wrede, *ZfdA* 43 (1899) 346.

[3] *ZfdA* 43 (1899) 346–60.

[4] It no doubt was in some positions, but not in all. The same phenomenon is found in Old English verse; it was probably conventional.

[5] Op. cit.

[6] E. Rooth, 'Zur Heliandsprache', *Fragen und Forschungen im Bereich und Umkreis der germanischen Philologie, Festgabe für Theodor Frings zum 70. Geburtstag* (Berlin, 1956), pp. 40 ff.

of the archetype from a study of the common portion of all four manuscripts. He believed that the genuine Saxon phonology and morphology was overlaid by southern spelling. Much earlier Wrede had assumed an artificial language for which he used the term *Bibelsächsisch* instead of *Altsächsisch*. Frings[1] associated the poem closely with Fulda, and Baesecke went so far as to hold that it was composed there,[2] but if two languages as different as those of the *Tatian* and the *Heliand* were being written at the same monastery at approximately the same time, it is difficult to see what standards can be established at all.

Although it is impossible to prove from the evidence provided by the language, style, manner, or matter precisely where the poem was composed or where the poet's home was located, it is at least likely[3] that it was composed under the influence of the Fulda movement and therefore connected with the plans of Louis the Pious and Rhabanus. So much is clear to most scholars from the extensive use the poet apparently made of Rhabanus's commentary on St. Matthew's Gospel. As the commentary was completed in 822, and as the manuscripts M and V are copies made in the ninth century, the poem can be dated with some accuracy. If it was directly inspired by the Emperor, it is unlikely to have been begun later than 840, the year of his death, but of that there is no proof. Baesecke, believing that it was composed at Fulda, maintained that it could not be earlier than the *Tatian* translation. Even if there were definite evidence of the precise date of the *Tatian*, which there is not, this method of reasoning would be fundamentally unsound, for it could be retorted that no great work of any kind appears to have been produced at Fulda later, and that therefore the *Tatian* might equally well mark the beginning of a decline.[4]

Attempts have been made to establish the connection between Louis the Pious and the *Heliand* through two short texts written in Carolingian Latin, one in prose and the other in verse, and entitled respectively *Prefatio in librum antiquum Saxonica lingua*

---

[1] *PBB* 59 (1935) 455–8.
[2] *Vocabularius Sancti Galli*, pp. 120–1.
[3] Though some, like Krogmann, *NddJb* 79 (1956) 1 ff., have denied it.
[4] The uncertainty of such speculations is augmented when one considers that the poet at least had access to readings not found in either the Fulda or the St. Gall versions of Tatian, and that Fulda is not universally accepted as the home of the Old High German translation (see above, pp. 158–68).

conscriptum and *Versus de poeta et interprete huius codicis*.[1] These are generally considered to refer to the *Heliand*, although they are not found in any manuscript of the poem, and their origin is unknown. They appeared for the first time in the year 1562, when the humanist Matthias Flaccius Illyricus printed them in the second edition of his *Catalogus testium veritatis*, a collection of excerpts which he made in order to show that the need for a reform of the Church had long been felt.

The prose Preface contains certain contradictions, and only a portion of it is original.[2] This states that 'Ludouuicus piissimus Augustus',[3] being most zealous to promote true religion and healthy minds among his people, and desiring to enable all his German-speaking subjects to read the Scriptures, a privilege formerly enjoyed only by the educated, 'praecepit cuidam viro de gente Saxonum, qui apud suos non ignobilis vates habebatur, ut vetus et novum Testamentum in germanicam linguam poetice transferre studeret'.[4] The man obeyed all the more readily as he had already received a call from God. He began with the Creation and selected the most important facts, adding, where he thought fit, mystical interpretations, until he had completed the Old and New Testaments, 'more poetico satis faceta eloquentia'. In accordance with the custom of this style of poetry he divided the work 'per vitteas quas nos lectiones vel sententias possumus appellare'. The poet, then, was well known among his people. The interpolated passages of the prose Preface contradict this, for they represent him as having been inspired in a dream when still entirely ignorant of his art and as having then produced the most wonderful poem that had ever been written in the German language. Presumably the interpolation was made in order to reconcile the prose Preface with the following verses.

The verse Preface describes the poet as a simple peasant who peacefully tended his flocks with no thought of glory, royal

---

[1] Printed in Sievers' edition, pp. 3–6, and in Behaghel's, pp. 1–3.

[2] For details see Sievers' edition, p. xxix, and *PBB* 50 (1912) 416–23. Like all Sievers' work that depends on his rhythmic theories, this latter must be used with caution.

[3] This is usually taken to refer to the Emperor Louis the Pious.

[4] Baesecke, *Vocabularius Sancti Galli*, p. 121, argued that the words 'de gente Saxonum' prove that the poem was not written in Saxony. This is fallacious. No one has doubted that Otfrid was a Frank on the ground that he uses the words *Frankon* and *frenkisg* repeatedly.

palaces, wordly wealth, or greed. In a dream he was summoned by a voice from Heaven, which said:

> Incipe divinas recitare ex ordine leges,
> transferre in propriam clarissima dogmata linguam.

The peasant became a poet. Beginning with the origin of the world, he told the story of the Five Ages and the coming of Christ, who rescued the world from hell. The idea of a miraculous summons is undoubtedly taken from Bede's account of the calling of Caedmon.[1]

Flaccius Illyricus did not state where he found the prefaces, and there is no positive evidence to connect them with the *Heliand*. It is certainly most improbable that he forged them, for the Latin is Carolingian, not humanist, and he could hardly have known or invented the word *vitteas*. Though not found in any Old Saxon or Old High German text, the word is Germanic and connected with OE *fit* 'song', 'poem' and *fittan* 'to sing'. The fact that manuscript C has numbered divisions seems to agree with the reference to *vitteas* in the prose Preface. The argument that the prefaces can refer only to the *Heliand*, because no other great work exists to which they could refer, is weak. Much medieval work has been lost, and as a matter of fact they do not entirely suit the *Heliand*, as the poem contains only matter from the Gospels and treats neither the Old Testament nor the remainder of the New.[2] The original portion of the prose Preface, then, cannot refer to the *Heliand* unless its author was inaccurate, or unless the poet had produced at least one other religious poem. In fact, this passage in the Preface has been used as an argument in favour of the unity of authorship of the *Heliand* and the *Genesis*. Such arguments, though interesting and plausible, are obviously inconclusive, and they may easily degenerate into a vicious circle. The prefaces merely show that there existed in the ninth century a tradition or belief that, at the command of the Emperor Louis, a Saxon had produced poems dealing with the Old and New Testaments.

The **Genesis** must have been a lengthy biblical epic. Altogether over 1150 lines are extant. Of these, 851 exist in an Old English

---

[1] *Historia Ecclesiastica Gentis Anglorum* IV. 24. On the Caedmon story see C. L. Wrenn, *The Poetry of Caedmon* (London, 1947).
[2] See G. Baesecke, *Vocabularius Sancti Galli*, pp. 138–40.

translation (known to English scholars as 'The Younger Genesis' or 'Genesis B'); one fragment of just over twenty-six lines (corresponding to ll. 791–817a of the English version) is preserved in both languages; the remainder, comprising two fragments of 123 and 187 lines respectively, survives in Saxon only. The discovery of the three Saxon fragments in 1894 confirmed the opinion expressed by Sievers in 1875[1] that the Old English text was a translation.

The first of the Old Saxon fragments contains Adam's lament after the Fall. The second recounts the murder of Abel, the cursing of Cain, the grief of Adam and Eve, and the birth of Seth; it then tells of their descendant Enoch, and looks forward to his contest with Antichrist. The third fragment describes the destruction of Sodom and the petrifaction of Lot's wife. All are tragic themes which would appeal to the Germanic mind, and their inclusion in the Vatican manuscript together with two fragments from the *Heliand* (ll. 958–1006a, treating of Christ's baptism, and 1279–1358a, containing the beginning of the Sermon on the Mount) is hardly fortuitous. Perhaps the compiler intended a contrast between fallen humanity and Christ's work of redemption. There are strong echoes of the *Genesis* in fitt 13 of the *Heliand*, which describes the Temptation of Christ, the second Adam. The destruction of the cities of the plain is mentioned in the *Heliand* (ll. 4366 ff.) and compared with the coming of Mutspelli. It is perhaps significant too that through the *Muspilli* we have a further link between the two Saxon poems: the second *Genesis* fragment, like *Muspilli*, tells of the death of a witness in the struggle with Antichrist, though in the latter poem the witness is named as Elias, not Enoch. It may indeed be that the thematic links between the *Genesis* and the *Heliand* were intended by their author (or authors), though it is clear from the opening lines of the *Heliand* that it is an independent work.

The treatment of the biblical narrative in the *Genesis* is often highly lyrical and dwells on the states of mind of the characters. Adam rails at Eve for what she has done: now she can see black hell gaping greedily and hear its tumult. Hunger and thirst, heat and cold torment the pair as they stand naked. Eve, who has suckled Abel at her breast, washes his bloody garments and grieves for him; Adam and Eve mourn not only because one of their

---

[1] E. Sievers, *Der Heliand und die angelsächsische Genesis* (Halle, 1875).

children is murdered, but because the other was his murderer. Often they stand lamenting that they will have no heirs; but the Lord consoles them and grants them descendants. In the third fragment Abraham's reverence towards God is developed in terms of feudal relationships:

Ik biun thin egan scalc,
hold endi gihorig,   thu bist mi herro so guod,
medmo so mildi: uuilthu minas uuiht
drohtin hebbian huat?   it all an thinum duoma sted.
Ik libbio bi thinum lehene,   endi ik gilobi an thi:
fro min the guoda,   muot ik thi fragon nu,
uuarod thu sigidrohtin   sidon uuilleas?[1]

The poet frequently expands, but sometimes abridges, the biblical source. Abraham's intercessions for the men of Sodom are reduced from six to three, no doubt for artistic reasons. The omissions in the third fragment are more puzzling; the exchanges between Lot and the men of the city are absent, and it is not at all clear what sins the citizens practised or how the angels learned of them.

As mentioned above, the controversies about the authorship of the *Heliand* and the value of the Latin prefaces are connected with the dispute over the authorship of the *Genesis*. One party holds that the *Genesis* was written by an inferior and slightly later poet who was an imitator, perhaps a pupil, of the author of the *Heliand*, while the other party maintains that both poems were written by the same man.[2]

Those who believe that there were two authors have collected many quotations in order to show that the poems differ in many details: words are used in different senses; prepositions are differently employed; the proportion of long sentences and subordinate clauses is said to be higher in the *Heliand*; there are

---

[1] 'I am Thine own servant, faithful and obedient. Thou art my Lord, so good and so generous with gifts. Wilt Thou, Lord, have ought of mine? It all stands at Thy command. I hold my life in fief from Thee and I believe in Thee. My good Lord, may I now ask Thee whither Thou, the Lord of victory, wilt journey?'

[2] See O. Behaghel, *Der Heliand und die altsächsische Genesis* (Giessen, 1902); F. Pauls, *Studien zur altsächsischen Genesis* (Leipzig, 1902); id. 'Zur Stilistik der altsächsischen Genesis', *PBB* 30 (1905) 142–207; A. Heusler, *ZfdA* 57 (1919–20) 1–48, esp. 44; W. Bruckner, *Die altsächsische Genesis und der Heliand das Werk eines Dichters* (Germanisch und Deutsch 4, Berlin/Leipzig, 1929).

differences in the use of epic variation and in other points of style and metre. Their opponents reply that their observations are inaccurate and their conclusions unjustified. Even if certain abstract nouns, for instance, occur in the *Heliand* in the singular only, whereas in the *Genesis* they are always plural, other nouns of the same kind occur in the plural in the *Heliand*, so the lack of examples of the former may well be due to chance; the same argument applies to the use of prepositions. Differences of style and treatment, they argue, are due to the difference between the sources, for the Book of Genesis lends itself to brisker narration, while the New Testament invites treatment in detail. There is weak alliteration in both works, and the Germanization is on precisely the same level.[1] Above all, they attribute to their opponents the fundamental errors of assuming that the style and poetic qualities of the *Heliand* are on the same level throughout, and of comparing parts only of the *Heliand*, especially the beginning, with the *Genesis*. Both poems, they say, were written by the same man, but the *Genesis* is a later work and has much in common with the latter part of the *Heliand*. Such differences as exist are due to the differences in the material. Metrical divergences too have been observed: the *Heliand* is remarkable for its extensive use of the 'Hakenstil'; in the *Genesis* it is less prevalent, and there are fewer 'Schwellverse'.[2]

The view that the *Genesis* is the work of a later and inferior writer appears to be generally accepted, though some may still feel that the evidence is insufficient. Conclusions drawn from the minutiae which have been so industriously collected would be more convincing if the *Genesis* had been better preserved. The supposed 'inferiority' of this work is, of course, a matter of taste: some might feel that certain passages in it are as fine and as powerful as anything else written during the period.

---

[1] See Bruckner, op. cit., against Braune, *PBB* 32 (1907) 26.
[2] See A. Heusler, op. cit., esp. pp. 14 and 44 f.; G. Berron, *Der Heliand als Kunstwerk* (Würzburg, 1940).

XI

Louis the German

LOUIS THE PIOUS died on 25 June 840, having just put down the rebellions of his third son, Louis of Bavaria, and of his grandson Pippin the Younger, who claimed the kingdom of Aquitaine. Just before his death, the Emperor had made the partition of Worms, the last of several by which he had sought to divide his realm among his future successors. By the partition of Worms, Pippin was entirely disinherited, and Louis was deprived of all but his Bavarian duchy. The bulk of the Frankish dominions were divided between his eldest son Lothar and his youngest, Charles (the only one by his second marriage), who was later to be known as Charles the Bald (Charles II of France). Lothar received Italy, Swabia, Saxony, and all the Frankish territories on the Meuse and the Rhine; Charles received Neustria and Aquitaine. The imperial office naturally went to Lothar, whom his father had already made co-regent.

The accession of the new emperor was followed by renewed contention between the brothers. Lothar had designs on the territory of Charles and attempted to prosecute them with military force. This led to an alliance between Louis and Charles, and Lothar was joined by the disinherited Pippin. On 25 June 841, exactly one year after the previous Emperor's death, there took place a disastrous confrontation between Lothar and his enemies at Fontenoy (Fontenoy-en-Puisaye or Fontanet), where the Austrasian army of Lothar was ranged against Louis's Saxons and Bavarians, while the Neustrian army of Charles faced Pippin's Aquitainians. The imperial forces were defeated after tremendous carnage. Lothar withdrew to Aachen and Pippin to Aquitaine. On 14 February 842 Charles and Louis met at Strasbourg and swore the oaths of alliance known as the **Strasbourg Oaths** (*Die Straß-burger Eide* or *Les Serments de Strasbourg*).[1] The meeting took

---

[1] *MSD* LXVII; *Ahd. Lb.* XXI. 1; *Kl. ahd. Spdmr.* XV. Facsimiles Enneccerus;

place between the two armies of the contracting parties (*untar heriun tuem*, as it were). First of all the kings explained the reason for the meeting, namely to make a compact that they might the better resist the aggression of Lothar. Then, each king swore 'by the love of God, the Christian community and their common salvation' that to the full extent of their powers they would maintain brotherly friendship with each other, and that neither would ever make common cause with Lothar to the injury of the other. Louis swore first, as the elder, and in French, so that Charles's French-speaking followers might understand. Charles, for a similar reason, took the oath in German. Then, the followers of each swore in their own languages that, if their respective king were false to his oath, they would not support him.

The German oaths are in the Rhenish or Middle Franconian dialect (probably the former in view of the *b* in the word *furgibit*). The orthography of the text is confused, the division between the German words being frequently so faulty as to suggest that the scribe did not understand the language. When writing Latin and French too he ran some words together (as was not unusual), and sometimes divided a trisyllabic words into three, but he never produced such confusion as

> in dimit luheren in nohein
> iut hingnege gango

for *indi mit ludharen in noheiniu thing negegango* 'and will enter into no dealings with Lothar'.

The oaths were recorded in Book III, Chapter v, of the *Historiarum Libri Quattuor* by Nithart, the son of the scholar Angilbert and Bertha, the daughter of Charles the Great. Nithart was thus a grandson of Charles the Great, a nephew of Louis the Pious, and a cousin of the contracting monarchs and their imperial rival. He attached himself to Charles, who commissioned him to write the book in 841. It deals with the reign of Louis the Pious and with later events down to 843, when the great reconciliation took place which produced the treaty of Verdun. This treaty was concluded after Lothar had been driven from Austrasia to Lyon and at last sued for peace. By it Lothar retained Austrasia, Burgundy,

F. Steffens, *Lateinische Paläographie*, p. 69. For an interpretation of the difficulties in the French text, the earliest document extant in that language, and a discussion of the form of the oaths, see A. Ewert, *TPS* (1935) 16–35, and M. Roques, *Med. Æv.* 5 (1936) 157–72.

Provence, and Italy, while Charles retained Neustria and Aquitaine, and Louis kept all the German lands on the right bank of the Rhine—Saxony, Thuringia, Swabia, and Bavaria—together with an area on the left bank containing Worms, Speier, and Mainz. Charles's territories thus corresponded approximately to the area of present-day France without Burgundy, Provence, Flanders, and Alsace-Lorraine, while Louis's comprised most of present-day Germany. The Emperor ruled over a kingdom extending from the Frisian coast to just north of Naples; this narrow strip of land had little ethnic cohesion, and it survived as a political entity no longer than Lothar himself.

For ten years after the treaty of Verdun the brothers lived in comparative amity, but in 853, the Aquitainians revolted against the rule of Charles the Bald and were abetted by Louis the German (as we may now call him), who sent an abortive expedition to their aid under his son Louis the Saxon. In 855 Lothar died. His eldest son Louis (the Emperor Louis II, who reigned until 875) succeeded as Emperor, but he lost the Frankish heartland of Austrasia, together with Burgundy and Provence. His younger brothers, Lothar and Charles, divided their father's cisalpine domains between them: Lothar took Austrasia, becoming king of Lotharingia (Lothar II of Lorraine), while Charles became king of Provence; Burgundy they partitioned between them. Louis II was thus Emperor in name, but in fact he was king of Italy and no more.

Civil wars continued in the Empire for many years. Louis the German in 857 made a bid to gain control of the western part of the Frankish lands, choosing just the moment when Charles the Bald was occupied in confronting a Danish incursion into the valley of the Seine. He quickly won Neustria, but just as quickly lost it. In 863 Charles of Provence died, and his kingdom was divided between Lothar II (king of Lorraine) and the Emperor Louis II. In 869 Lothar II died, and in consequence Louis the German and Charles the Bald began to contend for the middle kingdom (i.e. Lotharingia or Lorraine). Charles at once seized it, but when Louis the German marched against him he offered to negotiate. The outcome of the ensuing negotiations was the partition of Meersen, agreed in 870.[1] By this partition Charles took western Austrasia as far as the Meuse, together with Burgundy, while

---

[1] Meersen lies on the river Geul and is a few miles north-east of Maastricht. It had a royal palace in Frankish times.

Louis the German took the eastern part of Austrasia and Frisia. Charles thus got Lyon, Vienne, Besançon, Toul, Verdun, Cambrai, Liége, Tongres, and Malines, while Louis acquired Aachen, Cologne, Trier, Strasbourg, Utrecht, Nijmegen, and Maastricht. Although the middle kingdom thus ceased in the ninth century to be an independent political entity, the territories continued until modern times to be the object of Franco-German rivalry.

The partition of Meersen coincided approximately with the completion of the next great contribution to German letters, the *Evangelienbuch* of Otfrid of Weissenburg (Wissembourg in Alsace), a version of the life of Christ in over 7,000 lines of rhyming verse.[1] This book is of immense historical importance, and to the author's contemporaries it must have represented a literary innovation as significant as the first three cantos of Klopstock's *Messias* seemed to the readers of the *Bremer Beiträge*.

The text of the work has been exceptionally well preserved, for there exist three manuscripts and fragments of a fourth, all of which are contemporary or almost contemporary. Of these, the best is considered by most scholars to be the Vienna manuscript, known as V (Codex Vindobonensis 2687. Theol. 345 of the Austrian National Library); it is complete, and from it all the other manuscripts were copied. Five scribes can be distinguished, of whom the third wrote only a few lines, but corrected the whole after the completion of the work, adding and deleting letters and insert-

---

[1] There are four modern scholarly editions of the work. That of Johann Kelle, *Otfrids von Weißenburg Evangelienbuch* (3 vols., Regensburg, 1856–81) contains the text and an extensive introduction (vol. I), a grammar of the language (vol. II) and a full glossary (vol. III). That of O. Erdmann, *Otfrids Evangelienbuch*, Germanistische Handbibliothek 5 (Halle, 1882), contains the text, an introduction, and some valuable notes. That of P. Piper, *Otfrids Evangelienbuch mit Einleitung, erklärenden Anmerkungen und ausführlichem Glossar* (2 vols., Freiburg/Tübingen, 1878, 2nd edn. 1882–4) has an extensive introduction, a full apparatus, a valuable commentary, and a glossary. There is also a student's edition by O. Erdmann, *Otfrids Evangelienbuch*, Altdeutsche Textbibliothek 49, 5th edn. rev. by L. Wolff (Tübingen, 1965); this has the biblical sources and excerpts from relevant commentaries at the foot of each page, a short preface with bibliographical references, a short glossary, but no critical apparatus. Kelle and Erdmann base their text on the Vienna manuscript, Piper on the Heidelberg manuscript. For a discussion of the editions see Wolfgang Kleiber, *Otfrid von Weißenburg. Untersuchungen zur handschriftlichen Überlieferung und Studien zum Aufbau des Evangelienbuches* (Berne/Munich, 1971), pp. 19–39. There is a facsimile of the Vienna manuscript, Otfrid von Weißenburg, *Evangelienharmonie. Vollständige Faksimileausgabe des Codex Vindobonensis 2687* (Graz, 1972).
    Selections are to be found in *Ahd. Lb.* xxxii, facsimiles in Kelle (vol. II), Enneccerus, Petzet–Glauning, *Schrifttafeln* 18 and Kleiber, op. cit.

ing the accents and dots to which reference will be made later. It is a pleasant but unproven surmise that this corrector was Otfrid himself.[1] Second in value is the Heidelberg manuscript, known as P (Codex Palatinus No. 52 of Heidelberg University Library); it is thought to have been copied from V after the corrections had been made, but it differs from V in the placing of accents. Some leaves are missing. The third manuscript, known as F (now Cgm. 14 of the Bavarian State Library, Munich), formerly belonged to the Cathedral Library at Freising, where it was discovered by Beatus Rhenanus in 1530. Its text is inferior to the others, in that the scribe copied V, but also made use of P; he also introduced Bavarian forms and a considerable number of errors. The approximate date of the manuscript can be deduced from the scribe's statement at the end: 'Uualdo episcopus istud euangelium fieri iussit. Ego Sigihardus indignus presbyter scripsi.' Waldo was archbishop of Freising from 884 to 906. Between this entry and the end of the work are inserted two German prayers in verse, known as *Sigihards Gebete*, which will be considered in the next chapter. In addition to the three principal manuscripts, there are fragments of a fourth dispersed in Berlin, Wolfenbüttel, and Bonn. This manuscript, known as D (Codex Discissus), was cut up, like so many handsome manuscripts, to make the bindings of books. There is evidence that other manuscripts existed which are now lost.[2]

Otfrid is the first German author whose work bears his name. He was a monk at Weissenburg, but he was not one of the celebrated ecclesiastics, and the little we know of his life emerges from the three dedications to his book—to Louis the German, to Salomo, who was Bishop of Constance from 837 to 871, and to his friends Hartmuat and Werinbert, who were monks at St. Gall— and from his letter to Archbishop Liutbert of Mainz, inserted after the dedication to the king, in which he explains his purpose and, in effect, seeks archiepiscopal leave to publish.[3] Towards the

---

[1] Kleiber, op. cit., like many scholars, believes this hand to be Otfrid's own and identifies it with others found in several other Weissenburg codices, mainly biblical in content. He concludes that Otfrid's was a biblical scholar of considerable stature, probably the master of the monastery school and responsible for the efflorescence of biblical learning to which the growth of the monastery's library during his lifetime bears witness.

[2] For details of the manuscripts see the editions and Kleiber, op. cit.

[3] For a translation and a commentary on this letter see F. P. Magoun, Jr., 'Otfrid's "Ad Liutbertum"', *PMLA* 58 (1943) 869–90. See also A. J. Ansen,

end of this letter he states that he was educated by Rhabanus Maurus, Liutbert's predecessor as archbishop of Mainz. This indicates that Otfrid probably attended the monastery school at Fulda before 824, when Rhabanus was its master. One may further conclude that the *Evangelienbuch* must have been completed between 863, when Liutbert became archbishop, and 871, when Bishop Salomo died. The reference to the times of peace in the dedication to the king are of dubious value for dating, because such references were common form in poems composed in praise of a ruler. The connections with St. Gall and Constance need not indicate that Otfrid had visited those places, nor can we conclude, from the image of the mariner returning home (used in the last chapter), that Otfrid had sojourned on Lake Constance, since this image is found elsewhere in similar use.

German literature was growing ever more national and independent. The great glossaries had been importations and, by their nature, afforded little scope for originality. The OHG *Isidor* was a translation of a Latin work, and the Tatian translation distorted the natural idiom out of fidelity to the sacred text. Even the author of the *Heliand*, who was independent enough to tell the story of the Gospels in his own words to his countrymen, no doubt borrowed the form of the alliterative book epic from England. Strange as it may appear at first sight, the monk of Weissenburg, whose tribe had been Christian for centuries and for whom only Latin culture had any value, was more openly national than the Saxon had been. Otfrid was not propagating a newly imported cult, but nationalizing an established culture. He had therefore no inducement to adhere to a traditional native style, but was able to adopt a manner that in all probability was new in the vernacular and derived from the tradition of Christian Latin poetry. He was a patriotic Frank, as we see from his dedication to Louis and the first chapter of Book I of his work, which bears the heading 'Cur scriptor hunc librum theotisce dictaverit', and it was his ambition to give his countrymen an elegant literature in their own tongue such as other nations already possessed.[1] 'Why must the Franks

MLN 59 (1944) 513 f., O. Springer, *Symposium* I (1947) 54–81, and A. E. Schönbach, *ZfdA* 39 (1895) 383–5.

[1] On Otfrid's use of metrical terms in this chapter, see P. von Polenz, 'Otfrids Wortspiel mit Versbegriffen als literarisches Bekenntnis' in *Festschrift für Ludwig Wolff zum 70. Geburtstag*, ed. W. Schröder (Neumünster, 1962), pp. 121–34.

alone', he asks (1. 1. 33–4), 'fail to indite God's praises in their own tongue?' They are as brave as the Romans, and it is useless to maintain that the Greeks can rival them (ibid., ll. 57–60); not even the Medes and Persians could prevail against them (l. 86). They may be compared to Alexander, who dominated the world (ll. 87–90). They dominate their neighbours by martial prowess and will be ruled by none but their own native king (ll. 93–4); they fear none as long as he is alive (l. 98), and none can harm him as long as his Franks defend him (ll. 103–4). They dwell in prosperity in a land of plenty, where copper, iron, crystals, silver, and gold are won (ll. 65–72). Moreover, they are a pious people, diligent in learning what the Scriptures have to tell them and acting accordingly (ll. 104–12). Yet, this gifted and exemplary people has no direct access to the Scriptures. It is Otfrid's purpose to supply their need (ll. 119–22).

In marked contrast to Otfrid's praise of the Franks as a people is the contempt expressed in his letter to the archbishop for their language, characterized by its barbarity ('hujus linguae barbaries') and ungrammaticality ('ut est inculta et indisciplinabilis atque insueta capi regulari freno grammaticae artis'): it did not, for instance, observe the Latin genders, and it was difficult to spell in Latin letters. Furthermore, Otfrid had no regard for existing Frankish 'literature'; he spoke of unedifying secular song ('rerum sonus inutilium, laicorum cantus obscenus, ludus saecularium vocum') which he hoped his work would supplant. In his endeavour he was encouraged, he says, by certain notable brothers and, especially, by a certain lady named Judith, of whom we know nothing more. It may be that the secular song to which Otfrid refers included the *uuinileudos* which Charles the Great had forbidden abbesses to send or write.

Otfrid divided his work into five books, justifying this division to Liutbert in typically medieval fashion: although there are four Gospels, he has composed his work in five books, because the holy even number of the four Gospels adorns our uneven five senses, and all things superfluous in us, both deeds and thoughts, are turned heavenwards. What we do amiss through our senses we may cleanse through remembrance of our reading of the Gospels.[1]

---

[1] 'Hos (sc. libros), ut dixi, in quinque, quamvis evangeliorum libri quatuor sint, ideo distinxi, quia eorum quadrata aequalitas sancta nostrorum quinque sensuum inaequalitatem ornat, et superflua in nobis, quaeque non solum

The five books, of which Otfrid gives Liutbert a brief synopsis,[1] contain respectively twenty-eight, twenty-four, twenty-six, thirty-seven, and twenty-five chapters. The first presents the Annunciation and Nativity, the childhood of Christ, the Baptism, and the teaching of John. The second opens with expositions of the doctrine of the Logos, the role of John, and the significance of Christ's Coming; then follow the Temptation, the calling of the Apostles, the marriage at Cana, the meeting with the Samaritan woman, and the Sermon on the Mount. The third book deals with the miracles and the teaching of Jesus to the Jews—the healing of the nobleman's son, the feeding of the multitude, the healing of the Canaanite woman, the woman taken in adultery, the man born blind, the raising of Lazarus, and the examination by the priests and pharisees. The fourth is devoted to the Passion, beginning with the annointing of Jesus' feet by Mary and ending with the sealing of the Sepulchre. The fifth book treats of the Resurrection, Christ's subsequent appearances and teaching, the Ascension, the Day of Judgement, and the life everlasting. Before the first book Otfrid places a dedication to the king, the Latin letter to Archbishop Liutbert and a dedication to Bishop Salomo of Constance; at the end he adds a dedication to his friends Hartmuat and Werinbert, monks of St. Gall.

Otfrid does not provide a harmony of the Gospels. He selects his matter carefully, adhering faithfully to the chosen portions of Scripture and the commentaries in use at the time. At the beginning and at the end, as he tells Liutbert,[2] he made a careful choice of matter from the four Gospels, arranging it in order to the best of his ability. In the middle, however, fearing to overload his book and to overstrain his readers, and being himself wearied, he reluctantly passed over many of Christ's parables and miracles and

actuum verum etiam cogitationum vertunt in elevationem caelestium. Quicquid visu, olfactu, tactu, gustu, audituque delinquimus, in eorum lectionis memoria pravitatem ipsam purgamus.'

[1] 'Volumen namque istud in quinque libros distinxi, quorum primus nativitatem Christi memorat, finem facit baptismo doctrinaque Johannis. Secundus jam accersitis ejus discipulis refert quomodo se et quibusdam signis et doctrina sua praeclara mundo innotuit. Tertius signorum claritudinem et doctrinam ad Judaeos aliquantulum narrat. Quartus jam qualiter suae passioni propinquans pro nobis mortem sponte pertulerit dicit. Quintus ejus resurrectionem, cum discipulis suam postea conlocutionem, ascensionem et diem judicii memorat.'

[2] Scripsi itaque in primis et in ultimis hujus libri partibus inter quatuor evangelistas incedens medius, ut modo quid iste quidve alius caeterique scriberent, inter illos ordinatim, prout potui, penitus pene dictavi.'

much of His teaching, no longer endeavouring to observe the
former order, but relying on his poor memory (or modest judgement).[1] By 'order' Otfrid apparently meant the chronological order
of events in the Gospels, as it had been established by St. Augustine in his work *De Consensu Evangelistarum*, of which Otfrid's
monastery library possessed a partial copy. Augustine had concluded that John was the most reliable of the Evangelists in the
matter of chronology, although he was the last to write; Matthew's
Gospel was written first, and Mark's (which modern scholarship
considers of great importance) was an abridgement of it. Accordingly, Otfrid hardly drew upon Mark and used John as his chief
source from the beginning of Book II onwards, inserting matter
from the other two Gospels into the framework provided by the
fourth. Naturally he relied upon Matthew and Luke in Book I,
since only they supplied accounts of the events anterior to the beginning of Jesus' ministry. It appears that Otfrid may have been
guided in his choice of scriptural passages by a lectionary and by his
knowledge of Augustine's chronology, but the question is complicated by the probability that Otfrid had access to many works of
biblical exegesis. He was clearly steeped in the divinity of his day.
Recently, for instance, it has been shown that he was probably
familiar, through Latin versions, with some of the writings of the
Syrian father, Ephraem.[2]

Otfrid was not content merely to relate the Gospel story, but
he also explained and interpreted it according to the theology of
his generation. Some of the chapters in which he does this and
some sections of others are accordingly headed 'Spiritaliter',
'Mystice', or 'Moraliter'.[3] The distinction between the modes of

---

[1] 'In medio vero, ne graviter forte pro superfluitate verborum ferrent legentes,
multa et parabularum Christi et miraculorum ejusque doctrinae, quamvis jam
fessus (hoc enim novissime edidi), ob necessitatem tamen praedictam pretermisi
invitus et non jam ordinatim, ut caeperam, procuravi dictare, sed qualiter meae
parvae occurrerunt memoriae.'
    On the sense of *memoria* in this passage see K. Dieter Goebel, *ZfdA* 96 (1967)
260–3.
    Kleiber, op. cit., pp. 306 ff., identifies the 'middle' as ch. 15 of Book III
together with the three preceding and the three following chapters.
[2] See R. Schmidt, 'Neue Quellen zu Otfrids Evangelienbuch', *ZfdA* 96
(1967) 81–96. M. Schmidt, *PBB* 94 (1972), traces Otfrid's linking of the Coming
of Christ with the destruction of Satan in 1. 5 to similar ideas in two of Ephraem's
hymns.
[3] Kleiber, op. cit., pp. 308 ff., attempts to elicit the structural principles
governing the placing of these exegetical chapters.

interpretation characterized by the first two of these headings is not sharp, and sometimes they merge. It may be said that *spiritaliter* denotes the spiritual interpretation of the story, as opposed to *corporaliter*, the literal sense, the story itself. Thus, in v. 6 Otfrid interprets the race of Peter and John to the Sepulchre *spiritaliter* as representing the progress of Jews and Gentiles towards faith: John, though a disciple, represents the Jews, for they were the first to know God; yet, just as John looked into the Sepulchre but remained outside, so the Jews failed to appreciate the message of their Scriptures. Peter, on the other hand, represents the Gentiles, at first outstripped by the Jews; he, however, entered the Sepulchre and believed. Finally, seeing Peter enter, John followed him in: this symbolizes the eventual conversion of the Jews, which will come with weeping and remorse. Further significance is found in the fact that the linen clothes and the napkin that was about Jesus' head are lying separately, and that the napkin is wrapped together: the napkin represents Christ's divinity, which is removed from our endeavours (*arabeitin*); moreover, it is wrapped together, so that its ends cannot be seen, and thus signifies that Christ's divinity has neither beginning nor end. Such interpretations are, of course, never Otfrid's invention: they follow those of the well-known Fathers; in this instance the ideas derive from Alcuin's commentary on St. John's Gospel and were repeated in one of the homilies of Otfrid's teacher Rhabanus.

Otfrid's treatment of the Marriage Feast at Cana, related in II. 8 and expounded in II. 9, is a typical example of the contemporary method of exegesis. In order that we too may partake of the feast, Otfrid gives an interpretation, based on Bede and Alcuin. Christ is the bridegroom, and His friends, designated as the bride, are His faithful in Heaven. The stone jars are the hearts of the saints, full of the Scriptures, with which they refresh us as with a pure spring. The jars are six in number, thus representing the six ages of the world. Choosing the third age, that of the Patriarchs, Otfrid recounts the story of the sacrifice of Isaac by his father Abraham. The reader is then enjoined to emulate Abraham's readiness to do God's will; he will then taste the pure water. If we wish to taste the wine made out of this water we must interpret more subtly (*kleinor reken*): Abraham represents God the Father Who, as Paul reminds us, 'spared not His only Son', and Isaac represents Christ. The wood with which Isaac was to have been burned represents the Cross; the ram caught by the horns in the thorns represents Christ on the Cross, and the thorns represent the people who placed Him there. Thus two kinds of drink are afforded by the Scriptures: pure water by emulation and heavenly wine by contemplation. Finally, the capacity of the jars is significant; holding 'two or three firkins apiece', they represent the Saints, some of whom write of the Father and the Son, while others write of the Holy Ghost too.[1]

Such is the manner of interpretation *spiritaliter*.[2] The interpretation *mystice*, on the other hand, introduces a matter of dogma, for example I. 11. 55–62: the Lord decided to come when all the world was counted (Luke 2: 1) so that we should all be enrolled in heaven. He was laid in a manger, where the cattle feed, because He wishes to see us at the eternal feast. Had he not been born, the world would have perished; Satan would have seized it if He had not come. We were in bonds, in the hands of the Devil. 'Thou, Lord, didst help us', exclaims Otfrid, 'in our greatest need.' Here the ideas can be traced to one of Gregory's homilies. The Wise Men's return to their own land by a different way teaches us *mystice* (I. 18) to seek our own land, namely Paradise, by a different way; we lost it through our pride and wilfulness, but we may return there through purity, goodness, humility, charity, and abstinence. The seamless garment of Christ is interpreted *mystice* (IV. 29) as representing the united company of His followers; it was woven by Charity which is always present in the Church. (The unity and uniqueness of the Church is a matter of dogma.)

The sections headed 'Moraliter' relate theology to our private lives. Thus, I. 26 expounds the purpose of baptism and the benefits derived from it. In IV. 37, which closes the fourth book, we are enjoined to guard Christ's grave, not like the soldiers appointed to do so (Matt. 27: 62 ff.), but with unremitting faith. In III. 3, after a chapter describing the healing of the nobleman's son, Otfrid draws a contrast between the nobleman, who wished Christ to go to his house, and the humble centurion who did not presume

---

[1] On Otfrid's interpretation of the Marriage Feast at Cana and the problem of knowing for what kind of public he designed his work, see Xenja von Ertzdorfer, *PBB* (Tübingen) 86 (1964) 62–82.

[2] Other examples are III. 7 (the Feeding of the Five Thousand), III. 21 (the Healing of the man born blind), IV. 5 (the Entry into Jerusalem), V. 25 (the Crown of Thorns), V. 8 (the Angels at the Sepulchre), and V. 12 (the Mystery of the Resurrection).

to invite Him; Jesus did not accede to the nobleman's invitation but was ready to visit the centurion's servant: this teaches us not to be respecters of persons.

A modern reader, educated to prize originality of thought and imagery, is inclined to accredit Otfrid's apparent inventiveness to the Fathers from whom he borrowed his ideas and to dismiss him as a slavish copier. It would, however, be wrong to deny him inventiveness simply because we have sought it in the wrong place. Otfrid's claim to originality resides in the skill with which he manipulates his material and gives it a new form. This skill may be illustrated by a brief analysis of one chapter, the thirteenth in the fourth Book. Under the heading 'Petrum dixit negaturum' this chapter recounts Jesus' warning to Peter that he will deny Him thrice before the cock crows. The biblical sources are John 13: 31, 33–5, and 37 (for ll. 1–10 and 46), Luke 22: 31–3 (for ll. 11–24), and Matthew 26: 33–5 and 69–74 (for ll. 25–54); in addition Otfrid may have used Rhabanus's commentary on Matthew. Otfrid arranges the matter provided by these sources in such a way as to produce a regular alternation of narrative and direct speech in the following manner:

ll.		
1–2	Narration	2 lines
3–10	Speech of Jesus	8 ,,
11–12	Narration	2 ,,
13–20	Speech of Jesus	8 ,,
21–2	Narration and words of Peter in indirect speech	2 ,,
23–8	Speech of Peter	6 ,,
29–30	Narration and words of Jesus in indirect speech	2 ,,
31–8	Speech of Jesus	8 ,,
39–40	Narration	2 ,,
41–8	Speech of Peter	8 ,,
49–50	Narration	2 ,,
51–2	Disciples' words in indirect speech	2 ,,
53–4	Disciples' words in direct speech	2 ,,

A rather different analysis of the passage is suggested by the scribe's use of large initials for the first two letters of the first word in ll. 7, 11, 21, 26, and 49. If we regard these, with Kleiber, as indicating structural groupings of lines,[1] we arrive at the following analysis:

---

[1] Kleiber, op. cit., pp. 50–67 and 181 ff. For a sceptical view of Kleiber's findings see W. Schröder, 'Neues zu Otfrid von Weißenburg', *PBB* (Tübingen) 96 (1974) 59–78.

ll. 1–6 Introductory narrative and Jesus' prophecy of His death   6 lines
7–10 Jesus gives the disciples His new commandment   4 ,,
11–20 Jesus enjoins Peter to comfort his brethren   10 ,,
21–8 Peter swears loyalty to Jesus   8 ,,
29–48 Jesus warns Peter that he will deny Him, and Peter reaffirms his loyalty   20 ,,
49–54 The disciples join Peter   6 ,,

The passage illustrates Otfrid's habit of anticipating direct speech by indirect speech (ll. 22, 29, 51–2) or by abstract nouns (ll. 29, 40, 49–50). Another characteristic of Otfrid's presentation, namely his use of variation, is amply illustrated here. The word *mánnilih*, l. 9 is varied by *ellu uuórolt*, l. 10; *húg es ubar ál*, l. 13, by *harto thénki tharazúa*, l. 14; *in gilóubu ni giuuángtis* by *múates thih gihártis*, l. 18; *báldlicho* by *théganlicho*, l. 22; *báldi sines múates* by *éllenes gúates*, l. 30; *er hinaht háno krahe*, l. 35, by *er thaz húan singe*, l. 36; *min*, l. 35, by *thes héreren thines*, l. 38; *suért . . . so harto bízenti*, l. 43, by *spér . . . so uuás*, l. 44, and *uuáfan*, l. 45. Some of these variations, of course, provide the author with convenient rhymes (but those used by the poet of the *Heliand* similarly help preserve the 'Hakenstil' so essential to the external form of that work). Another feature of Otfrid's style is cumulative repetition: for instance, *thú gilougnis hárto . . . thero uuórto*, l. 32, reappears three lines later as *lóugnis min zi uuáre*, l. 35, and, most fully, as *lóugnis thrín stunton   mit thínes selbes uuórton | . . . thes héreren thines*, ll. 37 f. Otfrid's use of variation may derive partly from the technique of alliterative verse; it may, alternatively or in addition, owe something to that of the Psalmist.[1]

In some chapters Otfrid employs a refrain, sometimes modified in length, wording, and even the position of the rhyming words at its successive occurrences. One such is v. 19, in which the full refrain of four lines (ll. 11 ff., 41 ff., and 63 ff.) alternates with a half-refrain of two lines (ll. 19 f. and 55 f.) and in which the rhyme-words *thingon* and *mennisgon* are transposed at the central recurrence of the refrain (l. 41).[2]

---

[1] See Klaus Schulz, *Art und Herkunft des variierenden Stils in Otfrids Evangeliendichtung*, Medium Ævum 15 (Munich, 1968). This chapter is discussed on pp. 26–9, and the influence of the Psalms on pp. 77 ff.

[2] For a structural analysis of this chapter see Kleiber, op. cit., pp. 229 ff.

The chapter 'Petrum dixit negaturum' discussed above might perhaps be interpreted as an attempt to accommodate the biblical account to Germanic taste; however, if one compares it with its sources, there is little that they do not contain but the variation (which is dictated by the poet's technique) and the insistence on the master–servant relationship. This insistence on the distinction between master and servant is found earlier (though it may be said to be immanent in the source) in IV. 11; there Peter's words 'Domine, tu mihi laves pedes? . . . non lavabis mihi pedes in aeternum' (John 13: 6, 8) are rendered (ll. 21–4):

'Ist, drúhtin,' quad, 'gilúmplih, thaz thú nu uuásges mih;
 inti íh bin eigan scálk thin, thu bist hérero min?
Thuruh thin héroti níst mir iz gimúati,
 thaz io fúazi mine zi thiu thin hánt birine.'[1]

When Otfrid comes to tell of Peter's behaviour on Jesus' arrest, he cannot contain his admiration for the servant who, unarmed, defends his Master against His enemies (IV. 17. 7–14):

Níst ther uuidar hérie so héreron sinan uuérie,
 ther úngisaro in nóti so báldlicho dáti;
Ther ana scílt inti ana spér so fram firlíafi in thaz giuuér,
 in githréngi so ginóto sinero fíanto!
Uuérit er inan giuuísso hárto filu uuásso,
 unz imo drúhtin thuruh nót thaz uuig sélbo firbot.
Soso éin man sih scal uuérien ioh héreron sinen nérien:
 so áht er io ginóto thero Kristes fíanto.[2]

Furthermore, there is a striking similarity between the terms in which the Disciples swear their loyalty to Jesus in IV. 13. 53–4 (based on Matthew 26: 35: 'similiter et omnes discipuli dixerunt')—

'Níst er', quadun, 'tháre ther ío thih so irfáre,
 gisúnten uns thir dérien; uuir uuóllen thih in uuérien'[3]

[1] '"Is it seemly, Lord," he said, "that thou now shouldst wash me, I being thy bond-servant and thou my lord? Because of thy lordship it is displeasing to me that my feet should ever for this purpose be touched by thy hand."'

[2] 'There is none who thus defends his master against an army, who would act so boldly in need, being unarmed, who would so rush into the fray without shield and without spear, compulsively into the throng of his enemies. He defended Him indeed with great mettle until the Lord himself of necessity forbade the combat. As one man ought to defend himself and rescue his lord, so did he always of necessity pursue Christ's enemies.'

[3] '"There is", they said, "no man who will ever so endanger thee as to harm thee while we are alive; we will defend thee against them."'

—and those used by the poet to describe the Frankish people's loyalty to its king (I. 1. 103):

Ni sínt thie ímo ouh dérien,   in thiu nan Fránkon uuerien.[1]

That Otfrid, like the poet of the *Heliand*, responded readily to anything resembling the warrior mentality of the Germanic hero seems clear; but lest we should claim the passages just quoted as reflecting an unadulterated Germanic tradition, we should remark that the phrase *gisúnten uns* (IV. 13. 54) is an adaptation of the Latin 'ablative absolute' construction.

Like the author of the *Heliand*, Otfrid endeavours to make the Gospels less alien in outward appearance. He omits names when they are unnecessary for his purpose, for example those of Jesus' ancestors (I. 3) and Anna's ancestors (I. 16). Bethlehem, having been mentioned once at I. 12. 15, is not named at I. 13. 3, where the shepherds say:

Ílemes nu alle   zi themo kástelle[2]

In II. 9 Abraham becomes 'a friend' (*wini, drut*) of God. Egypt is mentioned by name at I. 19. 5, but referred to simply as *elilenti* at I. 21. 3; shortly after this the biblical 'in terram Israel' is rendered by *zi iro heiminge* and *heimort(es)*, and Herod's successor Archilaus becomes simply *ander kuning*. Even Nazareth is here called *ein burg ziari* and not named. The words 'Samaritanus es tu' (John 8: 48) are rendered *bist elibenzo fremider* 'You are a foreigner' (III. 18. 14). The name 'Samaria' is given when necessary, as at II. 14. 5, but later the Samaritan woman says *ih bin thesses thietes* 'I am of this people', where the Gospel has 'sum mulier Samaritana' (John 4: 9). The desert ('eremus') is *uuasti, uuastinna*, but also *uuastinna uualdes* (I. 23. 19), and *uuastuuald* (I. 27. 41), *uuastuueldi* (I. 23. 9).[3]

Germanic customs cast their shadows; thus the magistrates (*heroti*) judge in the *ring* (III. 20. 53–4). The *thing* assembles in the *ring* in Caiaphas' courtyard (*frithof*, III. 25. 6). Christ defeats Satan in single combat (*in einuuigi*, IV. 12. 62). However, the Germanization does not extend beyond inessential details. Jesus is the King, but he is not portrayed as a wordly king;[4] in fact, He is

---

[1] 'Nor are there any who will harm him while ever the Franks defend him.'
[2] 'Let us all now hasten to the city.'
[3] As already observed, the word *uuald* does not necessarily mean 'wooded land'.   [4] See H. Göhler, *ZfdPh* 59 (1935) 1–52.

contrasted with other kings at 1. 20. 34, where Otfrid says that
another king would not shed his blood for us. The Disciples are
thegana, drutthegana (IV. 10. 1 *et passim*), but in Christian writings
all Christ's followers are 'milites Christi'. Even the comparison
of Jesus to a giant—

> Er quam so risi hera in lant   joh kreftiger gigant (IV. 12. 61)

is based on Psalm 18: 6 'exultavit ut gigas' (A.V. 19: 5 'a strong
man'). It is noteworthy that here Otfrid uses the native word *risi*
and the Latin word side by side. Caiaphas the Chief Priest and
Pilate the Governor, representing the spiritual and temporal
power, are designated as *biscof* and *herizoho* respectively (IV. 20. 2)
and the centurion become *ein scultheizo* (III. 3. 5).

Otfrid omits the Circumcision from his German text, though
the words 'De circumcisione pueri' appear in the heading of 1. 14,
contenting himself with a reference to fulfilling the Law. In
v. 20. 31–2 the Lord separates the good and the bad as the shepherd separates his sheep; the bad are not *called* goats as in Matthew
25: 32, but they stink like goats (l. 58). The omission of the Agony
in the Garden and the sleep of the Disciples need not be due to
Otfrid's Germanic instincts, for both episodes are wanting in
John's Gospel which he is following at this point.

There is a little more warrant for seeing native colouring in
Otfrid's treatment of the Last Judgement. As in the *Muspilli*, we
are told that nothing can help us at that Judgement—not gold or
fine clothes, not social position or kinship, not rewards or riches:

> Ni lósent thar in nóti   góld noh diuro uuáti,
>   ni hilfit gótouuebbi thár   noh thaz sílabar in uuar;
> Ni mag thar mánahoubit   helfan héreren uuiht,
>   kínd noh quéna in uuare,   sie sorgent íro thare;
> Odo íauuiht helphan thánne   themo fílu richen mánne:
>   sie sint al ébanreiti   in theru selbun árabeiti.
> Giuuísso thaz ni híluh thih: thar sorget mánnilih bi síh,
>   bi sines sélbes sela;   nist uuíht in thanne méra.
> Skálka ioh thie ríche   thie gént thar al gilíche,
>   ni si thíe thar bi nóti   gifórdoront thio gúati.
>   Uuard uuóla in then thíngon   thie selbun ménnisgon,
>   thie thar thoh bigónoto   sint síchor iro dáto!
> Thar nist míotono uuiht   ouh uuéhsales níauuiht,
>   thaz íaman thes giuuíse,   mit uuíhtu sih irlóse;

Ni uuari thu ío so richi ubar uuóroltrichi,
 thóh thu es thar bigínnes: ther scáz ist sines síndes.
Uuanta drúhtin ist so gúat, ther thaz úrdeili duat;
 er duat iz sélbo, ih sagen thir, éin, ander bótono nihein.[1]

What Otfrid emphasizes here is that the Last Judgement will be unlike all earthly legal proceedings; we shall not be able to invoke the aid of those who would help us here, for all the natural and feudal bonds will be dissolved, and we shall have no earthly possessions to bargain with. Every man will stand on his own, and only his good deeds will avail him anything. Some of these ideas are repeated in the succeeding chapter (v. 20. 37 ff.) where Otfrid describes how the Judge will divide mankind; again the dissolution of the bond between master and servant is mentioned specifically—

Giscéident sih in alauuár hérero inti thégan thar
 fon álteru líubi[2]   (ll. 43 f.)

—and so is the bond of kinship—

Gisíbbon filu líebe, thie uuárun hiar in líbe
 mit mínnon filu zéizen, ni múgun siez thar giwéizen.[3]

Otfrid's style is inclined to be diffuse. Not only did he allow the need to find a rhyme to lead him to insert formal phrases, such as *so ih thir zellu* and irrelevant parenthetical statements, but the second line of a couplet frequently repeats in other words the sense of the first; even couplets are repetitive. The portion of

---

[1] 'There gold and costly clothes will work no release in need, nor indeed will precious cloth or silver. The bondman will not be able to help his lord there, nor will child or wife: they will be anxious about themselves there. Nor will anything then help the very rich man: they will all be equal in the same distress. Assuredly I will not conceal it from you: every man will be anxious about himself, about his own soul; nothing will be more important to them then. Servants and rich men will all be levelled, except those who of necessity are advanced by their virtues. It will have been well, in those proceedings, for these same men, who are entirely justified in their deeds. There will be no rewards there and no *quid pro quo*, such that anyone may attempt to release himself by any means. Were you never so powerful in the world—even though you may attempt it there—your treasure is gone. For the Lord who will give the judgement is so good; he will give it in person, I tell you, alone; it will not be given by any deputy.'
This last line is taken to be an allusion to the Carolingian *missus*, who went on circuit through the realm, administering justice in the name of the sovereign.

[2] 'In truth master and retainer shall be parted from old affection.'

[3] 'Dear kinsmen who here in life were (united) with tender love will not be able to show it there.'

Otfrid's account of the meeting with the Samaritan woman (II. 14) which corresponds to the thirty-one lines of the fragment *Christus und die Samariterin* is just twice as long. On the other hand he could be brief: the expulsion of the money-changers from the Temple receives only two lines (IV. 4. 65 f.); it is a mere episode in Jesus' triumphal entry into Jerusalem. Otfrid does not indulge in wordy descriptions; his scenes and situations are dynamic, not static. In the account of the Annunciation, for example, the Angel (who is not named) flies *sunnun pad, sterrono straza, uuega uolkono* to Mary, who is singing the Psalter, holding the book in her hand while she embroiders rich fabrics (I. 5. 5–12). Otfrid no doubt had in mind three pictures such as he might have seen painted on an altar-piece—the Angel in flight, the Virgin reading, and the Virgin embroidering (there was a tradition that Mary wove the veil of the Temple, but Otfrid does not mention this)—and was not disturbed by the fact that the last two are incompatible. Other notable situations are the intended sacrifice of Isaac (II. 9. 29–62), the maternal pleasure of Mary (I. 11. 31–54), the lamentation of the mothers of the Holy Innocents (I. 20. 9–24), the women before the Cross (IV. 26), Jesus on the Cross commending His Mother to John (IV. 32). The Entry into Jerusalem is a triumphal procession; Otfrid's description (IV. 4) is as vigorous as that of the *Heliand* (ll. 3671–3757), but the detail is differently distributed.

Some have held that Otfrid intended his book to be sung, although it might seem unsuited for that purpose; this view has support in the musical notation (neums) inserted in the Heidelberg manuscript. It is more generally held that it was intended for reading—though whether for silent reading or 'performance' is not certain. The word *cantus* in phrase *hujus cantus lectionis* probably means 'song' only in the figurative sense that Virgil, Lucan, Ovid, Juvencus, Arator, and Prudentius, whom Otfrid names, 'sang' of famous men; the word *lectio* refers, like *lekza* (Sal. 5), to the reading matter, the text of the Scriptures, or to the contents, the subject matter. The whole phrase is likely to mean 'the reading matter', 'the reading of the Scriptures'. In his letter to Liutbert Otfrid repeatedly uses the word *legentes*, and in the course of his work he frequently advises independent reading in the Scriptures. In the Dedication to Hartmuat and Werinbert he refers several times to what can be learned by reading books. We may imagine his *memoriae digni fratres* in their cells, reading with their fingers in their ears, rather than singing lustily in competition with the light-hearted folk outside. It is, however, possible that portions of Otfrid's work may have been read aloud in the refectory at meal-times in place of the Latin sermons more commonly used. Though Otfrid was an outspoken nationalist he did not write his book for the ignorant common people. It is a literary production intended for educated men; these would most probably be clerics who, having some knowledge of the subject, would be able to appreciate both the matter and the art. They would read the book for their own satisfaction, and could accept its guidance in the method of their own teaching. The repeated injunctions to read for oneself would not be addressed to a congregation of simple people, but to such men as his friends Hartmuat and Werinbert. It has, however, been suggested that Otfrid's intended public was not confined to the clergy, but embraced parts of the educated laity: Otfrid at least envisaged that the king might have the work read to him, and perhaps the *veneranda matrona* Judith was a laywoman. It has been argued that Otfrid intended the *Evangelienbuch* to be read as a commentary on the Gospels, since it would be unintelligible without the text of the Vulgate. Some passages, notably IV. 6, support this view, but the obscurities which have been discovered are no doubt due rather to Otfrid's extreme familiarity with the Bible than to deliberate intention. His anxiety to make the text of the Scriptures fully intelligible led him, like the author of the *Heliand*, to answer the rhetorical questions of the Bible or to substitute statements. Thus, 'Dixit ei Jesus: nonne dixi tibi quoniam si credideris, videbis gloriam Dei?' (John 11: 40) becomes (III. 24. 85 f.):

'Thih deta ih míthont', quad er, 'uuís,   oba thu gilóubis,
    thaz thu gisíhis gotes kráft   ioh selbes drúhtines máht.'[1]

The *Evangelienbuch* is carefully constructed both as a whole and in detail. There are three dedications, each of which has an acrostic and a telestich. This form of virtuosity was very highly esteemed; poems exist with not only acrostics and telestichs, but with sentences running diagonally or forming crosses, diamonds, and other

---

[1] 'I have just told thee', he said, 'that if thou believest, thou wilt see the power of God and the might of the Lord Himself.' On Otfrid's treatment of rhetorical questions see D. A. McKenzie, *JEGPh* 44 (1945) 286 ff.; id. *Otfrid von Weissenburg: Narrator or Commentator?* (Stanford, 1946); J. K. Bostock, *Med. Æv.* 16 (1947) 53 ff.

patterns.[1] There are even examples in which each word in the whole text begins with the same letter.

It has already been shown that Otfrid paid considerable attention to the numerical balance of his lines. This preoccupation with 'the beauty of numbers' was typical of his age—and indeed of succeeding centuries. It is, for instance, not surprising that Otfrid's dedication to King Louis should be exactly twice as long (ninety-six lines) as that to Bishop Salomo of Constance (fourty-eight lines). Recently there have been attempts to show that Otfrid was concerned not only with the numbers themselves but with their symbolism; there is much to be said in principle for such a hypothesis, since it would be in keeping with contemporary ways of thought. It is almost certainly not fortuitous that Chapters 5–11 of Book I (encompassing the Annunciation and the Nativity) should comprise 276 lines, for Jesus was commonly reckoned to have spent 276 days in the Virgin's womb; furthermore, Chapters 6 and 7 of Book I, which tell of Mary's visit to Elizabeth, the quickening of the Child, and the words of Mary (the 'Magnificat'), comprise forty-six lines which, according to patristic opinion, corresponded to the number of days required by the embryo to form. It may be significant that the chapter headed 'Sol obscuratus et tradidit spiritum Jesus' is the thirty-third in the fourth book, since Jesus was thirty-three years old when He was crucified.[2]

Each dedication is written in an appropriate style and placed in order according to the rank of the person addressed: the king comes first, followed by the archbishop and the bishop. Hartmuat and Werinbert, the humblest personages involved, come at the end. To the king Otfrid writes as a loyal subject, to the archbishop as an ecclesiastical inferior, explaining the technical details of his work, to the bishop still as a subordinate, but gratefully acknowledging past help. To his friends at St. Gall Otfrid writes as an equal in a tone of pious exhortation and goodwill.

One of the unsolved problems is the origin of Otfrid's metrical

[1] One such work is Rhabanus's *De laudibus Sancti Crucis* (*P.L.* 107, 141 ff.). See E. R. Curtius, *Europäische Literatur und lateinisches Mittelalter* (1948), pp. 284 ff.

[2] For other possible instances of number symbolism see Kleiber, op. cit., pp. 298 ff., and W. Haubrichs, *Ordo als Form. Strukturstudien zur Zahlenkomposition bei Otfrid von Weißenburg und in karolingischer Literatur*, Hermaea NF 27 (Tübingen, 1969). See also H. Swinburne, 'Numbers in Otfrid's *Evangelienbuch*', *MLR* 52 (1957) 195–202.

form. It seems fairly clear that he progressed from beginner to adept in the art of versification as he composed his work: Chapters 3–6 and the first sixteen lines of Chapter 10 in Book I are technically primitive by comparison with other portions, which, presumably, were composed later; they contain a high proportion of unidiomatic constructions and violations of German grammar, e.g. present participles combined with the verb 'to be' but agreeing, for the sake of the rhyme, with the object, e.g. 1. 4. 5–7:

> Uuárun siu béthiu   góte filu drúdiu
>   ioh íogiuuar sínaz   gibot fúllentaz,
> Vuízzod sínan   ío uuírkendan . . .[1]

The dedications, together with the introductory Chapter 1 of Book I, are probably the last parts that Otfrid wrote. The problem of chronology is complicated and has not yet been fully solved.[2] While, however, it is agreed that Otfrid's technique improved as he went along, this improvement is not necessarily to be equated with progressive mastery of a foreign verse-form and increasing success in adapting it to German.

Whereas the poet of the *Heliand* had used alliteration as the constitutive element in his verse, Otfrid used terminal rhyme. There are indeed traces of alliteration, notably in the unrhymed line 1. 18. 9,

> Thar ist lib ana tod,   lioht ana finstri,[3]

which, interestingly enough, recurs in *Muspilli* (l. 14). There are also occasions when alliteration seems to be used as an ornament in lines whose halves are linked by normal rhyme, e.g. 1. 5. 5–7:

> Floug er súnnun pad,   stérrono stráza,
>   uuega uuólkono   zi deru ítis frono,
> Zi édiles fróuun,   sélbun s*ancta* Máriun . . .[4]

or 1. 5. 10–12:

> mit sálteru in hénti,   then sáng sị unz in énti,
> Uuáhero dúacho   uuerk uuírkento

---

[1] 'They were both very dear to God and everywhere fulfilling His ordinance, always carrying out His law . . .'
[2] See H. Bork, *Chronologische Studien zu Otfrids Evangelienbuch*, Palaestra 157 (Leipzig, 1927); L. Wolff, *AfdA* 48 (1929) 17–27.
[3] 'There there is life without death, light without darkness.'
[4] 'He flew along the path of the sun, the street of the stars, the ways of the clouds to the holy lady, to a lady of nobility, St. Mary herself . . .'

díurero gárno,   thaz déda siụ io gérno.[1]

It should be noted that some of these lines, even if deprived of rhyme, would still not conform with the rules of alliteration observed by the *Heliand* poet: in ll. 5 and 6 the alliterations on *st-* and *w-* are confined to their respective half-lines (unless one takes *súnnun* as alliterating with *stérrono* and *stráza*, which is not possible according to normal rules); the alliteration on the vowels and *f-* in ll. 6–7 not only links two long lines, but is crossed, as is also that on *d-* and *g-* in l. 12; and in ll. 5 and 11 there are two staves in the second half-line. It is not unthinkable that Otfrid was here employing the native technique of alliteration in addition to rhyme, since all the 'irregularities' just noted are attested in the OHG alliterative remains (together with occasional rhyme), and it is clear that the rules of versification deducible from OHG practice were different from those of Old Saxon. On the other hand, alliteration was a familiar ornament in Latin verse, and Otfrid may well have been imitating Latin practice.

The immediate source from which Otfrid derived his metre is uncertain. It is commonly thought that it goes back to the Ambrosian hymns.[2] Most of these were written in stanzas of four lines, each of which has four beats and a stressed final syllable:

> Iam súrgit hóra tértiá
> Et nós inténti cúrrimús,
> Psalléndi ópus ímplemús,
> Christúm laudámus dóminúm.

Regular rhyme does not occur in those hymns of St. Ambrose which are indisputably genuine, but it does in some others and in hymns of later composers.[3] The same metre is used by Prudentius in his hymns. Rhabanus Maurus' hymns also have four beats to the line, and the lines are often rhymed. Perhaps we need look no further than these hymns of Otfrid's revered teacher for his inspiration.

There are, however, several difficulties in the way of accepting the theory of Latin provenance. One is that in the Latin verse of the ninth-century rhyme was still exceptional, whereas in Otfrid

---

[1] '... with a psalter in her hand, she sang it to the end, working fabrics of rich cloths and costly yarns, she always did that gladly.'

[2] Ambrose was bishop of Milan from 374 until his death in 397. The hymns attributed to him may be studied in *P.L.* XVII. 1171–1222.

[3] See Raby, *Christian Latin Poetry*, p. 24 *et passim*.

it is the rule. Another is that Otfrid, while naming Rhabanus as his teacher, fails to mention the latter's use of rhyme, even though in his letter to the archbishop he has a good deal to say about the necessity for rhyme (Otfrid uses the grammatical term (*h*)*omoeoteleuton*) in German verse. An alternative suggestion is that Otfrid derived his verse-form from the 'leonine' hexameter, which had internal rhyme.[1] Otfrid himself names the Christian Latin poets Juvencus, Arator, and Prudentius, some of whose hexameters, though a minority, are of the leonine type; yet, again, he does not link the names with the subject of rhyme.

We cannot, therefore, be certain that Otfrid took his rhyming technique from Latin poetry. Indeed, it is possible to construe Otfrid's statement 'Quaerit enim linguae huius ornatus . . . a dictantibus omoeoteleuton id est consimilem uerborum terminationem obseruare' as describing not just his own poetic practice, but that of contemporary German poets (note the plural 'dictantibus'). This would accord with the view that Otfrid was not the first poet to use rhyme in German, while allowing us still to maintain that it was an import. It has, however, been argued that Otfrid's very failure to mention a model for his use of rhyme, in spite of his obvious interest in the problems it posed, might be taken to indicate that he found his verse-form in his native culture, perhaps even in the *laicorum cantus obscenus* which he affected to despise.[2] It is certainly true that Otfrid's verse bears a greater rhythmic resemblance to Germanic alliterative verse than to any Latin measure, though the main reason for this may lie in the differing accentuation patterns of the two languages.[3] Finally, it should be noted that rhyme is used together with alliteration in the Charms, and that it is an important feature of the idiosyncratic verse cultivated by the Icelandic 'skalds' or court poets during the Viking period.[4]

[1] P. Hörmann, 'Untersuchungen zur Verslehre Otfrids', *Literaturwissenschaftliches Jahrbuch der Görres-Gesellschaft* 9 (1939) 1 ff. On the rhythmic implications of this view, see Appendix, p. 326.

[2] See G. Schweikle, 'Die Herkunft des althochdeutschen Reimes. Zu Otfrids von Weißenburg formgeschichtlicher Stellung', *ZfdA* 96 (1967) 165–212. This provocative article gives the history and a powerful critique of the common opinion on this matter.

[3] Heusler, for instance, believed that Otfrid adhered to the Germanic sentence stress, even though the accents in the manuscripts do not necessarily correspond to the main lifts of the verse, *DVG* ii, §§ 467–72.

[4] On the mysterious origins of rhyme, see J. W. Draper, 'The Origin of Rhyme', *Revue de littérature comparée* 31 (1957) 74–85.

Whatever Otfrid's model or models may have been, his standards were Latin, and he discussed the problems of German versification in terms which suggest a comparison with those of Latin versification. One of these was the extent to which hiatus was permitted and elision required. He observed that the figure of *metaplasmus*, 'which grammarians call *sinalipha*' (i.e. *synalœpha*) is permitted, and that if this is not observed by the reader the sound of the words is distorted.[1] To Otfrid, as to such medieval grammarians as Donatus and Alcuin, *metaplasmus* meant an alteration in the form of the word for the sake of the metre, and *synalœpha* was a type of *metaplasmus*, namely the elision of a final vowel before the initial vowel of a following word. Sometimes, Otfrid adds, the letters are retained in writing, sometimes they are omitted 'in the Hebrew manner'.[2] This remark has a bearing upon the way in which, in manuscript V, final unstressed vowels and the initial vowels of such words as *inan* and *imo* were sometimes written (as in *horta er*) and sometimes omitted (as in *hort er*). The corrector of this manuscript sometimes left these final vowels as he found them, but sometimes he either crossed them out or placed a dot beneath them (as in (*sageta er*), or inserted them where the original scribe had omitted them. Detailed investigations make it appear likely that, when the vowel was either omitted by the scribe or crossed out by the corrector, it would have been elided in ordinary speech but, when the dot was placed beneath it by the corrector, the intention was to indicate that it was to be elided for the sake of the metre contrary to spoken usage. Manuscript P likewise has forms with the vowel, without the vowel and with the dotted vowel, and it agrees closely with V in the use of the full forms, but there are considerable differences in the use of the dotted forms. It is clear that the dots were intended to assist the reader, and that the corrector abandoned the attempt to use them. Although they occur throughout the text, they are for the most part concentrated in patches and, in Manuscript V, especially in Book I. It seems that, when the following initial vowel was stressed, there was no elision (*horta ér*), but if the initial vowel was unstressed, it was possible

---

[1] 'Patitur quoque metaplasmi figuram nimium (non tamen assidue) quam doctores grammaticae artis uocant sinalipham (et hoc nisi legentes praeuideant, rationis dicta deformius sonant), literas interdum scriptione seruantes, interdum uero ebraicae linguae more uitantes . . .'
[2] The reason for the omission of vowels in Hebrew writing has, of course, nothing to do with elision.

and, under some conditions, even usual (*hórt er*). The details, however, are too elaborate to be discussed here.[1]

The dialect of both the Vienna and the Heidelberg manuscript is called South Rhenish Franconian. Weissenburg is on the border of Alsace. The orthography shows signs of Alemannic usage, notably *ua* for Franconian *uo* (*firdruag*, *buah*, *guate*), and *iu* for *io* in *liub*. A characteristic feature of the vocalism is the assimilation of medial vowels to those either preceding or following them (thus *heilogo*, *gorugun*); this applies also to the second element in the diphthongs *ua* and *ia* (thus *iaman*, *iemer*, *liobo*, *lieben*). The consonant system is that of Rhenish Franconian: Gmc. *p* is unshifted initially (*pad* 'path') and appears after *l* both as *f* and as *ph* (*helfan*, *helphan*). Gmc. *þ* remains initially but becomes *d* medially and finally (*thiob*, *edil*, *sid*). WGmc. *d* remains initially but is usually shifted medially and finally to *t* (*duan*, *guati*, *gihialt*). This orthography represents the practice of the Weissenburg scriptorium, and it no doubt reflects the spoken language of the locality, though it should be noted that an unshifted initial *p* beside a shifted *pp* (e.g. *pad* beside *aphul*) would be anomalous in the present-day dialects.

It has been maintained with some show of reason that there was already popular German poetry in rhyme before Otfrid produced his work, but the evidence is slender. The only extant German verses which can be cited in support of this view are a lampoon preserved in a St. Gall manuscript of the ninth century. They were inserted into the manuscript in the same century, but late.[2] They run:

Liubene ersazta sine gruz   unde kab sina tohter uz.
to cham aber starzfidere,   prahta imo sina tohter uuidere.[3]

The name *Liubene* (from *Liubwine* formed from the words *liub* 'dear' and *wini* 'friend', 'beloved') was not uncommon. It occurs, for example, in a list of Reichenau monks.[4] *Starzfidere* ('start', 'stert', 'buttocks', and 'feathers') is evidently a name for a swaggering gallant, 'Cockstail', or may have an obscene significance. It is

---

[1] See H. de Boor, *Untersuchungen zur Sprachbehandlung Otfrids*, Germanistische Abhandlungen 60 (Breslau, 1928).
[2] *MSD* xxviiib, *Kl. ahd. Spdmr.* lxxxii. See H. Fränkel, *ZfdA* 58 (1921) 40–64; Schönbach, ibid. 40 (1896) 118–20; G. Baesecke, *PBB* 46 (1922) 436.
[3] 'Liubene set out his beer and gave his daughter in marriage. Later Starzfidere returned and brought him his daughter back again.'
[4] See G. Baesecke, *PBB* 52 (1928) 29, no. 323.

idle to speculate on the origin of the lampoon or on its exact meaning. It has the appearance of a vulgar jibe which has survived because it happened to have been scribbled in a manuscript instead of on a wall. It proves, if proof were needed, that 'popular' poetry existed, and shows why so little of such 'poetry' has survived. It is certainly an unsure foundation on which to erect a theory of the origins of a metre.

It is impossible to say how far Otfrid's influence extended or how long it endured. Of the shorter strophic poems only the *Petruslied* attains to the high level of technique exhibited by Otfrid's latest work. The remainder are cruder in their rhymes, though in rhythm they stand close to Otfrid,[1] and in the succeeding period a much freer technique prevailed. From the dedications it is known that the *Evangelienbuch* was sent to Constance and St. Gall, and from the language of the Freising manuscript it is clear that it was known in Bavaria. The text can thus be seen travelling south-eastwards, but there is no convincing evidence that it had any widespread or enduring influence. From the time when Sigihard wrote manuscript F, Otfrid vanishes from our sight until the manuscript was discovered by Beatus Rhenanus in 1530. An Augsburg physician, Pirminius Gassar, discovered and copied manuscript P in 1560, and from that copy Matthias Flaccius Illyricus caused the first printed edition to be published in 1571. The *Evangelienbuch* was, therefore, one of the first Old High German texts to become known in modern times, and since then interest in it has never lapsed. Few readers have accorded much honour to Otfrid as a poet, though Kienast has called him the greatest German lyric poet before the twelfth century,[2] and Ohly has praised his work for its formal beauty.[3] Even though Otfrid's aesthetic criteria are perhaps alien to us, his poetic technique, revealed in the construction of his lines, his chapters, and his books, is well worth studying. He was a bold innovator, both as a teacher and a writer,[4] a nationalist and a churchman, progressive in every respect according to the ideas of his age, and also a sensitive craftsman, conscious of the problems of his art.

---

[1] See Heusler, *Deutsche Versgeschichte* I. §§ 455, 469.
[2] R. Kienast, 'Die deutschsprachige Lyrik des Mittelalters', *DPA* II², col. 20.
[3] *ZfdA* 89 (1958–9) 20.
[4] Kleiber, op. cit., p. 154, says: 'Hinter allen Werken Otfrids steht der Pädagoge, der Schulmeister.'

XII

The Minor Religious Poems

BESIDE the monumental *Evangelienbuch* of Otfrid there is a number of short religious poems in rhyming verse. Three of these (the *Petruslied*, *Sigihards Gebete*, the *Augsburger Gebet*) are prayers, one is a rendering of a passage from St. John's Gospel (*Christus und die Samariterin*), one a metrical psalm (*Psalm* 138) and one a poem in praise of a saint of the Church (the *Georgslied*).

The **Petruslied** or *Bittgesang an Sanct Peter*[1] has been preserved in a Freising manuscript of Rhabanus's Commentary on Genesis. The manuscript is now in Munich. The hymn is entered on the verso of the last leaf by a different scribe. The date is late ninth or early tenth century, and the dialect is Bavarian, though the prefixes *fir-* and *gi-* suggest that the original may have been Frankish. There are three Otfridian strophes of two lines, each followed by the refrain 'Kyrie eleison, Christe eleison'. The first two state that the Lord has entrusted to St. Peter the power to save those to whom he will open the gates of Heaven. The third urges all to pray that Peter will be merciful to us sinners. The first two strophes are narrative and the third exhortation; the hymn has, therefore, some resemblance to the form of the charms. It is roughly contemporary with Otfrid, but there is disagreement on the question of priority. Some hold that l. 8 (*daz er uns firtanen   giuuerdo ginaden*), which is identical, except in spelling, with Otfrid i. 7. 28, derives from Otfrid, but it is a formal phrase and is not strong evidence, although it would help to account for the Frankish prefixes in a Bavarian text.[2] The metre is smooth, and Heusler considered it equal to Otfrid's best. The upholders of the theory of 'popular' origin claim it as evidence for their view. That the hymn was intended

---

[1] *MSD* ix.; *Kl. ahd. Spdmr.* xxi; *Ahd. Lb.* xxxiii. Facsimiles: *Schrifttafeln* 20, Enneccerus 39, Petzet–Glauning ix.

[2] See Steinmeyer's comments in *Kl. ahd. Spdmr.*, pp. 103 f.; G. Baesecke, *PBB* 46 (1922) 438; O. Behaghel, ibid. 56 (1932) 224 f.

to be sung is indicated by the provision of neums throughout.[1] The form of the neums has been taken to indicate a fairly early date, probably earlier than Otfrid, and the use of 'Kyrie eleison' as a refrain to suggest processional use, perhaps outside the church.[2] The two prayers called **Sigihards Gebete** also come from Freising: they were entered, as has already been stated, above the scribe's autograph at the end of the Freising copy of Otfrid's *Evangelienbuch*. There is nothing to indicate whether Sigihard composed them himself. They are merely formal prayers suitable for use at the conclusion of any undertaking.[3]

The four-line prayer known as the **Augsburger Gebet** is so called because it is found in a Latin manuscript now in Munich but formerly in Augsburg. It is preceded by a Latin prose prayer, of which it appears to be a syntactically awkward verse translation.[4] The prayer may have been entered in the manuscript, which probably belongs to the ninth or tenth century, some considerable time later.[5] The dialect is Rhenish Franconian.

Christus und die Samariterin is a rendering of the conversation between Christ and the Woman of Samaria recounted in the fourth chapter of St. John's Gospel. The text is incomplete, breaking off at a point corresponding to verse 20 of the biblical source. Its thirty-one lines have survived by a fortunate chance, being entered in a manuscript of the annals of Lorsch. The manuscript is now in Vienna.[6] The script belongs to the tenth century, and most scholars agree that two hands can be identified. The text is written continuously as though it were prose.

---

[1] See F. Gennrich, *ZfdA* 82 (1948) 140; J. Müller-Blattau, *Zs. f. Musikwissenschaft* 17 (1935) 129 ff.; O. Ursprung, 'Das Freisinger Petruslied', *Musikforschung* 5 (1952) 17 ff.; E. Jammers, 'Das mittelalterliche deutsche Epos und die Musik', *Heidelberger Jahrbücher* 1 (1957) 31–90, esp. 82 f.

[2] See L. Stavenhagen, 'Das "Petruslied". Sein Alter und seine Herkunft', *WW* 17 (1967) I. 21 ff.

[3] *MSD* xv; *Kl. ahd. Spdmr.* xx; *Ahd. Lb* xxxvii. 2.

[4] *MSD* xiv; *Kl. ahd. Spdmr.* xviii; *Ahd. Lb.* xxxvii. 1. It may be rendered: 'God, it is thy property always to be merciful. Receive our prayer; this we need straightway, that the mercy of thy goodness may quickly release us from the bonds of sins which bind us.' The Latin prayer reads: 'Deus cui proprium est misereri et parcere, suscipe deprecationem nostram, ut quos catena delictorum constringit miseratio tuae pietatis absolvat. Per . . .'

[5] See *Kl. ahd. Spdmr.*, pp. 92 f.

[6] Nationalbibliothek Cod. 515, fol. 5ʳ, with l. 5 entered on 4ᵛ. Printed in *MSD* x; *Kl. ahd. Spdmr.* xvii; *Ahd. Lb.* xxxiv. Facsimiles: *Schrifttafeln* 21, Enneccerus.

The translation follows the Vulgate text, but a few formal phrases have been inserted, and words have been added for the sake of the rhyme, e.g. *Lesen uuir*, l. 1, *uuizzun thaz*, l. 2, *thanna noh*, l. 4, *guot man*, l. 7, and the remarkable anachronism *uuizze Christ*, l. 8; *ze deru ih heimina liuf*, l. 12, *ubar tac*, l. 22. The diction is terse, without digressions or refrains. It may have been meant to be recited or read as a lesson from the Bible. The first six lines are narrative, and the remainder of the extant text is dialogue. No verb of saying is used to indicate who is speaking, except in l. 24, which is in reported speech, and in l. 6, where the Vulgate's 'Dicit ei Iesus: Da mihi bibere' is rendered indirectly by *bat er sih ketrencan   daz uuip thaz ther thara quam.*[1]

The lines do not always run smoothly, for the secondary stress often falls on a syllable normally unstressed, and the unstressed syllable of the foot is sometimes wanting. Alliteration in one or both parts of the line occurs in ll. 1, 3, 7, 13, 17, 26, 29; 9*a*, 9*b*, 15*a*. It does not conform to the rules of alliterative verse and is most probably due to chance.

In Otfrid's verse the lines form two-line strophes which sometimes combine to form larger units. In the present poem, as in other short texts in rhyming verse, the lines combine to form sometimes two-line and sometimes three-line strophes; these in turn are arranged and grouped in such a way that the number of lines, the grouping of the strophes, and the disposition of the subject matter produce a harmonious balance.[2] Each poem has its own distinctive pattern.

In *Christus und die Samariterin* the six opening lines introduce the persons involved and set the scene.[3] Lines 1–2 give Jesus' actions: the Saviour, weary with journeying, sat by the well; ll. 3–4 give the woman's actions: she came to draw water and found Him there; l. 5 (in its manuscript position) tells that the disciples had gone in search of food, and l. 6 gives Jesus' request for a drink.

[1] It is customary to transpose ll. 5 and 6 of the text, since they correspond to vv. 8 and 7 respectively of the biblical source. This custom is broken by the latest editor of *Ahd. Lb.*

[2] J. A. Huisman, *Neue Wege zur dichterischen und musikalischen Technik Walthers von der Vogelweide mit einem Excurs über die symmetrische Zahlenkomposition im Mittelalter* (Utrecht, 1950), endeavours to show that the short OHG rhyming poems were composed in groups of verses on purely arithmetical principles without much regard to the subject matter.

[3] This fact, together with the reference to authority in the first line, may remind us of the opening of the *Hildebrandslied*.

The subject matter of the introduction is thus evenly spread over three two-line strophes in narrative. The dialogue begins without a verb of saying, but the first two-line strophe (ll. 7–8), in which the woman expresses her surprise at Jesus' request, is in direct sequence to l. 6. There follow a three-line strophe spoken by Jesus (ll. 9–11), two three-line strophes spoken by the woman (ll. 12–17), one three-line strophe spoken by Jesus (ll. 18–20), and then a two-line strophe spoken by the woman. The strophes of ll. 7–22, therefore, balance each other, as shown in the analysis below.

At l. 23 the conversation is given a new turn by Jesus' abrupt demand (in one line) to see the woman's husband; this corresponds to v. 16 of the source. Her reply is reported, also in one line. This part, therefore, opens with a two-line strophe (ll. 23–4) half in direct speech and half in indirect speech. Jesus answers the woman in a three-line strophe (ll. 25–7), and we have four lines of her reply, the strophic division of which must remain uncertain. The system can be traced as far as l. 27:

A. INTRODUCTORY NARRATIVE

Lines		*Strophes*	
1–2	Actions of Jesus	1 two-line	2 lines
3–4	Actions of the Woman	1 two-line	2 lines
5	The absence of the Disciples ⎱	1 two-line	2 lines
6	Jesus' request for water ⎰		

B. DIALOGUE

7–8	The Woman's reply	1 two-line	2 lines
9–11	Jesus' words	1 three-line	3 lines
12–17	The Woman's words	2 three-line	6 lines
18–20	Jesus' words	1 three-line	3 lines
21–2	The Woman's words	1 two-line	2 lines

C. CHANGE OF THEME

23	Jesus' words (direct speech) ⎱	1 two-line	2 lines
24	The Woman's words (reported speech) ⎰		
25–7	Jesus' words	1 three-line	3 lines
28–31	The Woman's words	?	4–? lines

A plausible strophic analysis[1] would be $(3 \times 2)+(2+3)+(2 \times 3)$ $+(3+2)+(2+3)+(2 \times 3?)$— . . .

---

[1] Suggested by F. Maurer, 'Zur Geistlichendichtung des Mittelalters' in *Fragen und Forschungen im Bereich und Umkreis der germanischen Philologie. Festgabe für Theodor Frings zum 70. Geburtstag* (Berlin, 1956), pp. 338–41, but here slightly modified.

It has been argued that Otfrid knew the poem and was influenced by it, because in the corresponding passage of the *Evangelienbuch* (II. 14. 58) he uses the word *bita*, which occurs in l. 31 of our poem, instead of his usual *gibet*.[1] This is misleading, for the two words are different in sense: *gibet* means 'oratio', 'prayer', whereas *bita* denotes 'adoratio', 'cultus', 'the act of worship' (the Vulgate has the verb 'adorare' at this point, John 4: 20) and *beta* denotes a single and definite prayer. *Bita* was, therefore, the only word which Otfrid could have used, and the resemblance between the two texts proves nothing.[2]

As the rhymes are not strictly pure, they are of little help in determining the date and place of composition. Both vocalic and consonantal assonances occur in *ketrencan*: *quam*, l. 6, *uuissīs*: *gift ist* l. 9, *anauuert*: *uuirt*, l. 23. In ll. 14 and 16 *prunnan* (*brunnan*) rhymes with *man*, though one would expect for the former word either the earlier termination *-on* (or *-un* in UG) or the later *-en*. In l. 18 a short unstressed vowel rhymes with a long stressed vowel (*uuazzer*: *mēr*).

The unstressed vowels appear to be undergoing late OHG weakening, for we find *uuazzer* (earlier *uuazzar*) rhyming with *saz er*, l. 4, and with *smalenozzer* (with a plural termination that earlier had the form *-ir*), l. 17. In l. 11 *unnen* (earlier *unnan*) rhymes with *prunnen* (gen. sg., earlier UG *prunnin*). The poem therefore most probably belongs to the late ninth or early tenth century.

The orthography of the manuscript is, apparently, a mixture of Franconian and Alemannic elements. The evidence has convinced some scholars that the exemplar was Franconian and the scribe Alemannic,[3] and has led others to the opposite conclusion.[4] The former alternative appears the more probable.

Gmc. *b* has remained initially (except in *pruston*, l. 20, and in the second part of the compound *kecprunnen*, l. 11, *quecprunnan*, l. 14), e.g. *brunnon*, l. 2, *bat*, l. 6, and medially, e.g. *geba*, l. 7; it is also retained finally, e.g. *gab*, l. 16. In the loan-word *buzza* (from Lat. *puteus*) we also find *b*. The OHG labial affricate is written *ph*, e.g. *scephan*, l. 4, *kiscephes*, l. 13. Gmc. *g* is written *g*, *k*, or *c*, e.g. *geba kerost*, l. 7, *commen*, ll. 24, 25. Initial Gmc. *k* is written *k* or *c*, e.g. *kosotis*, *ercantis*, l. 10; after *n* it is written *k* (as in *trinkan*, l. 7) or

[1] *MSD* vol. II, p. 68.   [2] See W. Braune, 'Ahd. *bita*', *PBB* 32 (1907) 153–4.
[3] *Kl. ahd. Spdmr.*, p. 91; G. Baesecke, *AfdA* 31 (1907) 206.
[4] Ehrismann, pp. 207 f.

c (as in *kitrencan*, l. 6, *tranc*, l. 17) except in *trinchit*, l. 19. The geminate *gg* is written *ch* in *thicho*, l. 21 (this looks like a variant of *cch*).[1] The labiovelar *qu* appears five times beside one example of *k* in *kecprunnen*, l. 11. The UG *iu* as the reflex of Gmc. *eu* before labials appears in *tiuf*, *liuf*, l. 12, and *liufi*, l. 22. Unstressed *e* appears as *a* in *geba*, l. 7, *sina*, l. 16, *giborana*, *berega*, l. 29, *sagant*, l. 31; this happens in various dialects at different stages and proves little. An indication of Alemannic influence is the distinction between *-un* in the strong verb *uuizzun*, l. 2, and *-on* (*-ōn?*) in the weak verbs *betoton*, l. 29, *suohton*, l. 30. Another is the conjugation of the verbs *habēn*, *sagēn*, and *lebēn* partly according to class I: *habis*, l. 13, *hebist*, ll. 25, 27, *segist*, l. 25, *hebitos*, l. 26, *hebiti libiti*, l. 24.

The decisive evidence, however, is the treatment of Gmc. *þ*. This is represented by *th* thirty-one times in initial position and by *d* fifty-four times, but there is one example of *t* (*tu* 13), and two of *d* corrected from *t* (*daz*, l. 5, *dir*, l. 11). From this it appears that the exemplar had the Franconian *th*, which an Alemannic scribe changed to *d* more often than not, and that the two corrections of *t* to *d* probably represent an original *th*, not—as some have held— a *t* written in accordance with Notker's 'Anlautgesetz'. Medially Gmc. *þ* is represented by *d* and finally by *t* in the one example *quat*, l. 24.

Another explanation attributes the confusion in the orthography, not to copying from one dialect into another, but to the unsettled condition of the orthography in the scriptorium where the text was made. It has been compared with that found in the lists of names of monks who were on the Reichenau in the ninth and early tenth centuries. This orthography shows Franconian influence.[2] The manuscript contains also the annals of the monastery of Lorsch from 794 to 803, and pleasant but unprovable speculation has connected the entry of the poem with the fact that Hatto III was abbot of both monasteries from 900 to 913.

The German rendering of **Psalm 138** belongs to the early tenth century and is composed in the Bavarian dialect. It has been preserved complete on one leaf of a manuscript of theological matter

---

[1] On *ch* and *cch* in lists of Reichenau monks see *PBB* 52 (1928) 130.
[2] See F. Maurer, 'Zur Frage nach der Heimat des Gedichtes Christus und die Samariterin', *ZfdPh* 54 (1929) 175–9; G. Baesecke, 'Das Althochdeutsche von Reichenau nach den Namen seiner Mönchslisten', *PBB* 52 (1928) 92–148.

now in Vienna.[1] There are thirty-eight lines of Otfridian verse arranged in two-line and three-line strophes. The first word of each strophe has a red initial letter and projects into the margin. The translation is very free. It has vigour and feeling, and although naturally dependent on the Vulgate text it interprets the psalm in accordance with contemporary ways of thought.[2] As the order of the lines does not correspond to the order of ideas in the original, it has been proposed to change the order;[3] but the piece is a paraphrase rather than a translation, and the manuscript order yields a clear scheme of two-line and three-line strophes, as will be shown.

The poet introduces the words of the Psalmist by a two-line strophe:

> Uellet ir gihoren   Daviden den guoton,
>   den sinen touginon sin?   er gruozte sinen trohtin:[4]

He then renders the words 'Domine, probasti me, et cognovisti me' of v. 1, but omits v. 2 ('Tu cognovisti sessionem meam et resurrectionem meam'):

> Ia gichuri du mih, trohtin,   inte irchennist uuer ih pin,
>   fone demo aneginne   uncin an daz enti.[5]

The second line may have been suggested by the words 'tu cognovisti omnia novissima et antiqua' (v. 5). v. 3 'Intellexisti cogitationes meas de longe; semitam meam . . . investigasti' is freely rendered:

> Ne megih in gidanchun   fore dir giuuanchon:
>   du irchennist allo stiga,   se uuarot so ih ginigo.[6]

---

[1] Nationalbibliothek Cod. 1609, fol. 69ʳ–69ᵛ; *MSD* xiii; *Kl. ahd. Spdmr.* xxii; *Ahd. Lb.* xxxviii. Facsimiles: *Schrifttafeln* 23, Enneccerus.
  In the Authorized Version the psalm is numbered 139. For interpretation of some of the passages see E. Sievers, *PBB* 34 (1908) 571–5, A. Leitzmann, ibid. 39 (1914) 558–63. See also F. Willems, 'Psalm 138 und der ahd. Stil', *DVjs* 29 (1955) 429–46, and O. Ludwig, 'Der althochdeutsche und der biblische Psalm 138. Ein Vergleich', *Euph.* 56 (1962) 402–9.
[2] See O. Ludwig, op. cit., who thinks of it as missionary literature.
[3] In *Ahd. Lb.* the manuscript order is retained, and the rearrangement adopted in *MSD* and approved by other scholars is indicated by small figures in the right-hand margin.
[4] 'Would you hear David the Good, his secret thoughts? He addressed his Lord: . . .'
[5] 'Yea, thou hast tried me, Lord, and knowest who I am, from the beginning until the end.'
[6] 'I cannot escape from thee in my thoughts: thou knowest all the paths wheresoever I turn.'

The poet for the time being omits the words 'funiculum meum' (which is a faulty translation of the Hebrew, correctly rendered in the A.V. by 'my lying down'), though it may have suggested the word *zoum* 'rein' in the next line:

> So uuare sose ih cherte minen zoum,   so rado nami dus goum:
> den uuech furiuuorhtostu mir,   daz ih mih cherte after dir.[1]

This is again a free rendering of the Latin (v. 4) 'Et omnes vias meas praevidisti'. The rest of the verse, 'quia non est sermo in lingua mea', the poet expands in order to make sense of it:

> Du hapest mir de zungun   so fasto piduungen,
> daz ih ane din gipot   ne spricho nohein uuort.[2]

This brief examination of the first ten lines will have sufficed to show the extent of the poet's freedom. It will also have illustrated his interpretation of the text. Whereas the Psalmist expresses his wonder at God's omniscience and omnipotence, the German poet is concerned to show how these divine qualities provide the basis for David's relationship to his Lord. David is obedient to the Lord in all his thoughts, words, and ways, because his Lord is all-powerful. David is seen here, as he is in Otfrid's dedication to Louis the German, to be the ideal king, and it is perhaps not without significance that he is called 'David the Good', just as the other Louis of the *Ludwigslied* is called 'Louis the Good'. Moreover, David is pictured here as travelling wherever he went on horseback (whether or not because of the interpretation of 'funiculus' as *zoum* is immaterial). Later (in ll. 22–4) David begs God to protect him on both sides, and by His power to take away the enemy's missile, so that he will not have the opportunity to shoot it at him:

> Du got mit dinero giuualt   scirmi iogiuuedrehalp,
> mit dinero chrefti   pinim du mo daz scepti,
> ne la du mos de muozze   daz er mih se ane skiozze.

There is no basis for this martial image in the psalm, though it may have been suggested by Psalm 90, especially v. 6 with the 'arrow that flieth by day' ('a sagitta volante in die'). Again the poet has

---

[1] 'Whithersoever I turned my rein, thou quickly markedst it. Thou didst prepare my way for me, that I might follow thee.'

[2] 'Thou hast so firmly controlled my tongue that I speak no word without thy command.'

pictured the relationship between David and the Lord in terms familiar to his age. David is the obedient follower of his Lord, and the Lord protects His servant in battle.

It has been remarked that the poet on occasion makes his rendering more visual than the original. At one point, however, he mitigates the boldness of the Psalmist's imagery. This is in ll. 31-2:

> So uuillih danne file fruo   stellen mino federa:
> peginno ih danne fliogen,   sose er ne tete nioman.[1]

This renders 'Si sumpsero pennas meas diluculo' (v. 9). The rendering of the next words, 'et habitavero in extremis maris', again illustrates the poet's concern for vividness: *so fliugih ze enti ienes meres* (l. 34) 'then I will fly to the end of yonder sea'.

A yet more significant divergence between the Latin psalm and its German rendering is to be found in ll. 16-17:

> Nu uuillih mansleccun   alle fone mir gituon,
> alle die mir rieton   den unrehton rihtuom.[2]

While the Psalmist commands the 'bloody men' who speak against God to depart from him, averring that he hates them and praying that his righteousness may be evident to the all-seeing God, the German version shows him resolving to act righteously because, God being all-seeing, he can do no other. The German version, therefore, contains a moral lesson which is absent from the original, and which may even remind us of the message of the *Muspilli*: eschew evil, because God will surely find it out. Similarly, the mention of 'unjust riches', though present in other psalms, is not found in this one; it too is reminiscent of the corrupt rewards condemned in the *Muspilli*.

The poem has three main sections, each of which contains a number of two-line and three-line strophes, and an epilogue made up of one three-line strophe. The refrain *ne megih in nohhein lant, nupe mih hapet din hant* (ll. 15 and 35) closes the first and third sections, and the repeated lines 17-18 and 32-3 serve to connect subsections. (It should be noted that the syntactic functions of ll. 18 and 33 differ from those of ll. 17 and 32, even though they are word-for-word repetitions: l. 18 is a noun phrase subject of

---

[1] 'Then I will set my wings very early: I will then begin to fly, as no man has done before.'

[2] 'Now I will put away from me all murderers, all who counselled unjust riches.'

the verb in the next line, while l. 17 is a noun-phrase object of the verb in the preceding line; l. 33*a* is a conditional clause, whereas l. 32*a* is a principal clause.) The following is a structural analysis of the manuscript text:

SECTION A

Lines		Strophes
1–2	Introduction	1 two-line
3–12	Words of the Psalmist	5 two-line
13–15	Climax (with refrain)	1 three-line l. 15

SECTION B

16–21	Words of the Psalmist	3 two-line
22–4	Climax	1 three-line

SECTION C

25–32	Words of the Psalmist	4 two-line
33–5	Climax (with refrain)	1 three-line l. 35

SECTION D

36–8	Epilogue	1 three-line

The scribe was Bavarian, for he wrote *ch* for Gmc. *k*, e.g. *gichuri*, l. 3, *irchennist*, ll. 3, 6, *gidanchun, giuuanchon*, l. 5, *p* for Gmc. *b*, e.g. *pin*, l. 3, *hapest*, l. 9, and thrice the specially Bavarian *ch* for final *g* in *uuech*, l. 8, *mach, tach*, l. 30. The unstressed vowels have weakened considerably, but since the spelling is in some respects conservative, it is difficult to know how impure some of the rhymes really were. Some of them were clearly very weak, however; the weakest is probably *fruo : federa*, l. 31.[1]

Of all the minor religious poems the **Georgslied** is the least dependent on the Bible or church ritual.[2] It is narrative, like *Christus und die Samariterin*, and it employs refrains, like *Psalm 138* and some of Otfrid's chapters, but its source is in medieval hagiography. The following translation, which is kept fairly literal, embodies some of the conjectures which have been devised to fill supposed lacunae in the scribe's text; these conjectures are indicated by brackets.

[1] One might be tempted to wonder whether alliteration stood in for rhyme here, just as in *Muspilli* rhyme sometimes stands in for alliteration though, of course, this line does not conform with Germanic practice.

[2] *MSD* xvii; *Kl. ahd. Spdmr.* xix; *Ahd. Lb.* xxxv. Facsimile: *Schrifttafeln* 19.

George[1] went to the court with a great army, from the boundary land with a great host. He went to the ring,[2] to an important assembly. The assembly was most illustrious, most dear to God. He left the world, he gained the kingdom of Heaven. This did George, the illustrious governor,[3] himself. (ll. 1–6)

Then many kings tempted him. They wanted to make him apostate. He would not listen to them. George's mind was steadfast: he did not listen to them, I swear, but performed everything for which he prayed to God. This (the lord) St. George did himself. (ll. 7–11)

They consigned him at once to the dungeon. There he was accompanied by the fair angels. Two women (were starving) there. He saved their lives. Then so (beautifully and) gloriously he made food. This sign truly George worked there. (ll. 12–16)

George then prayed; the Lord granted him everything: (the Lord granted him everything) for which George prayed to him. He made the blind to see, the lame to walk, the dumb to speak, the deaf to hear. A pillar had stood there for many years; from it at once there sprouted leaves. This sign truly George worked there. (ll. 17–22)

This moved the rich[4] man to great anger. Tacianus the tyrant was exceedingly angered by it. He said that George was a sorcerer. He ordered George to be seized, ordered him to be stripped, ordered him to be struck with an exceedingly sharp sword. This I know in all truth: George raised himself up there. (George raised himself up there;) well did he preach there. George put the heathen men greatly to shame. (ll. 23–30)

This moved the rich[4] man to great anger. He then ordered George to be bound, to be wound upon a wheel. Truly I tell you, they broke him in ten pieces. This I know in all truth: George raised himself up there. George raised himself up there; well (did he preach) there. George put the heathen men greatly to shame. (ll. 31–6)

Then he ordered George to be seized, ordered him to be sorely flayed. He was ordered to be ground and burnt[5] entirely to powder. He was cast into the well. He was a blessed son.[6] They rolled a great multitude of stones over it. They began to walk round him. They ordered George to rise up. A great deed George did there, as truly he always does. This I know[7] in all truth: George raised himself up there.

[1] The scribe uses a number of spellings for the hero's name, which in Vulgar Latin was *Geor(g)io*.

[2] i.e. the ring of assembly, in accordance with German procedure.

[3] The text has *der mare crabo Georio*. The saint is presumably conceived of as a 'Markgraf', i.e. a governor of the marches.

[4] Or 'mighty'.   [5] 'hysteron proteron' for 'burnt and ground'.

[6] The translation here is based on the reading *saligker sun*. The alternative reading *salig herasun* carries little conviction.

[7] Here the manuscript repeats the words *daz uuez · ihk*.

Well (did he preach there.) George put the heathen men greatly to shame. George (raised) himself up there; out sprang the glorious man[1] at once.[2]   (ll. 37–45)
He ordered (a dead)[3] man to rise up. He ordered him to walk to him, he ordered him to speak at once. Then he said: 'Jobel was my name. I pray you believe him.'[4] He said they were all lost, entirely prey to the Devil's deceit. This (the lord) St. George made known to us himself.
                                                                    (ll. 46–50)
Then he went to the royal chamber, to the Queen. He began to teach her; she began to listen to him. Elossandria was virtuous. She hastened at once to do good works, to donate her wealth. She donated her treasure there; this is of benefit for many years. From everlasting to everlasting she will enjoy mercies. This the lord St. George obtained by prayer.
                                                                    (ll. 51–7)
George raised his hand: Abollinus[5] quaked. He charged the hound of Hell. He[6] went at once into the pit. Him[7] . . .   (ll. 58–9)

---

[1] This takes the manuscript reading to be *der . waehe* (OHG *wāhi* 'good, fine, excellent'). Steinmeyer read *der wāc* ('the water').

[2] The translation here orders the lines according to the manuscript. This order may well be incorrect.

[3] This conjecture is based entirely on the Latin legend in which a dead man is raised up.

[4] Again the interpretation relies heavily on the Latin legend in which the dead man's name is *Jovis* or *Jovius*. The manuscript at this point (l. 48) reads:

Do seGita : : *k*obet · ihz · ih betamo · Geloubet ehz ·

The single points are the scribe's punctuation; the double points represent spaces where no letters can now be discerned. The *k* of the third word is not clear. Since *ihz* for the verb *hiez* would accord with the scribe's orthographical system (see below), we may justifiably take the preceding word to be a proper name and identify it with that of the dead man in the legend. The last four words cause greater difficulty. In the translation *betamo* is taken to be equivalent to normal OHG *bit(tu) (i)mo*, the dative personal pronoun *(i)mo* being governed by the next word, the imperative *geloubet*. The NHG equivalent would therefore be 'Ich bitte, ihm glaubt es'. H. de Boor, on the other hand, identifies *bet* with the (later well attested) Frankish *bit* 'with', and *amo* he regards as a corruption of *namon*. He would then make *ih*, in spite of the expectation that the half-lines would be syntactically autonomous, into the subject of *hiez* (MS *ihz*), translating 'Then he said: "Jobel was I called by name. Believe it." ' See H. de Boor, 'Eine unerklärte Stelle des althochdeutschen Georgsliedes nebst Bemerkungen zu seiner Orthographie und Heimat', *Festschrift Josef Quint* (Bonn, 1964).

[5] The termination *-us* is required to produce a rhyme on *uf* (MS *uhf*). Abollin*us* is most probably to be identified with Apollyon 'the destroyer' mentioned in Rev. 9: 11, and to be identified with the hound of Hell, one of Satan's minions.

[6] Presumably one is to take this as meaning that, at George's command, the hound of Hell fled into the pit.

[7] The manuscript *ihn* is here taken to represent the first word of the next sentence of the poem; it would be in accordance with the scribe's system for *ihn* to stand for *hin*. Others associate *ihn* with the succeeding Latin word *nequeo*,

The poem is based on the legend of St. George as it was known in Germany in the ninth century.[1] George is one of the Church's more obscure saints, of whom the fifth-century Pope Gelasius said that 'their names are justly reverenced among men, but their acts are known only to God'. According to early Greek sources George was a young man of substance from Lydda (Lod) in Palestine, who served with distinction in the Roman army under the Emperor Diocletian. The Emperor had instituted the 'tetrarchy', under which the Empire was governed by himself and Maximian, both with the title 'Augustus', each having under him an assistant 'Caesar'. The eastern part of the Empire was ruled by Diocletian and his Caesar, Galerius, a native of Dacia and a fanatical opponent of Christianity. When, at the instigation of Galerius, the persecution of the Christians began in A.D. 303, George is said to have appealed on their behalf to the Emperor and to have appeared before an assembly of sixty-nine governors at Nicomedia, then the administrative capital of the Eastern Empire. He was enjoined more than once to abjure the Christian faith and, when he refused, he was subjected to a week of cruel torture and finally beheaded. George of Lydda was later confused with the Arian Bishop George of Alexandria, who was murdered by the mob in A.D. 361. Also, through the well-known phenomenon of syncretism between pagan and Christian cults, he was credited with having killed a dragon and thereby rescued a princess; this feat probably belonged originally to Perseus who (reputedly in the neighbourhood of Lydda) rescued Andromeda by killing a sea-monster. As the dragon-killer, his most famous role in later times, George was not known in the West until the age of the Crusades.

In Germany the saint was venerated in the ninth century. A Latin passion of St. George is found in a near-contemporary manuscript preserved in St. Gall. This contains all the details of the German poem, including the name of the pagan king Datianus or Dacianus (perhaps, 'the Dacian', i.e. Galerius). In 888 Abbot Hatto III of the Reichenau built a church at Oberzell on the Reichenau, dedicated to St. George. The supposed relics of the saint were given to Hatto by Pope Formosus when, as archbishop

and analyse it as the personal pronoun *ih* followed by the negative particle *n* (for *en* or *ne*).

[1] See F. Zarncke and W. Arndt, *Berichte der sächsischen Akademie der Wissenschaften, Phil.-hist. Klasse* 26 (1874) 41–70; ibid. 27 (1875) 256–76.

of Mainz, he accompanied Arnulf to Italy. (Arnulf was king of
Germany from 887 to 899, succeeding his uncle Charles the Fat
and becoming Emperor in 896.) The relics were translated to the
Reichenau in 896 and are still preserved there. It is widely held
that their translation was the occasion for the composition (or the
present redaction) of the German poem.

The historical connection between the Reichenau and the cult
of St. George, together with the location of the Latin life in nearby
St. Gall, provide good non-linguistic reasons for localizing the
text in the Alemannic area. An additional, literary, reason is
afforded by the existence of a Latin hymn in praise of St. Gall,
the patron of the famous monastery, known as the *Galluslied*.[1]
We know, on the evidence of Ekkehard IV, that this poem was
originally composed in German and later translated into Latin.
Although we cannot reconstruct the vernacular original, scholars
have discerned similarities between the *Galluslied* and the *Georgslied*. The orthography of the latter text is problematical, as we shall
see, but it is widely held to contain Alemannic features; whether
these belong to the original or were introduced at some stage in
the transmission is uncertain.

The extant text of the *Georgslied* was entered about the year 1000
on the last two leaves of the Heidelberg (Palatinus) manuscript of
Otfrid's *Evangelienbuch*. It is written continuously as though it
were prose. The hand is not, as has been said by some critics,
weak and childish. Only the first sixteen lines are available in facsimile, but the most that can be said against this portion of the
text is that the letters are irregular in size and that the lines are not
straight. Most of the text has now become almost illegible. It is a
most peculiar document, for at first sight the spelling appears to
be in complete confusion. Although the scribe was conscious of
failure and broke off abruptly with the admission *nequeo Vuisolf*,[2]
it may be said at once that all theories that attribute the confusion
to ignorance of the German language,[3] to a kink in the scribe's
mind,[4] or to an attempt to write down the text from uncertain
memory, are untenable. The words are rarely run together (an

[1] Printed *MSD* XII.
[2] As stated above, some critics associate the previous 'word' *ihn* with *nequeo*,
making Wisolf's admission bilingual.
[3] Kelle, I. 186; R. Koegel, *Geschichte der deutschen Litteratur bis zum Ausgang
des Mittelalters* (Strasbourg, 1894–7), I. ii. 95 sqq.; *Kl. ahd. Spdmr.*, p. 98.
[4] F. A. Wood, *Modern Philology* 12 (1914–15) 172–8.

error to which those who write in a strange language are very
liable); there are—so far as we can judge—no mistakes in vocabulary or idiom; and such apparent lacunae or misunderstandings
as there are may easily be due to faulty copying. It has been shown[1]
that the orthographical peculiarities are to a large extent consistent,
and Ehrismann came nearest the truth when he described the
spelling as 'eine lächerliche Manier'. We have encountered in the
Glosses examples of a crude cipher in which the vowels are replaced by the following consonants of the alphabet (e.g. *mfrb* for
mera). This is an eccentric orthography of another kind. It was his
fanciful system, not his ignorance, that defeated *Wisolf*.[2]

The most striking peculiarities in Wisolf's text are his use of *c*
and *z* for the affricate from Gmc. *t*, his use of *h* and *k* for the fricative from Gmc. *k*, and the misplacement of letters. There are also
a few errors in spelling, e.g. *munt*, l. 9, for *muot*, *kenerier*, l. 14, for
kenerit(a) er, *ehtle*, l. 59, for *ehlle* (i.e. *helle*). Partly because of his
use of the letter *k* where one would expect a High German *h* or *hh*
(e.g. *mikilemo*, ll. 1, 2, for *mihhilemo*, *rhike*, l. 5 (twice) for *rihhe*)
there appears to be a mixture of shifted and unshifted forms such
as is paralleled only in the *Hildebrandslied*. Moreover, as in the
Hildebrandslied, some of the shifted forms appear to be specifically
Upper German (e.g. *chuninginno*, *keteta*, *pilnten*—i.e. *plinten*).
When this apparent confusion is examined more closely, certain
principles emerge. The clue to the mystery of the system is concealed in the words *ihmil*, *ihk*, *ceiken*, *zehiken*.

The affricate from Gmc. *t* is written *z* before *u* (*zurenen*, l. 23,
zuhrentzes, l. 24, *zunrnen*, l. 31). Before *i* and *e* it is written *z* or
c: *ze*, ll. 1, 3, 12, 22, 38, 51, beside *ce*, ll. 10, 16; *zimo*, l. 18; *zehiken*,
l. 22 beside *ceiken*, l. 16; *ceuuei*, l. 14; *halcen*, l. 20, *uncin*, l. 56.
There is, therefore, reason to believe that the system required *c*
before *e* and *i*, but *z* before *u* and probably also before *a* and *o*,
a distinction that is found in a number of manuscripts. The combination of the two letters *zc* and the digraph *zs* for the fricative
from Gmc. *t* (e.g. *ferliezcer*, l. 5, *hiezcen* beside *hiezen*, l. 47, *imbizs*,
l. 15) are found elsewhere also.

---

[1] K. Siemers, *PBB* 39 (1914) 98 ff.
[2] See J. K. Bostock, *Med. Æv.* 5 (1936) 189–98. This article contains a number
of inaccuracies. See also F. Tschirch, 'Wisolf, eine Schreiberpersönlichkeit',
PBB 73 (1951) 387–422. Tschirch, without having read the author's article
reaches similar conclusions and offers additional speculations as to the scribe's
motives.

It is clear that the system which Wisolf was struggling to follow intended initial *h* to be placed immediately after the vowel which it normally preceded, or, in the case of a following diphthong, after its first element, thus *ehrte* l. 9, *ahrto*, l. 37 (for *herte* and *harto*) and *ihez*, l. 26, *uhob*, l. 58 (for *hiez* and *huob*). There are twenty-eight examples in twelve different words, whereas there are only five examples of *h* normally placed: *heuihemo*, l. 3, *halcen*, l. 19, *harto*, l. 37; *hiezcen*, *hiezen*, l. 47. As initial *h* has never been omitted entirely, it appears unlikely that the misplacement was due to unfamiliarity with the aspirate, such as one would expect of a Romance speaker, and there is no resemblance between Wisolf's spelling and the errors (or crude phonetic transcriptions—whichever they are) of the *Altdeutsche Gespräche*.[1]

It appears improbable that the system required a spurious initial *h* to be added after the vowel in words which did not begin with *h* (e.g. *ehz*, l. 48, *ihu*, l. 33, for normal OHG *ez*, *iu*; *ehngila*, l. 13), for it is correctly absent far more often than it is incorrectly present.[2] The *h* which occurs frequently after and before consonants (e.g. *fholko*, l. 2, *rhike*, l. 5, *shlahen*, *shuereto*, l. 27, *shie*, l. 52, *sihk*, ll. 28, 43, *chuninginno*, l. 51, *kuningha*, l. 7) requires examination in detail. There are three other examples of *gh* (*beghontez*, ll. 23, 31, and *mane ha*, l. 7, where a *g* might be postulated in the gap left by the scribe); *bh* does not occur, but *dh* is common (*dho*, ll. 7, 15, *dhar*, l. 14, etc.) for Gmc. *þ* beside *d* (*do*, ll. 12, 32, etc.), and there is one example of *th* (*thin*, l. 4, for *thing* beside *dinge*, l. 3).

The presence of *dh* beside *d* and of *gh* and *g* beside *k*, with the variations *gk* (*gkoto*, l. 4) and *kk* (*kkaen*, l. 47) has been taken by some scholars as evidence that the scribe was Franconian and the original text Alemannic, while others have taken the opposite view, namely that the scribe was Alemannic and the original text Franconian. Yet others have favoured Murbach, where Franconian and Upper German influences are thought to have met.[3]

---

[1] On prothesis and aphaeresis of *h* in OHG see H. Garke, *QuF* 69 (1891) and the review by W. Bruckner, *AfdA* 22 (1896) 164 ff. Garke ignores our text because he considers it to be in so bad a condition as to be worthless as evidence.

[2] This may argue that the prothetic *h* was present now and then in the text which the scribe copied.

[3] It is noteworthy that *dh* and *gh* are characteristic of *early* Frankish texts, whereas Wisolf was writing fairly late in the OHG period. If the inconsistencies noted above are due to copying, the simplest view would be that he was copying an early OHG text of Frankish provenance. This is the view of H. de Boor, op.

On the whole, it appears that the system of Wisolf's orthography was based on Upper German, but no definite conclusion can be drawn. It appears at least probable, nevertheless, that the significance of the mixture of *dh* and *d*, *gh* and *g*, *ch* and *k* (for initial Gmc. *k*) and the strange *k* and *hk* for post-vocalic Gmc. *k* (OHG *hh*), as in *mikilemo*, ll. 1, 2, *ceiken*, l. 16, *sprekenten*, l. 20, *sprecken*, l. 47, *ihk*, ll. 28, 34, 43) has been exaggerated; it may be due to the system Wisolf was trying to follow, and not to dialect or to the conventional orthography of any scriptorium. In order to understand these spellings, we must examine them in connection with the use of *c* and *z* for the affricate, e.g. in *ceiken*, l. 16, and *zehiken*, l. 22.

If the fricative from Gmc. *k* were written *ch* and the letters were transposed to *hc*, as is commonly done in OHG manuscripts,[1] confusion might easily arise between this *c* and the *c* representing the affricate from Gmc. *t*, for *zeichen* would become **ceihcen*. If *k* were used to avoid this, the result would be *ceihken*. Out of this Wisolf could have made *ceiken* (which appears in l. 16), forgetting the *h*, and *zehiken* (l. 22), with *z* for the affricate and the *h* misplaced by analogy with such words as *ihez* (*hiez*) and *uhob* (*huob*). The sequence *hk* actually occurs in *ihk*, ll. 28, 34, 43; *ihkzes*, l. 33; *sihk*, ll. 28, 34, 35, 43, 44 (beside *ih*, ll. 43, 48); *mihkil*, ll. 40, 42; beside *mikilemo*, ll. 1, 2, *sprekenten*, l. 20, *praken*, l. 33, in which the *h* has been omitted, whereas in *sprecken*, l. 47, the scribe has written both *c* and *k* but forgotten the *h*. In *rhike*, l. 5 (twice), 31, the *h* has been misplaced, while in *rike*, l. 23, it is missing. The *h* in *fhaen*, ll. 26, 37, is probably due to the scribe's transposition of *h* and *a*; contrast *sehenten*, l. 20. In *malo*, l. 1, the *h* has probably been inadvertently omitted, although its absence might be due to the Alemannic loss of *h* before *l*. The *h* in *fholko*, l. 2, is probably due to the UG *ch* for *k* after *l*; it is uncertain whether Wisolf's system required *folcho* to be written *folhko* or *fohlko*, but misplacement of the *h* in either would have led to the form he wrote. The form *makrko*, l. 2, is doubtless an error for *marhko*. In the

cit., who would place the original in an area of Frankish territory where Romance and non-High German influences were effective. The Upper German features he would ascribe to the copyist.

[1] See, for example, the Reichenau lists of monks printed by Baesecke, *PBB* 52 (1928), esp. p. 100, the list written by Ruadho about 880: no. 399 *Fridelohc*, no. 425 *Witprhet* (*Witperht*), no. 527 *Alberihc*, no. 594 *Thietprhet*, no. 599 *Otprhet*.

loan-words *karekare*, l. 12, and *kamero*, l. 51, the *k* is unshifted,
while in *ckoukelari*, l. 25, the scribe has used both *c* and *k* for the
shifted initial *g*.

The use of *dh* and *d*, *gh* and *g*, which has caused so much discussion, loses much of its significance when account is taken of two
other features of Wisolf's spelling, namely his tendency to spell
individual words always in the same way, and the presence in the
text of a series of patches in which particular spellings either do
or do not occur.[1] There are, for example, fifty-three instances of
initial *d* for Gmc. *þ* to nineteen instances of *dh*, to which must be
added *dh* medially in *gnadhon*, l. 56, and *dh* for Gmc. *ð* in *dheter*,
l. 20; *d* is therefore the regular spelling. The first *dh* (*dho*, l. 7) is
in the same line as one of the four examples of *gh* (*kuningha*).
Lines 17–20 contain numerous instances of *d* (*do, digita, Druhtin,
des, digita, dem den, den deter, den*) with only one *dh* (*dheter*, l. 20).
Then, with l. 21, an outburst of *dh* and *gh* spellings begins and
continues with little interruption until l. 33. There follow shorter
patches with and without *h*. There are other patches in the text
too. The *c* and *z* are present in patches, though not in connection
with the incidence of *h*. The saint's name is spelt *georio* in ll. 1, 6,
and 9, *gorio* in l. 11, *georio* again in ll. 16 and 17, and then *gorio*
in l. 18 to the end. Down to l. 35 the only capital letters which
occur are in the word *DRuhtin*, l. 17. Even the saint's name begins
with a small letter. From l. 36 onwards we find *GoRio* and
numerous capital *G*'s medially, e.g. *meGine*, l. 40, *beGonton*, l. 41.
There are even patches in the scribe's use of dots, which sometimes
divide clauses and sometimes, as in ll. 19 and 20, follow almost
every word.

Attempts to deduce the dialect of Wisolf or of the copy he had
before him cannot succeed until something more has been learnt
about the system he was trying to follow. The presence of *p* and *k*
for initial Gmc. *b* and *g* suggests Upper German.[2]

The motive of the person who devised the system can only be
conjectured. Such virtuosity was esteemed as a demonstration of
ingenuity, and it pleased the vanity of the learned to be unintelligible to the vulgar. In the grammar of Virgilius Maro Gram-

---

[1] See Bostock and Tschirch, opp. citt.

[2] Behaghel, *PBB* 57 (1933) 240 ff., esp. 242, claimed Wisolf as a Bavarian
because *b* is represented by *p* initially but by *b* after a prefix. Since he cites our
text as his prime witness, the argument appears to be circular. On *kobet* (l. 48),
see *PBB* 46 (1922) 334.

maticus[1] the chapter 'De scinderatione fonorum' furnishes an excellent example of such a mentality:

Ob tres causas fona finduntur: prima est ut sagacitatem discentium nostrorum in inquirendis atque in inveniendis his quaeque obscura sunt ad probemus. Secunda est propter decorem aedificationemque eloquentiae. Tertia ne mystica quaeque et quae solis gnaris pandi debent passim ab infimis ac stultis facile repperiantur, ne secundum antiquum sues gemmas calcent.

He describes many subtle methods; one example will suffice: 'Ubi sit regnem, ponatur germen.'

Even if the mystery of the orthography were solved, we should have penetrated at the most as far as the copy from which the present text was derived. Only the rhymes and, to a lesser degree, the scansion, could furnish evidence as to the language of the poet. The metre is regular, and the rhymes are for the most part pure, although there is consonantal assonance in *man : fram*, ll. 30, 36, 45; and *gān : sprehhan*, l. 47, can only be an impure rhyme, and Alemannic rather than Bavarian, for the latter would have had *gēn*.[2] The impure rhyme *tuon : spenton* inferred for l. 54 would be Franconian or later Alemannic, for the latter dialect retained *tuan* until the close of the ninth century. The rhyme *fuorren : skōnen*, l. 13, if it goes back to an earlier *fuorun : skōnun*, is likely to be Upper German, for earlier Franconian would have been more likely to have the form *skōnon*. Such evidence as there is, then, points to Upper German and more especially Alemannic origin. Apart from the rhyme with *tuon* in l. 54, the only evidence as to the date is the preservation of the instrumental case in *fholko*, l. 2, *shuereto*, l. 27 (the former with a dative adjective, the latter with the rarely used instrumental case of the adjective *uunteruuassho*). The apparent instrumentals *malo* and *ehrigo* (*herigo*), l. 1, may be original datives, since the scribe is unreliable in the distribution of *o* and *e*. The poet, it seems, was unsure about the use of the instrumental, but the forms still existed, a condition which points to the close of the ninth century and agrees with the historical connections already suggested.[3]

---

[1] *Virgilii Maronis Grammatici Opera*, ed. J. Huemer (Leipzig, 1886), pp. 76–82, esp. p. 78, l. 28.

[2] On the distribution of *gān*, *gēn*, *gangan* see *PBB* 59 (1935) 235–43.

[3] Sievers, however, relying as usual on his acoustic methods, assigned the composition to Weissenburg and the period before Otfrid. See *PBB* 52 (1928)

The style of the *Georgslied* is terse. The sentences are co-ordinate, and there is a swift sequence of events with little elaboration. A notable feature of the verse technique is the repetition of phrases with variation of individual words; for instance, the phrase *mit mikilemo herigo*, l. 1, is varied by *mit mikilemo folko*, l. 2, and *Georgio fuor ze malo*, l. 1, is varied by *fuor er ze demo ringe*, l. 3. The effect of this repetition with variation is to underline the parallelism between the lines, not, as with the variation in alliterative verse, to provide a syntactical counterpoint to the metrical form. The two halves of the line are similarly balanced, as for instance in ll. 5, 8, 19, 20, 26, 37, 52. The poem also employs repeated formulas, sometimes with slight variation, which sum up the content of the preceding lines; such are ll. 6 and 11, 16 and 22, 30, 36, and 45. These mark the ends of short sections. Some others, e.g. in ll. 23 and 31, mark the beginnings. Yet others extend over two lines, e.g. ll. 17–18, 28–9, 34–5, 43–4, and (in so far as we can be sure of the reconstruction of the text, which seems to have been abbreviated at points) they seem to employ chiasmus. All these repeated formulas seem to have the function of refrains. Lines 6, 11, 16, 22, 30, 36, 45, 50, and 57 appear to mark the end of sections (of six, five, five, six, eight, nine, five, and seven lines respectively). Since the manuscript text has lacunae (perhaps also incorrect repetitions) and breaks off before the end of the poem, we cannot be certain about the construction of the work. It can be seen, however, that there are two principal parts (ll. 1–45 and 46–59), and it may be conjectured that there were originally more. The poem appears to be working up to a climax, but it is idle to speculate about what is lost.

The metre is the same as that of Otfrid and the other short rhyming poems. The feet are regular, and there is neither enjambment nor hiatus (except possibly in the problematical l. 48). Numerous attempts have been made to group the lines into strophes, but none has been generally accepted. Zarncke suggested strophes of three, four, and five lines, Scherer and Koegel strophes of two and three lines.[1] Kolbe preferred strophes of two and three lines, interrupted at irregular intervals by a refrain.[2] Huisman divided the lines to form a strict mathematical balance, and inferred that

214–16. It may be noted that the rhyme in l. 13 would have been *fuorun*: *skōnun* in Otfrid's dialect.

[1] See the two arrangements given in *Ahd. Lb.*   [2] *MLN* 31 (1916) 19–23.

fourteen lines were missing at the end.[1] Sievers held that the
poem was not written in strophes, but was intended to be sung
by two choirs taking alternate lines, after the manner of the
Psalms.[2] Maurer envisaged a basic strophe of five lines like that of
the *Galluslied* but admitting extensions; he also imagined it sung
to the same melody (which has been preserved) as the Latin
poem.[3] Possibly the poem was intended to be chanted in sections
with short intervals during a procession of the relics, or to be read in
sections at successive services on the saint's day. The arrangement
offered below comes close to the views expressed by Steinmeyer.[4]

The poem may be divided into two sections, A and B, the latter
being incomplete. Section A (ll. 1–45) may be further divided into
three subsections, (*a*) dealing with George's appearance before the
tribunal, (*b*) with his imprisonment and ensuing miracles, and (*c*)
with the three torments and his repeated resurrections. Subsection (*a*) occupies eleven lines, the sixth and the eleventh being
a refrain. Subsection (*b*) occupies eleven lines too (ll. 12–22), the
fifth and eleventh (ll. 16 and 22) being a refrain. Subsection (*c*)
occupies twenty-three lines (ll. 23–45) and can be divided into
three parts (ll. 23–30, 31–6, 37–45), the last three lines of each
part being a three-line refrain, and the first two of these employing
chiasmus. Section B may likewise be divided into three subsections, (*a*) telling of the raising of a dead man, (*b*) of the conversion of the queen, and (*c*) of the banishing of Apollyon. These
subsections contain five, seven, and two lines respectively, though
the last is clearly incomplete. Both (*a*) and (*b*) conclude with a refrain (ll. 50 and 57). We may thus represent the structure of the
poem as follows: the figures denoting numbers of lines and the
asterisks indicating refrains:

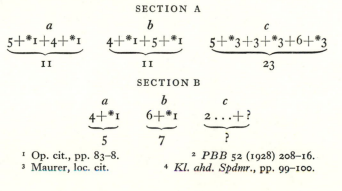

SECTION A

a	*b*	*c*
5+*1+4+*1	4+*1+5+*1	5+*3+3+*3+6+*3
11	11	23

SECTION B

a	*b*	*c*
4+*1	6+*1	2...+?
5	7	?

[1] Op. cit., pp. 83–8.   [2] *PBB* 52 (1928) 208–16.
[3] Maurer, loc. cit.   [4] *Kl. ahd. Spdmr.*, pp. 99–100.

This is perhaps the best we can do with the poem as it was recorded by Wisolf.[1] This analysis may be converted into a strophic
analysis by taking the refrains as closing the strophes, thus:

$$5+{}^*1+4+{}^*1 \qquad 4+{}^*1+5+{}^*1 \qquad 5+{}^*3+3+{}^*3+6+{}^*3$$
$$\underbrace{}_{6} \quad \underbrace{}_{5} \qquad \underbrace{}_{5} \quad \underbrace{}_{6} \qquad \underbrace{}_{8} \quad \underbrace{}_{6} \quad \underbrace{}_{9}$$

$$4+{}^*1 \qquad 6+{}^*1 \qquad 2\ldots+\,?$$
$$\underbrace{}_{5} \qquad \underbrace{}_{7} \qquad \underbrace{}_{?}$$

We cannot, however, be certain where to place the strophic divisions in Section A (*c*), since we cannot know whether the thrice-
repeated sequences of three lines (ll. 28–30, 34–6 and 43–5)
represent the beginnings or ends of strophes; a third possibility[2]
is that the chiastic ll. 28–9, 34–5, and 43–4 are to be divided between the strophes. Yet another possibility is that ll. 11, 30, 36,
and 45 open new strophes. This would give a slightly less uneven
strophic structure $(6+5+5+6+7+6+9+6+7+\,?)$ and would
make Section A (*c*) equivalent (with twenty-two lines) to Section
A (*a*) and A (*b*) together.[3]

---

[1] One of the difficulties facing the critic is the uncertainty about the com-
petence of the scribe. We cannot be sure whether his repetitions indicate a
feature of the construction (as is assumed for the analysis above) or rest upon
dittography. If the former is the case, we have to conjecture a missing half-line
in ll. 18 and 29.

[2] See Maurer, op. cit., who regards ll. 35–6 and 43–5 as spurious.

[3] The author of this handbook wished to rearrange the lines in the passage
ll. 17–22, placing l. 18 after l. 22, and thus enclosing the second and third miracles
with a chiastic refrain. Such interference with Wisolf's text seems unwarranted.

XIII

Louis III of France and the *Ludwigslied*

LOUIS THE GERMAN ruled the eastern realm from 843 to 876, while his half-brother Charles the Bald was king of Neustria from 843 to 877. During this time the imperial office was held first by Lothar, their eldest brother, from 840 to 855, and then by Lothar's son, Louis II, from 855 to 875. Louis II, who inherited the kingdom of Italy from his father, was entirely preoccupied south of the Alps in defending the Italian peninsula against the Saracens, who repeatedly attacked Sicily and southern Italy and even threatened Rome. Meanwhile, another race of heathens, the Vikings or 'Northmen' (Latinized as 'Nortmanni', 'Nordmanni', or 'Normanni') were ravaging the coasts of Western Europe from the Guadalquivir to the Elbe, sailing up the rivers in their shallow-draught boats and plundering every settlement within reach. The Northmen came from various parts of Scandinavia. Some, chiefly from Norway, concentrated their attacks on western Britain and Ireland, while others, mainly Danes, attacked eastern Britain and the continental coast. Their raids had been going on for generations, but it was not until the second quarter of the ninth century that they began to pose a serious threat to the safety of the Frankish dominions.

In 841 Danish raiders sailed up the Seine and took Rouen, and in 843 they entered the Loire and burned the town of Nantes. In 845 they burned Hamburg, and in 851 a great expedition sailed up the Elbe, defeated the Saxon armies, and ravaged the eastern part of Saxony. Every year they raided the Frisian coast, and in order to gain peace the Emperor Lothar gave the island of Walcheren in fief to the Danish chief Rorik so that he might defend the coast against other marauders.

Between 843 and 868 the Northmen established themselves in

Flanders and at the mouths of the Somme, the Seine, the Loire, and the Garonne. They were present in such force that they were able with virtual impunity to carry out raids deep into France, plundering Paris (in 845 and 857) and many other towns. They met with virtually no sustained resistance, since Charles the Bald was more concerned with territorial gains than with protecting his realm against the danger from without. On the one occasion when Charles offered strong resistance, in 857, besieging the Danes for three months on the island of Oissel in the Seine, Neustria was invaded by Louis the German; Charles had to raise the siege, losing his fleet and allowing the Danes to escape. During the Franco-German hostilities which ensued they were able to harry Flanders and the area round the mouth of the Rhine; a Danish force even entered the Mediterranean, sailed up the Rhône and devastated Provence. Charles made a number of futile attempts to bribe them to depart or to fight each other. In 852 he even granted them a large sum and a tract of land at the mouth of the Loire to settle in. During part of this period they were abetted by Pippin, Charles's nephew, who claimed the kingdom of Aquitaine and who is said to have even embraced the heathen religion.

From 868 onwards France enjoyed a respite from the incursions of the Danes, since they then began to concentrate their attacks on the England of Alfred the Great. Charles the Bald died in 877. His successor as king of France was Louis the Stammerer (Louis II of France). Shortly after Louis's accession the Danes began to return from England after the defeat of Ethandum. He showed some resolution in resisting their attacks, but he died in April 879, after reigning only two years. He left two young sons, Louis, who was seventeen, and Carloman, who was sixteen. In the September of that year a third son was born posthumously. (It was this third son, later known as Charles the Simple, who, as king of France from 893 to 929, finally delivered France from the Danish menace. In 911, by the treaty of Clair-sur-Epte, he ceded to them a great tract of land in the lower valley of the Seine. Their leader Hrolf, or Rollo, became the first duke of Normandy, a more or less loyal vassal of the king of France, and an adherent of the Christian faith. During the ensuing century the Normans—as we may now call them—forgot their Norse tongue and developed a variety of French, just as the West Franks had forgotten their Frankish tongue and established their own variety of Latin, which

we now call French. Just over a century and a half after the treaty
of Clair-sur-Epte, a successor of Hrolf invaded England and defeated King Harold at Hastings.)

The death of Louis II caused dissension: some of the nobles
wanted the succession to go to Louis of Saxony, but they did not
prevail. The late king's cousin, Abbot Hugo, wanted to install
Louis and Carloman as kings of France, having promised their
father that he would watch over their interests. Hugo was successful, and they were crowned by Ansegis, archbishop of Sens, in
September 879. At about the same time Hugo sent to Louis of
Saxony to beg him to settle for part of Lorraine. This was pro-
visionally agreed and confirmed at Saint-Quentin by Louis, Hugo,
and the two young kings in February 880. Shortly after this compact was confirmed, the two brothers met at Amiens and divided
the West Frankish lands between themselves: Louis III (as we
may now call him) took the northern part, while Carloman took
Burgundy and Aquitaine.

In 879 Count Boso of Vienne, encouraged by his wife Irmengard, daughter of the Emperor Louis II, had had himself made
king of Arles. Since the territory he had seized belonged to Carloman's portion of France, Louis and Carloman set off to the south
together to make war on him. They were half-heartedly aided by
Charles the Fat, who had his eye on the imperial office and knew
that Boso was favoured by the Pope. They laid siege to Vienne,
but suddenly Charles left them in the lurch and returned home.
Realizing that they could not prevail alone, Louis and Carloman
called off the siege, though Carloman remained in the south to
deal with the rebellion. Louis set off to the north in order to
oppose the Northmen who were causing havoc in his part of the
realm, and had been but ineffectually resisted by those whom the
king had left in charge. Louis celebrated Christmas in Compiègne,
and in the New Year he began to prepare effective resistance against
the invaders.

The Northmen, who had begun to return to France and the
Low Countries from England during the reign of Louis II
(877–9), profited greatly from the discord following upon his death,
as well as from the lack of leadership due to Louis III's absence in
Burgundy. At first they concentrated most of their forces on the
territory of Louis the Saxon. In 880 they defeated the Saxon and
Thuringian levies on the Lüneburg Heath and ravaged the valley

of the Elbe. Another army attacked the Low Countries and established itself at the mouth of the Scheldt. Some notion of the devastation they caused may be gathered from the following entry in the Annals of Saint-Vaast (in Arras)[1] for the year 880:

Timor quoque et tremor eorum [sc. Nortmannorum] cecidit super inhabitantes terram, et hac elati victoria die noctuque non cessant aecclesias igne cremare populumque Christianum iugulare. Tunc omnes intra Scaldum et Sumnam atque trans Scaldum monachi, canonici, sanctimoniales cum corporibus sanctorum et omnis aetas et conditio fugam ineunt. Ipsi enim Dani nemini nec etiam aetati parcebant, sed omnia ferro et igne devastant. Gozlinus[2] vero et hi qui cum eo erant videntes non posse eis resistere, mense Octobrio intrante dimisso exercitu, rediit unusquisque in sua. Nortmanni vero seu Dani sedem sibi mutaverunt et mense Novembri Curtriaco[3] sibi castrum ad hiemandum construunt. . . . Omnemque terram vorax flamma consumpsit.

One may imagine that the inhabitants of northern France longed for deliverance but saw little hope. In the first half of 881 the Danes continued their ravages. In July they crossed the Somme with a large army and marched almost as far as Beauvais. By this time Louis had assembled an army and crossed the Oise, marching in the direction of Lavier (on the Somme, below Abbeville). Learning from spies he had sent out that the enemy was returning laden with spoil, Louis directed his march towards Saucourt-en-Vimeu (*Sathulcurtis in pago Witmau*), where he met and engaged the Danes on 3 August 881. They were put to flight, pursued, and defeated. It seems, however, that at one stage in the fighting the Franks themselves were almost put to flight by the Danes, and that only the steadfastness of the king himself saved the day.[4] The Annals of Saint-Bertin, the relevant parts of which were written by

---

[1] Ed. B. de Simson, *Annales Xantenses et Annales Vedastini* (MGH Scriptores Rerum Germanicarum) (Hanover/Leipzig, 1909), pp. 48 f.

[2] The abbot to whom Louis III had entrusted the defence of the realm.

[3] Courtrai.

[4] The Annals of Saint-Vaast blame this reverse on the hubris of some of the Franks:

'Et patrata victoria ex parte coeperunt gloriari suis hoc actum viribus et non dederunt gloriam Deo. Paucique Nortmanni ex dicta villa egressi, omnem exercitum vertit [sic] in fugam, pluresque ex eis, videlicet usque ad centum homines, interfecerunt; et nisi rex citius equo descendens locum resistendi et audaciam suis donaret, omnes turpiter ex eodem loco fugiendo abirent' (*Annales Vedastini*, ed. cit., p. 50).

Hincmar of Reims,[1] belittle Louis's victory, mentioning only that he took flight when no one was pursuing. This proved to Hincmar that the Northmen were acting with the power of God.[2] However, although it brought only a temporary lull in the Danish ravages, it was clearly a decisive victory in the eyes of most contemporaries. The annalist of Saint-Vaast tells us that very few of the Danes returned to bring the news to their comrades and that the enemy began to fear the youthful King Louis.[3]

The career of Louis III, culminating in the glorious victory at Saucourt,[4] is celebrated in the *Ludwigslied*, a poem made up of fifty-nine lines of rhyming verse.[5] The following is a translation of the text:

I know a king—his name is Hluduig—who serves God zealously: I know He rewards him for it. As a young man he became fatherless. This was at once made good to him: the Lord took him and became his guardian. He gave him forces,[6] a lordly following, and the throne here in France.[7] Long may he enjoy it! This he then at once divided, the number of the enjoyments,[8] with Karleman his brother. (ll. 1–8)

When this was all accomplished, God desired to prove him (to see) whether he could endure hardships so young. He let heathen men journey across the sea to remind the Frankish people of their sins. Some at once perished, some were chosen.[9] He who had formerly lived amiss

[1] Ed. G. Waitz, *Annales Bertiniani* (MGH Scriptores Rerum Germanicarum), p. 150.

[2] 'Et ipse Hludowicus una cum suis retrorsum, nemine persequente, fugam arripuit, divino manifestante iudicio, quia quod a Nortmannis fuerat actum non humana, sed divina virtute patratum extiterit.' It is interesting to note that, whether the battle of Saucourt was regarded as a great victory or not, the Danes were thought to have been sent by God; set-backs for the Franks were interpreted as due either to human wickedness or to human impotence in the face of divine power.

[3] '. . . perpauci vero Dani, qui evasere, interitum suorum nuntiavere in castra, indeque Nortmanni Hludowicum regem adolescentem timere coeperunt' (*Annales Vedastini*, ed. cit., p. 51).

[4] See E. Berg, 'Das Ludwigslied und die Schlacht bei Saucourt', *RhVB* 29 (1964) 175–99, where the events and the background of contemporary thought are discussed in detail, with copious references to contemporary writings and a map of the theatre of war.

[5] *MSD* XI; *Kl. ahd. Spdmr.* XVI; *Ahd. Lb.* XXXVI. Facsimile: *Schrifttafeln* 22.

[6] Or 'power' or 'valour'.   [7] Or 'among the Franks'.

[8] The rendering 'enjoyments' is chosen to accommodate a possible legal sense of *wunniono*. For a possible territorial sense of the word see the article 'Wonne' in Kluge, *Etym. Wb.*, and the remarks of Braune, *PBB* 14 (1889) 370.

[9] Lachmann, and following him T. Schumacher, *PBB* (Tüb.) 85 (1963) 57–64, emend this line to *Uurdun sum erkorane, Sume sar verlorane* 'Some were chosen, some immediately lost'.

suffered punishment.[1] He who was then a thief and survived[2] took to fasting; later he became a good man. One was a liar, one a robber, one full of licentiousness, and he[3] mended his ways.[4]   (ll. 9–18)

The king was far off, the realm all in disarray. Christ was angered: alas, it paid for this. Yet God took pity on it: He knew all the distress. He bade Hluduig ride thither at once: 'Hluduig, my king, help my people. The Northmen have them hard pressed.' Then said Hluduig: 'Lord, I will do all that thou commandest, unless death prevents me.'
(ll. 19–26)

Then he took leave of God, raised the standard, and rode thither into France to meet the Northmen. Those who were waiting for him thanked God. They all said: 'My lord, we have waited for thee so long.' Then Hluduig the Good spoke loudly: 'Take comfort, comrades, my companions in adversity. God has sent me hither and commanded me Himself, if it should seem advisable to you, that I should fight here and not spare myself until I have saved you. Now I desire all God's servants to follow me. Our life here is allotted for as long as Christ wishes; if He wishes our departure hence, over that He has authority. Whoever does God's will here with courage—if he comes out of it alive—I will reward him for it; if he does not survive,[5] (I will reward) his family.' (ll. 27–41)

Then he took up shield and spear. Courageously he rode. He wanted to demonstrate the truth to his adversaries. Then, it was not long before he found the Northmen. He rendered praise to God: he sees what he has longed for. The king rode bravely and sang a holy song, and all together they sang 'Kyrie eleison'. The song was sung, the battle was begun, blood shone in cheeks,[6] the Franks romped there. There every warrior fought, but none like Hluduig: swift and brave—that was in his blood. This one he hewed through, that one he ran through. He at once poured out bitter drink for his enemies: so woe to them for ever!
(ll. 42–54)

Praised be the power of God! Hluduig was victorious. And thanks to all the saints! His was the triumph. Hail again to Hluduig, (our)

[1] *haranskara* is usually taken to be a term denoting secular punishment. Its OS cognate, however, is used to denote divinely inflicted punishment. Cf. *Heliand*, l. 240; the same is true of OE *hearmscearu* in the translation of the OS *Genesis*, ll. 432 and 781.

[2] It is not clear whether *thanana ginas* means 'survived the calamity' or 'returned to health after his wickedness'.

[3] It is not clear whether this refers only to the last-mentioned type of sinner or to all three.

[4] Or 'redeemed himself from it' sc. by penance. It might also mean 'made amends for it'.

[5] Literally 'if he remains in it'.

[6] Or, just conceivably, 'fields'. See T. M. Andersson, 'Blood on the Battlefield: A note on the Ludwigslied v. 49', *Neophil.* 56 (1972) 12–17.

fortunate[1] king. As ready as he has always been wherever there has been need of it, may the Lord in His mercies save him!   (ll. 55–9)

The poem is a glorification of the Church Militant, and of the king, its servant. The author was almost certainly a cleric with a theodicean view of history: the destiny of the young king is in the hands of God, and the apparent evil of the Viking invasion is part of God's design. Just as in old times God punished his people, the Jews, so He punishes His people (*minan liutin*), the Franks; and just as God, after His anger, was moved to pity for the Jews, so He is moved to pity for the Franks. The effect of the visitation is salutary: the wrongdoers turn back and forsake their wicked ways. It can be shown conclusively[2] that the poet's interpretation of the invasion is in accord with contemporary ecclesiastical thinking. Archbishop Hincmar of Reims had shortly before Saucourt, in a synodal address to Louis, emphasized penitence as a prerequisite victory. He had also urged Louis to restore law and justice.[3]

Also reminiscent of the Old Testament is the depiction of Louis as a warrior king: we may recall that Otfrid compared *his* Louis with David. God speaks to him as he spoke to the prophets of old. He chooses Louis as His champion against the heathen, and Louis rallies his people to God's cause, reminding them that Christ has power over life and death. He praises God when he sights the enemy. He rides to battle singing a hymn, and his followers, instead of uttering a battle-cry, join in with 'Lord have mercy'. He wants to 'tell the truth to the foe'—the truth that God is on his side, and none can prevail against Him. At the end of the poem God is praised and the Saints are thanked for Louis's victory; only then is Louis himself extolled, with a prayer that God may save him.

The king is God's lieutenant, ready to risk his life for his lord. The relation between God and the king is seen in the feudal terms of service and reward. So is the relation between the king and his people: although those who follow him are God's servants, doing

---

[1] The lacuna in the text at this point prevents us from being certain whether *salig* means 'endowed with good fortune' or 'endowed with divine blessing'.

[2] See E. Berg., op. cit., and W. Schwarz, 'The "Ludwigslied", a Ninth Century Poem', *MLR* 42 (1947) 467–73.

[3] For references see Berg and Schwarz, opp. citt. Schwarz also argues, with less conviction, that the poet, by making God communicate directly with the king, was contradicting the clerical opinion that God spoke to the king only through the Church.

God's will, the king promises to reward them for their service, or, if they perish, to reward their kin. The ideal feudal king was not an autocrat, and although Louis receives his orders from God, their execution is subject to the approval of his followers. Louis, then, is presented as a model of Christian kingship, acting as God's plenipotentiary on earth, vindicating the Faith against the heathen, coming to the aid of his people, leading them fearlessly in battle, and honouring his feudal duties towards them.

Yet, in spite of the obviously clerical presentation, some scholars have discerned 'Germanic' elements both in the style and the content.[1] Louis's ruthlessness in battle has been thought un-Christian and to amount to Germanic battle fury.[2] Much has been made of the notion that God becomes the young king's *magaczogo*; it has been conjectured that this motif refers to a Germanic custom of giving a young man into the care of a tutor, possibly a maternal uncle.[3] The historical basis for the poet's statement seems to be the fact that, when Louis was orphaned, his interests were looked after by his father's cousin, Hugo, who was an abbot, and who had both brothers, Louis and Carloman, made kings by Archbishop Ansegis. It could be maintained that God, acting through the Church, became the boy's guardian and gave him his throne.[4] Admittedly the metaphor by which Louis 'pours out bitter drink for his enemies' has a 'heroic' ring. It has parallels in the *Nibelungenlied* and *Beowulf*.[5] On the other hand, it is not inconceivable that the poet found the motif in the Old Testament.[6] There have been attempts to find traces of alliteration and variation in the poem, but such echoes of Germanic technique as have been discerned are faint and may be in the heads of the critics.

Whether one is convinced on this score is ultimately a matter of temperament. So too is the determination of the genre to which

[1] An extreme position is taken by T. Melicher, 'Die Rechtsaltertümer im Ludwigslied' (*Anzeiger der phil.-hist. Klasse der österreichischen Akademie der Wissenschaften*, Jahrgang 1954, Nr. 18, pp. 254–75).   [2] Ibid. 272.

[3] Tacitus, *Germania* 20, states: 'Sororum filiis idem apud avunculum qui apud patrem honor. quidam sanctiorem artioremque hunc nexum sanguinis arbitrantur.' It is worth noting that the word *magaczogo* might be a calque on *paedagogus* (Gr. παιδαγωγός); formationally it is partnered only by *herizogo*, which corresponds to Lat. *dux, strategus* (Gr. στρατηγός).

[4] See Schwarz, op. cit., p. 470.

[5] *Nib.*, str. 1960, 1981; *Beow.*, l. 769.

[6] Cf. Job 21: 20; Ps. 74: 9 (A.V. 75: 8); Jer. 25: 15; also Rev. 14: 10. Such a metaphor could, of course, occur to any poet at any time: in Kipling's poem *Danny Deever* the condemned soldier drinks 'bitter beer' before he is hanged.

the poem belongs. Many scholars have held the *Ludwigslied* to be a representative of the ancient genre of the *Preislied*, a song of praise addressed to a ruler.[1] This kind of song certainly existed in Norse literature, where it may have been preserved from Germanic times, and there is evidence in *Beowulf*[2] that the deeds of a king might be celebrated in song soon afterwards. In Germany, apart from the *Ludwigslied*, we have only Latin poems on such themes, notably one celebrating the victory of Charlemagne's son Pippin over the Avars in 796 and another, concerned with the capture of the Emperor Louis II at Benevento in 871.[3] It is not clear what connections exist between the German and the Latin poems; there are certainly similarities: all employ dialogue, and both the poem in praise of Pippin and the *Ludwigslied* render praise to God at the end. If there was no tradition of *Preislieder* in Germany, one would be inclined to think that the Latin poems— or others like them—had furnished the model for the German poem. If such a tradition did exist, one might surmise that it was continued in both languages.

Pleasing though it is to imagine that, among the scanty remains of Old High German literature, fortune has preserved for us not only one heroic lay (the *Hildebrandslied*), but also one example of yet another ancient genre, it is certain that the poet was inspired chiefly by the Bible. Moreover, if we are to believe, as is commonly supposed, that rhyming verse was a recent importation from Latin, we may assert that the poet chose a medium of expression which was relatively new in his day, deliberately eschewing whatever traditional forms may have been current.

A more plausible view of the genre has recently been advanced, namely that we should regard the *Ludwigslied* as an example of 'Christian heroic poetry' such as we find in the French *chansons de geste*.[4] In such poetry the hero is a Christian warrior fighting in God's cause against a heathen foe. It is not represented in any

[1] On the *Preislied* see A. Heusler, *Die altgermanische Dichtung* (Potsdam, 1926), pp. 119–44. For a recent attribution of our poem to the genre, see F. Maurer, 'Hildebrandslied und Ludwigslied', *Dichtung und Sprache des Mittelalters* (Berne, 1963, 2nd edn., 1971), pp. 157–67, esp. pp. 163 ff.   [2] ll. 867 ff.

[3] For a full discussion of the possible relation of these and other Latin poems to the *Ludwigslied*, see Heinrich Naumann, *Das Ludwigslied und die verwandten lateinischen Gedichte* (Halle, 1932).

[4] See M. Wehrli, 'Gattungsgeschichtliche Betrachtungen zum Ludwigslied', in *Philologia Deutsch. Festschrift zum 70. Geburtstag von Walter Henzen* (Berne, 1965).

extant German work—other than the *Ludwigslied* perhaps—until the twelfth century, when Pfaffe Konrad rendered the *Chanson de Roland* into German. The first great German work on such a theme is Wolfram's *Willehalm*, and the source of this is a French *chanson de geste*. It must be remembered that the Franks had been Christians for nearly three centuries when Charlemagne became Emperor, and it is not unlikely that their kings would have been celebrated in song as Christian warriors. Indeed it is possible[1] that the 'barbara et antiquissima carmina' mentioned by Charlemagne's biographer Einhard, 'quibus veterum regum actus et bella canebantur', were not 'heroic lays' like the *Hildebrandslied* (as is commonly supposed), but works not unlike the *Ludwigslied*. In that part of Charlemagne's dominions which became Germany, it seems, the older 'secular' themes continued to be cultivated, providing ultimately the sources for the heroic epic of the Middle High German period. The heroes of German poetry, where they can be identified with historical figures, belong in large measure to the period of the Migrations of the Peoples—though figures from later periods, like Herzog Ernst, could still become legendary heroes. Whatever heroic traditions grew up in Christian Carolingian times were preserved, not in Germany, but in the western part of Charlemagne's Empire which became France. The reason for this divergence is to be sought in the historical situation in Europe after the division of the Empire. The great military threat to Christendom came from the Saracens in Italy, Spain, and southern France, whereas Germany had little to do with religious wars until the age of the Crusades. In Germany, therefore, there was no grand new heroic theme to replace the traditional tales of dynastic conflict, internecine feuding, exile, and divided loyalty. Moreover, there was no German patriotic idea comparable to *la dulce France*, which might have fostered a new kind of national poetry. The two kinds of heroic literature may have coexisted in Carolingian times, but the evidence is inconclusive. It is perhaps significant that the battle of Saucourt was remembered in French literature and is supposed to lie behind the Old French *Gormont et Isembart*, although the French work is in no way connected with the German poem and does not resemble it in any particular.[2] It is

---

[1] See Wehrli, op. cit.

[2] *Gormont et Isembart. Fragment de chanson de geste du XIIe siècle.* Ed. by Alphonse Bayot (2nd edn., Paris, 1921). In this poem the Normans have become Saracens, but the locale is still northern France.

perhaps significant that the *Ludwigslied* not only celebrates the victory of a French king on French soil, but was most probably composed in France for performance at a French court. If this view of the genre of the poem is correct, we may characterize it as the only representative of the *chanson de geste* in German, and the first attestation of the genre on French soil.[1]

The text is exceptionally well preserved in a manuscript of the ninth century which is now in the public library at Valenciennes in Flanders and was formerly in the monastery of Saint-Amand nearby. The manuscript is the work of several scribes; it contains some theological matter and also the oldest surviving French poem, the *Sequence of St. Eulalia*, followed by the *Ludwigslied*. The two poems were entered by the same scribe in a beautifully legible hand; this scribe wrote neither the preceding nor the following pieces. It is the only known example of an Old French and an Old High German work occurring together in a manuscript. We cannot know whether the scribe spoke both languages, but at any rate he could write and no doubt understand both. His French is Picard-Walloon, and his German is essentially Rhenish Franconian.

The Gmc. voiceless dental fricative appears initially as *th*, medially and finally as *th*, *dh*, or *d*. Gmc. *ð* is represented by *d* initially, by *d* or *t* medially (*holoda*:*tholota*), and by *t*, occasionally *d*, and once *th* finally (*got*, *god*, *hinavarth*). The voiced labial is written *b*. The affricate from Gmc. *p* appears as *ph* after *l* and as *f* after *m* (*hilph*, *sigikamf*). The fricative from Gmc. *t* appears only once medially, and then it is spelt *zs* (*heizsit*); in final position it appears as *z* (*uueiz*), but there is apparent confusion between *s* and *z* in *imoz* (l. 40) beside *imos* (l. 2). In one word, *lietz* (l. 11), we should expect a fricative (normal *liez*). The *tz* here has been interpreted as a compromise between Low German *t* and High German *z* (this is improbable), or as representing an intermediate stage in the shift from stop to fricative. It is, however, probably due to scribal confusion between the fricative and the affricate, which were often not distinguished in spelling. Both *c* and *z* were commonly used for the dental affricate; the scribe of our text uses the former before front vowels (*uncih*, *cehanton*) and a combination of the two before back vowels (*magaczogo*, *czala*). Initial

---

[1] On the provenance of the poem and the related question of its language, see R. Harvey, 'The Provenance of the Old High German Ludwigslied', *Med. Æv.* 14 (1945) 1–20.

pre-consonantal *h* occurs only in the proper name *Hluduig* (and in its Latinized form in the title), but there are numerous examples of the unhistorical prothetic *h* before vowels (e.g. *heigun, hiu, hin, hio*). The sequence *sl* appears as *skl* in *thuruhskluog* (l. 52). The *k* may represent a glide such as is found in Romance between *s* and *l*; on the other hand *sk* may represent the merger, attested in later German, of *s* and *sk* in the palato-alveolar [ʃ].

One feature of the phonology which may be explained as a sign either of archaism or of proximity to Low German is the regular retention of post-consonantal *j*, written *i* (as in *uuuniono, gendiot, gisellion*). Standard editions of the text print *frano* in l. 46. This would be the Low German form of *frono*, but it appears to rest upon a misreading of the manuscript.[1]

In the morphology the most noteworthy feature is the occurrence of the pronoun *he* (l. 40) beside the normal *her* and the enclitic *-er* (as in *uuolder*). In the syntax there is syncretism of the dative and accusative cases of the personal pronoun *ir*, the form *hiu* (with prothetic *h*) representing both (ll. 42 f.).

There is in the linguistic peculiarities of the text some support for the view that it was written in an area where High German, Low German, and French influence met. On the other hand, the archaic retention of post-consonantal *j* would accord with the view that the text represents a form of Rhenish Franconian that was spoken by the Frankish conquerors of Northern France and had become isolated from the main stock. As the poem celebrates in German the victory of a French king on French soil, and as the scribe wrote in both languages, it would be natural to suppose that it was composed in a bilingual area. That the Franks spoke German for some time after the conquest is not in doubt, but how long German survived there we do not know. Nor do we know whether this postulated 'West Frankish' was similar to the language of the *Ludwigslied*.[2]

Even if we cannot localize the language, we can date the composition of the poem with unusual accuracy. It cannot have been written before the victory of 3 August 881, and it must have been composed before the king's death (see ll. 2, 6, and 59). Louis died

---

[1] See R. N. Combridge, *ZfdA* 97 (1968) 33 ff.

[2] On the relevance of the language of the poem to the West Frankish problem, see R. Schützeichel, 'Das Ludwigslied und die Erforschung des Westfränkischen', *RhVB* 31 (1966–7) 291–306.

on 5 August 882, so the *Ludwigslied* must have been composed between these dates. It was entered in the manuscript after his death, for the Latin title calls it a memorial (*Rithmus teutonicus de piae memoriae Hludouico rege filio Hludouici aeque regis*).

The poem is composed in the same metrical form as Otfrid's work, though there is a high proportion of assonances and impure rhymes. It is true, of course, that we cannot be sure how impure some of the rhymes were; for instance the rhyming of *ih* or *gelih* with *Hluduig* in ll. 1, 25, and 50 may indicate a fricative *g*, and the rhyme *urlub* : *uf* a fricative *b* (less probably an originally unshifted *up*). The confusion between -*z* and -*s* mentioned above is matched by the rhymes -*los* : *buoz*, l. 3, and probably indicates an approximation between the two sibilants in the poet's speech.

The poet for the most part operated with two-line strophes, as Otfrid did, though sometimes (ll. 33–5, 36–8, 39–41, 52–4, and 57–9) the syntax requires a three-line strophe.[1] There can be no absolute certainty about the structure of the poem, though the following seems a reasonable analysis. There are two sections of almost equal length. The first, consisting of ll. 1–30, refers to the events preceding the king's return. The last strophe of this section, ll. 29–30, connects it with the second section, which treats of the events subsequent upon the king's return. The first section, containing only two-line strophes, may be divided into three subsections. The first introduces the king and covers his early life in eight lines. The second deals with the visitation by the Northmen in ten lines. The third describes God's summons to Louis and his return to France in twelve lines. The second main section is more elaborate. The king's speech occupies a subsection of eleven lines, made up of one two-line and three three-line strophes. Then follows a subsection of thirteen lines, dealing with the preliminaries to the battle and the battle itself; this is made up of five two-line strophes and one of three lines. The conclusion consists of a two-line and a three-line strophe. We may thus represent the plan of the poem as follows:

Section A: $(4 \times 2) + (5 \times 2) + (6 \times 2)$ $= 30$
Section B: $(1 \times 2 + 3 \times 3) + (5 \times 2 + 1 \times 3) + (1 \times 2 + 1 \times 3)$ $= 29$

Other groupings are, however, also possible.

---

[1] Some editors place a full stop at the end of l. 58, though this makes the line difficult to construe. It is perhaps best taken, as in the translation given above, as a subordinate clause, and should be followed by a comma.

The remnant of the Danish army defeated at Saucourt withdrew to Ghent. Then, having repaired their ships and been reinforced by new arrivals from England, they entered the Meuse and wintered at Elsloo, below Maastricht. In 882 they harried the whole area from the mouth of the Scheldt to the Eifel; they even burned and plundered the imperial city of Aachen. An imperial army led by the egregious Charles the Fat marched against them and besieged them at Elsloo, but the Emperor (as Charles now was) chose to treat with the Danish leader Godefrid. He bought off further attacks on his own territory by ceding Frisia and his cousin Gisela, the illegitimate daughter of Lothar II, to the Dane, who, in return consented to be baptized and do homage to Charles.

The following winter the Danes were back in northern France. The victory at Saucourt had given the French a respite of just over a year. However, the great deliverer of Saucourt was now dead. He had died on 5 August 882 as the result of a frivolous adventure,[1] and his brother Carloman reverted to the disastrous policy of bribing the enemy to depart. For 12,000 pounds of silver the Northmen were prepared to quit France, but they returned after Carloman's death in 884.

---

[1] 'Sed quia iuvenis erat, quandam puellam, filiam cuiusdam Germundi, insecutus est; illa in domo paterno fugiens, rex equo sedens iocando eam insecutus scapulas superliminare et pectus sella equi attrivit eumque valide confregit. Unde egrotare coepit et delatus apud Sanctum Dionisium, Nonis Augusti defunctus maximum dolorem Francis reliquit, sepultusque est in aecclesia Sancti Dionisii' (*Annales Vedastini*, ed. cit., p. 52).

XIV

The Ottonian Renaissance

AFTER the death of Louis the German in 876, his kingdom was divided between his three sons, but two of them soon died, leaving the third son, the diseased and imbecile Charles the Fat, as the only residual heir to Louis the German's kingdom. In 884 Carloman of France died, leaving as heir only his five-year-old brother Charles (who succeeded to the French throne nineteen years later in 893). The French nobles decided to invite Charles the Fat to become king of France. Charles had already obtained the imperial dignity in 882; thus, for a short time, Charlemagne's empire, with the exception of the independent kingdom of Provence, was reunited under one of his descendants.

Charles the Fat embraced the disastrous old policy of trying to bribe the Danes to depart, but this naturally encouraged them to come in greater numbers. Disgusted by his incompetence, the German nobles set up Arnulf, the duke of Carinthia and illegitimate son of Louis the German, as king, and Charles was forced to abdicate in 887, only a few months before his death. Arnulf ruled Germany for the next twelve years. He had greater success against the Danes than his predecessors, defeating them decisively at Louvain in 891, after which their incursions were confined to the coastal area and the immediate hinterland. Arnulf had less success in his attempt to conquer Italy, though he did obtain the imperial crown in 896.

He was succeeded in 899 by his six-year-old son Louis, known as Louis the Child, who was king until 911. During Louis's necessarily feeble reign the Magyars, driven westwards by pressure of tribes in their rear, overran what is now Austria. As he left no heir, the Franks, Saxons, Swabians, and Bavarians united in electing a Frankish count named Conrad as their king. The reign of Conrad (911–18) was disturbed by personal feuds among the nobles. On his death he was succeeded by the powerful duke of

Saxony, Henry the Fowler (Henry I). The royal dignity thus passed from the Frankish to the Saxon dynasty, from Caroling to Ludolfing. Henry reigned from 918 to 936 and warred successfully against the Danes, the Magyars, and the Wends. He devoted much energy to establishing the royal power in Germany, which for centuries to come was to remain divided into separate nations, but he never sought to be made Emperor.

On Henry's death in 936 the royal power passed to his son Otto I, who ruled Germany until 973. Two years after his accession civil war broke out, Otto being opposed by his younger brother Henry, who had pretensions to the throne. The rebellion was put down, and Henry was reconciled with Otto at the Christmas feast of 941. In 947 Otto made Henry duke of Bavaria, a title which he held until his death in 955. Otto's policy was directed to extending the royal power and confining that of the duchies. To this end he sought to make use of the Church. He put members of his own family into the important ecclesiastical posts. He appointed his brother Bruno archbishop of Cologne and his son William archbishop of Mainz, making such ecclesiastics responsible for the temporal administration of their territories. Great reforms were achieved, but the policy was not wholly successful because it depended on the continuing support of the Pope who, being in Italy, was not entirely under the Emperor's control, and would sometimes support a bishop who did not acquiesce in the Emperor's plans. Italy was in a state of anarchy at this time, and both Otto's son Ludolf, duke of Swabia, and his brother Henry of Bavaria had territorial ambitions there. In order to thwart these ambitions, Otto invaded Italy in 951 and took the crown of Italy for himself. He was now a widower, and while in Italy he married Adelaide, the widow of Lothar, the former king. He was unsuccessful in his attempts to get himself crowned Emperor, and when he departed there was still contention in Italy. In 952 peace was made and, though Otto remained overlord in Italy, the crown went to Berengar, marquis of Ivrea, and Henry of Bavaria obtained the lands between the Adige and Istria, including Verona and Aquileia. Otto's intervention in Italy and the subsequent settlement caused disaffection among some of the German princes and led to another revolt in 953. In 962 he again entered Italy. This time he succeeded in obtaining the imperial crown and founded the Holy Roman Empire of the German Nation, which lasted until 1806. After some difficulties Otto at length acquired the control over the Papacy that he needed, but the connection with Italy was a source of weakness for Germany throughout much of the Middle Ages.

The south of Italy was the territory of the Eastern Empire. In 972 Otto established a dynastic claim to this territory by marrying his son Otto, who succeeded him a year later, to the Byzantine Princess Theophano, the daughter of the late Eastern Emperor Romanus II. With Theophano there came to Germany Greek scholars and knowledge of the Greek language. How extensive this knowledge was is not certain. It seems that Notker of St. Gall knew little Greek. However, the continual contacts with Italy during the tenth century and the revival of learning associated with such reformers as Bruno, the brother of Otto I, fostered an interest in scholarship which is exemplified in the work of Notker.

Otto II (973–83) continued his father's policy of maintaining close relations with the Papacy. He engaged in wars in Italy in order to expel the Saracens from the south. His attempts to weld the Empire into a unity were so successful that in 983 at a diet held in Verona, the main occasion for which was a projected war against the Saracens, Germans and Italians met together as a single body. At home, however, he had to contend with the rebellious national dukedoms. Henry I of Bavaria had died in 955, after which Bavaria was ruled by his widow Judith in the name of her son Henry II, later called the Quarrelsome ('der Zänker'). Judith's daughter was married to the aged duke Burkhard of Swabia. Seeing a threat to the royal power in a close association between Bavaria and Swabia, Otto secured the Swabian succession, on Burkhard's death in 976, to his own nephew Otto. This provoked a revolt among the Bavarians, who sought help from the Bohemians and Poles. The Emperor put down the revolt, deposed Henry the Quarrelsome, consigned Judith to a convent, and set up his nephew Otto as duke of Bavaria. Henry went into exile, whence he made several attempts to recover his position; none of them was successful while Otto II lived.

Otto II died in Italy in 983 at the age of twenty-eight, leaving as his successor the four-year-old Otto III (983–1002). His widow Theophano became regent. In the following year Henry the Quarrelsome came out of exile and claimed the regency; he even had pretensions to the crown itself. He had the support of several German bishops, the French king, and his old allies the dukes of

Poland and Bohemia. He managed to secure the person of the boy king himself, and appeared to be in a strong position. Against him, however, he had the mass of the Saxons and the powerful Archbishop Willegis of Mainz. Before long he lost ground and was forced to submit. At Easter 985 he was reconciled with Otto at Frankfurt and restored to his Bavarian duchy. From then on, until his death ten years later, he was a reformed character, showing exemplary loyalty to his young sovereign. Theophano died in 991 and a council of regency was set up; one of its members was Henry's son, later Henry IV of Bavaria and the prince who, as Henry II, succeeded Otto III on the German throne. In 996, having attained his legal majority, Otto visited Rome and was crowned Emperor by Pope Gregory V, his own cousin and protégé. Gregory collaborated closely with Otto, and so did the next Pope, Sylvester II. During the last years of his reign there was dissension in Italy and Germany, due to some extent to displeasure at Otto's support for papal authority. He died in Italy in 1002 at the age of twenty-two.

During the tenth century a number of works composed at an earlier date were committed to parchment, but there is little evidence that new works in the vernacular were composed. The small trickle of German literature—in the narrow sense of the word, meaning works *written* in German—which had continued beside the main stream of Latin literature, from the age of Charles the Great to the end of the ninth century, seems virtually to have dried up. Doubtless oral poetry flourished, but no one troubled to write it down. There began what is called the 'Ottonian Renaissance', when classical learning flourished. The longest, though in most respects negligible, work from this period employing the vernacular is a curious composition, commonly called **De Heinrico,** which is preserved in an eleventh-century manuscript in Cambridge University Library.[1] The manuscript includes forty-seven poems in Latin, many of which relate to events in German history down to the second quarter of the eleventh century. *De Heinrico* is the nineteenth in the collection. It consists of twenty-seven lines of rhyming verse, divided into strophes of four and three lines, the division being indicated by large initials at the beginning of each strophe. In all but two of the lines (ll. 1 and 22)

---

[1] Edited by K. Strecker, *Die Cambridger Lieder*, 2nd edn. (Berlin, 1955) (*MGH*); also *MSD* xviii; *Kl. ahd. Spdmr.* xxiii; *Ahd. Lb.* xxxix.

the first half is in Latin and the second in German; in the remaining two, as preserved in the manuscript, Latin and German alternate. In the following translation italics are used where the original is in Latin:

> *Now may the generous son* of the everlasting Virgin, *my kindly protector, assist me,* that I may tell of a certain duke, the lord Henry, *who with dignity* ruled the realm of the Bavarians.
>
> *A messenger entered*[1] and exhorted the Emperor thus: '*Why do you remain seated,*' he said, '*Otto* our good Emperor? *Henry is here.* He brings a kingly host, *worthy to be yours,*[2] to be your own.'
>
> *Then Otto arose,* our good Emperor. *He went to meet him* with a large number of men *and received him* with great honours.
>
> *He also spoke first:* 'Welcome, Henry, *you two of the same name,*[3] both to God and to me, *and your companion too.* I bid you welcome.'
>
> *After a reply had been given* by Henry so becomingly, *they joined hands.* He led him into the church. *They both prayed* for God's grace.
>
> *After they had prayed,* Otto welcomed him again. *He led him into the council chamber* with great honours *and conferred*[4] *upon him* whatever he had, *except the royal power,* which Henry did not desire.
>
> *Then was* the whole council *subject to the steadfast* Henry. *Whatever Otto did* was counselled by Henry, *and whatever he bestowed*[5] was counselled by Henry too.
>
> *Here*[6] *there was not one person* (I have good support *from nobles and freemen* that this is all true) *to whom Henry did not accord* every entitlement.

In this poem an Emperor called Otto appears together with one Heinrich, a former[7] duke of Bavaria. It was once held that the occasion celebrated in the poem was the reconciliation between Otto I and his rebellious brother Henry at Christmas 941. There were objections to this theory, for the historical facts differed from

---

[1] The word *nempe* is not translated here; it suggests a foregoing narrative.

[2] This translation takes *fore* to be a Latin infinitive (= *esse*). Others take it to be a German preposition (= *vor*); in this case the line, which would be incomplete, would mean: 'worthy of you . . . to be before you yourself'.

[3] On the meaning of *ambo vos equivoci* see p. 254.

[4] Some emend (unnecessarily) to *omisit,* but *amittere* is attested in the sense 'to give away, bestow, confer'.

[5] Here the context (contrast with *fecit*) more strongly suggests emendation to *omisit,* but *amisit* makes sense; see note 4 above.

[6] If the poem was composed in Bavaria, this statement would accord with Henry II's good repute as a just administrator of his duchy.

[7] The use of the past tense *beuuarode* in l. 4*b* must indicate that Heinrich is either dead or no longer ruling Bavaria at the time of composition. We cannot tell whether Otto is still alive or not.

what is stated in the poem. Henry did not come regally attended, but barefoot and by night, accompanied by a single ecclesiastic. He was not received with deference and fraternal affection, but at once placed in strict confinement. Otto was not crowned Emperor until 962, long after Henry's death in 955. He should not, therefore, have been called *unsar keisar guodo*. To avoid this difficulty, it was argued that the poem, though referring to a reconciliation between Otto I and his brother Henry, was written by a follower of the latter's son, Henry II of Bavaria ('the Quarrelsome') at a later date.

The chief prop for this theory, however, was removed when it was discovered[1] that the faded half-line 7*b* should properly read *bringit her hera kuniglich*, and not *bruother hera kuniglich*, as had formerly been thought. It was no longer necessary to look for a pair of brothers called Otto and Henry. A further difficulty in interpreting the poem is posed by the words *ambo vos equivoci* in l. 13*a*. The obvious sense of the words is 'both of you bearing the same name', though it would not be impossible to construe the phrase as meaning 'both of you belonging to the same lineage' or even 'both of you holding the same rank or title'. If Otto and Henry are meant, the phrase can only be a harsh parenthesis by the poet ('You are both of the same lineage'). Since Otto is ostensibly the speaker, it has been proposed to read *nos* for *vos* ('We are both of the same lineage'), but such emendations are a confession of failure. If the words are indeed Otto's, he is most probably addressing two men by the name of Henry.

The most attractive suggestion (we need not mention them all)[2] is that the poem was composed after the death of Henry II (which would account for the past tense of *beuuarode*) in celebration of his loyalty to Otto III after his reinstatement as duke of Bavaria in 985 and that ll. 7–8 are a reminiscence of Henry's military support for Otto III in his war against the Slavs (994–5). The problematical words *ambo vos equivoci*, uttered by Otto, would then most probably apply to Henry II and his son Henry IV of Bavaria, who in 1002 succeeded Otto III as Henry II, the last Saxon Emperor.[3]

The manuscript was in all probability written in England. This

---

[1] R. Priebsch, *Deutsche Handschriften in England* (Erlangen, 1896–1901) I pp. 25–7, and *AfdA* 20 (1894) 207.

[2] For a full account of the many interpretations, see Strecker, *Die Cambridger Lieder*, pp. 116–19, and the article by Dittrich cited in n. 3 below.

[3] See M.-L. Dittrich, 'De Heinrico', *ZfdA* 84 (1952–3) 274. On *ambo vos equivoci* see ibid., p. 282.

would account for the use of the letter *þ* for *th* (once) and perhaps also for the form *hafode* in l. 20.[1] The rhymes are mostly impure, and afford little help in establishing the original dialect. In view of the representation of Gmc. *þ* by *th*, Gmc. *ð* by *d* (e.g. *godes genatheno*), and Gmc. *b* by *v* (in *selvemo*) the dialect of the extant text appears to be West Middle German; western provenance is also suggested by the preposition *fane*. The pronominal form *tid* (l. 26) for *thid* or *thit* might belong to Middle Franconian, but in this dialect one would expect an unshifted *t* instead of *z* in *iz* and *allaz* too. If the original came from the Lower Rhine, one might be inclined to associate its composition with the fact that Henry II spent part of his exile in Utrecht. On the other hand, some have held[2] that the original was composed in the Saxon dialect. Some of the features of the consonantism already mentioned would accord with this view. The most obvious 'Saxonisms' are the pronominal forms *mi* (ll. 13 and 14) and *gi* (l. 14), but it has been thought[3] that these might have been inserted by the poet to characterize the Saxon speech of the Emperor.

Since Henry II was duke of Bavaria, one might expect the original poem to have been in the Bavarian dialect. If this is so, one can only observe that the original dialect has been very successfully concealed.

We shall never know the circumstances that inspired the composition of the poem or the precise events that it refers to. All we can say is that it was composed in a mixture of Latin and German sometime in the last sixty years of the tenth or the early years of the eleventh century, and that it commemorates the meeting and collaboration of one of the Ottos with one of the Henrys (who was perhaps accompanied by another Henry at the time of the meeting). The principal figure, Henry, is depicted as having the necessary attributes of a good ruler: he is a faithful subject of the Emperor, a humble Christian, a wise counsellor, and a just administrator. It is difficult to identify an individual behind the type. However, the poet's statement that his hero did not desire the royal power might be an oblique reference to Henry II's renunciation of his former pretensions.

---

[1] Dittrich, relying on the rhyme with *illi*, suggests that the original had the OHG pret. subj. form *habeti*. See op. cit., p. 290.

[2] H. Meyer and W. Seelmann, *NddJb* 12 (1898) 70 ff.

[3] G. Ehrismann, *PBB* 29 (1904) 125, cited with approval by Steinmeyer, *Kl. ahd. Sprdmr.*, p. 113.

The mixture of Latin and the vernacular is not unique. It is found in another poem in the Cambridge collection which will be referred to shortly.[1] In most of the lines the first half is Latin and the second German; in ll. 1 and 22 neither language is confined to one half (though the former may be emended and thus made to conform). It has been held that the poet thought in German and translated the first half of nearly every line into Latin. On the other hand it may be observed that many of the German halves (e.g. in ll. 5, 6, 8, 9, 11, 14, 19) are either padding or consist of formal phrases. This has suggested to one scholar[2] that the poet worked from a Latin prose original couched in the style of a chronicle, where one would not be surprised to find sentences beginning with such phrases as 'intrans nempe nuntius', 'dato responso', or 'oramine facto'.

The purpose of the poem is uncertain. It was formerly regarded as a political poem, the oldest in the German language. This designation is unobjectionable, since the poem does deal with political events, but it may well have been intended as a memorial, rather than as propaganda for a particular cause.

The twenty-eighth poem in the Cambridge collection is composed, like *De Heinrico*, in a mixture of Latin and German. Unfortunately it has largely been erased and only fragments can be read. What survives, however, reveals that the poem consisted o a dialogue between a man and a nun. It is usually called **Kleriker und Nonne**,[3] though some have held that the man is intended to be a layman, perhaps a knight. The man tries to persuade the nun to make love, invoking the grass which is turning green (*tempus adest . . . gruonot gras in . . .*). The nun is unwilling (*Quid uis ut faciam . . .*). The man renews his suit, telling her of the birds singing in the wood (*. . . miner minn . . . silue nu . . . uualde*). Again the nun demurs, declaring that she heeds (?) only the nightingale of Christ (*. . . philomela kristes . . . cui me deuoui*). Again the man tries to persuade her, but is rejected. He begs her to test his love and makes some extravagant promise of bliss (*nunna choro miner minno . . . dabo tibi super hoc uuerelt*). The nun rejects his advances once more, declaring herself for eternal joy alone. The remainder of the text is difficult to piece together, but it is clear that virtue

---

[1] The OE *Phoenix* closes with eleven lines in which OE and Latin alliterate, and there are other examples of bilingual poems.

[2] Dittrich, op. cit., pp. 292 ff.

[3] Ed. cit.

triumphs and it appears that the nun converts her lover to virtue. Why it should have been felt necessary to obliterate it is difficult to understand. The poem has been called the first German love-song, but such a designation is not entirely just, since the poem seems rather, like the last two strophes in Walther's *Alterston*, to involve a rejection of *amor carnalis* in favour of the eternal love of God, *amor verus*. It is clearly, in view of the use of Latin, not popular poetry, though the invocation of nature as a persuasion to enjoy may echo a popular note. The last poem in the collection, which is also in a bad state of preservation, may also treat an amorous theme, but it employs no German words.

Only one entirely German fragment of what is perhaps a love-song has survived from the Old High German period. This is pre-served among a number of Latin poems in a manuscript now in the Royal Library of Brussels. It is known as **Hirsch und Hinde**:

> Hirez runeta   hintun in daz ora
> 'uildu noh, hinta . . . ?'

('A hart murmured in the ear of a hind: "Wilt thou yet, hind...?"') Whether the fragment comes from a narrative poem or is part of a lyric meant to be sung we cannot tell. The latter possibility is suggested by the fact that neums are placed above some Latin verses in the same manuscript. The only complete line seems to employ not only rhyme but alliteration too; the latter may well be fortuitous, for a hart and a hind appearing in one line cannot fail to produce alliteration. Whether this fragment is evidence of popular poetry in the Old High German period is a question we must answer according to our inclination.[1]

The six plays and eight legends in Latin composed by the nun **Hrotsvitha** of Gandersheim, though a product of the Ottonian Renaissance, are also a reaction against it.[2] The convent of Gandersheim in Brunswick was a Benedictine foundation for women of noble birth. The Abbess Gerberga, a distinguished classical scholar, was a daughter of Henry, duke of Bavaria, and therefore a niece of the Emperor Otto I. Hrotsvitha lived from about 935 to 973. She refers to herself in the Prologue to her plays as 'Ego clamor validus

---

[1] *MSD* vi; *Kl. ahd. Spdmr.* lxxix.
[2] Ed. by P. von Winterfeld, *Hrotsvithae opera* (Scriptores rerum germani-carum in usum scholarum 17), 1902; K. Strecker, *Hrotsvitae Opera Omnia*, 2nd edn., 1930. See also Bert Nagel, *Hrotsvit von Gandersheim* (Sammlung Metzler) (Stuttgart, 1965).

Gandersheimensis'. They were printed by Conrad Celtes in 1501. The repeated suggestion that they were part of an immense Humanist forgery is not usually taken seriously.[1] In recent years Hrotsvitha's plays have received much attention, especially from those who are interested in the origin of the drama.[2]

Of the six plays, *Gallicanus*, *Dulcitia*, and *Sapientia* deal with the conflict between paganism and Christianity in Rome, *Callimachus*, *Paphnutius*, and *Abraham* deal with unlawful love. Hrotsvitha's purpose was, as she states in her Prologue, to divert the attention of Catholics from the licentious women and worldly intrigue of Terence's plays to the laudable chastity of Christian virgins and the fortitude of Christian martyrs. Like Otloh, to whom reference will be made in Chapter XVI, she regarded classical authors as a snare.

Her plays have only a slight and superficial resemblance to those of Terence. They are written in brisk and vivid dialogue with rapid slap-dash action. There is much humour ranging from clowning to erudite logic and arithmetical puzzles.

---

[1] See E. H. Zeydel, *MLN* 61 (1946) 50–5.

[2] See id., 'Knowledge of Hrotsvitha's Works prior to 1200', *MLN* 59 (1944) 282–5; 61 (1946) 281–3; G. R. Coffman, 'A new Approach to Mediaeval Latin Drama', *Modern Philology* 22 (1924–5), esp. pp. 261–4; A. Wright and T. A. Sinclair, *Later Latin Literature*, pp. 183–90; Raby, *Secular Latin Poetry* i. 277–8; id., *Christian Latin Poetry*, p. 208; H. E. Wedeck, *Humour in Varro and other Essays* (Oxford, 1929), pp. 75–9; M. Rigobon, *Il teatro e la latinità di Hrotsvitha* (Padua, 1932); Hugo Kuhn, 'Hrotsviths von Gandersheim dichterisches Programm, *Dichtung und Welt im Mittelalter* (Stuttgart, 1959), pp. 91–104.

XV

Waltharius and *Ruodlieb*

IT is usual in histories of German literature to distinguish between the 'heroic epic' and the 'court epic' or 'courtly romance'. The former drew its material from native tradition, whereas the latter was of French provenance and treated stories of French, Celtic, or classical origin. The two works considered in this chapter, though composed in Latin, have affinities with these genres—the *Waltharius* with the heroic epic, and the *Ruodlieb* with the courtly romance, though perhaps also with the heroic epic.

The native lays of the period of the Great Migrations are no longer extant; nor are the lays and epics of the ninth, tenth, and eleventh centuries which are postulated as the sources and fore-runners of the Middle High German heroic epics and of certain texts in other Germanic languages, and much learning and in-genuity has been devoted to attempts to reconstruct them. Apart from the *Hildebrandslied*, heroic poetry does not appear in German until the twelfth century. There are a number of Carolingian and later poems dealing with persons and events in German history, but these are not usually included in the history of German litera-ture, because their language is Latin, and because there are no related works in German. An exception is made in favour of the **Waltharius,** a Latin epic in 1456 hexameters, because the story it tells was part of Germanic heroic tradition and was transmitted to England, Scandinavia, and Poland.[1]

The *Waltharius* is the life-story of Walther and Hildegunde. The central matter is the pair's journey home from the land of the Huns, and the chief event within this is the encounter of Walther with Gunther and Hagen and their eleven followers, who attempt to detain and rob him. The argument is as follows:

Attila, king of the Huns, marches with an invincible host against three kingdoms—Francia, ruled by Gibicho, Burgundia,

[1] For details of editions see p. 280.

ruled by Herericus, and Aquitania, ruled by Alphere. All three kings think it wise to submit; they agree to pay tribute to Attila and to send hostages. Gibicho's son Guntharius is too young to be parted from his mother, and so Hagano of the noble race of Troia is sent in his stead; Herericus sends his daughter Hiltgunt; and Alphere delivers up his son Waltharius, who has already been betrothed to Hiltgunt.

Waltharius becomes the foremost warrior in Attila's host, and Hiltgunt the controller of the treasure of his queen, Ospirin. When Guntharius succeeds Gibicho as king of the Franks, he denounces the treaty made by his father, and Hagano, hearing of this, flees by night. Lest Waltharius should also be lost to them, Attila is persuaded by Ospirin to propose to Waltharius an advantageous marriage with a Hunnish noblewoman and to give him a permanent high position. Waltharius, being in love with Hiltgunt and planning to elope with her, evades the offer, pointing out that, if he married, he might become less willing to risk his life in battle.

One day, having returned from a successful military enterprise, he makes sure of Hiltgunt's willingness to elope, and then gives a banquet at which all the Huns become incapable with drink. Hiltgunt meanwhile has collected as much of the queen's treasure as can conveniently be carried, together with provisions for the journey and fishing tackle. All this, and Hiltgunt, are loaded on to Waltharius's horse, and they set out on their flight to his home. When their flight is discovered, none of the Huns dare pursue them.

They travel unmolested for forty days until they enter the territory of Guntharius. As a fee for being transported across the Rhine, Waltharius gives the ferryman some fish. The ferryman passes them on to the king's cook. Guntharius finds them to be of a kind not known locally and inquiries are made. When the ferryman explains that he obtained them from a lone warrior whose horse bore a maiden and a load which jingled like gold coin, Hagano guesses at once that the warrior is his comrade Waltharius. Guntharius's cupidity is aroused. Against the advice of Hagano he sets off in pursuit, accompanied by Hagano (who resolves not to fight) and eleven others, in order to secure the gold which he claims as the treasure extorted from his father by Attila.

Waltharius is overtaken in a defile in the Vosges, where he can be attacked by only one man at a time. He offers to pay a fee in gold arm-rings for leave to pass through Frankish territory. His offer is refused and the attack begins. Ten of the attackers are killed, including Hagano's kinsman Patavrid. Hagano sits all the while on his shield, refusing to fight against his friend. At last, however, in order to save the Franks from the disgrace of being defeated by one man, and mindful of his own reputation, he consents to help his king.

On his advice Waltharius is allowed to believe that they have abandoned the attack. In the morning Waltharius leaves the defile to continue his journey. He is surprised from the rear by Guntharius and Hagano simultaneously. Hagano justifies himself to Waltharius by the pretext that the latter has killed one of his kinsmen. Guntharius is a feeble fighter. His spear merely scratches his opponent's shield. While he is trying to recover the weapon by stealth, Waltharius cuts off his leg, and is about to kill him when Hagano interposes his own helmet. Waltharius's sword breaks on it. He flings away the fragment, carelessly stretching out his right hand. Hagano seizes the opportunity to strike it off. Waltharius fits the shield on the stump of his right arm, draws his short Hunnish dagger with his left hand, and therewith slices off half of Hagano's face, depriving him of one eye and six teeth. They call off the fight. Hiltgunt bandages their wounds and brings them wine. The two comrades jest about each other's disabilities. Guntharius is then loaded on to a horse and led home to Worms by Hagano. Waltharius and Hiltgunt continue their journey. On reaching home they marry, and Waltharius reigns, after succeeding his father, for thirty years.

The *Waltharius* is, in the main, the story of an exile's return. Exile was a potent heroic theme which is treated in many works— the *Hildebrandslied*, *Herzog Ernst*, *König Rother*, the Dietrich epics, and *Wolfdietrich*. The hero is the solitary, self-sufficient individual who is dependent on his manly virtues and his wits for survival. He is the bold man, who by valour and guile carries off his bride from the enemy's stronghold. Hagano has to face the tragic problem of divided loyalties: he feels obliged to fight his sworn blood-brother in order to maintain his honour as a warrior and the honour, not of his king, as has sometimes carelessly been assumed, but of his people, the Franks. He is in this respect comparable with Hildebrand, Rüdiger, and Dietrich. The ending is burlesque. The author does not take his characters quite seriously. They are to him shadowy figures from the remote past, and while he can tell his story with verve, he cannot enter into the heroic spirit with full commitment. He prefers to use his story to point useful morals. Guntharius represents the disastrous result of avarice, Attila the folly of drunkenness. Before his nephew Patavrid is slain, Hagano deplores the baleful effect of cupidity which lures men to their death. Guntharius is thrice given the derogatory epithet *demens*. Waltharius, though a ruthless fighter, is chaste (ll. 426 f.), and, after uttering presumptuous words, he immediately begs God's forgiveness (ll. 559–65). After the first day of battle he gives thanks to God for his deliverance and prays for the salvation of those he has slain (ll. 1161–7). Hiltgunt has the domestic virtues of the Christian maiden, of the 'sexus fragilis' (l. 1209). Too much should not be made of the words 'timidam puellam' (l. 1407) as evidence of Christian influence, for they are a standing phrase of classical Latin, but this Hiltgunt is a contrast to her counterpart Hildegyth in the OE *Waldere*, who encourages her man before battle: Hiltgunt is frightened by the nocturnal rustlings in the trees (ll. 351–3), and advises her hero to flee before Guntharius and Hagano (l. 1213).

The poem begins pompously with the statement, addressed to the poet's 'fratres', that the third part of the globe is called Europe; it is inhabited by races differing in customs, languages, names, dress, and religion, among whom dwell the people of Pannonia, whom we are accustomed to call the Huns. We can visualize the teacher, beginning with the general ('orbis') and progressing steadily to the particular ('Europa'—'gentes'—'gens Pannoniae'). He knows the correct honorifics: the Huns are mighty both in their virtue and their valour; they dominate not merely the neighbouring peoples—like Otfrid's Franks—but have even crossed the ocean; they overthrew all who resisted, but granted treaties of peace to all who submitted. Their rule lasted a thousand years. Thus, in ten lines the Hunnish nation is paraded for our inspection: we see its situation in Europe, its qualities, its actions; it shall endure for ever.

From this introduction the poet passes on to his story. Each episode is varied to avoid monotony, as pupils are instructed should be done. The shifts of scene, for example from the banquet to the lovers' journey through the forest, then back to court for the 'morning after', are neatly contrived; and pleasing variety is introduced into the series of single combats and the inevitable *Reizreden* which precede them. All the details of the action have full logical motivation; the disposition is flawless, and one might say of the poet, as he says of the ferryman (l. 448), 'causam ex ordine pandit'. The plan must have been clear in his mind down to minor details. In his literary style the poet's originality is slight: both the wording and the imagery arise from the conventional erudition of the school. The description of the battle in which Waltharius wins a great victory over Attila's enemies (ll. 173–214) is Virgilian in language and conventional in detail, an exercise in forty-two lines. To celebrate his victory, Waltharius crowns himself with a laurel wreath. The poet was undoubtedly well read in the Latin poetry of the classical and later Christian writers, as the many literary echoes perceived by critics clearly indicate.

Because the *Waltharius* is the oldest surviving account of the doings of Walther, it is just conceivable that the story was made up by the poet by adapting various episodes in Virgil, Ovid (the rescue of Andromeda by Perseus), Statius' *Thebaid* (the fight in the defile between Tydeus and fifty pursuers), Prudentius, and other poets. This view has found little favour.[1] It is generally held that the poet knew a German lay of Walther, though the form in which this lay told the story is a matter for conjecture.[2] Other works on the same theme are the OE *Waldere* (of which two fragments, amounting to sixty-three lines, survive on two parchment leaves in Copenhagen, but which was probably a poem of at least 1,000 lines), and a thirteenth-century German epic of which likewise only fragments survive. The Norse *þiðrekssaga* tells a rather different story of Walther's flight.[3] There Hǫgni (Hagen) pursues the lovers on

---

[1] It was advanced by F. Panzer, *Der Kampf am Wasichenstein. Walthariusstudien* (Speyer, 1948), and largely accepted by O. Schumann, 'Statius und Waltharius' in *Studien zur deutschen Philologie des Mittelalters, Festschrift für Friedrich Panzer*, ed. by R. Kienast (Heidelberg, 1950), pp. 12 ff. It was refuted by K. Stackmann in 'Antike Elemente im Waltharius. Zu Friedrich Panzers neuer These', *Euph.* 45 (1950) 231 ff.

[2] See H. Schneider, *GHS* I. I. 331–44, id., 'Das Epos von Walther und Hildegund', *GRM* 13 (1925) 14–32, 119–30; Betz in *DPA*, cols. 1536–9; G. Zink in *Kz. Grundriß*, pp. 42–4, id., 'Walther et Hildegund. Remarques sur la vie d'une légende', *Études germaniques*, I (1956) 193–201. See also the work by H. Geurts cited on p. 280, esp. pp. 54 ff.

[3] See F. Norman (ed.) *Waldere* (Methuen's Old English Library, London, 1933, 1949). For *þiðrekssaga* see p. 64, n. 2 above.

behalf of Atli (Attila); there is no defile, and Hǫgni flees after his eleven companions have been killed. He returns to surprise the pair as they are eating by their camp-fire. Valtari throws the ham-bone of the boar they are eating at Hǫgni with such force that it fells him, tears his cheek, and shatters his right eye. Hǫgni escapes back to Atli, and the lovers ride southwards over the hills to Erminrikr, Valtari's uncle.

There is also a Polish version of the story from the twelfth century.[1] In this version Walterus Robustus is a Polish count who falls in love with a French princess, Helgunda, while serving abroad. In order to gain her affection he sings outside her window on three successive nights. A German prince who is his rival leaves for Germany and orders all the ferries over the Rhine to be closed. Walterus and Helgunda flee to the east and cross the Rhine on horseback. Walterus is then attacked by the German, but defeats him and returns safely home. Some time later Helgunda takes a lover in her husband's absence. When he returns, he is imprisoned, but, with the help of the lover's sister, he is freed, kills the adulterous pair, and marries the sister.

There are a number of references to Walther in Middle High German works, namely the *Nibelungenlied, Biterolf und Dietleib, Alpharts Tod, Rosengarten, Dietrichs Flucht,* and the *Rabenschlacht.* The most celebrated reference, however, is in one of the songs of Walther von der Vogelweide (74, 19), in which the poet playfully breaks the convention of secrecy and reveals that his lady's name is Hiltegunde.

Though the *Waltharius,* the *þiðrekssaga,* and the first part of the Polish version all tell substantially the same story—the flight of two lovers to the hero's homeland and the defeat of those who would detain them—there are puzzling differences between the German and the Norse versions with regard to the role of Hagen: in the one he is the servant of Gunther, while in the other he acts on behalf of Attila. If we regard the Norse version as having preserved something old here, we may be inclined to link the legend, as some scholars have done, with the story of Hild, which is preserved in Norse and in the first eight adventures of the Middle High German *Kudrun.* In this story, Hild elopes with the envoy of her lover (Heðinn in Norse, Hetel in Middle High German), and is

[1] It is contained in the Latin chronicle of Bishop Boguphalus II of Poznán, *Monumenta Poloniae Historica* II, ed. A. Bielowski (Lwów, 1872) 510–14).

pursued by her father (Hǫgni in Norse, Hagene in Middle High German). Another link is provided by the Polish story: there Helgunda is wooed by her lover's sweet singing; in the *Kudrun*, Hild is wooed by the sweet singing of her suitor's messenger Horant (who seems to have had a counterpart in Old English legend). The chief reason, of course, for linking the two legends, which are separate in the extant versions, lies in the shared name Hagen and the shared name-element Hild. If we are disinclined to believe in an original connection, we may explain the triple serenading in the Polish version as due to a late contamination. As for the name Hild, we should remember that it was a common element in compound names for women, for example Brünhilt, Kriemhilt, and others.

Another problem is posed by the ending of the story. The three versions recounted above all end with the final triumph of the lovers over their adversaries. Burlesque though the ending of the *Waltharius* is, it seems unlikely that the poet substituted a happy ending for a tragic one. Unfortunately we cannot tell how the OE *Waldere* (written down about the year 1000 and therefore nearest in date to the *Waltharius*) ended, but nothing in the extant fragments points to impending tragedy.

It was once fashionable to mythologize heroic legend, that is to interpret its figures as representations of natural phenomena. In 1820 F. J. Mone expressed the opinion that Walther was a sun-hero, his horse a sun-horse, and his twelve fights symbolic of the path of the sun through the signs of the zodiac. Hagen the thorny (*Hagano spinosus*, l. 1421) was the thorn of sleep and death, the mistletoe which killed Baldr. In fact, Mone thought that the names Walther and Baldr were identical. The Walther story was just another version of the Nibelung story, where Sigfrid represented the sun. During the course of the nineteenth century there were further attempts to interpret the story as deriving from a myth. Another kind of interpretation sees Walther's flight from the Huns to the west and the consequent battles with various opponents as a historical myth, symbolizing the foundation of the Visigothic kingdom in the west.

We may dismiss such remote considerations and confine ourselves to speculations which go only a short distance beyond the tangible evidence. It seems most likely that in the seventh century a lay was composed in Bavaria, where Attila was viewed as a kindly ruler, telling the story of the elopement, tribulations, and safe home-coming of Walther and Hildegunde. The poet was acquainted with the pair Gunther–Hagen and probably with Dietrich (who appears as Ðeodric in the *Waldere*, but is for some reason not mentioned in the *Waltharius*). He knew of Weland the smith, who is credited in the *Waldere* and the *Waltharius* (*Wielandia fabrica* l. 965) with the fashioning of Walther's armour. He must have known the story of the Fall of the Burgundians, though whether the reference to the burning of Attila's hall when all his men are drunk (ll. 322 f.) presupposes a knowledge of the most ancient version is dubious. The lay combined the familiar motif of the exile's return with that of the fight between near friends or relations, as the *Hildebrandslied* does. The Walther lay became known in England, perhaps as early as the seventh century (the dating of the *Waldere* is difficult). Since the English version gives no indication that Guðhere (Gunther) is a weakling, it is probable that this feature was introduced in Germany under the influence of the Siegfried story. In Germany the story remained popular throughout the Middle Ages with substantially the same outlines as in our Latin version.

Long extracts from the *Waltharius* have been embodied in the *Chronicon Novaliciense*, a history of the monastery of Novalese written in 1027. A sequel has been added. Walther becomes a monk late in life to atone for his sins. He cultivates the monastery garden, while his old horse works in the mill. One day, when the servants of the monastery have been robbed, his martial spirit revives. With the abbot's blessing he takes his horse, the only one which can bear his weight, and sets out to recover the stolen goods. Having with due humility permitted himself to be smitten by the robbers and stripped of all but his drawers, he fights and confounds the knaves. This kind of monkish coda to a heroic story is not unusual: it is found in the extant version of *König Rother* and in version D of *Wolfdietrich*.[1]

The German heroic epic is usually anonymous, and this is true of the *Waltharius* too. There have, however, been attempts to ascertain the identity of the author. According to the *Casus Sancti Galli*, IX. 30, written by Ekkehardus IV of St. Gall (who lived from about 980 to 1057) a life of 'Waltharius de manu forte' was composed in verse as a school exercise by Ekkehardus I, who was born between 901 and 910 and died in 973:[2]

---

[1] The chronicle is to be found in *MGH Script.* II, chs. VII–XIII.

[2] 'And at school he wrote for his master a verse life of Walther of the Strong

Scripsit et in scolis metrice magistro, vacillanter quidem, quia in affectione, non in habitu erat puer, vitam Waltharii manu fortis, quam Magontiae positi, Aribone archiepiscopo jubente, pro posse et nosse nostro correximus; barbaries enim et idiomata ejus Teutonem adhuc affectantem repente Latinum fieri non patiuntur. Unde male docere solent discipulos semimagistri dicentes: Videte quomodo disertissime coram Teutone aliquo proloqui deceat, et eadem serie in Latinum verba vertite. Quae deceptio Ekkehardum in opere illo adhuc puerum fefellit, sed postea non sic.

If this school exercise is to be identified with the *Waltharius*, we must place the original composition in the second quarter of the tenth century and its correction during the archiepiscopate of Aribo (1021–31). Those who are inclined to favour this identification find support for it in the author's closing recommendation (ll. 1453–5):[1]

> Haec quicumque legis, stridenti ignosce cicadae
> Raucellam nec adhuc vocem perpende, sed aevum,
> Utpote quae nidis nondum petit alta relictis.

Those who are not so inclined would regard this as a conventional formula such as is frequently used by medieval poets as an expression of modesty.

The matter is complicated, however, by the fact that in three manuscripts the poem is preceded by twenty-two lines of verse in which one Geraldus presents a poem about Waltharius to a certain illustrious Erchamboldus. One manuscript, of the twelfth century, carries also the heading 'Incipit poesis Geraldi de Gualtario', though the writer does not claim to have composed the poem, but only to have resolved to provide it at great pains.[2] Some

---

Hand, haltingly however, since as a boy he was a learner, not an adept. This we corrected to the best of our ability when we were in Mainz, at the behest of Archbishop Aribo, for a German who has hitherto been a learner is prevented by his foreign origin and ways of speech from becoming a Latin speaker overnight. Hence, incompetent masters have a habit of saying to their pupils: "See how one ought to express oneself clearly to a German, and then translate the words into Latin in the same order." This wrong advice led Ekkehardus astray in the work in question when he was a boy, but not subsequently.'

[1] 'Whoever you are who read these lines, pardon the shrill cricket and pay no attention to its voice, which is still raucous, but to its age, for it has not yet left the nest and sought the sky.'

[2]　　　　Praesul sancte dei, nunc accipe munera servi,
　　　　Quae tibi decrevit de larga promere cura
　　　　Peccator fragilis Geraldus nomine vilis.

scholars have maintained that the Latin of this prologue cannot have issued from the same pen as the one that wrote the *Waltharius*; others, however, have maintained that the linguistic differences are due solely to the difference in genre. Such questions must be left to the Latinists, for the last word on the latinity of both poem and prologue has not yet been said.

Geraldus was a common name. If the writer of the prologue was passing off as his own a poem written by the young Ekkehardus, he was possibly the Geraldus who was master of the monastery school of St. Gall and died between 970 and 975. In this case, the Erchamboldus of the prologue was probably Bishop Erchambald of Strasbourg (965–93). The known work of this Geraldus is entirely ecclesiastical. If, on the other hand, the *Waltharius* was written not by Ekkehardus, but, as some maintain, by the man who names himself in the prologue, we are not bound to identify the author with Geraldus of St. Gall. The recipient for whom it was intended might have been Bishop Erchambald of Eichstätt (882–912). Though this Erchambald was a patron of the arts, it has been objected that the geography of the poem, such as it is, suggests familiarity with the west bank of the Rhine rather than with more easterly regions. Yet Erchambald need not have been a bishop: the words *summum pontificem* with which he is designated may have been applied as a compliment to a highly placed prelate of another degree. An Erchambald was chancellor to Lothar II (855–69), and that would bring the poem into the Aachen–Metz area.

The poem itself contains no definite reference to any contemporary historical personage or event, but it has been scrutinized for evidence of its date and place of composition. One piece of supposed evidence is Guntharius's description of his nation as *caput orbis* in l. 1083. It has been pointed out that this title, usually reserved for Rome, could hardly have been applied to the Frankish kingdom after the imperial dignity had passed from the Carolingian to the Saxon dynasty on the death of Conrad I in 918.[1] It should be remembered, however, that this is not the poet's description.

In making the historically and traditionally Burgundian Guntharius into a Frank, the poet was accepting the fact that Worms was in Frankish territory, as it had been since 443, when Aetius removed the remnant of the Burgundians to Savoy after their defeat by the Huns in 437. As he had to find a territory and a capital

---

[1] See Schumann, *ZfdA* 83 (1951) 35.

for Herericus, he may well have seized upon the familiar and now unattached name 'Burgundia'. He may have had no clear conception of Burgundy or of the geographical position of Herericus's capital, Chalon-sur-Saône (*Cabillonis*, l. 52). Nevertheless, the name of the city must have had associations for him, as he was under no obligation to mention it, rather than Vienne or Lyon.

By the Treaty of Verdun in 843, Chalon was included in Charles the Bald's kingdom. On the death of Lothar I in 855 it was an important city in the part of French Burgundy that passed to his youngest son Charles, whose title was king of Provence (not of Burgundy). On the death of Louis II (Louis the Stammerer), the territory of his three sons was invaded by Louis of Saxony, whose daughter Irmengard was married to Count Boso of Provence. Boso took the opportunity provided by the invasion to seize southern Burgundy in his wife's name, and succeeded in making himself king of Arles and Provence. In 887, Count Rudolf, who was the nephew of Judith, the mother of Charles the Bald, established the kingdom of Upper Burgundy. Chalon was not included in either of these states. It is therefore arguable that the poem must have been composed at a time before 'Burgundia' had acquired its new meaning, and when Chalon was known as one of the principal cities of the region, that is to say not later than 887.

Aquitaine, where Alphere and later Waltharius reigned, was a kingdom from 781 to 882.

These references appear to imply a date of composition not later than 918 (if the argument from the expression *caput orbis* carries conviction), and possibly between 843 and 882. The references to the expressed preference of the Huns for victory by negotiation rather than by force of arms are not strong evidence. It is true that their ravages in the tenth century would have made the words sound strange at that time. Nevertheless, there was a tradition that Attila was a merciful ruler. Furthermore, the embassy which was sent to submit begged Attila to cease from ravaging; his conventional reply that he preferred peace is to be expected of a successful invader, and the poet may have intended mild irony. It could be argued that the three surrenders and the payment of heavy tribute are consistent with the weak attempts of Charles the Fat to bribe the Vikings to depart. Such speculation is unprofitable. The poem reveals no clear perception of the Huns or of Pannonia.

It will be seen that, if one discounts as irrelevant the information that Ekkehardus I composed a poem about Waltharius, it appears more plausible to assign the epic to the ninth century than to the tenth, and to accredit it to an unknown Geraldus of the Carolingian period. As has already been stated, the problem of the date and authorship is one for the latinists.

Although attempts have been made to prove that the author was a French-speaking native of Lorraine, there is no reason to doubt that he was a German. He treats the *h* in the Latinized names of his characters as a German would, and he puns on the name *Hagano*: in l. 1421 he calls its bearer *Hagano spinosus* ('prickly Hawthorn'), and in l. 1351 he makes Waltharius address him with the words: *O paliure, vires foliis, ut pungere possis* ('O thorn-bush, you are verdant with leaves so that you may prick'). On the other hand, the opinion that his Latin shows the influence of German usage has been challenged.

As has already been stated, there is no reason to doubt the accepted opinion that the author of the epic knew one or more vernacular lays about Walther; but it is likely that much of the detail (for instance of the series of single combats) was his own contribution. Into the native story he infused the Christian ethic with a didactic purpose which is not unduly obtruded, and he adapted the subject matter to the literary style that he had imbibed from his scholarly reading. The old view that the poem was a school exercise may be an exaggeration, but there is no sign of strong personal emotion. The outstanding qualities of the poem are the facility, liveliness, and speed of the narrative, and the clarity of the argument. It was produced at a time when, according to common opinion, there were as yet no vernacular epics. If it had been written in German it would have been a superb example of an early 'heroic epic'.

The **Ruodlieb** is a Latin poem in leonine hexameters composed, probably at Tegernsee, about the middle of the eleventh century.[1]

---

[1] It was first edited in full by F. Seiler, *Ruodlieb, der älteste Roman des Mittelalters*, nebst Epigrammen mit Einleitung, Anmerkungen und Glossar (Halle, 1882). This edition is still valuable, though Seiler's ordering of the fragments was corrected by L. Laistner, *AfdA* 9 (1883) 70–106 and *ZfdA* 29 (1885) 1–25. More recent editions are: Edwin H. Zeydel, *Ruodlieb. The Earliest Courtly Novel (after 1050)*. Introduction, text, translation, commentary and textual notes (Chapel Hill, 1959); Gordon B. Ford, Jr., *The Ruodlieb. Linguistic introduction, Latin text, and glossary* (Leiden, 1966). Ford has also provided a facsimile edition.

If the account of the meeting between the two kings in the work is based, as has often been thought, on the meeting between the Emperor Henry II and King Robert of France in 1023, then we have a *terminus ante quem non*, but there are discrepancies as well as resemblances between the historical facts and the poem.

The *Ruodlieb* is a unique and valuable document of life in Germany before the impact of French culture, and despite its being written in a learned language it has a freshness lacking in most of the later vernacular works with which it is inconclusively compared. It also provides evidence of an attitude to chivalry which was ready to receive the 'courtly' ethos of the following century. The text has been only partially preserved in eighteen fragments on thirty-six leaves of an eleventh-century manuscript, written in Tegernsee and now in Munich (Clm. 19486), and on two leaves of a manuscript from St. Florian, near Linz. This latter contains only 140 lines, twenty-three of which coincide with the Tegernsee text, from which it was probably copied. The Tegernsee text may be the author's autograph. Both manuscripts were cut up and used for binding; consequently much of the text is mutilated. In addition, there are major and minor lacunae between the fragments; the order of the fragments is uncertain too, but the arrangement proposed by Laistner[1] is now accepted. In spite of the gaps, the drift of the story is fairly clear.

A certain nobleman (whom we later know as Ruodlieb) is forced into exile and takes service with a magnanimous king in Africa. He rises to a high position at the king's court, acting as army leader and diplomatist in a conflict with a lesser king. After ten years he receives word from his former masters and his mother that he may now safely return. The king sends him on his way with twelve precepts for right living and with much treasure concealed in what appear to be two loaves of bread. On his way home he has several adventures which prove the

The Ruodlieb: Facsimile Edition (Louisville, 1965). The work has been translated into German by M. Heyne, *Rudlieb, Übertragung des ältesten deutschen Heldenromans* (Leipzig, 1897), P. von Winterfeld, *Rudlieb*, in *Deutsche Dichter des lateinischen Mittelalters in deutschen Versen* (Munich, 1913, 1922³, and K. Langosch in *Waltharius, Ruodlieb, Märchenepen* (Basle/Stuttgart, 1956), pp. 86 ff. There are two English translations, one by Zeydel in his edition (see above), and one by Ford, *The Ruodlieb: the First Medieval Epic of Chivalry from Eleventh-century Germany, translated from the Latin with an Introduction* (Leiden, 1965). The former is very literal, the latter more elegant.
[1] opp. citt.

soundness of the king's precepts. He also meets his nephew, an exile like himself, whom he frees from the clutches of an evil woman. They visit a chatelaine, whose daughter turns out to be the godchild of Ruodlieb's mother. The nephew and the young lady fall in love, and Ruodlieb arranges a marriage. On his return he discovers the treasure in the African loaves and on his mother's advice, resolves to seek a wife. He is counselled by his kinsmen to seek the hand of a lady whom he does not know, and who proves to be a wanton. By a messenger he sends her, ostensibly as a present to be delivered after she has accepted his courtship, a parcel containing a hat and an intimate garment which she had discarded while entertaining a cleric. Ruodlieb's mother has two dreams which seem to presage for him tribulation and ultimate marriage. He has an encounter with a dwarf, whom he binds and who foretells his destiny: he will destroy two hostile kings, Immunch and his son Hartunch, and then he will marry Heriburg, the heiress to their kingdom.

The last fragment breaks off before the end of the page, and this has led some scholars to conclude that the poet did not complete his work.

The first part of the poem is the familiar story of an exile, with the difference that the hero is a young man who, though his family has property and position, has his way to make. The last part of the extant text seems to indicate that the hero is to win great glory and a bride after much bloodshed. This is clearly the theme of a heroic epic of the early 'spielmännisch' type, such as *König Rother*. The existence of a heroic tradition of this kind seems to be proved by the reference to Ruotlieb, the father of Herbort and the possessor of a valuable sword, in the much later *Eckenliet*.[1] It has recently, however, been argued that the mother's dreams and the poet's notions about dwarfs may derive from other, non-Germanic sources.[2]

The narrative is composed of a series of episodes, which are indeed told for the sake of the story, but equally for the sake of the moral they exemplify. The poem has thus two aspects, the didactic and the entertaining. Both elements were of equal importance to the author and have been fused with considerable skill. Although the didacticism is always present, it is never obtruded in a tiresome

---

[1] Ed. J. Zupitza, in *Deutsches Heldenbuch* v.
[2] W. Braun, *Studien zum Ruodlieb. Ritterideal, Erzählstruktur und Darstellungsstil* (Berlin, 1962), pp. 69–77.

manner. It accounts for the concentration of attention on the hero's experiences, and the absence of interest in his emotions. It no doubt also accounts for the anonymity of all the characters except the hero: they are representative types. The author was concerned to depict by means of typical incidents a number of typical characters, some wise, some foolish or even wicked, profiting for the most part by their errors, and to demonstrate thereby the efficacy of certain familiar moral principles. Part of this purpose was served by the illustration of the king's first three precepts: do not trust a red-head; do not go through sown fields to avoid a muddy road; do not take lodging with an old man who has a young wife. On his journey Ruodlieb meets a red-headed man who robs him of his coat. This man tramples a peasant's sown field and is belaboured by him; he then seduces the wanton young wife of an old man, kills the husband in a brawl, and is brought to justice. Ruodlieb meanwhile is well housed with a young man whose wife is old. Other precepts of the king are less directly illustrated. The sixth precept, warnings against familiarity with one's maid, is echoed in the episode with the wanton wife: before becoming mistress of the house she had been a servant. The seventh precept, which states that one should choose as a wife only a woman who is known (*cognoscibilis*),[1] and only on the advice of one's mother, bears upon Ruodlieb's own unsuccessful wooing: he sues for the hand of a lady who is not known to him and, apparently, without the advice of his mother.

An adequate account of the didactic elements of which the poem is full would require a commentary longer than the poem itself. Only a brief explanation can be attempted here. Sometimes the lesson is implicit, and obscure to the modern reader, although readily intelligible to contemporaries who were familiar with the traditional moral philosophy. Thus, to give only two examples, when Ruodlieb crosses the frontier into the territory of the greater king, he is joined by the king's huntsman, who tries in vain to get him to reveal his identity and his purpose. Such clumsy questioning was bad manners—Parzival, for example, was warned against asking too many questions—and Ruodlieb's taciturnity was correct. Then the overbold questioner, discerning that Ruodlieb is a man of strength and ability, and realizing from his behaviour that he has wisdom, loses no time in coming out into the open and securing

---

[1] On the meaning of *cognoscibilis*, see Braun, op. cit., pp. 12 f.

Ruodlieb's friendship, thus profiting by his initial error. Some-times, on the other hand, the philosophy is put into words, as for example when the king offers Ruodlieb the choice between material reward and wisdom. The hero sensibly chooses the latter (v. 425 ff.):

> '*Non cupio*, quod' ait 'conponderat usus honori.
> *Census habet* multos, ubi noscitur, insidiantes.
> *Pauperies miser*os cogit plures fore fures;
> *In consanguineos* parit invidiam vel amicos,
> *Vel fratrem* stimulat, fidei quod foedera rumpat.
> *Est melius*, censu careat quis quam quoque sensu,
> *Et quicumque* pia satagit florere sophia,
> *Ille vel argenti* semper sat habebit et auri,
> *Quae vult* expugnat, quia telis intus abundat.
> *At memini* multos vidisse creberrime stultos,
> *Qui opibus cunctis* per stulticiam nichilatis
> *Vivebant inopes*, vitiose degenerantes,
> *Quos non iuvisse* sed opes patuit nocuisse.
> Unde potes facile me verbu*m* ta*l*e docere,
> Quod si servabo, quod id ipsum non te*m*erabo,
> Tam karum quod erit, ceu pondo decem mihi quis det.
> Nemo mihi rapit id inimicaturve nec odit
> Propter id et latro me non occidet in arto.
> In camera regis census decet ut sit opimus,
> Pauper homo sat habet, si vi valet arteque pollet.
> Non volo peccuniam, sitio gustare sophiam.'[1]

---

[1] 'I do not desire', he said, 'what custom makes equal to honour. Wealth, when it is known, has many lying in wait for it. Poverty compels many poor men to be thieves; it brings envy to relatives and friends, and incites a brother to break the bonds of loyalty. It is better for someone to lack wealth than sense, and whoever tries to flourish in upright wisdom will always have enough silver and gold; whatever he wishes he will achieve, because he has an abundance of inner weapons. But I remember having very often seen many foolish men who, having lost all their wealth through stupidity, were living in want and de-generating into vice, and who had been harmed rather than helped by their riches. Therefore, you can easily teach me a lesson which, if I observe it and do not violate it, will be as valuable as if I were to be given ten pounds. No one will steal it from me or be hostile to me or hate me for it, and no robber will kill me in a narrow place. Great wealth is proper in a king's chamber; a poor man has sufficient if he has strength and skill. I do not want money; I thirst to taste of wisdom.' The thought in this passage derives ultimately from the Scriptures; cf. Prov. 8: 10–11: 'Receive my instruction, and not silver; and knowledge rather than choice gold. For wisdom is better than rubies; and all the things that may be desired are not to be compared with it.' Bauer, op. cit., pp. 55 f., draws attention to the similarity between the opening of this passage and Hagen's invective against greed in the *Waltharius* (ll. 857 ff.). This, together with the advice tendered to the greater king that he should marry off the hero

The greater king is clearly represented as an ideal Christian ruler. His dealings with his adversary the lesser king are generous in the extreme: he refuses to take vengeance for the attack upon his own kingdom; he protects the count who started the war by taking him into his own service; he sends back the prisoners of war with gifts of horses and weapons; he refuses to allow the lesser king to be subject to him, and he rejects all indemnities. Similarly, Ruodlieb takes no vengeance on the red-head who steals his coat or on the waiter who steals his spurs; nor does he openly denounce the lady who would have brought him dishonour, but contents himself with teaching her a lesson. In the portion dealing with his exile, he is overshadowed by the king, but the latter's subjects appreciate his virtues (v. 270 ff.):

> Dicunt, quod nunquam vidissent huic similem quem
> Maris honestate fidei vel in integritate
> Quod nec obest ulli sed, ubi quit, profuit omni.[1]

So does the king (v. 405 ff.), who even acknowledges himself to be inferior in one respect to Ruodlieb

> A quo sum numquam minimam commotus in *iram*,
> Quin irascentem me mitem reddit ut *agnum*.[2]

Similarly, his masters at home, when they recall him, avow (v. 238 ff.):

> Tunc in consilio dando par est tibi nemo,
> Qui vel tam iuste ius dicat tam vel honeste
> Et qui sic viduas defendat sive pupillos,
> Propter avariciam cum damnabantur iniquam,
> Qui lamentatur nimium *cum* quando premuntur.[3]

Another figure who exhibits exemplary virtue is the young man with whom Ruodlieb takes lodgings. By meekness he had earned

---

and so retain his services (v. 402 ff., cf. *Waltharius*, ll. 135 ff.) suggests to Bauer that the poet may have been familiar with the earlier epic.

[1] 'They said that they had never seen his like in manly loyalty, honesty, or integrity, and that he had never harmed anyone, but helped everyone wherever he could.'

[2] '... by whom I have never been moved to the slightest anger; rather does he make me as mild as a lamb when I grow angry.'

[3] 'Then there is no one equal to you in giving advice, no one who passes judgement either so justly or so honourably, and who so protects widows or orphans, who lament greatly whenever they are condemned through unjust avarice and are oppressed.'

himself a place in the household, and on the death of his par-
simonious master he inherits the land and marries the mistress. Yet
another model of Christian virtue is given by the old peasant who
forgives his murderer. The red-head is the type of the foolish and
wicked man who will not profit by teaching. The young wife,
whose wanton flirtation with him led to the crime, repents and
mortifies her flesh until she dies. She represents the type of the
penitent sinner. The long account of her penances in horrible
detail is another example of the didactic element. It is of the same
encyclopedic class as the detailed description of old age as seen in
her husband, and foretold for herself by Ruodlieb's mother.

The episodes which compose the narrative are in many cases
traditional stories which appear with manifold variations in many
languages and many periods.[1] The 'origin' of these international
stories or *Wandermotive* is a problem for the folklorist. The study
of it leads into pleasant bypaths, though these may easily lead the
inexperienced traveller astray. There is an extraordinary similarity
between the account of Ruodlieb's departure from court with the
'loaves', the king's advice, and the murder of the old peasant, and
a Cornish folk-tale of about 1700. How our poet came to hear such
a story is a matter for speculation.

In addition to such stories and the strong didactic element, the
poem contains an immense store of information about the details of
life at court, such as the formalities of sending and receiving em-
bassies and negotiating treaties, of sports and pastimes such as
hunting, fishing, chess, and music-making, in all of which, of course
Ruodlieb excels; one is reminded of the accomplished hero of
Gottfried's *Tristan*. We learn much, too, about ordinary life and
customs—the manner of negotiating and solemnizing marriages, of
travel, judicial procedure, and domesticity. This has led to the work's
being praised for its 'down-to-earth realism'.[2] Realistic treatment
is, however, mingled with conventional literary motifs, like that
of the speaking jackdaw which brings Ruodlieb's mother the first
news of her son's return; such motifs occur in the later 'Spiel-
mannsepos'.[3] There is a good deal of 'scientific' information, too,
which is no doubt the product of monkish learning, but of a kind

[1] See Seiler, ed. cit., pp. 45–74; Zeydel, ed. cit., pp. 9 f.; Bauer, op. cit.,
pp. 9–17.

[2] See Zeydel, ed. cit., Preface and pp. 16–20.

[3] See P. Wareman, *Spielmannsdichtung, Versuch einer Begriffsbestimmung*, (Amsterdam, 1951).

that is also found in some of the court epics such as those of
Wolfram.

The most remarkable, and to us the most interesting, parts of
the poem are the domestic scenes, and the most striking of these is
the entertainment accorded to Ruodlieb and his nephew by the
chatelaine. The nephew and the daughter of the house fall violently
in love at first sight. (The *coup de foudre* is a frequent motif in the
court epic.) As part of the entertainment, they dance beautifully,
representing the pursuit of a swallow by a hawk.[1] Then they cast
dice for rings; first the girl wins the young man's ring, and then
with the next cast he wins hers; she throws it to him with exu-
berance, whereupon they enjoy a grammatical jest involving
genders and cases. The poet adds (xii (Seiler x)) 29 ff.:

> Nec iam celarunt, se quin ardenter amarent,
> Mater si sineret, uel in ipsa nocte coirent.
> Illa tamen sineret, sibi si non dedecus esset.
> Ut praestoletur, tunc virgo vix superatur.[2]

The formalities of betrothal soon follow, but now the young man,
who has been rather notoriously sowing his wild oats, receives
a sharp lecture from his bride before she consents.

One passage, formerly held to be of great importance as evidence
for the existence of love poetry in German at this early period, is
the famous *Liebesgruß*. When Ruodlieb's friend has conveyed his
proposal of marriage to the lady, she replies: (xvii. 11 ff.):

> Dic illi nunc de me corde fideli
> Tantumdem liebes, veniat quantum modo loub*es*,
> Et volucrum vvunna quot sint, tot dic sibi m*inna*,
> Graminis et florum quantum sit, dic et honorum.[3]

These lines employ the 'quot . . . tot' formula which appears first

---

[1] There is no need to regard the dance as a survival of ancient peasant nature
ritual, or to read into the description more than the natural pleasure of two
healthy young people in a flirtatious dance. See E. Schröder, *ZfdA* 61 (1924) 29.

[2] 'They no longer concealed their ardent love for each other or their desire
to be united that night, if her mother would allow it. The mother would have
allowed it if it had not been dishonourable to them. Then the girl could hardly
be prevailed upon to wait.'

[3] 'Speak to him now from my faithful heart of as much love as there are
leaves, as much affection as birds have joy, and as much honour as there are
grass and flowers.' These words are repeated with slight differences in ll. 66–9.
Printed in *MSD* xxviii.

in Ovid. It was very common in Carolingian Latin for expressing greetings and good wishes. One example is:

> Quot caelum retinet stellas, quot terra lapillos,
> Quot saltus ramos, folia, aut quot pontus harenas,
> Quot fluvius pisces vel sunt quot in orbe volucres,
> Quot flores prati vel quot sunt gramina campi,
> Tot tibi praestantes det virtus tibi salutes.[1]

It is true that most of these complimentary greetings are not used in the service of love, but are addressed to male friends and colleagues, and no motive for the introduction of the German words has been suggested. It is of course impossible to prove, or even to believe, that the Germans did not compose love poems in their native language, but these lines cannot be used as evidence; once more the written word is found to be derived from the written Latin, not from an oral vernacular tradition. Likewise the lady's indignant repudiation of her consent when she discovers the nature of Ruodlieb's gift is couched in the 'si . . . non' formula (VII. 43 ff. and 79 ff.):

> Tunc ait illa: 'tuo dic contribuli vel amico:
> Usquam si nullus vir plus foret, is nisi solus,
> Ille vel in dotem mihi mundum si daret omnem,
> Nubere nolo sibi, dic tu veraciter illi.'[2]

The language contains numerous graecisms in its vocabulary, and apart from the words already cited there are other German words in the text, notably the names of fish in x (Seiler XIII), 47 ff. There is also a number of Germanisms in the syntax. Unlike the *Waltharius*, the work evinces little dependence on Virgil. A striking feature of the poet's narrative technique is the repetition of certain episodes; the account of the friend's visit to the lady, for instance, is first given directly by the poet and then verbatim by the friend to Ruodlieb. Another feature is his love of long descriptions, especially of jewels. Such descriptions are a feature of the works of

---

[1] 'May virtue give you as many excellent greetings as the sky holds stars and the earth stones, as the forest has branches and leaves and the sea has sands, as many as there are fish in the river or birds in the world, as many as the flowers of the meadow or the grass of the field.' This example is quoted by H. Walther, *ZfdA* 65 (1928) 269, from *Poetae Latini Aevi Carolini* IV. i. 349 ff.

[2] 'Then she said: "Tell your relative or friend: if there were never any man but he alone, and if he were to give me the whole world as a wedding present, I would not marry him. Tell him that faithfully."'

Gottfried and Wolfram. He enjoys, too, displaying his store of curious knowledge as, for instance, when he describes how the ligure is made out of the urine of the lynx. Such information was no doubt culled from Isidor's *Liber Etymologiarum* and other learned sources.

We have already remarked upon the 'realism' of the poet's presentation. It has, however, been rightly pointed out that there is a good deal of idealization too. Much of the account of the meeting between the two kings or of the hospitality dispensed by the young peasant is probably in accord not so much with how things were actually done, but how the didactic poet thought they should be done. Hospitality is given in much the same manner as is recommended in the Rule of St. Benedict, and it has been shown that the ethic underlying the poem, especially in the conduct of the hero and the greater king, is the same as that found in the Life of St. Gerald of Aurillac by Abbot Odo of Cluny.[1] Gerald was a knight whose knighthood was pleasing to God, who never stained his sword with blood, who sought reconciliation with his enemies, and who protected the poor, the widows, and the orphans. As seen by Odo of Cluny and by the poet of the *Ruodlieb*, the career of a knight need not conflict with the service of God. In the century which saw the launching of the First Crusade (1099), a new concept of knighthood was emerging: the Christian knight, the *miles Christi*, was no longer just a fighting man who was also a member of the Church, but one who, by virtue of his martial calling, had a duty to defend the helpless and succour the oppressed. This ideal of knighthood is first embodied in a secular work by the author of the *Ruodlieb*. The earlier type of the Christian warrior, who fears God but vindicates his right, is exemplified in the hero of the *Waltharius*.

Although they are so close to each other in date (though not so close as was once thought), these two epics could scarcely be more different in spirit: the one tells a native tale of derring-do in the pagan Roman style, though with a certain monkish aloofness; the other is inspired by a contemporary ideal, and pays only a half-hearted tribute, if any at all, to the native heroic tradition.

Yet a century and a half divide the *Ruodlieb* from the Middle High German court epic. We cannot call the work 'courtly' in the

---

[1] *P.L.* 133, 639–704. The poet's probable debt to Odo is discussed by Bauer, op. cit., pp. 35 ff.

sense that properly attaches to the word in a discussion of Middle High German literature, even though part of the action takes place in a courtly milieu. Here already women are treated with respect, and the daughter of the chatelaine even seems to enjoy a remarkable degree of emancipation. What is absent, however, is any trace of the elevating, educative function of love between the sexes. Unless one was foolish, like the red-head or the hero's nephew in his unregenerate phase, one sought out a woman only 'causa karorum generandorum liberorum' (v. 485). The chatelaine's daughter is an eligible spinster, and all the other women are either venerable matrons (her mother, the hero's mother, the young peasant's wife) or wantons (the old peasant's wife, the nephew's harlot, Ruodlieb's lady).

The author was a learned man, probably a cleric—unless such a person cannot be credited with defaming the cloth in XVII. 30. The circumstance that only the clergy were allowed to accept gifts from the lesser king (v. 210–19) is not evidence, for it means only that the greater king was prudently making provision for prayers to be said for himself, his new friend, and their followers.[1]

As has been stated, the poem is most conveniently regarded as a forerunner of the chivalric romance of the later Middle Ages. The last fragment, however, is widely taken to indicate an affinity with the heroic epic, and the author may have drawn upon material heard from the professional entertainers (*joculatores* or *mimi*) of the day, with whose activity he was familiar, as we learn from v. 87; XI. 26. 43.

---

[1] On the genre of the *Ruodlieb*, see Zeydel, ed. cit., pp. 13 ff., and K. Ruh, *Höfische Epik des deutschen Mittelalters*, I: *Von den Anfängen biz zu Hartmann von Aue* (Berlin, 1967), pp. 27–32.

EDITIONS of *Waltharius*. Those by H. Althof, *Waltharii Poesis* (2 vols., Leipzig, 1899–1905) and K. Strecker, *Ekkehards Waltharius* (2nd edn., Berlin, 1924) are full and scholarly. Strecker also provided a popular edition with a German translation by P. Vossen (Berlin, 1947). A translation into German hexameters is given by K. Langosch, *Waltharius, Ruodlieb, Märchenepen* (Basle/Stuttgart, 1956). For a recent discussion of the work and its affinities see H. Geurts, *Der lateinische Waltharius und die deutsche Walthersage* (Bonn, 1969).

XVI

The Close of the Period

HENRY II, the last of the Saxon Emperors, acceded to the German throne in 1002. He concentrated much of his energy on laboriously rebuilding the royal power in Germany, which had been seriously eroded during the reign of Otto III. He also paid three visits to Italy, where, after the death of Sylvester II in 1003, there was contention about the papal succession and about the tenure of the Italian crown. On his first visit he obtained the crown of Italy (1004), and on his second, in 1014, he was crowned Emperor by Pope Benedict VIII. Between his coronation and a visit which Benedict paid to Germany in 1020 there was further contention in Italy for both the temporal and the spiritual power. Accordingly, in the next year Henry mounted a great expedition in order to assert both his own and Benedict's authority. Militarily and politically he met with success, but in Apulia his army was attacked and decimated by the plague. In 1022 the army recrossed the Alps, bringing the plague with it. One of the victims of this deadly sickness was the greatest figure in German letters of the period, Notker III of St. Gall. Henry and Benedict both died in 1024. Both had been advocates of the ideas of ecclesiastical reform which emanated from Cluny, ideas which were unpopular in some church quarters in Germany and whose propagation under royal favour had brought Henry into conflict with the German bishops.[1]

Notker was known to his contemporaries as 'Teutonicus' because of his zeal for the German language,[2] and later as 'Labeo' because of a thick lip. He was a schoolmaster, who wrote for the benefit of his pupils. He came of a noble Thurgau family, many

[1] The echo of the Cluniac reforms is hardly perceptible in Old High German literature, but some critics have credited Cluniac ideas with responsibility for the ascetic tone of much early Middle High German literature.

[2] At the end of Notker's translation of the Athanasian Creed is entered the epitaph:

'Notker Teutonicus domini finitur amicus,
Gaudeat ille locis in paradysiacis.'

These lines reappear in the passage quoted on p. 282, n. 3 below.

members of which were connected with the monastery, either as monks or in a lay capacity.[1] As there had been two others of his name at St. Gall, he is sometimes called Notker III. Notker I, called 'Balbulus' ('The Stammerer'), was a well-known author of Latin sequences,[2] and Notker II, called 'Piperis Granum' because of his fiery temper, was a distinguished physician.[3] Like his contemporary Abbot Purchard, Notker III was a nephew of Ekkehard I, who was formerly supposed to have written the *Waltharius*. The few details of his life which are known are recorded in a number of contemporary documents, notably the *Annales Sancti Galli Maiores*,[4] the *Casuum Sancti Galli Continuatio* of Notker's pupil Ekkehard IV,[5] and the latter's *Liber Benedictionum*.[6] He was born in the year 950 and spent his life as a respected teacher in the monastery school,[7] where he made many notable translations into German. His versions of the Psalter and the Book of Job earned

---

[1] A short pedigree of Notker's family is given in a footnote on p. 118 of *MGH* II. On the life of the monastery, see J. M. Clark, *The Abbey of St. Gall as a Centre of Literature and Art* (Cambridge, 1926).

[2] On Notker I see W. von den Steinen, *Notker der Dichter und seine geistige Welt* (Berne, 1948). This work is in two volumes, the second being an edition of the poems.

[3] A fourteenth-century hand entered the following punning lines in a St. Gall manuscript at the end of a collection of Latin verses 'Ad picturas claustri Sancti Galli', i.e. characterizations of people whose portraits were displayed in the monastery:

> 'Panditur ecce liber: solvit signacula Notker,
> Abdita perspicuis septem speculatus ocellis.
> Gusta quam sapiant, quia quarto vase nec obstant.
> Balbus erat Notker, piperis granum fuit alter;
> Tercius hic labio datus est agnomine lato,
> Pectore mandatum gestans labio quoque latum:
> Lacior hinc labio puto nemo videbitur illo.
> Ecce favos! labio qua stillat *mel* tibi lato.'

(*Mitteilungen zur vaterländischen Geschichte* XXXI (St. Gall, 1909), p. v). The insertion of *mel* in the last verse restores the metre; for this emendation I am indebted to my colleague John Carter. On the meaning of 'quartum vas', see p. 290 below.

[4] *MGH Script.* I. 72–85, and *Mittheilungen zur vaterländischen Geschichte* XIX (St. Gall, 1884), pp. 265 ff.

[5] *MGH Script.* II. 149 ff.; transl. by L. G. Meyer von Knonau, *Geschichtsschreiber der dt. Vorzeit. 10. Jahrhundert*, Bd. 11.

[6] Ed. J. Egli in *Mittheilungen zur vaterländischen Geschichte* XXXI.

[7] The Annals of St. Gall call him 'Notker nostrae memoriae hominum doctissimus et benignissimus' (*MGH Script.* I. 82). The affection in which he was held is attested by Ekkehardus IV's moving account of the grief caused by his death in an interlinear gloss to a poem which also treats of his death. See *Liber Benedictionum*, ed. cit., pp. 230 ff., and *MGH Script.* II. 57 f.

the admiration of the Empress Gisela.[1] He died of the plague just
after completing the translation of the Book of Job.[2] Having con-
fessed his sins, one of the most serious being that he had once
as a young man killed a wolf while wearing his habit, he died on
St. Peter's Day, 29 June 1022. He was buried in his habit with the
iron chain which he wore round his waist. Abbot Purchard and
several other monks also died of the plague.

Notker was purely and simply a pedagogue. As such he was
distinguished. His knowledge of Latin was profound, and he was
a highly resourceful translator with a rich vocabulary and an un-
surpassed facility in manipulating the German language. His
erudition was immense and his scheme of education novel. Moreover, he used, and probably devised, a remarkably consistent and
phonetically exact system of orthography for German. He was not
otherwise what would be considered an original thinker. He was
a compiler of knowledge and a translator of standard Latin texts.
Of his own compilations only *De Musica* was, as far as we know,
composed in German. All the rest were written in Latin, and some
were translated into German, the *De Arte Rhetorica* less fully than
the others. His subject matter was the Bible (the Psalms and the
Book of Job), the Creeds and Prayers, as well as the subjects of the
trivium (grammar, logic, and rhetoric) and the quadrivium (arith-
metic, geometry, astronomy, and music), which were studied in
schools as a preparation for the service of the Church. The translations are accompanied by exegetical commentaries in German.
These too are for the most part not original, but are based on, even
translations of, the commentaries of an earlier scholar, Remigius of
Auxerre (*c*. 840–905).[3]

---

[1] The interlinear gloss mentioned on p. 282, n. 7 contains the words: 'Kisila
imperatrix operum eius avidissima, psalterium ipsum et Iob sibi exemplari sol-
licite fecit.'

[2] 'Henricus . . . victor rediit in Germaniam. Pestilentia in exercitu orta,
multos extinctit; inter quos Ruodhardus Constantiae episcopus, et Purchardus
noster obierunt. Notkerus quoque magister et alii prestantes fratres apud
Sanctum Gallum decesserunt' (*MGH Script.* II. 155).

[3] Notker's works have been edited by P. Piper, *Die Schriften Notkers und
seiner Schule* (Freiburg/Tübingen, 1882–3), 3 vols. This is still the standard
edition. The first volume contains the philosophical works, the second the
Psalms and catechistic pieces, and the third the derivative texts (the Wessobrunn
Psalms, etc.). A new edition by E. H. Sehrt and Taylor Starck, *Notkers des
Deutschen Werke* began to appear in 1933. Sehrt and Starck together edited *De
Consolatione* (Altdeutsche Textbibliothek, vols. 32–4, 1933) and *De Nuptiis*
(ibid., vol. 37, 1935). Sehrt edited the Psalter (vols. 40, 42, and 43, 1952–5);

Notker gives a list of his books in a letter to his friend Hugo, bishop of Sitten, and in this letter he also declares his aims.[1] Many of the texts he mentions have perished. Of the original Latin compositions named in the letter the following have been preserved: *De Arte Rhetorica, De Partibus Logicae*, the fragment *De Disputatione*, and *Computus* (a work on the calendar). All these he translated more or less completely into German, or at least provided them with German notes. *De Musica* was, apparently, composed in German. Of Notker's translations into German we have Boethius' *De Consolatione Philosophiae*, the *Categories* and *De Interpretatione* of Aristotle (both made from Boethius' Latin translation with commentary), and the first two books of *De Nuptiis Mercurii et Philologiae* by Martianus Capella.[2] In his letter to Hugo Notker refers to a number of other translations which are now lost, including the *Disticha Catonis*, Virgil's *Bucolics*, and Terence's *Andria*. He also translated the Psalter together with some of the Canticles, the Lord's Prayer, the Apostles' Creed, and the Athanasian Creed. His last work, the translation of the Book of Job, has not survived. Notker's industry was obviously prodigious. It was formerly held that much of the labour of translating was done by assistants under his supervision, but it has been established that there are no divergences in the language such as would lend credence to this view, and all the work is now attributed to Notker himself.

Boethius' *Consolation* and Martianus Capella's *Marriage of Mercury and Philology* were both standard works in the schools and excellent examples of the medieval conception of the higher

unfortunately Sehrt and Starck present a normalized orthography and relegate 'abnormal' spellings to the foot of the page. This project is being continued by J. C. King and P. W. Tax, who have now edited the *Categories* (Altdt. Textbibl., vol. 72, 1972), and are going to bring out Notker's Latin writings. King and Tax present a virtually diplomatic text. E. H. Sehrt and W. K. Legner have provided a full lexicon of Notker's language, their *Notker-Wortschatz* (Halle, 1955), with references to Piper's edition. Mention should be made, too, of the useful *Notker-Glossar* by Sehrt (Tübingen, 1962), which dispenses with textual references. Extracts: *Ahd. Lb.* xxiii; facsimiles: *Schrifttafeln* 11 a and b.

[1] Piper, 1. 859–61. On this letter see I. Schröbler, 'Zum Brief Notkers des Deutschen an den Bischof Hugo von Sitten', *ZfdA* 82 (1948–50) 32–46.

[2] Martianus (or Marcianus) Capella was a Carthaginian writer who flourished at the end of the fifth century, and became famous on account of this one work which is a celebration of the liberal arts. See Pauly–Wissowa, *Real-Lexikon der classischen Altertumswissenschaft* xiv, cols. 2003 ff. *De Nuptiis* is edited by F. Eyssenhardt (Leipzig, 1856), rev. A. Dick (1925). See also C. E. Lutz, 'Remigius of Auxerre and Martianus Capella', *Med. Stud.* 19 (1957) 137–56.

learning. Both are composed in the form known as 'Menippean satire' (*satura Menippea*), in which portions of prose and verse alternate. Both are admirably suited to the kind of philological instruction given in medieval schools; the *Consolation* employs the whole range of rhetorical devices, and the first two books of the *Marriage* are a mine of information about classical mythology allegorically interpreted. In his translation of the former Notker accentuates the rhetorical element by frequently interrupting the argument to point out the rhetorical device which is being employed at a given point. He also gives a Christian interpretation to parts of the work, which is, at least on the surface, profane.[1] The work has thus become, in his hands, to a large extent a treatise on the art of Rhetoric. Both works had been provided with commentaries by Remigius of Auxerre. Notker appropriated these commentaries and acknowledged his debt at the opening of his translation of the *Marriage*. For the *Consolation* he also used another commentary, which has not been identified, and contributed some details of his own which can be distinguished from both. Occasional chapters in German interpolated by Notker explain and summarize the arguments concluded in the preceding chapters.

Anicius Manlius Severinus Boethius (*c.* 480–524) was a Roman aristocrat who became consul in 510 under Theodoric the Great, an office which his father before him had held under Odoacer. He had already distinguished himself in the service of the state and continued to do so, becoming *magister officiorum*, i.e. head of the civil service and chief of the palace officials. In 522 both his sons were appointed consuls together. In the very next year his fortunes changed: he was accused of conducting treacherous dealings with the Empire and found guilty. He was exiled to Pavia, where he was imprisoned and where he composed his *Consolation of Philosophy*. He was finally tortured and killed in 524 or 525. Not long afterwards, his father-in-law Quintus Aurelius Memmius Symmachus was also put to death, as was Pope John I.[2]

---

[1] See Ingeborg Schröbler, *Notker III von St. Gallens als Übersetzer und Kommentator von Boethius' De Consolatione Philosophiae* (Hermaea N.F. 2. Tübingen, 1953), pp. 1–20.

[2] The Latin and German Prologues to Notker's Boethius record these crimes of Theodoric (Piper, I. 4 and 6; S.-St. I. 6):

'contradicentes occidit. Inter quos symmachus patricius . et gener eius boetius gladio perierunt. Sanctissimum quoque papam iohannem . usque ad necem carcere afflixit.'

('. . . únde dîen râten án den lîb . tîe ímo dés neuuâren geuólgig. Fóne díu

Boethius was not only a statesman, but a prodigiously gifted scholar with a profound knowledge of Greek philosophy. It was his ambition to translate all the work of Aristotle and all Plato's dialogues into Latin, and this ambition he partly fulfilled. Indeed, it was to Boethius that later scholars, including Notker, owed their access to the philosophy of Aristotle, for few western scholars of the Middle Ages knew enough Greek to read the original works. He also wrote four, possibly five, theological tractates in which he applied the methods of philosophy to questions of Christian dogma. It was, however, his last work, the *Consolation of Philosophy*, which earned him his lasting reputation. It might be said that, next to the Scriptures themselves, it was the most important book of the Middle Ages.[1] This 'golden volume', as Edward Gibbon called it, was translated into many languages; among those who translated it into English were King Alfred, Chaucer, and Queen Elizabeth (who is reputed to have completed her translation in twenty-seven hours).

The *Consolation* belongs to the originally Greek genre of the *consolatio*, a kind of composition designed to provide a philosophical remedy for the reader's ills. It is couched in the form of a dialogue between the imprisoned Boethius and his nurse, the Lady Philosophy. Philosophy at first applies the remedy of persuasion to her patient, showing him that Fortune is by nature unstable, and that he has no right to complain of reverses suffered at Fortune's hands.[2] Afterwards, when his mind has been partly healed, she administers the sharper remedies of philosophical disputation. The argument is skilfully developed into an elaborate treatise on the relations between God and Man, on the nature of

slûog er boetium . únde sînen suêr symmachum . únde dáz óuh uuírsera uuás . iohannem den bâbes.')

The origin of this account, which interprets history in the light of St. Paul's prophecy of the coming of Antichrist, is unknown. See K. Ostberg, *GLL* N.S. 16 (1962–3) 256–65.

[1] On the place of Boethius in western thought, see F. P. Pickering, *Augustinus oder Boethius?* (Phil. Stud. u. Qu. 39, Berlin, 1967). A convenient edition of the *Consolation* is to be found in the Loeb Classical Library together with an English translation of 1609 revised by H. F. Stewart (London/New York, 1918). A modern translation with a valuable introduction and bibliography is provided by V. E. Watts in the Penguin Classics (1969).

[2] See H. R. Patch, *The Goddess Fortuna in Medieval Literature* (Cambridge, Mass., 1927); F. P. Pickering, 'Notes on Fate and Fortune', *Medieval German Studies presented to Frederick Norman* (London, 1965), pp. 1–15.

Providence, Fate, and Free Will, and on the proper attitude of the individual towards the problem of evil.

To a modern reader the *Consolation* is a puzzling work, for, though written by a Christian, who might be expected to find his consolation in Christ and the Church, it is strictly pagan in character with no overt reference to Christianity. Boethius belonged to an age when pagan philosophy and Christian doctrine could coexist without being thought to conflict. He seems to have believed that rational thought could provide a true understanding of the governance of the universe, and a conviction that it was ruled by a benevolent God. Such rational thought existed on a different plane from that of revealed truth: it could not confer grace, and it was not concerned with sin and redemption. Philosophy was not yet the handmaid of theology that she was to become later in the Middle Ages.

We may illustrate Notker's method of translation by his treatment of the first metre of the *Consolation*, which opens with the following lines:

> Carmina qui quondam studio florente peregi,
> Flebilis heu maestos cogor inire modos.
> Ecce mihi lacerae dictant scribenda camenae
> Et ueris elegi fletibus ora rigant.
> Has saltem nullus potuit peruincere terror,
> Ne nostrum comites prosequerentur iter.

These Notker treats as follows:[1]

Qui peregi quondam carmina florente studio . hev flebilis cogor inire mestos modos. Íh tir êr téta frôlichív sáng . íh máchôn nû nôte chárasáng. Ecce lacerę camenę dictant mihi scribenda. Síh no . léidege musę lêrent míh scríben. Táz mír uuíget . táz uuíget ín. Tîe míh êr lêrton iocunda carmina . tîe lêrent míh nû flebilia. Et rigant ora elegi . i. miseri . ueris . i. non fictis fletibus. Únde fúllent sie mîniv óugen . mít érnestlichên drânen. Has saltim comites nullus terror potuit peruincere . ne prosequerentur nostrum iter. Tíse geuértun nemáhta nîoman eruuénden . sîe nefûorîn sáment mír. Quasi diceret. Úbe íh ánderro sáchôn beróubôt pín . mînero chúnnôn nemáhta míh nîoman beróubôn.

Here we see that Notker reorders the words so that they may be the more easily construed; he even on occasion modifies the Latin syntax, as when he assigns *comites* to the foregoing clause, and he

---

[1] Piper, I. 7; S.-St. I. 7.

frequently supplies synonyms (here 'miseri' and 'non fictis') to aid comprehension.[1] His German translations of the Latin words are often quite free: 'cogor inire' is represented by *máchôn nû nôte*, 'lacerę' by *léidege*, 'nullus terror' by *nîoman*, 'ne prosequerentur nostrum iter' by *síe nefûorîn sáment mír*. If the translation fails to render the full sense of the Latin (as for instance that of l. 5), he provides an explanatory gloss and sometimes a periphrastic summary. If (as in l. 6) he discerns an implicit purport, he makes it explicit.

Sometimes Notker's explication is incorporated into the Latin text, while his German version is exceedingly bald, though rendering the sense accurately and often idiomatically. At times he is at pains to give a logical sense to the Latin, even at the expense of over-interpretation. These features are to be noted in his version of the following lines:

> Et dolor aetatem iussit inesse suam.
> Intempestiui funduntur uertice cani
> Et tremit effeto corpore laxa cutis.

Notker renders them as follows:[2]

Et dolor iussit inesse suam ętatem . s. ideo suam . quia citius cogit senescere. Únde léid hábet míh álten getân. Funduntur uertice intempestiui cani. Fóne dîen díngen grâuuên íh ze únzite. Et laxa cutis . tremit effeto corpore. Únde sláchiu hût. rîdot an chráftelôsemo lîchamen. Táz chît . mîne lîde rîdont únder sláchero híute.

(The poet in fact says that his skin trembles, not his limbs!) Notker was clearly not concerned to furnish an elegant German translation (not until over a century and a half after his death was elegance sought in the vernacular) but to reproduce faithfully the sense and what he considered to be the purport of the original. His German versions were intended as aids to understanding rather than to translating.

Notker had yet another aim, namely to familiarize his pupils with rhetorical figures and dialectic techniques by indicating their use in the text. Thus we find the following commentary on the last line of the first metre ('Qui cecidit stabili non erat ille gradu'):[3]

---

[1] Relying on Remigius, from whom the gloss 'miseri' derives, Notker seems to have parsed 'elegi' as a genitive. It is in fact a plural noun ('elegiac verses') and properly the subject of 'rigant'.

[2] Piper, I. 7; S.-St. I. 8.   [3] Piper, I. 8; S.-St. I. 8.

Qui cecidit . non erat ille stabili gradu. Tér dóh îo uîel . fásto nestûont .
úbe er fásto stûonde . sô neuîle er. Argumentum a repugnantibus.
Repugnant enim stare et cadere.

Such comments abound throughout his translations, and show how
he saw the literary texts as vehicles for the inculcation of rhetorical
and dialectical principles. He also used them as a means for con-
veying to his pupils useful knowledge about etymology, history,
astronomy, and other subjects. Thus, when Philosophy reminds
Boethius of the infinitesimal dimensions of the earth in relation
to the heavens, Notker seizes the opportunity to interpose first
a reminder of Aristotle's definitions of a point and a line, and then
a lengthy disquisition on geography and astronomy, in which he
refers to a globe which has recently been constructed in St. Gall.[1]
Sometimes the pedagogue, as it were, lays aside his book in order
to summarize the argument as it has developed up to the point he
has reached and to draw useful lessons from it. One such interpolation occurs after the fifth metre in the second book of the *Consolation*; here Notker contrasts rhetorical persuasion (*rhetorica
suadela*) and philosophical disputation (*philosophica disputatio*), il-
lustrating his lesson by instances of the former culled from ancient
history, and goes on to discuss the divisions of philosophy.[2]

It has already been said that Notker is content with a free rendering of the Latin and not concerned to produce anything like a
stylistic equivalent in German. In matters of terminology, however, he spares no pains in trying to render the exact sense. An
example of his punctiliousness is afforded by his treatment of the
following passage (*Cons*. v. i):

'Si quidem,' inquit, 'aliquis euentum temerario motu nullaque
causarum productum casum esse definiat, nihil omnino casum esse
confirmo et praeter subiectae rei significationem inanem prorsus uocem
esse decerno. . . .'

Notker's translation and commentary runs as follows:[3]

Si quidem inquit aliquis diffiniat casum esse productum euentum
temerario motu . et nulla conexione causarum. Úbe îoman héizet
casum . éina stúzzelingun uuórtena geskíht . únde âne állero díngo
máchunga. Nihil omnino casum esse confirmo. Sô chído íh páldo . dáz

---

[1] Piper, I. 110 ff.; S.-St. I. 121 ff.   [2] Piper, I. 98 ff.; S.-St. I. 109 ff.
[3] Piper, I. 305 ff.; S.-St. I. 332 ff. On Notker's treatment of the concept *casus*
and the associated vocabulary, see Schröbler, op. cit., pp. 107–17, esp. 114 ff.

casus nîeht nesî. Et decerno prorsus inanem uocem esse . preter significationem subiecte rei. Únde héizo íh iz éinen báren námen . âne bezéichennisseda. Causa íst îo conexa zû dero euentu. Fóne díu . dáz man chît temerario motu . únde sine causa . álde sine conexione causarum . dáz íst ál éin. Táz chît állez . stúzzelingûn . árdingun . úndúrftes . âne úrhab . âne úrspríng . âne scúlde . âne réda. Temerarius motus mág óuh chéden sélbuuaga . álde sélbhéui . íh méino . álso dáz íst . úbe síh îeht fóne ímo sélbemo erhéuet . únde fóne ímo sélbemo uuírdet. Uuélez íst áber dáz? Uuír múgen iz spréchen . uuír nefíndên is îo nîeht. Temeritas íst úmbedéncheda . únde úngeuuárehéit . únde gâscrécchi . únde únórdenhafti . fráuali . únúnderskéit . únrihti. Temerarius .i. mentis preceps íst tér . dér nerûochet uuáz er tûot . únde dér âne rât tûot . táz ímo míttundes ûfuuírdet. Tén héizên uuír rágare. Fóne temnendo íst kespróchen temeritas per sincopam . quasi temneritas.

In his version of the Psalter Notker expounded the spiritual meaning of the text in accordance with an exegetical tradition going back to Augustine, whose authority he acknowledged in his letter to Hugo.[1] He did not, however, incorporate the whole of Augustine's *Enarrationes in Psalmos* into his exegesis, and he drew upon a number of other commentaries. How he gathered his material together is a question which cannot be answered with confidence.[2] His aim was, as a contemporary poet put it, to 'transfuse' the biblical books (the Psalter and the Book of Job) into a 'fourth vessel', namely the German language, the first three vessels being the sacred languages, Hebrew, Greek, and Latin.[3] As an example of his method we may take his treatment of vv. 8 and 9 of Psalm 136, which read:

Filia Babylonis misera! beatus qui retribuet tibi retributionem tuam quam retribuisti nobis! Beatus qui tenebit et allidet parvulos tuos ad petram!

[1] 'totum psalterium et interpretando et secundum Augustinum exponendo' (Piper, i. 560).

[2] A large number of parallels are adduced by Sehrt in his edition. For an account of the latest work see P. W. Tax, *Notker Latinus* (Tübingen, 1972 (Altdt. Textbibliothek 74)).

[3] The *Rhythmi de Sancto Otmero* (*MHG Script.* ii. 57 f.) describes his achievement as follows:

'Primus barbaricam scribens, faciensque saporem,
Notker mox obiit, ubi Iob calamo superavit,
Quem vas in quartum transfundens fecit apertum.'

Ekkehardus glossed these lines with the words: "Teutonice propter caritatem discipulorum plures libros exponens, ipsa die, qua obiit, librum Iob finivit, opus mirandum librum Iob in quartam linguam exponens . . .'

Cassiodorus had commented on v. 8:

> Filia Babylonis bene caro nostra dicitur . . . sed postquam de Baby-
> loniae filia dixit, iustissimam compensationem ei asserit esse reddendam;
> ut sicut nos luxuria concitat ad vitia, ita repressam ieiuniis atque tribula-
> tionibus subditam faciamus esse virtutibus.

And on v. 9 Augustine had commented:

> Qui sunt parvuli Babyloniae? nascentes malae cupiditates. sunt enim
> qui cum vetere cupiditate rixantur. quando nascitur cupiditas . . . elide
> illam. sed times, ne elisa non moriatur: ad petram elide. petra autem
> erat Christus.

Notker's version reads:[1]

> Filia babilonis misera. id est caro . uel carnales . beatus qui retribuet
> tibi retributionem tuam quam retribuisti nobis. Uénega tóhter babilonis .
> kesah in gót ter dír lônot nah temo lône . sô dû úns lônotôst. Úbe únsih
> caro álde carnales scúndent ze áchusten . tîe uuír uuólton chêren ad
> uirtutes . únde uuíder uns sínt . uuíder dîen súln uuír uuésen uuáchendo
> únde fástendo . únz uuír sîe úber uuínden . álso sîe únsih úber uuínden
> uuólton. Beatus qui tenebit et allidet paruulos tuos ad petram. Sâligo
> der dîniu chínt nímet únde siu chnístet an den stéin. Babilonis chínt sínt
> kelúste únz sîe nîuue sínt. tîe súln uuír in christo ferchnísten . êr sie
> álteren uuerden.

As in his translations of secular works, so too in the Psalms, though
less frequently, Notker inserts items of general knowledge which
will promote understanding of the text. For instance, on the
words 'petra refugium erinaciis' (Ps. 103: 18) Augustine had commented: 'Quid significant nisi peccatores?' Notker incorporates
this interpretation into his commentary, together with some
zoological information about the 'erinacius' which he identifies
with the familiar marmot:[2]

> CHRISTVS ist petra . er sî fluht erinatiis . id est peccatoribus. Erinatius

[1] Piper, II. 573 f. The text quoted above is taken from the Basle fragment
(S.-St. III. 995 f.) given by Sehrt in his apparatus and also in *Ahd. Lb.*

[2] The animal the Psalmist had in mind was no doubt the Syrian rock-badger
(*Hyrax syriacus*), which the A.V. identifies with the cony. In Notker's version
one sees his etymological interest in play: the *erinaceus* is of the same size as the
hedgehog (*ericius*), though it is evidently not the hedgehog that the Psalmist
intends. The later glossator provides *murmento* 'marmot' as the German equivalent of *mus montis*. On the German designation for the marmot see the article
'Murmeltier' in Kluge, *Etym. Wb. der dt. Sprache*. The passage quoted is to be
found in Piper, II. 438; S.-St. III. 757 f.

ist animal magnitudine ericii . daz chit des ígeles . similitudine ursi et muris . daz heîzen uuir murem montis . uuanda iz in foraminibus alpium sîna festi hábet.

Notker's technique was in all respects the result of the didactic purpose which his books were designed to serve. The medieval scholar was expected to dispute, so writers were naturally inclined to present their matter in the form of question and answer. This technique is often found in Notker's commentaries. It is a method familiar from the Catechism and, in a more elaborate form, from Plato's dialogues. These have a long line of successors through the Middle Ages to the present day. Manuscripts, as Notker points out in his letter to the bishop, were costly; a book was, therefore, a precious possession not easily acquired. Notker's works are a record of his teaching. The teacher would read aloud first a sentence of the Latin (or a clause or a few words at a time if the passage was especially difficult), then he would give his translation, and finally present his exegesis. The pupils would have to rely on their memories and on such notes as they could take on waxed tables or on waste scraps of parchment.

A notable feature of Notker's style is his use of Latin words among the German, whence his language is known as *Mischprosa*. It is not peculiar to him, and indeed it may well reflect the oral medium in which he conducted his lessons, not unlike that in which Luther conducted his table-talk centuries later. The Latin words occur in both the translation and the commentary. They are to a large extent technical terms which the scholar would encounter in the course of his studies and would have to use in his disputations. To have replaced them by German terms, even if the vernacular could have provided exact equivalents, would have frustrated Notker's purpose, which was to make his pupils familiar with them. He usually explained and translated a new term on its first occurrence and then reverted to the original Latin when his pupils had understood its meaning and use.

Notker had a taste for etymologies, and these he often expounded by means of loan-formations. This was a technique practised throughout the Old High German period. Some of the loan-translations found in his works, e.g. *uuíolíchî* for 'qualitas' were already well established. Others are not encountered earlier, but one can never be sure that they are Notker's inventions. Examples are *bûochkámera* for 'bibliotheca', *bûochlíste* for 'liberales artes', *zéigorûota* for 'virga', *héimegezógeno* for 'alumnus', *uuíghórn* for 'classicum'. He was particularly adept at matching Latin abstract nouns with comparable German formations. Thus we find *geuángeni* for 'comprehensio', *gnôtmárchunga* and *gnôtmézunga* (also *úndermárchunga*) for 'definitio', *uuíderechêreda* for 'relatio', *ábanémunga* for 'remotio', and many others. In the matter of linguistic inventiveness Notker was at least the peer of more recent creators of German words, such as J. H. Campe, but his aims were different: while Campe wished to provide effective substitutes for foreign words, Notker sought only to clarify the meanings and derivations of the Latin words that were to be encountered in the reading of standard texts.[1]

In an age when Latin was the language of learning and German had in scholarship only an auxiliary function, it is not surprising that Latin constructions such as the ablative absolute and the accusative and infinitive were imitated, the dative being substituted for the ablative in the former. Thus the clause 'tunc discussa nocte . liquerunt me tenebre' is rendered by *sâr . hína uertríbenero náht . pegáb mîh tiu uínstri*,[2] and 'quod amitti posse non dubitat' by *dáz er síh uuéiz múgen uerlíesen*[3] (there is no attempt to render the passive infinitive exactly). Even if there is no infinitive construction in the original, Notker may use one in German. Thus 'respexi nutricem meam philosophiam' is rendered by *Pechnâta íh sia uuésen mîna ámmûn*.[4] Similarly, Notker imitates participial constructions, sometimes with modification, e.g. 'et uibratus subito lumine . ferit radiis mirantes oculos', which is rendered by *Únde sî gâes skînende . skíuzet tien líuten síh uuúnderônten únder diu óugen*.[5]

The use of such Latinate syntax in German represents a development beyond that found in the interlinear translations of an earlier period. The German version of Tatian's gospel harmony provided in the main a word-for-word rendering of the original. The translator was not concerned to produce a piece of German prose which could stand by itself. Notker, though regarding German only as a means to a better understanding of the Latin texts

---

[1] On his loan-formations, see Evelyn S. Coleman, 'Die Lehnbildungen in Notkers Übersetzungen', *Festschrift Taylor Starck* (The Hague, 1964), pp. 106–29.
[2] Piper, I. 17, l. 4; S.-St. I. 18, l. 22.
[3] Piper, I. 85, l. 20; S.-St. I. 95, l. 20.
[4] Piper, I. 17, l. 29; S.-St. I. 19, l. 21.
[5] Piper, I. 17, l. 21; S.-St. I. 19, l. 12.

he translated, was no slave to them. He produced a real translation, altering, where necessary, the cases of any Latin words he employed in order to make them accord with the rules of German syntax. Yet his German continually bears witness to the influence of the Latin language; German was not yet a learned language and had to be adapted if it was to become a vehicle of learning. It was natural for a learned man to express himself in Latin and, if he wrote German, to carry over into it some features of Latin syntax. Notker was doing no more than many learned men have done in the history of Western culture: he was trying to make his mother tongue adequate to the requirements of a kind of discourse normally confined to Latin. Whether a particular alien construction becomes naturalized and ceases to appear 'unidiomatic' depends to a large extent on continuity of literary tradition. Notker's German seems unidiomatic in many respects because the foundations he laid were not built upon: it was many centuries before German became a medium of learned discourse again, and when it did Notker was forgotten.

It is important to understand that Notker did not intend his translations to be substitutes for the original works. Thus, both the Latin and the German words in his versions have their place. Philosophical terms are often explained and delimited by German words, none of which are exact equivalents: for instance, in the *Categories* he renders 'positio' by *gelégeni, státa, sképfeda, légerstát,* and *sézzi,* but none of these replaces it as the authoritative technical term. Because the key words remain in Latin, Notker is not obliged to build up a consistent system of terms in German, though he shows skill in constructing small sub-systems which answer to groups of related Latin terms: thus 'opponi'–'oppositus'–'oppositio' are reflected by *gágenstéllet uuérden–gágenstált– gágenstélle, gágenstélleda,* and 'habere'–'habitus', 'habitudo'–'habilis' by *hában–hába–hábemáhtíg.*

Sometimes, we can observe Notker at work, improving on his first renderings of Latin terms. Unlike a modern translator he does not later eliminate these from his work, since they remain legitimate attempts to capture the sense. Translation is for Notker a process, just as his teaching, for which it served as a means, was a process. He experimented with the German language and allowed his pupils to witness his experiments; like all experienced linguists, he realized that a clearer understanding might be arrived at by a series of attempts to capture the sense of a foreign word than by a single accurate but unexplained rendering.[1]

Notker's use of accents, to which he refers in his letter to Hugo,[2] is remarkably regular in some of the manuscripts, especially that of the *Consolation*.[3] The acute accent is placed on short stressed vowels and on the first element in each of the digraphs *éi*, *óu*, and *íu*. (The spelling *iu* now represents the high front rounded vowel [y:], and is used both for the continuant of the older diphthong *iu* and for the Umlaut of *ū*, thus *líute* < *liuti* and *híute* < *hūti*.) The circumflex accent is placed on long vowels which are represented by a single letter, and also on the first element of the digraphs *íe*, *ío*, *úo*. The use of the circumflex is not confined to stressed syllables.

In unaccented syllables, except in uncovered final position, all the earlier short vowels merge in one, usually written *e*, but sometimes *i*. In uncovered final position the old short vowels *e*, *a*, and *o* remain, but *i* and *u* merge with *e* and *o* respectively. Unaccented long vowels retain their original quality and in many instances their original length, marked by a circumflex; sometimes they carry no accent, but the phonetic significance of this is difficult to determine.[4]

Most characteristic of Notker's orthography is the so-called 'law of initial consonants' ('Notkers Anlautgesetz'). According to this, an initial *b*, *d*, or *g* (from Gmc. *b*, *þ*, or *g*) appears only in words that are not preceded by a pause,[5] and that follow a word

---

[1] On Notker as a translator, see E. Luginbühl, *Studien zu Notkers Übersetzungskunst* (Zürich, 1933), and the review by Starck, *AfdA* 53 (1934) 143–5. A study of his philosophical vocabulary is provided by J. Jaehrling, *Die philosophische Terminologie Notkers des Deutschen in seiner Übersetzung der Aristotelischen 'Kategorien'* (Phil. Stud. u. Qu. 47, Berlin, 1969). For a detailed discussion of one conceptual complex see K. Ostberg, 'Interpretations and Translations of *animal/animans* in the Writings of Notker Labeo', *PBB* (Tübingen) 81 (1959) 16–42.

[2] 'Oportet autem scire quia uerba theutonica sine accentu scribenda non sunt preter articulos. Ipsi soli sine accentu pronuntiantur acuto et circumflexo' (Piper, 1. 861).

[3] It was this striking regularity that enabled Sehrt and Starck, with very few alterations, to normalize the spelling in their edition.

[4] The principal features of Notker's vocalism are set out in Braune, *Ahd. Gramm.* §§ 8 A. 2, 42, 59 A. 1.

[5] By a 'pause' is meant the silence between the end of one speech-group and the onset of the next. All sentences are presumed to be preceded by a pause, as are many shorter units, though there is some discrepancy between the incidence of punctuation and the operation of the substitutions described above.

ending in a vowel, a nasal, or a liquid. If a pause or a word ending in any other sound precedes, the initial *b*, *d*, or *g* is replaced by *p*, *t*, or *k*. There seems to have been a similar, though far less regular, replacement of *u* by *f* (< Gmc. *f*) under the same conditions. It should be noted that, while one may speak of a conditioned alternation of *b*- and *p*- or *g*- and *k*-, one cannot extend such a description of the facts to the incidence of *d*- and *t*-, since the former spelling is normally used only for the continuant of Gmc. *þ*, Gmc. *d*- being normally represented by *t*- except after a word ending in -*n*, when it appears as *d*-. There is thus only a partial merger of Gmc. *t*- and *d*- in Notker's spelling. There is no merger of Gmc. *k*- and Gmc. *g*-, since the former appears regularly as *ch*-, and the latter, as already stated, either as *g*- or as *k*-. Nor is there a complete merger of Gmc. *f*- and Gmc. *p*-, since the latter is regularly represented by *f*-, and only the former sometimes appears as *u*-.[1]

Most of the orthographical features just described may be observed in the following passage:[2]

Uuér ne bechénnet tíz kechôse . únde dáz ze dísemo gechôse háftêt . ál tréfen ze oratoris officio? Únde uuér neuuéiz rhetorice facundie . díz uuésen éigen spíl? Uués sínt únmûozîg iudices . únde iurisconsulti . âne súsliches strítodes? Tíz genus cause . héizet forense. In foro skéllent tîe sô getânen controuersie. Án dísen íst suasio . únde dissuasio. Mít uuíu mág man in dínge suadere . álde dissuadere . âne mít iusto . únde iniusto? Mít uuív máhti sî ín nû stíllen . âne mít tíu dáz sî in dûot pechénnen . dáz er án fórtunam nehéin réht nehábe? Sô man dáz pegínnet óugen . uuîo réht . únde uuîo únréht táz sî . dáz éinêr den ánderen ána fórderôt . sô spûot tero suasionis . únde dero dissuasionis. Únde uuánda sî ímo nû hábet úbernómen sîn sêr . mít téro satisfactione . pedíu stépfet si nû ába dero suasione ze dero disputatione . dáz si ímo dâr míte fólle héile sîn mûot. Nû fernémên dáz uuóla . dáz man in sprácho dâr man ín dero deliberatione sízzet . úbe dáz únde dáz zetûonne sî . álde zelâzenne . mít utili . únde mít inutili . suasionem tûon sól únde dissuasionem.

Other details of Notker's language may be found in the standard handbooks. The phonetic realities that lay behind his orthography are keenly debated by historical linguists, dialect-geographers,

---

[1] For an account of the 'Anlautgesetz' see Braune, *Ahd. Gr.*, § 103. For a discussion of its phonetic and phonological implications, see H. Penzl, 'Zur Erklärung von Notkers Anlautsgesetz', *ZfdA* 86 (1955) 196–210.

[2] Piper, I. 99; S.-St. I. 109f.

phoneticians, and phonologists, but the solutions of the problems it presents have no bearing on the dating and localizing of the texts and cannot properly be discussed here.

The special significance of the teaching and writing of Notker was that he brought to the notice of the average scholar the Latin authors and the Latin translations of Aristotle which, though known to the exceptionally gifted, were not generally studied at first hand. The purpose of his labours and his own attitude of mind can be seen in the letter to Hugo, who had evidently urged him to devote himself to the study of the Arts. Notker replies that, although he would gladly do so, he is obliged to read the books of the Church in his school. These are essential, whereas the Arts are merely desirable as means (*instrumenta*) towards the understanding of the former.[1] Notker, therefore, was not concerned with the beauties of literature, but with the Latin philosophers such as Cicero, of whose *Topica* he made extensive use, and with the Logic and Ethics of Aristotle. He would have liked, as some thoughtful clergy would like today, to study at first hand and in detail the sources of the ethic and theology he taught, instead of limiting himself mainly to the conclusions. His attitude to the poets will not have differed much from the attitude of Philosophy to the muses who are keeping Boethius company when she enters and whom she calls tragical harlots and sirens. It is not the poets, but the didactic works, which Notker offers to send to the Bishop (if the latter will pay for the copying). He expects him to be taken aback at the unusual nature of his books, but he hopes that after reflection he will think better of them. It is not the subject matter, but the presentation which is novel, and Notker justifies his innovation by pointing out that 'cito capiuntur per patriam linguam quae uix aut non integre capienda forent in lingua non propria'.[2] It is therefore misleading, if not entirely untrue, to describe Notker as 'a humanist before his time'. There was no thought in his mind of creating a national German literature by imitating an established classical model. Otfrid's aspirations were to a certain extent those of a ninth-century Klopstock, but Notker had not the slightest desire to be a tenth-century Gottsched, Lessing, or Wieland.

[1] 'Artibus autem illis quibus me onustare uultis ego renunciaui neque fas mihi est aliter quam sicut instrumentis frui. Sunt ecclesiastici libri, et precipue quidem in scolis legendi, quos impossibile est sine illis prelibatis ad intellectum integrum duci' (Piper, 1. 860).

[2] Piper, 1. 861.

Though the reforms of Cluny prevented further development on the lines laid down by Notker, his work was not doomed to disappear altogether: at least his Psalter survived, adapted to suit the reformers' taste. Psalms 1 to 50 and 101 to 150 have been preserved in a manuscript now in Vienna which was probably produced at Wessobrunn in the eleventh century.[1] In this revised version the verses of the Psalms are no longer split into sentences, and the Latin words of the commentary have been translated. Often other words have been substituted in the text for those originally used by Notker. Notker's original text is preserved in a St. Gall manuscript of the twelfth century. In this manuscript a large number of the Latin words of Psalms 1 to 108 and a few others have been furnished with interlinear glosses attributed to Ekkehard IV. Some of the words used in the Vienna manuscript for the Latin technical terms of the commentary correspond to those of the glosses, but it is not certain that the new text was prepared from a glossed manuscript. The dialect of the Wessobrunn text is Bavarian. There is also an adaptation of Notker's text made in the fourteenth century.

A number of sermons of various types, all probably composed in Wessobrunn in the first half of the eleventh century, appear to be dispersed elements of a collection once united in the Vienna manuscript of Notker's Psalter. A St. Gall manuscript of the eleventh century contains a document which is commonly supposed to be a school exercise. This consists of a number of Latin words and sentences with German translations.

Notker had only one successor with a comparable mastery of the German language. This was the anonymous composer of the **Bamberg Creed and Confession,** who is thought to be also the author of the uniquely powerful description of Heaven and Hell which follows it in the manuscript.[2] The manuscript in which these two pieces are entered contains nothing else, though it was later

---

[1] Piper, III.

[2] *MSD* xxx and xci; *Kl. ahd. Sprdmr.* xxviii and xxix; Piper, *Die Schriften Notkers und seiner Schule* I. xi–xxi. The Wessobrunn version of the Creed and Confession are to be found in *MSD* xc, Piper, op. cit., 389–96, and in *Kl. ahd. Sprdmr.* xxviii in parallel with the Bamberg version. *Himmel und Hölle* is also printed in Fr. Wilhelm, *Denkmäler deutscher Prosa des 11. und 12. Jahrhunderts.* The texts are printed virtually diplomatically by Piper and Wilhelm. Since it was once thought that *Himmel und Hölle* was composed in unrhymed verse (a belief due to the extremely rhythmic character of the language but now discarded), it is printed as such in *MSD.*

bound together with three others of various dates. It once belonged to the Dominican monastery founded at Bamberg in 1310 and is now in Munich. There is an abridged and modified version of the Creed and Confession in the Wessobrunn manuscript which also contains the revision of Notker's Psalter. We do not know whether **Himmel und Hölle** was also included in this manuscript, since a gap occurs before the end of the Confession.

The Creed and Confession are remarkable not only for their unusual length, but also for the skilful exploitation of the resources of German word-formation in naming the many varieties of sin listed. These include a number of secular pursuits, such as *iagides lussami* ('the delights of hunting'), which were forbidden to the clergy and are subsumed under the concept of *werltminna*.[1] (The Wessobrunn version seems to have been made for women, since feminine pronouns are substituted for masculine forms.)

The description of Heaven which makes up the first part of *Himmel und Hölle* is based on the account of the New Jerusalem in Rev. 21. It also draws upon commentaries, none of which can be identified with certainty.[2] It is made up of a number of short sentences containing much variation and many noun-phrases in apposition to each other. It ends with the words *So ist taz himelriche eînis teîlis getan*. The description of Hell draws upon a number of biblical passages and has affinities with one of the sermons of Honorius Augustodunensis, though the connection with Honorius is not clear. It differs from the first part in being made up largely of one enormous sentence consisting of an accumulation of noun-phrases which conform to a small number of syntactic patterns. Despite the syntactical disparity between the two parts, the second closes with the words *So ist taz hellerîche eînis teîlis getan*. The author operates with a number of rhetorical devices such as paradox (Hell is not only *daz serige elilentduom*, but *diu leîtliche hêima*), and he also takes up and modifies concepts already used in the Confession. Nevertheless, the piece has a strangely improvised character, which is especially striking in the second part. In both pieces there is a large number of otherwise unattested words, some of which were no doubt coined by the author.

---

[1] One is reminded of the aged Notker's revulsion at his youthful hunting exploit.

[2] See I. Schröbler, 'Zu "Himmel und Hölle"', *Festschrift Georg Baesecke* (Halle, 1941), pp. 138–52.

The two pieces were entered in the manuscript by the same twelfth-century scribe, but, although they are thought, on linguistic grounds, to be the work of one author, there are orthographical differences suggesting that they may have been copied from different manuscripts. If so, it is difficult to understand how they came to be reunited. Perhaps the differences may be explained by a change of scribes in one and the same source. The language is usually thought to be East Franconian, but at any rate the Creed contains hints of Alemannic provenance. It seems likely that the author knew Notker's version of the Psalter, but this in itself would prove nothing about the place of composition.

We know nothing about the circumstances in which the Creed and Confession were used. It has been suggested[1] that the Confession may represent a form of 'Offene Schuld' which the congregation recited after the bishop or the priest on Maundy Thursday. *Himmel und Hölle* is an even greater mystery. It may be a fragment (it is followed by a blank space in the manuscript) or it may be complete. It may be a sermon or a devotional piece. We do not know what connection it was intended to have with the Creed and Confession: the linguistic links indicate nothing more than common authorship.

The ascetic movement which began at Cluny reached St. Gall in 1030, eight years after the death of Notker. The change of outlook which had taken place throughout the country by the middle of the century may be observed in the autobiography and in the other works of the Bavarian Otloh of St. Emmeram.[2] Otloh lived from about 1010 to 1070. He was born at Freising, went to school at Tegernsee, lived at St. Emmeram, Fulda, Amorbach, and finally at St. Emmeram. He was reluctant at first to become a monk, preferring to be a secular priest, but finally took the vows as a result of a vision. Owing to his great learning he was placed in charge of the school.

In his poem *De doctrina spirituali*, capitulum xi, 'De libris gentilium et de studio sacrae lectionis',[3] he issues a warning against worldly study:

---

[1] See H. Pörnbacher, 'Bamberger Glaube und Beichte und die kirchliche Bußlehre im 11. Jahrhundert', *Festschrift für Max Spindler zum 75. Geburtstag* (Munich, 1969), pp. 99–114.

[2] *P.L.* 156. See Manitius, *Geschichte der lateinischen Literatur des Mittelalters* (Munich, 1923) II. 83–103. G. R. Coffman, *Modern Philology* 22 (1924–5) 264–71.   [3] Ed. cit., col. 270.

Libros devita qui dant carnalia scita,
Ut sentire queas librorum dicta sacrorum.

Though some pretend that the study of authors like Horace, Terence, and Juvenal aids piety, such books are really Satanic influences, as he knows from his own experience:

Haec ita nonnulli perverso more fatentur.
Ast equidem dico, cognoscens experimento,
Hostic ab antiqui stimulis hos exagitari
Qui studio vanam recolentes philosophiam
Avertunt sensum de libris catholicorum.

Otloh left descriptions in Latin of a number of visions. In one of these, he says, he saw the Empress Theophano suffering in Purgatory for having introduced Greek luxury into Francia.[1]

He wrote much on theological matters in beautiful Latin prose and in good Latin verse. His sole contribution to the German language was a general prayer for himself and for all classes of his fellow men.[2]

[1] *Liber visionum*, Visus xvii (ed. cit., col. 372).
[2] German text and three Latin versions, ed. cit., coll. 427–30. The manuscript is Clm. 14490. *MSD* lxxxiii; *Kl. ahd. Spdmr.* xxxv; *Ahd. Lb.* xxvi.

Appendix on Old Saxon and Old High German Metre

GENERAL

THE poetry of the Old High German period is composed in two different forms of verse. The constitutive element in the one is alliteration and in the other, terminal rhyme. (The common German designations are 'Stabreim' and 'Endreim'; in English we may conveniently use the term 'rhyme' for the latter.) It is generally thought that alliterative verse was a heritage from Germanic times, while rhyming verse was an import from the Latin culture that came with Christianity, but this is not proven. The only Germanic cultures which can be shown to have a flourishing tradition of alliterative verse are those of England and the Scandinavian countries, especially Iceland; it is possible to imagine that the Old Saxon biblical epics, *Heliand* and *Genesis*, are imitations of their Old English counterparts, the obvious metrical differences being due to divergences in the structure of the two languages; and the alliterative remains in Old High German, the *Wessobrunner Gebet* (which some have believed to derive from an English poem), the *Hildebrandslied*, and the *Muspilli*, have been thought by some scholars to exhibit such a corrupt state of alliterative technique as even to raise doubts about the existence of a native tradition. In the following pages, however, we shall assume that there was a native tradition of alliterative poetry among the Saxons, Franks, and Bavarians, and we shall use the term 'Germanic' to refer to it.

The principal work of the period composed in rhyming verse is Otfrid's *Evangelienbuch*. There are also shorter poems, the chief of which are the *Ludwigslied, Christus und die Samariterin, Psalm* 138, and the *Georgslied*. Since the verse form used in all these is roughly identical with that used by Otfrid, we sometimes refer to it as 'Otfridian verse' ('Otfridverse'). Rhyming lines are found too in the *Hildebrandslied* (where they are almost certainly fortuitous), in the *Merseburg Charms* (which offer one certain instance of a rhyming pair together with some regular and some irregular alliterative lines) and in the *Muspilli* (which is composed principally in alliterative lines, some of them apparently irregular, interspersed with hybrid forms and one or two Otfridian lines). Conversely, Otfrid occasionally employs alliterative phrases, though these are ornamental and might well have been imitated from Latin poetry, together with one rhymeless alliterative line which, interestingly, recurs in the *Muspilli*. The sporadic contamination of the two types of verse is usually held to be the product of the transition from Germanic to Latin-based German culture. There are difficulties in the way of this common opinion, the chief of which is that not only the *Merseburg Charms* (generally, though not universally, believed to be pieces of venerable antiquity), but also the idiosyncratic verse cultivated by the Icelandic 'skalds' or court poets during the Viking period, employ a mixture of rhyme and alliteration. Furthermore, most of the Latin verse of Otfrid's period was unrhymed; only in the eleventh century did rhyme become a regular constitutive feature of most Latin poetry. It is worth recording that the common assumption that German rhyming verse had a Latin origin was not held by Jacob Grimm who, with roughly the same evidence before him as modern scholars, believed that alliterative verse and rhyming verse both belonged to the native German tradition, though the former was of greater antiquity.

Whatever may have been their respective sources, the two verse forms are strikingly different except, perhaps, in the length and linguistic structure of the lines, which are divided into two halves. While the alliterative line derived its unity from the distribution of stressed syllables with identical (or in some cases similar) initial sounds over roughly the first three-quarters of its length, the rhyming line is identified by the vocalic agreement of the cadences occurring at the ends of its two halves. While the alliterative line owes its metrical structure to the exploitation of German word stress and sentence stress in a regular pattern and treats word-endings with indifference, rhyming verse places primary importance on these word-endings, without whose agreement the verse would amount to little more than a succession of word groups with approximately equal numbers of syllables and some sort of elementary accentual balance. It is, however, possible to over-emphasize the differences and underestimate the similarities. One can easily scan many Otfridian lines, especially those that Otfrid composed early in his poetic career, in the same way as alliterative lines, though one has to do this without the guidance provided in the latter by the incidence of alliterating (and therefore strongly stressed) syllables. All scholars are aware of this fact, and some have sought to show how Otfrid's verse form may have grown out of the earlier measures and been adapted to rhyming practice. Conversely it is possible to scan many lines in the *Hildebrandslied* according to the accentual pattern presumed to underlie Otfrid's verse. This is a less common pursuit among modern scholars than it was in the last century, since it is now believed that, while Otfrid operated with half-lines of four stresses, the alliterative measure was essentially based on half-lines of two. Andreas Heusler, whose views we shall discuss later, credited the alliterative foot with a secondary stress which was not always realized, yet although he found alternations of primary and secondary stress in Otfrid's verse too, he insisted on an essential difference: Otfrid's verse emulated the smooth, regular, alternating rhythm of medieval Latin writing, while Germanic verse, despite the regularly recurring stresses, was emphatic, operating with feet of varying rhythmic patterns, with long-drawn-out syllables and rests as in music.

A. ALLITERATIVE VERSE

1. *Normal Verses*

The basic unit of alliterative verse[1] is the so-called 'long line' ('Langzeile') here called more simply the 'line'. This contains four principal metrical stresses or 'lifts' ('Hebungen') and several stretches of unstressed or lightly stressed material known as 'dips' ('Senkungen'). Each line falls into two approximately equal parts known as 'short lines' ('Kurzzeilen'), 'half-lines' ('Halbzeilen') or 'verses'. Here we shall use the last of these terms, calling the first verse of the line the *a*-verse and the second the *b*-verse (in German the terms 'Anvers' and 'Abvers' are commonly used). The two verses are separated by a caesura but bound together by alliteration. Identical initial consonants of syllables bearing a lift alliterate except in the combinations *sp-*, *st-*, and *sk-*, which behave as units, alliterating neither with single *s-* nor with each other. Any vowel may alliterate with any other, identical or not. The alliterating sounds were known to medieval Icelandic metricists as *stafir* and are consequently sometimes called 'staves' ('Stäbe'); this term will be used here.

In a normal line the alliteration coincides with the first and third lift or with the first three lifts, never with the fourth. In a minority of lines it may fall on the second and third. Since the third lift always bears a stave, this is known as the 'main stave' (OIcel. *hǫfuðstafr*, 'Hauptstab').

---

[1] The most useful brief account of the subject, with extensive bibliographical references, is given by Klaus von See, *Germanische Verskunst*, Sammlung Metzler (Stuttgart, 1967). Valuable introductions to the subject are given by U. Pretzel and H. Thomas, 'Deutsche Verskunst' in *DPA* III (1st edn.), 2327 ff., (2nd edn.) 2357 ff., and by W. P. Lehmann, *The Development of Germanic Verse Form* (Austin, 1956); Lehmann's work is particularly useful for its treatment of the effect of linguistic changes on versification. The basic work on the subject is still E. Sievers, *Altgermanische Metrik*, Sammlung kurzer Grammatiken germanischer Dialekte. Ergänzungsreihe II (Halle, 1893). Heusler's system, which is discussed below, is set out in his work *Deutsche Versgeschichte mit Einschluß des altenglischen und altnordischen Stabreimverses*, Grundriß 8/1, 2nd edn. (Berlin, 1956), vol. 1. Other works referred to below are: A. J. Bliss, *The Metre of Beowulf* (Oxford, 1958); J. C. Pope, *The Rhythm of Beowulf* (New Haven, 1942, 2nd edn., 1966); P. B. Salmon, 'Stress, Time and Quantity in Early German Narrative Verse' in *TPS*, 1967, 125–53.

If we represent a lift bearing a stave as *a* and a lift without a stave as *x*, we may denote the three varieties of normal line, in descending order of frequency, as *a x a x*, *a a a x*, and *x a a x*. These three varieties may be conveniently illustrated by ll. 42–4 of the *Hildebrandslied*, the lifts being marked by accents and the staves by bold type:

dat ságetun mí   séolídante
wéstar ubar wéntilseo,   dat *in*an wíc furnám:
tót ist **H**íltibrant,   **H**éribrantes súno.

There were strict rules determining which words might carry staves. These rules no doubt derive from the ancient pattern of Germanic sentence-stress, but are sometimes disregarded in the Old Saxon and Old High German poems of the ninth century with which we shall be principally concerned; whether this is due to changes in the stress patterns of the spoken language, to poetic licence or to degenerate technique, we cannnot say. The conventions and some of the deviations from them may be illustrated from the following thirty-one lines from the *Heliand*:

Thō telét that líuduuerod   aftar themu lánde állumu,
2900 tefór fólc mikil,   sidor iro fráho giuuét
an that gebírgi úppan   bárno ríkeost,
uuáldand an is uuílleon.   Thō te thes uuátares stáde
sámnodun thea gesídos Cristes   the he imu habde sélbo gicórane,
sie tuéliui thurh iro tréuua goda: ni uuas im tuého nigién
2905 nebu sie an that gódes thíonost   gérno uuéldin
obar thene séo sidon.   Tho lētun sie suídean strōm
hóh húrnidskip   hlúttron údeon
skédan skír uuater.   Skréd líoht dages,
súnne uuard an sédle;   the séolídandean
2910 náht nébulo biuuarp;   nádidun érlos
fórduuardes an flód;   uuard thiu fíorde tíd
thera náhtes cúman   — nériendo Críst
uuárode thea uuáglīdand —:   thō uuard uuínd míkil,
hóh uueder afhában: hlámodun údeon,
2915 strōm an stámne;   strídiun féridun
thea uuéros uuider uuínde: uuas im uuréd húgi
sébo sórgono ful: sélbon ni uuándun
lágulídandea   an lánd cúmen
thurh thes uuéderes geuuín.   Thō gisahun sie uuáldand Críst
2920 an themu sée úppan   sélbun gángen,
fáran an fádion: ni mahte an thene flód ínnan,
an thene séo síncan,   huand ine is sélbes cráft
hélag anthábde.   Húgi uuard an fórhtun
†thero mánno módsebo: andrēdun that it im máhtig fíund
2925 te gidróge dádi.   Thō sprak im iro dróhtin tó,
hélag hébencuning,   endi sagde im that he iro hérro uuás
mári endi máhtig: 'nū gi módes scúlun

fástes fáhan;   ne sī iu fórht húgi,
gibáriad gi báldlico: ik bium that bárn gódes . . .'

It will be observed that of the thirty-one lines in this passage only four (2901, 2905, 2912, 2920) contain fewer than the maximum number of three staves; such alliterative density is not typical of Germanic verse as a whole. Of the eighty-nine staves in the passage, seventy-one are provided by nominal forms (i.e. nouns, adjectives, numerals, infinitives and participles) and only ten by finite verbs. Of the remaining eight, four are accounted for by the pronoun *self* in its inflected forms, and four by the adverbs *gerno, baldlico* (which are of adjectival origin), *strīdiun* (which is a dative plural of the noun *strīd*), and *forduuardes*. This predominance of nominal over verbal forms is found in the placing of stresses too: of the 124 lifts in the passage, ninety-five fall on nominal forms and only sixteen on verbs; of the remaining thirteen, five are occupied by pronouns and eight by adverbs. It will be observed too that, while only six nominal forms in the whole passage lack a principal metrical stress, there are no fewer than fifteen finite verbs that are unstressed, not only common verbs like *uuas* and *uuard*, but more significant words like *andrēdun*.

This passage, then, illustrates clearly the prominence given in versification to nominal forms. It is a general rule that, if a verse contains two such forms, both bear a lift and either the first or both alliterate (naturally only the first may alliterate in a *b*-verse); any finite verb in the verse is relegated to a dip or a position of secondary stress. This rule is here illustrated by ll. 2903*b*, 2906*b*, 2909*a*, 2910*a*, 2911*b*, 2913*b*, 2916*b*, 2919*b*, 2923*b*, 2924*b*, 2928*b*, 2929*b*. It is disregarded in ll. 2900*a*, 2903*a*, 2908*b*, 2910*b* and 2914*b*.[1]

If three nominal forms occur in a verse, only two can be accommodated under principal lifts. It is then usual for the two which are most closely related syntactically to form a unit and to behave for metrical purposes like a compound noun: this happens in ll. 2904*a*, 2914*a*, and 2917*a*. Such treatment may be accorded also to two nominal forms occurring in the same verse as an alliterating verb, as we see in ll. 2900*a*, 2903*a*, and 2908*b*. Conversely, if a verse contains only one nominal form and no other word which may bear a lift, this nominal form (usually a compound noun) bears both the lifts, thus behaving for the purpose of the verse like two units; an example is found in l. 2909*b*. If such a compound occurs alone in an *a*-verse it may even contain two staves, e.g. *lagulīdandea* 2918*a*.

If a verse contains one nominal form and one finite verb, the former must normally bear a stave and the latter may share in the alliteration, whether it precedes or follows the nominal form; examples are ll. 2899*a*,

[1] See Sievers, op. cit., p. 44, on these lines.

2913*a*, 2923*a*, 2925*a*. In a *b*-verse there can, of course, be only one stave, and this must coincide with the first lift; since the nominal form (which may be an adverb) must bear the stave, the verb may not normally alliterate but it may, if it follows the nominal form, occupy the second lift. Such verses are ll. 2900*b*, 2905*b*, 2915*b*, 2917*b*, 2926*b*, 2927*b*. Deviation from this rule is to be observed in ll. 2910*b* and 2914*b*, where, as in l. 2908*b* discussed above, the verb is accorded special prominence.

In addition to the nominal forms and finite verbs which we have discussed hitherto, there is a third class of words known as 'form-words' or 'proclitics' (comprising pronouns, prepositions, the commoner adverbs, and conjunctions) which normally fall in the dips (like the pronouns in ll. 2903 f.); if necessary they may bear a lift (as, for instance, *uppan* does in l. 2901*a* or *tō* in l. 2925*b*; similarly *mī* in l. 42 of the *Hildebrandslied* cited above), but they seldom alliterate.[1]

We must mention briefly the problems of apparent alliteration between stressed and unstressed syllables and of crossed alliteration. It might be thought that the words *uuider* and *uuas* shared in the alliteration in l. 2916 above; although it is impossible to know whether the poet or his audience found such lines particularly pleasing because the staves were, as it were, echoed in the dips, these echoes have no structural role in the verse, and are almost certainly due to chance. Similarly, we might be tempted to regard l. 2912 as exemplifying an alliterative pattern *a b a b*, with additional alliteration on *cuman* and *Crist*; again, the likelihood is that such crossed alliteration, where it occurs, is fortuitous: the instances of it are sufficiently uncommon and its location so apparently haphazard as to render its significance dubious. This is not to deny the possibility that a line like the following may have generated additional aesthetic pleasure through the gratuitous alliteration on the second and fourth lifts (and that the poet may even have foreseen that pleasure):[2]

hímil endi értha   endi al that sea bihlídan ĕgun (*Hel.*, l. 41)

[1] Exceptions are found occasionally, e.g. 'thícchero thórno   an thému dáge' (*Hel.*, l. 2407); 'éndi gihórien,   that uui it áftar thí' (ibid., l. 2425).

[2] Comparable phenomena in modern verse are non-structural alliteration and non-structural internal rhyme such as are to be observed in the following lines from Poe's poem *The Raven*:

'And the silken, sad, uncertain rustling of each purple curtain
Thrilled me, filled me with fantastic terrors never felt before.'

We know that Poe intended the alliteration and the unexpected rhyme in the second line (that in the first is structural), but Poe's intention is irrelevant, and any beauty lies in the reader's inner ear. All we can know of the Germanic poet's intentions is that he followed certain conventions. Since the use of supererogatory alliteration is not conventional, we cannot know whether it was intended. If, however, it pleases, we are grateful to the poet and tempted to impute to him the intention of seeking to please us by this means.

While the line must be regarded as the basic unit of composition, since the alliteration is realized only within the line, the basic metrical unit is the verse. (The verse bears a similar relation to the line as the English iambic pentameter does to the heroic couplet.)

The analysis of Germanic verse rhythm is controversial, since we do not know how the poetry was performed. It is, however, possible to analyse the linguistic structure of the verses and, on the basis of this analysis, to classify them into various types. In doing this we use our knowledge of the accentual patterns of Germanic words and the observations already mentioned concerning the hierarchy of word classes which determines the distribution of staves. Verse rhythms and speech rhythms are not necessarily identical: as we have seen, for instance, a secondary speech stress may be raised to the status of a principal verse stress, and a principal speech stress may be reduced to that of a secondary verse stress; moreover, there were undoubtedly other and more subtle gradations of stress in actual speech which seem to have been irrelevant to the construction of the verses. We cannot, of course, know whether any compromise was made in recital in order to approximate the verse rhythm to the freer patterns of speech; if, as seems probable, the verse was spoken and not sung, it is likely that a skilled performer would make some such accommodation rather than do unnecessary violence to natural speech rhythms. As will be seen, the linguistic structure of the verses is remarkably flexible, and this flexibility ensures that the rhythmic patterns of speech are not subjected to undue constraints when ordered into a succession of two-stress verses.

The system of classification most generally accepted is that of Eduard Sievers; he discerned five types of verse in Germanic poetry (together with a number of sub-types), and his system is consequently called the 'Fünftypenlehre'.[1] A common criticism of Sievers's analysis is that it avoids, as far as possible, a strictly metrical interpretation of the data, and offers mainly a linguistic description of the verses actually found. This supposed weakness is, in fact, a strength: Sievers endeavoured to avoid mixing observation and interpretation (though, of course, any classification must involve a modicum of interpretation), and he reserved his views on the probable mode of recital until a late stage in his presentation.

Each of Sievers' five types consists of two feet, each foot containing a principal lift. Each verse contains, in addition to the lifts, one or two dips, and it is the disposition of the dips in relation to the lifts that forms the basis of his classification. If the verse is made up of two lifts, each followed by a dip (/ × / ×), it belongs to type A. If the lifts are preceded by the dips (× / × /), the verse belongs to type B. If the lifts both occur in the centre of the verse, and are embraced by the dips (× / / ×), the

---

[1] See Sievers, op. cit., pp. 22 ff.

verse belongs to type C. Since a lift seems to have required for its realization a duration equivalent to that of a long syllable (or, at the end of a verse, a close syllable of indifferent length), it is usually denoted by the complex symbol $\perp$; and since Sievers divided these verses into two (approximately) equal feet, he denoted types A, B, and C respectively as $\perp \times \mid \perp \times$, $\times \perp \mid \times \perp$, and $\times \perp \mid \perp \times$. The two remaining types consisted of unequal feet, one of which contained no dip, while the other had, in addition to the dip, a secondary lift. Those verses which have the basic pattern $\perp \mid \perp \perp \times$ or $\perp \mid \perp \times \perp$ (of which there are several varieties) belong to type D. Those with the basic pattern $\perp \perp \times \mid \perp$ or $\perp \times \perp \mid \perp$ belong to type E. We may illustrate all these types with the help of a few modern English phrases: *hándsome húsbands* (type A); *a hándsome mán* (type B); *a smárt lády* (type C); *smárt schóol-chìldren, smárt lády's-màids* (type D); *íll-fàvoured mén, bádly drèssed mén* (type E).

As has already been mentioned, a lift requires for its realization a duration equivalent to a long syllable. If, therefore, it falls on a short syllable, this must be followed immediately by an unstressed syllable which counts, not towards the dip, but towards the lift. The sequence $\smile \times$ is thus metrically equivalent to $\perp$, and the substitution of the former for the latter is known as 'resolution' ('Auflösung') of the lift. This phenomenon accounts for much of the rhythmic variety in Germanic verse. Again we may use English examples to illustrate the rhythmic possibilities: *clèver accóuntants, hándsome mŏnitors, clèver ecŏnomists* (type A); *a hándsome wŏman, a clèver replý, a gènerous gíver* (type B); *a clèver téacher, a clèver grắduate, a smárt grắduate* (type C); *smárt Lắtin-màsters, clèver Lắtin-màsters, hárd Lắtin exàms, smárt clèaning-wŏmen, clèver clèaning-wŏmen,* and even *clèver cŏvering lètters* (type D); *mŏney-cràzy mén, íll-fàvoured wŏmen, lĕmon-jùice and hŏney* and even *mŏney-grùbbing profèssors* (type E).

Another source of rhythmic variety is the so-called 'free filling' of the dips by any manageable number of unstressed syllables. It might be said that, while the use of resolution gives a tripping quality to the verse, free filling (especially to the degree practised by the poet of the *Heliand*) gives it extra weight. Thus, in English, type A might be represented by *téachers and their púpils*, type B by *for the bĕnefit of the póor*, type C by *for the most pervérse réasons*, type D by *smárt schóol-mìstresses, hárd hístory exàms*, and type E by *Lắtin màsters and their wíves*. Yet further variety is afforded by the addition of hypermetric unstressed syllables or 'anacrusis' ('Auftakt') before the first lift of types A, D, and E, thus: *with the téachers and their púpils* (type A), *to the smárt Lắtin mìstress* (type D), *for the íll-fàvoured wŏmen* (type E).

Yet even resolution, free filling, and anacrusis do not provide all the rhythmic variety found in Germanic verse. Further modifications may be made by the replacement of unstressed syllables in type A by syllables normally bearing a secondary word stress, thus: *whíte màn's búrden, táx-frèe gíft-shòp, pŏsitive páy-tàlks.* The first of these sub-types may have a lightened second foot, e.g. *whíte màn's wŏman.* Such lightening, by the substitution of a short for a long stressed syllable, is also found in types C, D, and E, thus: *to extréme límits* (type C); *lárge lŏoking-glàss, dull dóg-Làtin* (type D); *góod-lŏoking gírls* (type E).

Finally, we must mention Sievers' 'extended types', in which extra dips are introduced between syllables which bear main or secondary lifts and are contiguous in the basic types or in those 'heavy' varieties mentioned in the last paragraph. Type A may be extended to ⊥ ⊥ × | ⊥ × (e.g. *páy-frèeze propósals*), type D to ⊥ × | ⊥ ⸰ × (*stúpid stóol-pìgeon*), type E to ⊥ × ⊥ × | ⊥ (e.g. *íncome-tàx retúrns*).

These are by no means the only variations which Germanic poets could play on the five basic types, but it should be clear from what has been said that the Germanic poet enjoyed, within the limits set by the two-beat verse and the need for alliteration, as much rhythmic freedom as many of his most modern colleagues. This freedom was exploited to the full by the poet of the *Heliand,* whose use of free filling, anacrusis, and extended types now and then makes it difficult to decide how a particular verse should be classified. It will be seen, however, that in the passage quoted above most of the verses fall clearly into the rhythmic patterns discussed above. We may now illustrate, where possible from this passage, Sievers' five types and some of their varieties.

Type A	gérno uuéldin 2905b	⊥ × | ⊥ ×
	hĕlag anthábde 2923a	⊥ ×² | ⊥ ×
	gibăriad gi báldlico 2929a	× | ⊥ ×² | ⊥ ×²
	fáran an fădion 2921a	⸜× × | ⊥ ×
	the he imu habde sélbo gicórane 2903b	×⁶ | ⊥ ×² | ⸜× ×
	sínlìf sŏkean 2083a	⊥ ⊥ | ⊥ ×
	sălig sínlìf 1024a	⊥ × | ⊥ ⊥
	únrèht ĕnuàld 3747a	⊥ ⊥ | ⊥ ⊥
	gódspèll that gúoda 25a*	⊥ ⊥ × | ⊥ ×
Type B	sidor iro fráho giuuét 2900b	×⁴ ⊥ | ×² ⊥
	endi sagde im that he iro hérro uuás 2926b	×⁹ ⊥ | × ⊥
	nu gi mŏdes scúlun 2927b	×² ⊥ | × ⸜×
	thurh thes uuéderes geuuín 2919a	×² ⸜× | ×² ⊥
	tho te thes uuátares stáde 2902b	×³ ⸜× | × ⸜×
Type C	an thene séo síncan 2922a	×³ ⊥ | ⊥ ×
	te gedróge dădi 2925a	×² ⸜× | ⊥ ×
	nebu sie an that gódes thíonost 2905a	×⁵ ⸜× | ⊥ ×
	uuas im uurĕd húgi	×² ⊥ | ⸜×
Type D	the séolfdàndean 2909b	× | ⊥ | ⊥ ⊥ ×
	lágulfdàndea 2918a	⸜× | ⊥ ⊥ ×

náht nébulo biuuàrp 2910*a*	⊥ | ⌣x ×̲² ⊥
sébo sórgono fùl 2917*a*	⌣x | ⊥ ×̲² ⊥
skédan skír uuàter 2908*a**	⊥ × | ⊥ ⌣ ×
hélag hébencùning 2926*a**	⊥ × | ⌣x ⌣ ×
Type E	nérièndo Críst 2912*b*	⌣x ⊥ × | ⊥
fórduuàrdes an flód 2911*a*	⊥ ⊥ ×̲² | ⊥

(In the notation used here, asterisks indicate extended types; superscript figures give the number of unstressed syllables in dips and anacruses; subscript loops indicate resolution.)

It is interesting to note that the alliteration on the finite verbs (which presupposes a primary lift) imposes the scansion of ll. 2900*a* and 2908*b* as verses of type D with the pattern (×) ⊥ | ⊥ ⌣ ×, although if the verbs were unstressed both verses would belong to the lightened type C. Similarly, the first stave in l. 2899 compels us to scan the verse either as a heavy type A with resolution of the secondary stress in the second dip or as an extended type D with a lightened second foot; if the verb bore no stave, this verse too would belong to the lightened type C with an initial dip of four syllables.

Two verses in the passage present another difficulty: ll. 2903*a* and 2904*a* do not fall obviously into any of the normal types. If the verb of the former fell in the anacrusis, and the postposed adjective in the latter were deleted, both would be acceptable representatives of type A; the former would have an anacrusis of five syllables, and the latter an inner dip of four. As they stand, we might take them to be particularly heavy extended A-types, with secondary lifts on the nominal forms *Cristes* and *gōda*, each embraced by extra dips. On the other hand, we might interpret them as tripodic, crediting the last nominal form in each with a main lift. We will return to the question of these so-called 'Schwellverse' below.

Sievers seems to have imagined that Germanic verse was performed as a kind of heightened prose in which the word-groups, represented by the verses, were of approximately equal length. He rejected the notion that it followed a regular metronomic beat which would have meant giving equal duration, say, to such segments as *hōh* and *hurnidskip* in l. 2907. Andreas Heusler, however, maintained that the verse was 'measured', and that there must have been equal spacing between the main lifts.[1] On the analogy, therefore, of musical time, Heusler proposed a division of the verse into two bars of equal length, each containing, as in 'common time', four beats and having a secondary ictus on the third beat of the bar. Since the bar must begin with a down-beat, all unstressed syllables preceding it, whether anacrusis or initial dip, were for Heusler hypermetrical. A consequence of Heusler's assumption of isochronicity was that dissyllabic feet which Sievers had noted as ⊥ ×

[1] See Heusler, op. cit., *passim*.

were now interpreted as the metrical equivalents of two minims, or a minim and a crotchet followed by a rest, and Sievers' monosyllabic feet became equivalent to a semibreve (though Heusler envisaged the possibility of a half-bar rest in such cases). For the heavier feet Heusler employed units of shorter duration, equivalent to quavers or even semi-quavers. Least satisfactory perhaps is his interpretation of verses of type C; here the two main lifts were adjacent, and so, in order to achieve equal spacing, Heusler had to operate generously with rests.

We may now attempt to scan two lines of the passage (ll. 2909–10) according to Heusler's principles:

sunne uuard an sedle;   the seolīdandean | ˮx̌ × x̌ ¹× | ⁻ x̌ : × | ⌣ˮ |⊥ x̌ ×

naht nebulo biuuarp;   nādidun erlos | ⁻ ₍ₐₐ₎ | ℓ⌣⌣¹⌣ x̌ ₍ₐ₎| ⁻ x̌ × | ⊥ x̌

(where × is metrically equivalent to a crotchet, ⌣ to a quaver, − to a minim, ⌐⌐ to a semibreve, and ₍ₐ₎ to a crotchet rest; and where ' denotes a principal lift without a stave, ˮ a principal lift with a stave, ` a secondary lift, ¹ a division between speech-groups, which are the spoken equivalents of musical phrases and: the verse-boundary). Taking the whole line as a unit and presuming synapheia between the two verses, Heusler was often able to accommodate the anacrusis of the *b*-verse in the latter part of the second bar of the *a*-verse, as we have done here; sometimes it might even occupy the secondary lift on the third beat of that bar.

In one respect Heusler's scansion represents a welcome advance on Sievers': the secondary stress is no longer confined to the second parts of compounds and to heavy suffixes, but can be accredited to the more significant elements, notably finite verbs, which occurred among suc-cessions of what were for Sievers unstressed syllables. In order, how-ever, to be consistent, Heusler has to presume secondary stresses on many linguistically unstressed syllables in dissyllabic feet. (Since this is frequently done in order to account for the shorter lines in Otfrid's verse, this is not necessarily wrong, though it does open the way to the interpretation of alliterative verses as four-beat units, an interpretation which Sievers, with the approval of most modern scholars, had decisively rejected.)

In general, scholars are now inclined to reject Heusler's views con-cerning the equal spacing of the main lifts as doing violence to the verse. Pretzel, for instance, believes that it owes its effect largely to the variable spacing of an invariably recurring pair of lifts, now widely separated, now close together, so that the very irregularity of the rhythm, which Heusler with his complicated notation sought to regularize, is to be regarded as an essential feature of the poetry.[1]

One problem which neither Sievers nor Heusler solve satisfactorily is

[1] Op. cit. (1st edn.), 2360 f. (2nd edn.), 2390 f.

the metrical interpretation of the long strings of supposedly unstressed syllables (anacruses or initial dips) which occur in Old Saxon and Old High German poetry. While Heusler was able to accommodate those of modest proportions into second bar of the *a*-verse when they preceded the third lift of the line,[1] he could do little with those containing six or more syllables. Thus, while l. 2919 in the passage quoted above might be interpreted as follows

thurh thes | uuéderès ge- | uuín: thō gisàhun sie | uuáldànd | Kríst,

it is less easy to know what to do with lines like the following (*Heliand*, ll. 4702–3):

> Thuo im eft mid is uuordon gibōd   uualdand selbo,
> hēr hebancuning,   that sia im ni lietin iro hugi tuíflian.

Heusler would, no doubt, have scanned l. 4703*b* with eight hypermetric syllables and half a bar's rest after *hugi*. He believed that such strings of pretonic syllables stood outside the metre (though he continually thought in musical terms, he failed to adduce the analogy of grace-notes which compel a pause before the down-beat), and recommended a gentle *legato* reading leading up to the resumption of strict tempo on the third lift.[2] With his recommended *legato* we may compare Sievers' suggestion of a *staccato* recital of these strings![3] It is interesting to note that Sievers too felt the need for a pause in recital though not, like Heusler, in order to space out the lifts, but in order to balance the long initial dip: Sievers' pause, therefore, came at the end of the verse. Salmon, on the other hand, has recently suggested that we might invoke Heusler's secondary stresses in interpreting ll. 4702*a* and 4703*b*, placing both of them before the first main stress, namely on *thuo, eft, that*, and *liet-*.[4] (This would, in fact, provide a practical use for Sievers' theoretical type F, in which both dips precede the first of two lifts, though only the Heuslerian presumption of a secondary stress in each dip makes this type realizable.) If we adopt this attractive suggestion, we may be able to make greater metrical sense of ll. 2900*b*, 2903*b*, 2905*a*, 2919*b*, 2921*b*, 2924*b*, 2925*b*, 2926*b* in the passage quoted than with the more traditional scansion.

2. *Verses of Abnormal Length*

Among the verses that Sievers regarded as normal and credited with two main lifts, some contain only one nominal form which appears so late in the verse that we are bound to seek the first lift among the words preceding it. If we consider the following lines—'that gī ne uuilleat ōðrun   erlun alātan' (*Heliand*, l. 1621); 'tho bigan is thero erlo   ēn

[1] See op. cit., § 215.   [2] See Heusler, op. cit., §§ 216–18.
[3] See Sievers, op. cit., pp. 203 ff.
[4] See Salmon, op. cit., *passim*, but esp. pp. 147–9.

frāgoian' (ibid., l. 2417) —we find it somewhat embarrassing to determine the place of the first lift. Sievers located it on the first word of l. 1621, which is a conjunction; others might favour the verb. In the second example one might imagine that the verb bore the first lift, though the fact that the alliteration is vocalic might lead us to suppose that, exceptionally, the pronoun *is* is stressed. It has been suggested recently by Bliss[1] that comparable verses in Old English in fact contain only one lift and are to be designated as 'light verses', in contradistinction to 'normal verses' (in a more restricted sense than that intended by Sievers), which contain two words both capable of stress and actually stressed. Those containing three such words, one of which is subordinated for metrical purposes, and has its stress reduced to the rank of a secondary lift (e.g. ll. 2908a and 2914a in the passage quoted above), count for Bliss as 'heavy verses'. Now, all these types—light, normal, and heavy—are regarded by Sievers as 'normal', and indeed they make up the vast bulk of the Germanic corpus. However, there is in addition a small number of verses in Old English and Old Saxon, possibly also in Old High German, which contain three words capable of bearing lifts, and can only with difficulty (i.e. by presuming excessive extensions of the basic types) be scanned dipodically.[2] Two such were suspected in the passage quoted. Let us now consider the following passage from the *Heliand*:

<blockquote>

          The cuning is gifōdit,
giboran bald endi strang: uuī gisāhun is bōcan skīnan
600 hēdro fon himiles tunglun,   sō ic uuēt that it hēlag drohtin
marcoda mahtig selbo.   Uui gisāhun morgno gihuilikes
blīcan thana berhton sterron,   endi uuī gengun aftar them bocna
                      herod
uuegas endi uualdas huuīlon.   That uuāri ūs allaro uuilleono
                      mēsta
that uui ina selbon gisehan mōstin,   uuissin huār uuī ina sōkeạn
                      scoldin
605 thana cuning an thesumu kēsurdōma.   Saga us, undar huilicumu
                    hē sī thesaro cunneo afōdit.'
Thō uuard Herodesa   innan briostun
harm uuid herta: bigan im is hugi uuallan,
sebo mid sorgun . . .
</blockquote>

It is noteworthy, first of all, that in l. 606a the narrative resumes, after the words of the Wise Men, with a 'light verse' (the alliteration being on *Herodesa*, with a silent *H*-, and *innan*) which contrasts markedly with

---

[1] See Bliss, op. cit., pp. 6–23 and 61–75. Among the 'light verses' Bliss also reckoned those which have only one 'stressed element', e.g. ll. 2909b and 2918a in the passage quoted on p. 305.

[2] On such verses see Sievers, op. cit., pp. 135–44, 162–4; Heusler, op. cit., §§ 239–48; Bliss, pp. 88–97; von See, op. cit., pp. 67–71.

lengthy forms preceding it. Of the verses quoted, all the *b*-verses fall easily into the normal patterns, though the quantity of unstressed material before the main stave is striking, rising in l. 605*b* to no fewer than fourteen syllables (or thirteen if we take the Cotton text, with its short form *huilicon* in lieu of *huilicumu*). The first *a*-verse can be scanned as an example of type D although, as Sievers remarks,[1] the metrical subordination of a co-ordinate nominal form (*strang*) is rare. However, the next six *a*-verses seem at first sight to have three lifts apiece and the alliterative pattern *a a x*. In order to make the responding *b*-verses metrically equivalent, we should have to presume a lift on each of the verbs (contrary to the normal rules) and an alliterative pattern *x a x*— this in spite of the similarity of structure between l. 599*b* and l. 601*b* (which might be a reason for regarding l. 599*a* as comparable with the next six *a*-verses).

Verses of such abnormal length are called 'Schwellverse' or 'hypermetric verses'. The analysis just given is that of Sievers and his followers. Its chief weakness is that it disregards the hierarchy of word classes which can be seen to be valid elsewhere. Heusler and his followers prefer to regard such verses as extensions of the normal types, in which the staveless stressed elements (here *tunglun, selbo, sterron, huuilon, mōstin, -dōma*) are reduced in status to secondary metrical stresses.

Although it is true that the responding *b*-verse usually has its stave late enough to enable us, if we wish, to locate the first lift in the syllables preceding it, there are some in which the stave appears early, e.g. *Heliand*, ll.3066–7:

sō **d**iapo bi **d**rohtin thīnen.   **D**iurlico scalt thu thes lōn antfāhen,
hlūttro habas thu an thīnan **h**erron gilōbon,   **h**ugiskefti sind thīne
stēne gelīca

and which are not markedly lighter—except in having only one stave— than their partners. (Here Heusler would interpret the syllables *-fā-* and *-lī-* as bearing the secondary stress.) Indeed, the *b*-verse is occasionally weightier than its partner, as in the lines which follow the last (*Heliand*, ll. 3068–9):

sō **f**ast bist thū sō **f**elis the hardo,   hēten sculun thī **f**iriho barn
sancte Peter: obar themu stēne scal man mīnen **s**eli uuirkean.

Apart from the alliterative status of *hardo* and *hēten* here (cf. the staves in the preceding line), how can the noun *stēne* possibly be unstressed? Yet, if l. 3069 is to be scanned as a two-beat verse, this noun must go in the anacrusis (unless the tradition is corrupt or the poet was nodding— making *st-* and *s-* alliterate and giving a *b*-verse two staves).

[1] Op. cit., p. 43.

Finally we must consider the possibility of even longer verses than those just described. Consider the following line (*Heliand*, l. 3062):

'Sālig bist thu Sīmon' quad hē, 'sunu *Ionases*;   ni mahtes thū that
                                                      selbo gehuggean.

Disregarding the extra-metrical *quad hē*, Sievers found the *a*-verse here equivalent to a whole line, apparently forming a triad with the *b*-verse.[1] Heusler, less convincingly, took the first three words to be extra-metrical.[2]

Perhaps one should be content to regard Germanic metres as almost infinitely flexible, ranging from Bliss's 'light verses' through his 'normal' and 'heavy' verses to 'hypermetric' verses and perhaps even longer forms. The likelihood is that the poet and the reciter were conscious not so much of discrete verse types as of subtle gradations of metrical weight. The weightier lines in the *Heliand* (most notably the nineteen or twenty describing Mary Magdalene's encounter with the risen Christ, *Heliand*, ll. 5916 ff.) occur in passages of special significance. Perhaps they were recited, as Heusler believed, at a slower tempo but with continued observance of the two-beat measure; or perhaps they were accorded an extra stress, as Sievers believed.[3] Perhaps neither poet nor reciter knew the machinery of their effect, and, as we have just seen and as Sievers admitted, it is often impossible to tell the difference between normal and hypermetric verses. The effect of the lengthier types was no doubt at times a weightier and more deliberate style. Bearing in mind the fact that all our notions of Germanic verse rhythm derive from our knowledge of Germanic speech rhythm (reflected both in historical phonology and in the accentual patterns of the modern languages), we shall get the greatest aesthetic pleasure from the poetry if we imagine it performed in such a way as to do the least possible violence to the accentual patterns of natural speech.

3. *The Structure of the Line*

We have up to now discussed the alliteration which binds the verses together in lines, and the rhythmic patterns encountered in the verses. It must not be forgotten, however, that the line too has a rhythmic shape

---

[1] Op. cit., p. 164.   [2] Op. cit., § 219.

[3] Pope knew that an extra foot might have a retarding effect, when he described the alexandrine

        'That, like a wounded snake, drags its slow length along'
—but

        'Not so, when swift Camilla scours the plain,
        Flies o'er th'unbending corn, and skims along the main.'
                                    (*Essay on Criticism*, ll. 357 and 372 f.)

imposed upon it by the alliteration and the verse-types chosen for its two halves. In the first place, the fourth lift has no stave, while the third invariably has. This means that the *b*-verse contains the most powerful and the weakest of the four lifts, and therefore moves from the highest to the lowest point of accentual intensity. (This drop in intensity is, as we shall see, counterpoised by the common selection of a rising rhythm for the *b*-verse.) In Old Saxon the *a*-verses usually have alliteration of the pattern *a x* or *a a*, the former predominating in types B and C, the latter in type A. Since the pattern *x a* is unusual and accounted for mainly by 'light verses', we may regard the first lift in the line as being the second strongest, and the second lift as being the second weakest. We may say, therefore, that *a*-verses with alliteration only on the first lift show a slackening of intensity which is less extreme than that found in *b*-verses, that those with double alliteration maintain an even intensity, and that those with delayed alliteration are characterized by a gathering intensity. Again, it is noteworthy that the even intensity produced by double alliteration is most commonly associated with a falling rhythm (types A and D), while the slackening intensity of the pattern *a x* is more often found in conjunction with the rising rhythm of type B; the pattern *x a*, which generates a rising intensity, is almost exclusively confined to verses of type A.

Another matter is the incidence of the different types in the two halves.[1] Types A, D, and E are much more common in *a*-verses than in *b*-verses, while types B and C occur more frequently in *b*-verses than in *a*-verses. We may regard types A and D as falling (trochaic-dactyllic) measures, and type B as a rising (iambic-anapæstic) measure. Apart from the fact, already noted, that a falling rhythm tends to accompany what we may call a level or a rising stress pattern, and that a rising rhythm more often than not goes together with a falling stress pattern (so that the rhythm, as it were, tends to mitigate the extreme acoustic effects of the staves), it is obvious that the rising rhythm of type B is well suited to the *b*-verses of a work like the *Heliand* in which enjambment is common and few clauses close with the end of the line.

Type C is roughly twice as common in *b*-verses as it is in *a*-verses.[2] This, too, may be satisfactorily explained. Even among the *a*-verses of this type, fewer than a quarter have double alliteration, and this fact is undoubtedly connected with the relative weakness of the second stave in the immediate shadow, so to speak, of the first. A consequence of this

[1] Statistics are given by Sievers, op. cit., pp. 156 and 162.
[2] In the Old English *Beowulf*, type C with unlightened second foot is seven times as frequent in the *b*-verse as in the *a*-verse, and the variety with the lightened second foot is four times as frequent. In the *a*-verse the former type has double alliteration in three-quarters of the cases, while the latter has it only in one quarter. See Bliss, op. cit., pp. 53–4.

relative weakness is the frequent incidence of the lightened second foot (in 40 per cent of all verses of type C). Clearly this type was easier to handle in the *b*-verse, where only one stave was permitted, and where the second lift was inevitably weaker than the first.

A further point of interest is that the longer types, D and E, especially their extended varieties together with extended type A, are far more often encountered in the *a*-verses than in the *b*-verses. If, therefore, we disregard for a moment the lengthy anacruses and initial dips which, at any rate in the *Heliand*, proliferate in the *b*-verses, we may say that the *b*-verses are lighter than their partners in that they contain less phonic material. This naturally enhances the centralizing effect of the main stave. One might even account for the preceding strings of unaccented (and, if Salmon is right, weakly accented) syllables by regarding them as contributory to this effect, leading up to the peak represented by the main stave and balancing, as it were, the weak fourth lift.

We may say, therefore, that the main body of the average *a*-verse (i.e. what falls between the first lift and the end) is heavier in terms of phonic material than that of the *b*-verse, but that the *b*-verse balances this phonic weight by the accentual intensity of its one alliterating lift and its greater syllabic concentration. If we are right in believing the fourth-century Gallehus inscription to be a line of alliterative verse, we shall no doubt be right too in regarding this equipoise of length and accentual intensity between the two half-lines as an ancient feature of Germanic poetry.[1]

A feature of the Old English and Old Saxon book-epics which has a lesser claim to antiquity (and might even have been developed in England and passed on to the Saxons) is the so-called 'Hakenstil' (or 'Bogenstil' as Heusler preferred to call it). This is a mode of composition which employs copious enjambment, and places syntactic breaks preferably not at the end of the line but at the end of the *a*-verse. This style produces a pleasing counterpoint (at least when it is not carried to excess) between the metrical and syntactic structures of the poetry. It may be observed in the passage quoted on pp. 305 f., the last line of which is not, incidentally, the end of a sentence. This device of composition is essentially linked with a feature of poetic diction known as 'epic variation', i.e. the synonymous repetition of the same idea (couched in one word, a pair of words, a phrase, or even a clause) at different points in the sentence. The epic poets carried about in their heads a veritable arsenal of synonyms in order to meet the needs of this variational style. Thus, the clause *telēt that liuduuerod* is varied in the next line by *tefōr folc mikil* (ll. 2899 f.), and *iro frāho* by *barno rīkeost* and *uualdand*. Frequently,

---

[1] This inscription, with suggested scansion, runs: 'ek HléwagàstiR hóltijaR hórna táwiðo.'

the variants link a *b*-verse with the succeeding *a*-verse, as *uuind mikil— hoh uueder* (ll. 2913 f.), *uurēd hugi — sebo sorgono ful* (ll. 2916 f.), *ne sī iu forht hugi — gibāriad gī baldlico* (ll. 2928 f.).

Other devices are used in the service of the 'Hakenstil'. One is the separation of noun and adjective by the end of the line, e.g. *craft | hēlag* (ll. 2922 f.), sometimes as discontinuous pairs, e.g. *mōdes . . . | fastes* (ll. 2927 f.). Another is the separation of noun and dependent genitive, e.g. *thiu fiorde tīd | thera nahtes* (ll. 2912 f.), another the suspension of the subject, e.g. *feridun | thea uueros* (ll. 2915 f.), yet another the transposition of subject and object, e.g. *the seolīdandean | naht nebulo biuuarp* (ll. 2909 f.).

4. *Special Features of the* Hildebrandslied

It is not surprising that there should be differences of poetic technique between the *Heliand*, a book epic on a Christian subject, and the *Hildebrandslied*, a heroic lay based on traditional Germanic material. We will try here to describe the versification and composition of the lay, indicating how it differs from the model we have used hitherto, but without attempting to account historically for the divergences.

The first fact that strikes the reader about the alliteration is that it is far less dense than that of the *Heliand* passage from which most of our earlier illustrations were taken. The pattern *a x a x* predominates markedly over the denser *a a a x*: even if we credit the incomplete lines 10, 28, 38, and 68, each of which has two staves, with the latter pattern, it is still outweighed by the former in a proportion of 1:2. It tends to occur in single lines embraced by others with the lighter pattern, though ll. 5 and 6, 20 and 21 form pairs. The following verses are 'light' according to Bliss's classification, as they contain only one 'stressed element' apiece; 2*a*, 4*a*, 17*b*, 19*a*, 23*a*, 25*a*, 26*b*, 42*b*, 48*a*, 51*a*, 55*a*, 58*b*, 62*a*, 63*a*, 67*a*. We may add 30*a* and 58*a* if *quad Hiltibrant* is extra-metrical. Line 60 is anomalous in having the alliterative pattern *x a x a* and may be corrupt; l. 51, on the other hand, can be justified by Norse parallels, though it is often held to be faulty. There are three certain instances of cross-alliteration (*a b a b*) in ll. 9, 24, and 40, and one is produced in l. 7 by the customary deletion of the phrase *Heribrantes sunu*. Whether these are accidents or an intentional ornament we cannot tell. Yet another instance occurs in l. 6, though this is removed by the customary editorial restoration of initial *h-* to the manuscript reading *ringa*, giving three normal staves to the line.

The placing of the staves deviates at some points from the normal rules. In ll. 5, 33, and 40 the verbs *gurtun*, *want*, and *spenis* take precedence over the nouns *suert*, *arme*, and *wortun*, though the first instance is in a *b*-verse and has parallels in Old Saxon (as we have seen) and in Old English. In l. 44 the second rather than the first of two nominal forms bears the stave; a similar formula appears in *Beowulf* (ll. 1323-4), though with the division at the line-end and with 'correct' alliteration on the adjective.

A striking feature of the alliteration is the use of what has been called 'Hakenreim', i.e. agreement between the initial consonant of the staveless fourth lift of one line and the staves of the next. This is found in ll. 39 and 40, 48 and 49 (though these lines are often reordered), 63 and 64, 64 and 65, 65 and 66 (if we construe the manuscript *chludun* as a spelling for *hludun*), and 67 and 68, possibly also in ll. 14 and 15. The incidence of 'Hakenreim' in such density in the last few lines of the poem has been held to be a deliberate ornament, and Krogmann went so far as to see in it a constitutive feature of the verse. One might be struck too by other alliterative links between the lines—by the fact, for instance, that ll. 8-10 all alliterate on *f*-, or that l. 15*b* contains a non-alliterating word, *ūsere*, which anticipates the staves in l. 16, that ll. 34 and 35 are apparently linked by internally staveless syllables beginning with *t*- and *g*-, that ll. 35 and 36, 44 and 45 form pairs with identical staves, that *gap*, *gibu*, and *geba* (only the last bearing an internal stave) seem to link ll. 34, 35 and 37, and that the isolated half-line *ort widar orte*, l. 38, anticipates the alliteration of its successor.

All the features we have mentioned in the last paragraph may be accidental. It is, however, possible to conceive of them as formal devices for linking lines which are not, like those of the *Heliand*, regularly interlocked by the 'Hakenstil' and copious variation. Whereas in the book-epic we may observe an almost continuous counterpoint between the verse-structure and the syntactic structure, here we might be tempted to view the overlapping semantic content of the syntactically autonomous lines as being carried by ornamental devices which are extraneous to the structure of the lines.

As for the rhythmic patterns found in the verses, all Sievers' types are found, as well as a number of their variants and extensions, e.g. the greatly extended type A in l. 5 (*gǎrutun se iro gǔðhǎmun,   gúrtun sih iro suért ǎna*) with tetrasyllabic filling in the first dip of each verse and resolved secondary stress in the second. A few lines like ll. 15, 31, and 46 appear to be corrupt (though it has been held that the last of these belongs together with its successor, the two forming a longer unit). There are several isolated half-lines, viz. ll. 1, 10, 32, 38, and 68, which may have lost their partners in the course of transmission or may never have had any: a few such are found in the *Heliand*, and they are a regular feature of some Norse strophic forms. In addition to these five, which all have two stresses, l. 28 appears to have three and can be credited with a supposedly missing second foot if one wishes. Two others, ll. 11 and 29, would appear to have two stresses, with *welihhes* and *wāniu* unstressed, though Sievers thought l. 29 might be a 'Schwell-vers' (in which case *wāniu* would have to be stressed), presumably with the *a*-verse missing. Possibly 'Schwellverse' are to be found in ll. 17, 18, 27, 40, and 41. All five present difficulties. Sievers tentatively offered the following scansions:

```
17   dat Híltibrant hǽtti mīn fáter,        ih héittu Hádubránt
18   fórn her ő̄star giwéit,        flő̄h her Ő̄tachres níd
27   hér was eo fólches at énte:        ímo was eo féhta ti léop
40   spénis mih mit dínēm wórtun,        wíli mih dīnu spéru wérpan:
41   pist álsō giáltēt mán,        sō dū ewīn ínwit fúortōs
```

Heusler and most other scholars would be inclined to regard the verbs in l. 17 and the second verb in l. 40 as carrying at most a secondary stress. They would regard the first two words in each verse of l. 18 as preliminary to the first lift, and the pronouns in l. 27 as incapable of principal stress, like the adverb of degree *also* in l. 41. Similarly, the possessives in l. 40 would normally be postposed if they were to carry a principal lift. Sievers found the double alliteration in the *b*-verse of l. 41 offensive (but he was offended too by the same phenomenon in *wēwurt skihit*, l. 49*b*). Now, Sievers objected to this feature no doubt because it was alien to the verse technique best represented in what has survived. Others might see in the supererogatory alliteration of ll. 17, 18, 40, and 41, whether it falls technically under a lift or not (note that Sievers provided *wili* in l. 40 with a lift but did not mark its initial consonant as a stave), a pleasing and perhaps significant feature of the style. There may have been no precise prescriptions about the performance of such lines; at all events we do not know them. In the last resort one has to rely on whatever 'linguistic feeling' one thinks one has and decide what would be the most natural reading. As a reminder of how subjective such a decision is likely to be, let us quote Heusler's scansion of l. 17 ('die trotzig hervorstürzende Zeile mit ihrer eigenwilligen *Füllung*'):

dat | Híltibrant hǽtti mīn | fáter: ih heittu | Hádu- | bránt.

(Here the words *ih heittu* are equivalent to triplet crotchets and the second syllable of *Hadu-* to a dotted minim.) Some might think this scansion grotesque, but at the same time applaud Heusler for having given at least some prominence to the pronoun *ih*. Pronouns are after all significant in dialogue, especially when, as here and in l. 54, there is a switch in the grammatical subject. In l. 54 there is no verb-ending like the one in l. 17 to help signal the change of subject, and although we should be unwilling to credit the pronouns in the line with a main stress, we might be grateful for Salmon's suggestions and allot each a secondary stress, thus:

bréton mit sinu bílliu,   eddo ih imo ti bánin wérdan

Some support for this view might be found in the fact that the poet introduces the possessive *sinu* and places the infinitive before the noun, even though this is the reverse of the order used in the phrase *suertu hauwan* in l. 53*b*, of which l. 54*a* is technically only a variation.

It seems as though, in l. 54 and elsewhere, the poet has marked the ends of sections by particularly weighty lines; other instances are ll. 6, 13, 24, 35, and 57, to which we might add ll. 48 and 62 with their powerful hexameter-like cadences. It is noteworthy too that l. 24*b* exhibits the unusual feature of a heavy internal dip in a verse of type B. In contrast with the *Heliand*, the lay contains a number of lines in which there is an almost perfect balance between the halves, e.g. ll. 5, 12, 13, 18, 27, 40, and 41; indeed, in l. 40 this balance is emphasized in effect (if not in intention) by the cross-alliteration.

There are a few hints of the 'Hakenstil', namely in ll. 7–10, 21–2, 33–4, 37–8, 59–60, and 67–8, but it is not highly developed. Epic variation is used sparingly, notably in ll. 2–6, 53–4, 59–60, 64–7; we might wonder at the significance of its distribution.

Doubtless editors are right to print the work, as far as the text allows, in long lines, but it is questionable whether they are justified in suggesting by the square brackets in l. 7 and by the omission dots in ll. 10, 11, 28, 29, 38, and 68 that the whole poem was originally composed in long lines but corrupted in the transmission. It may well be that this ancient lay, perhaps originating among the Lombards in Italy, was composed in a form which admitted, among the predominant verse pairs, a few isolated half-lines and a few triads of verses linked by alliteration. It may be that the small number of similar 'irregularities' found in the *Heliand* are to be explained likewise as survivals from a freer form of composition which was largely regularized in the book-epic.[1]

B. RHYMING VERSE

The basic unit of Otfrid's verse and of the other Old High German poems which employ rhyme may be said to be the 'long line' made up of two 'short lines' linked by terminal rhyme. Some scholars prefer to take the short line as the basic unit and to speak of rhyming couplets; this enables them to see Otfrid as a precursor of the Middle High German poets who composed in couplets. That Otfrid and the scribes thought in terms of long lines is clearly indicated by the fact that each

---

[1] This is not to suggest that the tradition may not be corrupt at points, but simply to warn against the too easy assumption that everything which deviates from the regularity of *Beowulf* is necessarily a blemish introduced by incompetent scribes or even deriving from an ill-schooled poet.

line of the manuscript accommodates one long line, with only a point dividing the halves. It is further evident that Otfrid composed in pairs of long lines, for the even lines are indented and begin with a small letter, while the odd lines are not indented and begin with a majuscule. Moreover, Otfrid's acrostics and telestichs employ the first and last letters of pairs of long lines. These pairs are sometimes referred to as strophes. It is likely that Otfrid operated also with larger units of four, six, eight, ten, and twelve long lines, for in parts of the text the scribes employed a larger majuscule for the first letter of some lines and at times for the first two letters. The structural implications of this scribal practice, which seems linked with the incidence of the Latin marginalia, have recently been examined by Kleiber.[1] In what follows we shall be concerned only with the structure of the long line and the short line, which we will call respectively the line and the verse.

The rhymes employed by Otfrid may be confined to the final syllables of the verses or they may extend backwards to encompass the last two or three syllables. They may occupy syllables which in speech carry a main stress, or endings which, for the purposes of versification, have to be credited with a metrical stress. Sometimes a stressed syllable may rhyme with an ending. The principal varieties of rhyme may be conveniently illustrated in the following passage (from iv. 11):

```
   So síe tho thar gázun       noh tho zi dísge sazun:
      spíohota ther díufal      selbon Iúdasan thar.
   Dét er sos er ío duat,       uuárf iz hárto in sinaz múat,
      thes náhtes er gisítoti,   er drúhtinan firséliti.
 5 Krist mínnota thie síne      unz in énti themo líbe,
      thi er zi zúhti zi imo nám,   tho er erist brédigon bigan.
   Er uuéssa thaz sin fáter gab   so uuit so hímil umbiuuárb,
      ál imo zi hénti,           zi síneru giuuélti;
   Uuest er sélbo ouh so iz zám,   tház er uns fon góte quam,
10    ioh ávur, sos er uuólta,   zi ímo faran scólta:
   Er stúant yr themo múase     tho zi themo ábande,
      légita sin giuuáti,       er in mandát dati.
   Nám er einan sában thar,     umbigúrta sih in uuár,
      nam áfter thiu ein békin,   goz er uuázar tharin.
15 Fíang tho zi iro fúazin,     gibót sie stíllo sazin,
      thio síno diurun hénti    vvúasgin se unz in énti.
   Druhtin sélbo thaz biuuárb,  mit themo sábane ouh gisuárb;
      thíu sin hoha gúati       lerte sie ótmuati.
   So er érist bigán,          er sar zi Pétruse quam;
20    yrscíuht er filu thráto   súlichero dáto.
   'Ist, drúhtin', quad, 'gilúmplih,   thaz thú nu uuásges mih;
      inti íh bin eigan scálk thin,   thu bist hérero min?
```

---

[1] See pp. 198 f. above.

Thuruh thin héroti   níst mir iz gimúati,
    thaz io fúazi mine   zi thiu thin hánt birine.'
25 Gab er mo ántuuurti   mit mámmenteru mílti,
    thaz uuérk er thar tho sítota,   iz súazo imo giságeta:
'Thaz íh nu méinu mit thiu,   unkund hárto ist iz íu;
    iz uuirdit éthesuuanne   thoh iu zi uuízanne.'
'Firságen ih iz', quad er, 'frám,   ouh ío ni meg iz uuérdan,
30   theiz io zi thíu gigange   theih thíonost thir gihénge.'
'Ni uuasgu ih síe', quad er, 'thír,   ni habest thu déiles uuiht mit mír,
    ouh bi thía meina   giméinida níhéina!'
'Drúhtin', quád er, 'uuásg mih ál,   ob iz súlih uuesan scál,
    hóubit ioh the fúazi;   thin náhuuist ist mir súazi;
35 Thaz iz ío ni uuerde   thaz ih thín githarbe,
    noh, liobo drúhtin min,   theih io gimángolo thin!'

Of the rhymes in these thirty-six lines, eighteen are pure by modern standards, having perfect agreement between the vowels and the following consonants. Nine are masculine (in ll. 3, 9, 13, 17, 22, 27, 31, 33, and 36), and nine are feminine (in ll. 1, 10, 12, 16, 18, 20, 24, 32, and 34). Of the remainder, three (in ll. 14, 21, and 28) are pure but involve matching a stressed syllable with one that in speech does not carry a main stress. Seven (in ll. 4, 15, 23, 25, 26, 30, and 35) are confined to the final syllables of the verses, and one (in l. 11) to the last vowel only. Seven lines have only assonance, i.e. partial rhyme in which the vowels agree but not the consonants; three of these (ll. 6, 7, and 19) have masculine cadences, two (ll. 5 and 8) have feminine cadences, and two (ll. 2 and 29) match syllables with differing levels of speech-stress. There happens to be no example in the passage of the trisyllabic rhyme (e.g. *uuélita* : *zélita*) which Otfrid sometimes employs. It is noteworthy that the feminine cadences, whether they contain dissyllabic rhyme or assonance, or a rhyme or assonance confined to the last syllable, have the form ⊥ × (to be interpreted metrically as ⊥ ◡), never ◡ ×.

As for the rhythm, we have some guide to its nature in the accents entered in the manuscripts. In the passage quoted above, forty-eight verses are furnished with two accents apiece, twenty-one with one, one with three, and one with four. The usual number of accents to the line is three or four, though four lines (24, 28, 35, and 36) have only two, while one (l. 3) has five and one (l. 33) has six. Even if these accents indicate a rise in musical pitch (as some scholars think, supposing that the text was intoned), we must presume that they correspond with metrical stresses, and can therefore make use of them for metrical analysis, whether or not we believe in their alleged musical significance.

Each verse is commonly held to have four metrical lifts. All four are occasionally indicated in the manuscripts, as in l. 33 above. They are separated by dips usually comprising one syllable; Otfrid allows himself less freedom of 'filling' than the alliterative poets. If the cadence is masculine, the metrical pattern of the verse is thus ($\times$) $\acute{\times} \times \acute{\times} \times \times \acute{\times} \times \acute{\times}$ (where $\times$ stands for a long or short syllable). If the cadence is feminine, the last lift falls on the last syllable, which is normally an ending and presumably bore little stress in speech (though it is unlikely, in view of the syntactical information carried by the OHG endings, that they were always completely unstressed); the preceding stressed syllable, which is always long, is then allotted a duration equivalent to that required for a normal lift and a succeeding dip. The metrical pattern for a feminine line is thus ($\times$) $\acute{\times} \times \acute{\times} \times \overset{\_}{\times}$. If the cadence is trisyllabic, the pattern is ($\times$) $\acute{\times} \times \acute{\times} \times \acute{\times} \times \times$. These last two patterns, which involve raising the accentual status of the last syllable are commonly known as 'klingend'.

Although monosyllabic feet appear regularly only in feminine cadences, they can appear in any position in the verse. Thus, in l. 19 above, the words *érist* and *Pétruse* probably had two metrical lifts apiece, and in l. 25 the word *ántuurti* probably had a lift on each of its three syllables. In some of Otfrid's early lines it is particularly difficult to accommodate four metrical stresses in each verse without making it appear to plod. One cannot, for instance, be entirely happy with the following lines, if scanned with four lifts, though they do not read badly if one takes the hint provided by the manuscript accents and gives approximately equal stress and duration to the last word in each of the four verses:

> Uuízzod sínan   ío uuírkendan
> ioh réht mínnonti   ana méindati.

Perhaps at this early stage in his career as a versifier Otfrid still had the two-beat alliterative measure in his head but later succeeded more often in achieving the smoothly alternating four-beat measure at which he is thought to have aimed.[1] Most of the verses in the passage quoted above can be scanned easily as four-beat units, though clearly the scribes regarded two out of three verses as having only two principal stresses.

The presumption of a four-beat measure is popular not just because of its inherent probability, but also because of the common belief that Otfrid's model was the Ambrosian hymn, itself a four-beat measure. Otfrid is thought to have adapted the native verse-form as nearly to this supposed model as the speech-rhythm of German permitted, retaining only as much 'free filling' and as many monosyllabic feet as German accentuation patterns imposed upon him. This belief was not shared by

---

[1] Had Otfrid succeeded in composing in a regular alternating rhythm, with alternating feminine and masculine cadences containing only pure rhymes, he would have anticipated Walther's *Reichston* by over three centuries.

Hörmann,[1] who argued from Otfrid's reference to Juvencus, Arator, and Prudentius that the poet's model was the rhymed 'leonine' hexameter of which these three were exponents (though most of their hexameters were unrhymed). Hörmann, therefore, interpreted Otfrid's lines as six-beat units with internal rhyme. This makes scansion rather more difficult, and the result is remarkably unlike a hexameter. Hörmann's interpretation has found little favour.

As with the alliterative poetry, we must refrain from trying to force everything Otfrid wrote into too rigid a metrical pattern. The two essential features of his verse are the balance between the two halves of each line and the usually pure, though sometimes rudimentary, rhyme which links them. As for the rhythm, the best we can do is to imagine the lines read as naturally as possible. Like Otfrid, we shall find that the natural speech rhythm of German sometimes has to be distorted in order to maintain the metrical balance between the verses and the accentual congruence of the rhyming words.

[1] See above, p. 209.

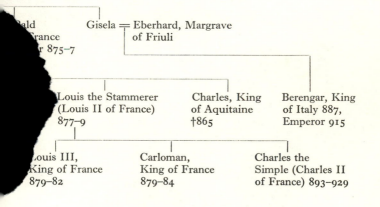

ald	Gisela = Eberhard, Margrave
rance	of Friuli
r 875–7	

Louis the Stammerer (Louis II of France) 877–9

Charles, King of Aquitaine †865

Berengar, King of Italy 887, Emperor 915

Louis III, King of France 879–82

Carloman, King of France 879–84

Charles the Simple (Charles II of France) 893–929

THE DESCENDANTS OF CHARLES MARTEL

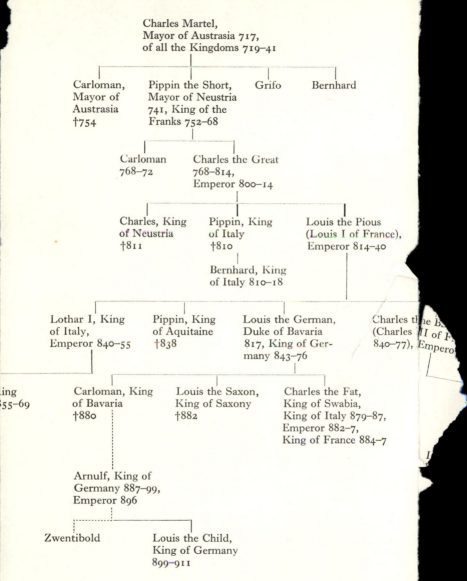

Charles Martel,
Mayor of Austrasia 717,
of all the Kingdoms 719–41

Carloman,
Mayor of
Austrasia
†754

Pippin the Short,
Mayor of Neustria
741, King of the
Franks 752–68

Grifo

Bernhard

Carloman
768–72

Charles the Great
768–814,
Emperor 800–14

Charles, King
of Neustria
†811

Pippin, King
of Italy
†810

Louis the Pious
(Louis I of France),
Emperor 814–40

Bernhard, King
of Italy 810–18

Lothar I, King
of Italy,
Emperor 840–55

Pippin, King
of Aquitaine
†838

Louis the German,
Duke of Bavaria
817, King of Ger-
many 843–76

Charles the B...
(Charles II of F...
840–77), Empero...

...ing
...55–69

Carloman, King
of Bavaria
†880

Louis the Saxon,
King of Saxony
†882

Charles the Fat,
King of Swabia,
King of Italy 879–87,
Emperor 882–7,
King of France 884–7

Arnulf, King of
Germany 887–99,
Emperor 896

Zwentibold

Louis the Child,
King of Germany
899–911

```
        ┌──────────────────┬──────────────────┬──────────────────┬──────────
Guido, ═ Rothilde      Louis II, King    Charles, King     Lothar II, K
Duke of │              of Italy,         of Provence       of Lorraine 8
Spoleto │              Emperor 855–75    855–63
        Guido,                │
        Emperor          Irmengard ═ Boso, King of
        891–4                       │ Provence 879–87
        │                           │
        Lambert,              Louis, King of
        Emperor               Provence 887–905,
        896–9                 Emperor 901
```

THE DESCENDANTS OF HENRY THE FOWLER

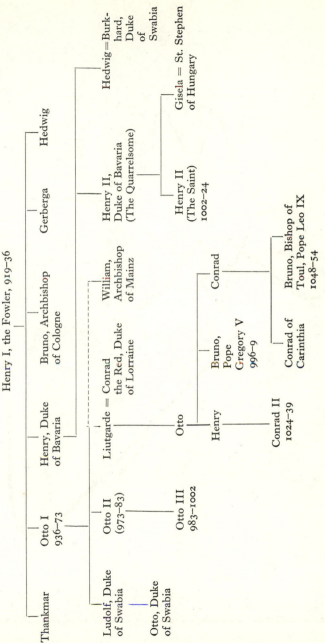

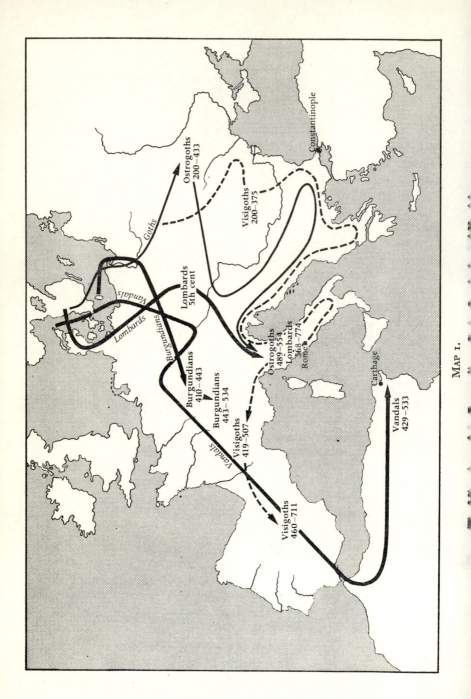

MAP 1.

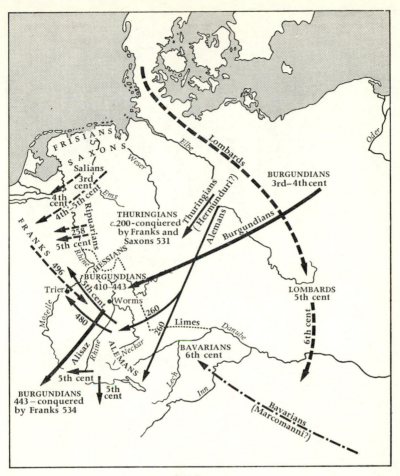

MAP 2.

The Migrations of the Alemans, Bavarians, Burgundians, Franks, Lombards
and Thuringians

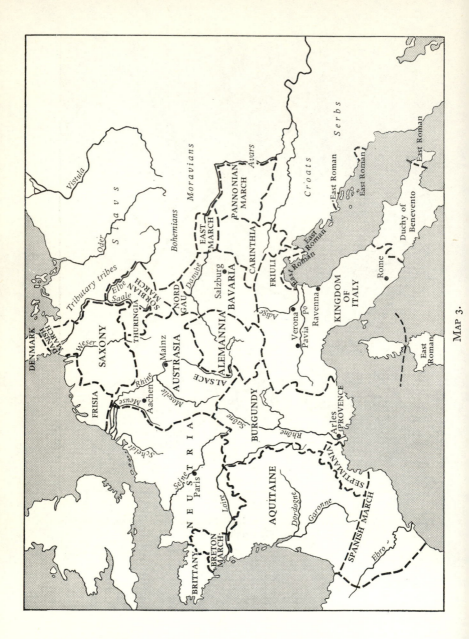

MAP 3.

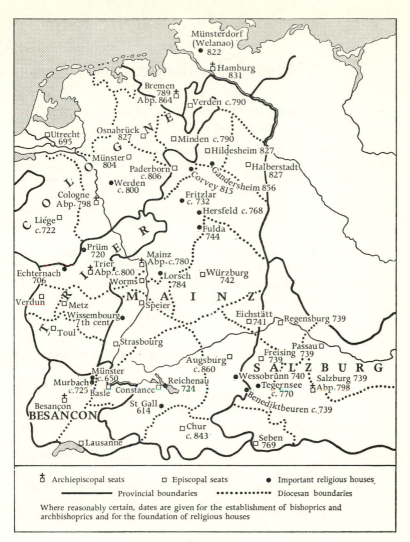

Münsterdorf
(Welanao)
● 822

⌖ Hamburg
831

Bremen
789 ⌖
Abp. 864 □

□ Verden c.790

N·E

□Utrecht
695

Osnabrück
827 □

G

□ Minden c.790

Münster □
804

Paderborn □
c. 806

● Werden
c. 800

□ Hildesheim 827

□ Halberstadt
827

Co

Corvey
815

Gandersheim 856

Fritzlar
● c. 732

● Hersfeld c. 768

Cologne
○ Abp. 798 □

L

R

● Fulda
744

C Liége □
c.722

● Prüm
720

Trier
⌖ Abp. c.800

Mainz
⌖ Abp. c.780

E

Echternach
706

Worms □

● Lorsch
784

□ Würzburg
742

Verdun

R

□ Metz

M · A · I · N · Z

□ Speier

Eichstätt
□ 741

□ Regensburg 739

● Wissembourg
7th cent.

T

□ Toul

□ Strasbourg

Passau □

Freising 739
□ 739

Augsburg □
c. 860

S · A · L · Z · B · U · R · G

Murbach ● ●
c.725

Münster
c. 650

Reichenau
724

● Wessobrunn 740

Salzburg 739

● Tegernsee
c. 770

⌖ Abp. 798

⌖
Basle

□ Constance

Benediktbeuren c. 739

Besançon

BESANCON

St Gall
614 ●

□ Chur
c. 843

Seben
□ 769

□ Lausanne

⌖ Archiepiscopal seats   □ Episcopal seats   ● Important religious houses

———————— Provincial boundaries   •••••••••• Diocesan boundaries

Where reasonably certain, dates are given for the establishment of bishoprics and
archbishoprics and for the foundation of religious houses

MAP 4.

The Ecclesiastical Division of Germany in the Ninth Century

General Bibliography

A. WORKS OF REFERENCE, COMPENDIA, ENCYCLOPEDIAS, ETC.

HOOPS, J. (ed.), *Reallexikon der germanischen Altertumskunde*, 4 vols. (Strasbourg, 1911–19); 2nd completely revised edn. by H. Jankuhn, H. Kuhn, K. Ranke, and R. Wenskus (Berlin, 1973–). (An encyclopedic work covering all aspects of Germanic antiquities.)

KOSCH, W. (ed.), *Deutsches Literatur-Lexikon*, 4 vols. (2nd edn. Berne, 1949–58), 3rd edn. by B. Berger and H. Rupp (Berne and Munich, 1966–).

LÜDTKE, G., and L. MACKENSEN (eds.), *Deutscher Kulturatlas*, 5 vols. (Berlin/Leipzig 1931–8). (Vol. 1 covers the period to A.D. 1000.)

MERKER, P., and STAMMLER, W. (eds.), *Reallexikon der deutschen Literaturgeschichte*, 5 vols. (Berlin, 1925–31); 2nd revised edn. (Berlin, 1955–).

PAUL, H. (founder and first ed.), *Grundriß der germanischen Philologie*, 3rd edn. (Strasbourg, 1911–). (A collection of scholarly works on different aspects of Germanic philology. After the third edition it continued as a collection of individual works published separately under a general editor.)

SCHMITT, L. E. (ed.), *Kurzer Grundriß der germanischen Philologie bis 1500* (Berlin, 1970–). (A collection of monographs on various aspects of Germanic philology; the first volume deals with language, the second with literature. It is in many respects a modern equivalent of the foregoing item.)

STAMMLER, W. (ed.), *Die Literatur des Mittelalters. Verfasserlexikon*, 5 vols. (Berlin/Leipzig, 1933–55).

—— (ed.), *Deutsche Philologie im Aufriß*, 3 vols. and register (Berlin, 1952–9; 2nd edn. 1957–62). (An encylopedic work consisting of lengthy treatments of the most diverse subjects falling within the compass of 'German philology'.)

B. OLD HIGH GERMAN AND OLD SAXON TEXTS

Details of the standard editions of the major OHG and OS texts are to be found in the footnotes to the appropriate chapters in this handbook. Selections from these texts are given in the collections of Barber, Braune, and Mansion listed below. The shorter texts are edited in the following collections:

BARBER, C. C., *An Old High German Reader with Notes, List of Proper Names, and Vocabulary* (Oxford, 1951).

BRAUNE, W. (ed.), *Althochdeutsches Lesebuch*, 15th edn. revised by E. A. Ebbinghaus (Tübingen, 1969).

HEYNE, M. (ed.), *Kleinere altniederdeutsche Denkmäler*, 2nd edn. (Paderborn, 1877, repr. Amsterdam, 1970).

MANSION, J. (ed.), *Althochdeutsches Lesebuch für Anfänger* (Heidelberg, 1912).

MÜLLENHOFF, K., and SCHERER W. (eds.), *Denkmäler deutscher Poesie und Prosa aus dem VIII.–XII. Jahrhundert*, 3rd edn. revised by E. von Steinmeyer (Berlin, 1892, repr. as 4th edn. in smaller format Berlin/ Zürich, 1964).

SCHLOSSER, H. D. (ed.), *Althochdeutsche Literatur mit Proben aus dem Altniederdeutschen. Ausgewählte Texte mit Übertragungen und Anmerkungen* (Frankfurt/Hamburg, 1970).

STEINMEYER, E. VON (ed.), *Die kleineren althochdeutschen Sprachdenkmäler* (Berlin, 1916, repr. Berlin/Zürich, 1963).

C. FACSMILES OF OLD HIGH GERMAN AND OLD SAXON TEXTS

ENNECCERUS, M. (ed.), *Die ältesten deutschen Sprachdenkmäler. In Lichtdrucken herausgegeben* (Frankfurt a. M., 1897).

FISCHER, H. (ed.), *Schrifttafeln zum althochdeutschen Lesebuch* (Tübingen, 1966).

PETZET, E., and GLAUNING, O. (eds.), *Deutsche Schrifttafeln des IX. bis XVI. Jahrhunderts aus Handschriften der K. Hof- und Staatsbibliothek in München* (Munich, 1910–30).

Other facsimiles are mentioned in the footnotes of this handboook.

D. GRAMMARS

BRAUNE, W., *Althochdeutsche Grammatik*, 12th edn. revised by W. Mitzka (Tübingen, 1967).

FRANCK, J. *Altfränkische Grammatik* (Göttingen, 1909).

GALLÉE, J. H. *Altsächsische Grammatik*, 2nd edn. (Halle/Leiden, 1910).

HOLTHAUSEN, F., *Altsächsisches Elementarbuch*, 2nd edn. (Heidelberg, 1921).

NAUMANN, H., and BETZ, W., *Althochdeutsches Elementarbuch*, Sammlung Göschen 1111/1111a, 4th edn. (Berlin, 1967).

SCHATZ, J. *Altbairische Grammatik* (Göttingen, 1907).
—— *Althochdeutsche Grammatik* (Göttingen, 1927).

WEINHOLD, K., *Alemannische Grammatik* (Berlin, 1863, repr. Amsterdam, 1967).

E. DICTIONARIES

GRAFF, E. G., *Althochdeutscher Sprachschatz oder Wörterbuch der althoch-deutschen Sprache* . . ., 6 vols. (Berlin, 1834–42). (Reprint, see Massmann below).

HEFFNER, R.-M. S., *A Word-Index to the Texts of Steinmeyer: Die kleineren althochdentschen Sprachdenkmäler* (Madison, 1961).

KARG-GASTERSTÄDT, E., FRINGS, TH., and others (eds.), *Althochdeutsches Wörterbuch auf Grund der von Elias von Steinmeyer hinterlassenen Sammlungen* . . . (Berlin, 1952–). (When completed this will be the authoritative dictionary of Old High German. Meanwhile the fullest collection of OHG vocabulary is that made by Graff in the last century, listed above and provided with an alphabetical Index, by Massmann.)

MASSMANN, H. F., *Gedrängtes althochdeutsches Wörterbuch oder vollstän-diger Index zu Graff's althochdeutschem Sprachschatz*, Vollständiger alphabetischer Index zu dem althochdeutschen Sprachschatze von E. G. Graff (Berlin, 1846. Reprinted with Graff's *Althochdeutscher Sprachschatz* (Hildesheim, 1963)).

SCHADE, O., *Altdeutsches Wörterbuch*, 2nd edn., 2 vols. (Halle, 1872–82, repr. Hildesheim, 1969).

SCHÜTZEICHEL, R., *Althochdeutsches Wörterbuch* (Tübingen, 1969). (This work is a useful aid to the student if used in conjunction with the special glossaries provided for various OHG texts.)

F. THE OLD HIGH GERMAN AND OLD SAXON LANGUAGES

BACH, A., *Geschichte der deutschen Sprache*, 8th edn. (Heidelberg, 1965).

EGGERS, H., *Deutsche Sprachgeschichte I. Das Althochdeutsche* (Reinbek bei Hamburg, 1963).

KROGMANN, W., 'Altsächsisch und Mittelniederdeutsch', *Kz. Grundriß* I. 211–52.

MOSER, H., 'Deutsche Sprachgeschichte der älteren Zeit', *DPA* I.

SONDEREGGER, S., 'Althochdeutsche Sprache', *Kz. Grundriß* I. 288–346.

G. STUDIES OF OLD HIGH GERMAN AND OLD SAXON LITERATURE

DE BOOR, H., *Die deutsche Literatur von Karl dem Großen bis zum Beginn der höfischen Dichtung, 770–1170*. (Vol. I of H. de Boor and R. Newald, *Geschichte der deutschen Literatur von den Anfängen bis zur Gegenwart*). 7th edn. (Munich, 1966). (The fullest modern treatment of the subject.)

—— 'Von der karolingischen zur cluniazensischen Zeit', *Annalen der deutschen Literatur* (ed. by H. O. Burger), 2nd edn. (Stuttgart, 1971), pp. 37–97.

EHRISMANN, G., *Geschichte der deutschen Literatur bis zum Ausgang des Mittelalters*. Erster Teil: *Die althochdeutsche Literatur*, 2nd edn. (Munich, 1932). (A fundamental work in its time, still valuable, though in many respects out of date.)

KELLE, J., *Geschichte der deutschen Litteratur von der ältesten Zeit bis zur Mitte des elften Jahrhunderts*, 2 vols. (Berlin, 1892–6). (An old work, still profitable if used with caution.)

RATHOFER, J., 'Altsächsische Literatur', *Kz. Grundriß* II. 242–62.

SONDEREGGER, S., and BURGER, H., 'Althochdeutsche Literatur', *Kz. Grundriß* II. 326–83.

STAMMLER, W., 'Mittelalterliche Prosa in deutscher Sprache', *DPA* II. 1299–1632.

H. HISTORY

The Cambridge Medieval History, vols. I–III.

DEANESLY, M., *A History of Early Medieval Europe*, 2nd edn. (London, 1969).

OMAN, SIR CHARLES, *The Dark Ages, 476–918*, vol. 1 of *Periods of European History*, ed. by A. Hassall (London, 1893–).

SCHMIDT, L., *Geschichte der deutschen Stämme bis zum Ausgang der Völkerwanderung*, 2nd revised edn. (Munich, 1934).

THOMPSON, E. A., *A History of Attila and the Huns* (Oxford, 1948).

TOUT, T. F., *The Empire and the Papacy, 918–1273*, vol. 2 of *Periods of European History*, ed. by A. Hassall (London, 1893–).

I. GERMANIC ANTIQUITIES AND ETHNOGRAPHY

BETZ, W., 'Die altgermanische Religion', *DPA* III. 2467–2556.

MAURER, F., *Nordgermanen und Alemannen*, 3rd revised edn. (Berne/Munich, 1952). (One of many attempts to establish the relations between the Germanic tribes.)

SCHWARZ, E., *Germanische Stammeskunde* (Heidelberg, 1956). (A modern synthesis of knowledge about the movements and interrelationships of the Germanic tribes.)

—— *Goten, Nordgermanen, Angelsachsen* (Berne/Munich, 1951). (Another attempt to establish the relations between the Germanic tribes.)

VRIES, J. DE, *Altgermanische Religionsgeschichte* (*Grundriß der germanischen Philologie* XII, 2 vols.), 2nd edn. (Berlin, 1956–7).

J. MEDIEVAL LATIN

CURTIUS, E. R., *Europäische Literatur und lateinisches Mittelalter* (Berne, 1948); translated by W. R. Trask, *European Literature and the Latin Middle Ages* (London, 1953).

MANITIUS, M., *Geschichte der lateinischen Literatur des Mittelalters*, 3 vols. (Munich, 1911–31) (*Handbuch der Altertumswissenschaft*, ed. I. von Müller and W. Otto, IX. 2).

RABY, F. J. E., *A History of Christian Latin Poetry from the Beginnings to the Close of the Middle Ages*, 2nd edn. (Oxford, 1953).

—— *A History of Secular Latin Poetry in the Middle Ages*, 2 vols., 2nd edn. (Oxford, 1957).

STRECKER, K., *Einführung in das Mittellatein*, 3rd revised edn. (Berlin, 1939); translated into English and revised by R. B. Palmer, *Introduction to Medieval Latin* (repr. Dublin/Zürich, 1968).

WRIGHT, F. A., and SINCLAIR, T. A., *A History of Latin Literature from the Middle of the Fourth Century to the End of the Seventeenth Century* (London, 1931).

A Concordance of the Collections of Braune, Barber and Schlosser

(In the body of this Handbook references are given to the collections of Old High German texts in *MSD, Kl. ahd. Spdmr.*, and *Ahd. Lb.* In recent years two other collections have come into use: C. C. Barber, *An Old High German Reader with Notes, List of Proper Names, and Vocabulary* (Oxford, 1951); and H. D. Schlosser, *Altdeutsche Literatur, mit Proben aus dem Altniederdeutschen. Ausgewählte Texte mit Übertragungen* (Frankfurt am Main, 1970). The following concordance will enable readers to locate texts in these two collections with the help of the references to *Ahd. Lb.* given in the Handbook. Where selections are given, the passages selected are not always the same in all three collections.)

Ahd. Lb.	Barber	Schlosser
I (selections)	1–3 (selections)	VI. 2 (selections)
II. 1	—	—
II. 2	—	—
II. 3	4a	—
II. 4	4b	V. 6
III	—	V. 1
IV	—	—
V. 1	2b	—
V. 2	—	—
VI	5	II. 4c (selection)
VII (selections)	13 (selections)	I. 5; V. 4 (selections)
VIII (selections)	12 (selections)	I. 10a (selections)
IX (selections)	11 (selections)	I. 10b; I. 18–21
X	6	II. 1
XI (selections)	9 (selections)	II. 5a (selections)
XII	14	II. 4f
XIII	15	II. 4a, b, e (selections)
XIV	18	—
XV	8	II. 5b
XVI. 1	17	II. 2a
XVI. 2. I	—	—
XVI. 2. II	—	II. 2b
XVII (selections)	16, 25 (selections)	I. 6–7 (selections)

Ahd. Lb.	Barber	Schlosser
XVIII	22	V. 1
XIX	26	V. 2
XX (selections)	20 (selections)	I. 11a, 12a, 13a, 14a, 16a, 24a, 25a, 26a, 29a, 31b (selections)
XXI. 1	21	V. 3
XXI. 2	23	V. 5
XXII (selections)	7, 27 (selections)	II. 3 (selections)
XXIII	28	I. 8b, 32
		VI. 3 b–f
XXIV (selections)	31 (selections)	—
XXV	32 (selections)	—
XXVI	30	—
XXVII	—	—
XXVIII	34	IV. 1
XXIX	35	I. 3
XXX	38	I. 33
XXXI. 1	33	III. 1, 2a
XXXI. 2	24a	III. 5
XXXI. 3	39e	III. 6
XXXI. 4	39 f	III. 3a
XXXI. 4a	—	III. 3b
XXXI. 5	—	—
XXXI. 6	—	—
XXXI. 6a	—	—
XXXI. 7	—	—
XXXI. 8	—	—
XXXI. 9 A	—	III. 2b
XXXI. 9 B, 1	—	III. 4c
XXXI. 9 B, 2	24b	III. 2c
XXXII (selections)	36 (selections)	I. 1, 2, 11b, 12b, 14b, 15a, 16b, 24b, 25b, 28, 29b; IV. 2; VI. 3a
XXXIII	39d	II. 6c
XXXIV	40	I. 15b
XXXV	41	II. 6b
XXXVI	37	IV. 3
XXXVII. 1	39b	II. 4g
XXXVII. 2	39a	—
XXXVIII	—	I. 8a
XXXIX	42	IV. 4
XL	—	—
XLI	43	—
XLII	45	—
XLIII	44	—
XLIV A (selections)	—	I. 13b, 17, 22, 23, 26b
XLIV B (selections)	—	I, 4

Index

Erchambald, bishop of Strasbourg, 268
Ermanaric, Gothic king, 20, 64
Eulalia, Sequence of St., 245
Euric, Visigothic king, 13
Exhortatio ad plebem christianam, 100, 110–11

Fontenoy, battle of, 187
Formosus, pope, 225
Fränkisches Taufgelöbnis, 26, 109–10
Franks, 9, 11, 15–19, 20, 21, 22, 23, 24–5, 65, 83, 85, 192–3, 249
Fredegunda, wife of Chilperich I, 86
Frederick I (Barbarossa), emperor, 19
Freisinger Paternoster und Credo, 111
Freyr, Norse god, 146
Friia, a goddess (ON Frigg), 29, 32
Frisians, 10, 23, 86, 87
Fuldaer Beichte, 156
Fylla, Norse goddess, 32

Galerius, Roman emperor, 225
Gallus (St. Gall), 86–7, 100, 226
Galluslied, 226, 233
Gailswintha, wife of Chilperich I, 86
Gegen Fallsucht, 31
Genesis, 2, 142, 169, 183–6, 302
George, bishop of Alexandria, 225
George, St., legend of, 225–6
Gepids, 11
Gerald, St., of Aurillac, 279
Geraldus, monk of St. Gall, 268
Gerberga, abbess of Gandersheim, 257
Germanic tribes, 7–25
Germanicus, Roman emperor, 9
Gisela, wife of Emperor Conrad II, 283
Gisela, illegitimate daughter of Lothar II, 248
Gislaharius, Burgundian king, 14
Glossae Salomonis, 99
glossaries, glosses, 90–107, 192, 227
Godefrid, Danish leader, 248
Godomarus, Burgundian king, 14
Gormont et Isembart, 244
Goths, 11–14, 15, 18, 22, 62–4, 66
Gottfried von Straßburg, *Tristan*, 276
Gregory I (the Great), St., pope, 141
Gregory III, pope, 87
Gregory V, pope, 252
Gundicarius, Burgundian king, 14, 64

Gundobad, Burgundian king, 14, 17
Gylfaginning, 146

Hadrian, Roman emperor, 9
Hamðismál, 13
Hamelburger Markbeschreibung, 113–14, 163, 164
Harold, king of England, 237
Hartmuat, monk of St. Gall, 191, 194, 204, 205
Hatto III, archbishop of Mainz, 218, 225
Heliand, 2, 3, 4, 5, 22, 29, 91, 126, 131, 135, 137, 140, 145, 167, 168–83, 184, 192, 199, 201, 204, 205, 207, 208, 302, 305–7, 310–19
Henry I, duke of Bavaria, 250, 253–4
Henry I (the Fowler), king of Germany, 250
Henry II (the Quarrelsome), duke of Bavaria, 251, 252, 254
Henry II, emperor (Henry IV of Bavaria), 252, 254, 271, 281
Hermeneumata, 100, 101, 103, 179
Herminafrid, Thuringian king, 21
Hermunduri, 20
Herzog Ernst, 67, 244, 261
Hessians, 11, 17, 24
Hildebrandslied, 4, 5, 13, 14, 15, 43–82, 115, 117, 126, 136, 149, 151, 152, 157, 163, 164, 215 n., 227, 243, 259, 261, 266, 302, 303, 305, 307, 319–22
Hildibrand, Lombard king, 80
Himmel und Hölle, 298–300
Hincmar, archbishop of Reims, 239, 241
Hirsch und Hinde, 257
Honorius Augustodunensis, 299
Horace, 301
Hrabanus, *see* Rhabanus
Hrolf (Rollo), duke of Normandy, 236–7
Hrotsvitha of Gandersheim, 257–8
Hruodolf, master of the abbey schoo at Fulda, 164
Hugo, abbot, 237, 242
Hugo, bishop of Sitten, 284, 295, 297
Hünengräber, 7
Huns, 10, 12, 13, 16, 17, 22, 268

Indo-European, 7, 8
Irenaeus, St., of Lyon, 85
Irmengard, wife of Boso, 237, 269